UNIVERSITY CASEBOOK SERIES®

ADJUDICATORY CRIMINAL PROCEDURE

CASES, STATUTES, AND MATERIALS

ROGER A. FAIRFAX, JR.

Senior Associate Dean for Academic Affairs

Professor of Law

George Washington University Law School

FOUNDATION
PRESS

University Casebook Series is a trademark registered in the U.S. Patent and Trademark Office.

© 2018 LEG, Inc. d/b/a West Academic
    444 Cedar Street, Suite 700
    St. Paul, MN 55101
    1-877-888-1330

Printed in the United States of America

ISBN: 978-1-62810-212-3

For #TeamFairfax. I love you.

PREFACE

This book is the product of years of my fascination with how the law is taught and how the law is learned. As a law student, I experienced varied approaches to transmitting to the next generation of students the essentials of the law. These were displayed by my criminal law professors Phil Heymann and Charles Ogletree, and the many other professors who helped shape the way I think about pedagogy and the student learning experience, including Chris Edley, Mary Ann Glendon, Morton Horwitz, Randall Kennedy, Arthur Miller, Alvin Warren, and the late Dan Meltzer and Detlev Vagts.

Immediately after law school, I encountered two more distinguished teachers of the substance and elegance of the law in the Honorable Patti B. Saris and the Honorable Judith W. Rogers, for both of whom I had the privilege of serving as a law clerk. My education continued as I entered practice as a federal prosecutor with the United States Department of Justice, where I had both the honor of serving my country and the great fortune of being trained by some of the finest lawyers in the profession. My time practicing primarily criminal defense (for both paying clients and indigent pro bono clients) with O'Melveny LLP was marked by almost daily lessons in lawyering and professionalism at the elbow of the finest lawyer I have encountered, the late William T. Coleman, Jr.

Since joining the legal academy, I have worked tirelessly to master the art of teaching. I am aware that it is a goal I never will achieve, yet it remains my motivating aim. At George Washington University Law School and other law schools at which I have taught, I have had the benefit of numerous colleagues who also display tremendous dedication to the craft of teaching. Some of the most successful of these teachers are able to integrate their scholarly interests and enthusiasm about the life of the law into their work in the classroom. As an academic dean overseeing the implementation of the recent substantial additions to, and revisions of, the American Bar Association Standards on Legal Education, I have had many meaningful conversations, at my own institution and with counterparts at law schools across the country, about pedagogical innovation, the changing nature of legal education, and the need to prepare law students for the modern practice of law.

Taking account of all of these experiences and data points, I embarked upon the project of this textbook. The textbook is meant to be different. Students and professors have at their disposal treatises and hornbooks that catalog every nuance of the law and provide the basis for deep exploration of even the most obscure and rarely-applied doctrines. This book is not intended to perform those functions. Instead, this book seeks to provide a nimble and highly-curated set of materials designed to contextualize and convey the core doctrines, principles, statutes, and rules animating the adjudication of criminal charges in the United States.

The textbook is informed by a rich engagement with the core sources of law and an understanding of what is most relevant to preparing students for practice in this area of the law. Another unique feature of this book is its reliance on a 13-member "Practitioner Advisory Panel" of distinguished federal and state judges, public defenders, private criminal defense attorneys, and federal and state prosecutors I recruited to review and critique the book. These practice experts—representative of those who ultimately hire, observe, and train our law students—have provided invaluable insight on the content of the book, and their professional generosity has enhanced immeasurably its efficacy as a tool for the professor to prepare students for modern practice in criminal law.

The approach taken within is an attempt to provide instructors the broadest opportunity to shape their own course content. As such, the textbook is designed to accommodate a variety of approaches—whether it is a high-level doctrinal treatment of the constitutional and statutory regulation of the criminal adjudicative process, or a more granular plunge into the particular rules and statutes that define the practice context in which criminal cases are adjudicated, or a skills-intensive approach that provides students with the opportunity to participate in exercises designed to bring the material to life, or a hybrid of all of these approaches. This textbook is meant to give the instructor maximum flexibility, from semester to semester, and even from class session to class session.

As what I expect is the case with the first edition of most textbooks, it is a work in progress. Subsequent editions are necessitated not only by changes in the law, but by the desire to improve upon how the book assists the professor in illuminating the law for the students. I look forward to feedback from those who teach from the book, and I eagerly anticipate opportunities to improve it in successive editions over the years.

I would like to thank Pamela Siege Chandler and Tessa Boury for their leadership on behalf of West Academic and Foundation Press, respectively, the Foundation Press editorial production team, led by Greg Olson, and my original acquisitions editor, Ryan Pfeiffer. I am further indebted to the members of my aforementioned Practitioner Advisory Panel, which includes Alvin Bragg, Esq., The Honorable Sharon V. Burrell, Paul B. DeWolfe, Esq., The Honorable Willie J. Epps, Jr., Kobie Flowers, Esq., The Honorable Ketanji Brown Jackson, Tamarra Matthews Johnson, Esq., Robert Livermore, Esq., Kwame Manley, Esq., Heather Pinckney, Esq., Philip Selden, Esq., Gina Simms, Esq., and The Honorable Edward Torpoco. Brief biographies of these distinguished jurists and attorneys can be found immediately following this Preface.

I would like to thank the several research assistants who, over the years, provided valuable support for this project—Maryam Casbarro, Rachel Clark, Julia Haigney, Surya Iyer, Iman Lyons, Melinda Momplaisir, and Brittany Norfleet. I am grateful to Delphine Harper for her expert and cheerful administrative assistance. I also appreciate the many students I have taught over the years who have provided insight on how a textbook's design affects their learning. Many of these students have offered suggestions on the Adjudicatory Criminal Procedure course materials I developed—and which evolved into this textbook.

Finally, I cannot even begin to quantify the support I have received from my family in this and every worthwhile endeavor I have been blessed to undertake throughout my lifetime. As my youngest brother often says about our family, we have been endowed with "spiritual wealth." That wealth was passed down from ancestors for whom liberty was an unrealized American ideal, to ancestors who were assigned a second-class status by law and custom and, despite their character, intellect, and talents, had many of their life opportunities either curtailed or extinguished. These family members invested their spiritual wealth into my parents, who, in turn, bestowed it upon my sister, my brothers, and me. Along with my wife, Lisa, without whom this book would not be possible, I strive everyday to pass that spiritual wealth upon our children, who serve as my inspiration for this book.

ROGER A. FAIRFAX, JR.
Washington, D.C.

October 2017

PRACTITIONER ADVISORY PANEL

Mr. Alvin Bragg is Chief Deputy Attorney General for New York State. He has served as an Assistant United States Attorney in the Southern District of New York, and as a criminal defense attorney with Morvillo Abramowitz in New York City. He clerked for a judge on the U.S. District Court for the Southern District of New York, and earned his J.D. at Harvard Law School.

The Honorable Sharon V. Burrell is a Circuit Judge on the Circuit Court for Montgomery County, Maryland. She has worked in private practice and served as Associate County Attorney for Montgomery County, Maryland. Judge Burrell clerked for a judge on the Court of Appeals of Maryland and earned her J.D. at Harvard Law School.

Paul B. DeWolfe is the chief Public Defender for the state of Maryland. He has served as Assistant Public Defender and District Public Defender in Montgomery County, Maryland, and as a defense attorney in private practice. He currently serves on the Board of Directors of the National Association of Criminal Defense Lawyers.

The Honorable Willie J. Epps Jr. is a U.S. Magistrate Judge for the Western District of Missouri and sits in Jefferson City. He has served as a U.S. Air Force Judge Advocate, Special Assistant U.S. Attorney, Assistant Special Counsel for The Waco Investigation, partner at two prominent Missouri-based law firms, and Head of Litigation for a leading financial services company. Judge Epps earned his J.D. at Harvard Law School.

Mr. Kobie Flowers is a partner at Brown Goldstein & Levy in Washington, D.C., where he practices criminal defense and civil litigation. He served as a Trial Attorney in the Criminal Section of the United States Department of Justice Civil Rights Division, as an Assistant Federal Public Defender in Baltimore, Maryland, and as a criminal and civil litigator at large and small law firms. He earned his J.D. at Georgetown University Law Center.

The Honorable Ketanji Brown Jackson is a District Judge on the U.S. District Court for the District of Columbia. She served as Vice Chair and Commissioner of the U.S. Sentencing Commission, an Assistant Federal Public Defender in Washington, D.C., Assistant Counsel at the Sentencing Commission, a criminal and civil appellate litigator at a large firm, and as an associate at two smaller firms. Judge Jackson clerked for judges on the U.S. District Court for the District of Massachusetts and the U.S. Court of Appeals for the First Circuit, and for an Associate Justice of the United States Supreme Court. She earned her J.D. at Harvard Law School.

Ms. Tamarra Matthews Johnson is a partner at Wilkinson Walsh + Eskovitz in Washington, D.C., where she practices civil trial litigation. She previously served as an Assistant United States Attorney and Deputy Chief of the Criminal Division in the U.S. Attorney's Office for the Northern District of Alabama, and in private practice at Latham & Watkins in Washington, D.C. She served as a law clerk to a Judge on the U.S. Court of Appeals for the D.C. Circuit and to an Associate Justice of the United States Supreme Court. A member of the American Law Institute, she earned her J.D. at Yale Law School.

Mr. Robert Livermore is an Assistant United States Attorney in the Eastern District of Pennsylvania. He served as an Assistant Commonwealth's Attorney in Virginia, and as a Trial Attorney in the Organized Crime and Racketeering Section of the Criminal Division and the Northern Criminal Enforcement Section of the Tax Division of the United States Department of Justice. He earned his J.D. at George Washington University Law School.

Mr. Kwame Manley is a partner at Paul Hastings in Washington, D.C., where he practices white-collar criminal defense and corporate internal investigations. He served as a criminal and civil litigator at a large firm in Washington, D.C., and as an Assistant United States Attorney and Chief of Major Crimes in the District of Maryland. He clerked for a judge on the U.S. District Court for the District of Columbia, and earned his J.D. from Harvard Law School.

Ms. Heather Pinckney is a partner at Harden & Pinckney, where she practices criminal defense litigation. She served as Deputy Chief of the Trial Division at the Public Defender Service for the District of Columbia. She earned her J.D. at George Washington University Law School.

Mr. Philip Selden is an Assistant United States Attorney in the District of Maryland, in the Fraud and Public Corruption Section. He served as an associate at a large law firm in Washington, D.C., and worked with at-risk youth in Philadelphia Family Court. He earned his J.D. from Columbia Law School.

Ms. Gina Simms is a shareholder at Baker Donelson in Washington, D.C. She served as an Assistant United States Attorney in Maryland and in the District of Columbia, and as Associate Independent Counsel in the investigation of a cabinet secretary. She earned her J.D. from George Washington University Law School.

The Honorable Edward Torpoco is a Judge on the Superior Court of California sitting in the City and County of San Francisco. He served as a Trial Attorney in the Public Integrity Section of the Criminal Division of the U.S. Department of Justice, an Assistant United States Attorney for the Northern District of California, a Deputy District Attorney in

Los Angeles, CA, and an in-house counsel at eBay, Inc. He earned his
J.D. at Harvard Law School.

SUMMARY OF CONTENTS

TABLE OF CONTENTS

TABLE OF CASES

The principal cases are in bold type.

UNIVERSITY CASEBOOK SERIES®

ADJUDICATORY CRIMINAL PROCEDURE

CASES, STATUTES, AND MATERIALS

CHAPTER 1

INTRODUCTION

I. THE ADJUDICATORY CRIMINAL PROCEDURE COURSE

The course in "Adjudicatory Criminal Procedure" (also named "Advanced Criminal Procedure," "Criminal Procedure II," "Federal Criminal Procedure," or the author's favorite, "Bail to Jail") is often overlooked by students seeking to deepen their engagement with criminal law-related courses. The traditionally more popular "Criminal Procedure" course focuses on how the Constitution and other legal rules regulate the state in its investigation of crime. In that course, sometimes nicknamed "Stops and Cops," students learn about how the Fourth Amendment governs the state's ability to encroach upon the privacy interests of the individual when seeking evidence of a crime or apprehension of an alleged offender. They also explore how the Fifth Amendment works alongside other provisions to limit the government's enlistment of an accused in the investigation of her own alleged offense. In a related vein, they grapple with how the Sixth Amendment ensures that an accused has the assistance of counsel when being interrogated about possible criminal activity. Of course, with all of these rights found in the federal constitution, the question often arises whether and how those rights apply to the states through the Fourteenth Amendment, and whether the states provide criminal defendants greater protection than they enjoy at the federal level.

At some law schools, the above-described course is named "Constitutional Criminal Procedure." This is unfortunate. The Constitution plays no more prominent a role in the "Stops and Cops" course than it does in the "Bail to Jail" course. The criminal adjudication process is governed by a host of constitutional, statutory, and judge-made rules and doctrines presenting knotty and fascinating issues as important as any in what some call the "Stops and Cops" course. Indeed, the adjudication of crime often implicates the Constitution both in ensuring due process is delivered to an accused and in shaping the substantive issues raised in the "Stops and Cops" course.

II. FEDERAL CONSTITUTIONAL CRIMINAL PROCEDURAL RIGHTS

This textbook focuses on federal criminal procedure, both because of its uniformity and because it has greatly influenced—and has been greatly influenced by—state criminal procedures. In the course of its coverage, this textbook will explore several core constitutional provisions defining criminal procedural rights enjoyed by the accused:

A. FOURTH AMENDMENT

The right of the people to be secure in their persons, houses, papers, and effects, against unreasonable searches and seizures, shall not be violated, and no Warrants shall issue, but **upon probable cause,** *supported by Oath or affirmation, and particularly describing the place to be searched, and the persons or things to be seized.*

The textbook will examine the procedures designed to enforce the Fourth Amendment's requirement of probable cause to support detention, as well as procedures made available to the defendant to challenge the constitutionality of evidence obtained by the state in violation of the Fourth Amendment.

B. FIFTH AMENDMENT

No person shall be held to answer for a capital, *or* **otherwise infamous crime, unless on a presentment or indictment of a Grand Jury,** *except in cases arising in the land or naval forces, or in the Militia, when in actual service in time of War or public danger;* **nor shall any person be subject for the same offence to be twice put in jeopardy of life or limb;** *nor shall be compelled in any criminal case to be a witness against himself, nor be deprived of life, liberty, or property, without* **due process of law,** *nor shall private property be taken for public use, without just compensation.*

The textbook will examine the requirement of grand jury indictment in serious federal criminal cases and the requirements of procedure and substance imposed by the Due Process Clause.

C. SIXTH AMENDMENT

In all criminal prosecutions, the accused shall enjoy the right to a **speedy** *and* **public trial,** *by an* **impartial jury** *of the* **State and district wherein the crime shall have been committed,** *which district shall have been previously ascertained by law, and to be* **informed of the nature and cause of the accusation;** *to be* **confronted with the witnesses against him;** *to have* **compulsory process for obtaining witnesses in his favor,** *and to have the* **Assistance of Counsel** *for his defence.*

The textbook will examine the requirement of notice of criminal charges, the right to a speedy and public trial, the right to counsel and standards of attorney effectiveness throughout the criminal process, and various trial rights including confrontation and subpoena authority.

D. EIGHTH AMENDMENT

Excessive bail shall not be required, nor *excessive fines* imposed, nor *cruel and unusual punishments* inflicted.

The textbook will examine bail and pretrial release, in the context of sentencing, the constitutional constraints upon various forms of punishment, including imprisonment and fines.

E. OTHER CONSTITUTIONAL PROVISIONS

In addition, other constitutional provisions occasionally are implicated by the various criminal procedure doctrines covered in this textbook. For example, Article III, Section 2 contains criminal procedural provisions related to the right to a criminal jury trial and the proper venue for a criminal case. U.S. CONST. art. III, § 2 ("**The Trial of all Crimes**, except in Cases of Impeachment, **shall be by Jury**; and such **Trial shall be held in the State where the said Crimes shall have been committed**; but when not committed within any State, the Trial shall be at such Place or Places as the Congress may by Law have directed."). Article I, Sections 9 and 10 contain the prohibition on ex post facto laws, which are laws criminalizing conduct that was innocent when undertaken or aggravating punishment for conduct after it was engaged in.

Likewise, the First Amendment figures into the discussion of media access to court proceedings or whether a reporter can be compelled under grand jury subpoena to disclose the identity of a source who has evidence of criminal activity. In addition, the Equal Protection Clause of the Fourteenth Amendment may be implicated by the discriminatory exercise of a peremptory challenge, or the allegation that an exercise of prosecutorial discretion resulted in a selective prosecution.

III. INCORPORATION

All persons born or naturalized in the United States and subject to the jurisdiction thereof, are citizens of the United States and of the State wherein they reside. **No State shall make or enforce any law which shall abridge the privileges or immunities of citizens of the United States;** *nor shall any State deprive any person of life, liberty, or property, without* **due process of law**; *nor deny to any person within its jurisdiction the equal protection of the laws.*

U.S. CONST., amend. XIV, § 1.

The Bill of Rights, where the aforementioned criminal procedural rights can be found, originally were construed to apply only to the federal government.[1] Thus, for a substantial portion of the nation's history, there was a question whether various criminal procedural rights set out in the Bill of Rights applied—through the Fourteenth Amendment—to the *states'* administration of criminal justice.

The Supreme Court, in *Hurtado v. California*, 110 U.S. 516 (1884), held that the Fourteenth Amendment's Due Process Clause did not require that a state obtain a grand jury indictment before pursuing serious criminal charges against a defendant. In that case, California's procedure of allowing a prosecutor to file a charging document called an "Information" against a defendant (rather than seeking an indictment from a grand jury) was held to be consistent with due process, and the requirements of the Fifth Amendment's Grand Jury Clause were inapplicable to the states.

The *Hurtado* case marked the beginning of a lengthy period of the Court grappling with the fundamental question whether the states would be bound by the same criminal procedural constraints binding the federal government. How the Court entertained varying approaches to this question is described in the following excerpt from the majority opinion in *McDonald v. City of Chicago*, 561 U.S. 742 (2010), a case in which the Court incorporated the Second Amendment's right to keep and bear arms to apply to the states.

McDonald v. City of Chicago

Supreme Court of United States, 2010
561 U.S. 742

■ JUSTICE ALITO announced the judgment of the Court and the opinion of the Court with respect to [Part II-D, which is excerpted below].

* * *

Two years ago, in *District of Columbia v. Heller*, 554 U.S. 570 (2008), we held that the Second Amendment protects the right to keep and bear arms for the purpose of self-defense, and we struck down a District of Columbia law that banned the possession of handguns in the home. The city of Chicago (City) and the village of Oak Park, a Chicago suburb, have laws that are similar to the District of Columbia's, but Chicago and Oak Park argue that their laws are constitutional because the Second Amendment has no application to the States. We have previously held that most of the provisions of the Bill of Rights apply with full force to both the Federal Government and the States. Applying

---

[1] *Barron v. Baltimore*, 32 U.S. 243 (1833).

the standard that is well established in our case law, we hold that the Second Amendment right is fully applicable to the States.

* * *

D

1

In the late 19th century, the Court began to consider whether the Due Process Clause prohibits the States from infringing rights set out in the Bill of Rights. * * * Five features of the approach taken during the ensuing era should be noted.

First, the Court viewed the due process question as entirely separate from the question whether a right was a privilege or immunity of national citizenship. See *Twining v. New Jersey*, 211 U.S. 78, 99 (1908).

Second, the Court explained that the only rights protected against state infringement by the Due Process Clause were those rights "of such a nature that they are included in the conception of due process of law." Ibid. See also, *e.g.,* * * * *Palko v. Connecticut*, 302 U.S. 319 (1937); * * * *Powell v. Alabama*, 287 U.S. 45 (1932). While it was "possible that some of the personal rights safeguarded by the first eight Amendments against National action [might] also be safeguarded against state action," the Court stated, this was "not because those rights are enumerated in the first eight Amendments." Twining, supra, at 99.

The Court used different formulations in describing the boundaries of due process. For example, in Twining, the Court referred to "immutable principles of justice which inhere in the very idea of free government which no member of the Union may disregard." 211 U.S., at 102 * * *. In *Snyder v. Massachusetts*, 291 U.S. 97, 105 (1934), the Court spoke of rights that are "so rooted in the traditions and conscience of our people as to be ranked as fundamental." And in Palko, the Court famously said that due process protects those rights that are "the very essence of a scheme of ordered liberty" and essential to "a fair and enlightened system of justice." 302 U.S., at 325.

Third, in some cases decided during this era the Court "can be seen as having asked, when inquiring into whether some particular procedural safeguard was required of a State, if a civilized system could be imagined that would not accord the particular protection." *Duncan v. Louisiana*, 391 U.S. 145, 149 n.14 (1968). Thus, in holding that due process prohibits a State from taking private property without just compensation, the Court described the right as "a principle of natural equity, recognized by all temperate and civilized governments, from a deep and universal sense of its justice." * * * Similarly, the Court found that due process did not provide a right against compelled incrimination in part because this right "has no place in the jurisprudence of civilized and free countries outside the domain of the common law." Twining, supra, at 113.

Fourth, the Court during this era was not hesitant to hold that a right set out in the Bill of Rights failed to meet the test for inclusion within the protection of the Due Process Clause. The Court found that some such rights qualified. * * * But others did not. * * *

Finally, even when a right set out in the Bill of Rights was held to fall within the conception of due process, the protection or remedies afforded against state infringement sometimes differed from the protection or remedies provided against abridgment by the Federal Government. To give one example, in [*Betts v. Brady*, 316 U.S. 455 (1942)], the Court held that, although the Sixth Amendment required the appointment of counsel in all federal criminal cases in which the defendant was unable to retain an attorney, the Due Process Clause required appointment of counsel in state criminal proceedings only where "want of counsel in [the] particular case . . . result[ed] in a conviction lacking in . . . fundamental fairness." Id. at 473. Similarly, in *Wolf v. Colorado*, 338 U.S. 25 (1949), the Court held that the "core of the Fourth Amendment" was implicit in the concept of ordered liberty and thus "enforceable against the States through the Due Process Clause" but that the exclusionary rule, which applied in federal cases, did not apply to the States. Id. at 27–28.

2

An alternative theory regarding the relationship between the Bill of Rights and § 1 of the Fourteenth Amendment was championed by Justice Black. This theory held that § 1 of the Fourteenth Amendment totally incorporated all of the provisions of the Bill of Rights. See, *e.g.,* * * * Duncan, supra, at 166 (Black, J., concurring). As Justice Black noted, the chief congressional proponents of the Fourteenth Amendment espoused the view that the Amendment made the Bill of Rights applicable to the States and, in so doing, overruled this Court's decision in *Barron.* * * * Nonetheless, the Court never has embraced Justice Black's "total incorporation" theory.

3

While Justice Black's theory was never adopted, the Court eventually moved in that direction by initiating what has been called a process of "selective incorporation," *i.e.,* the Court began to hold that the Due Process Clause fully incorporates particular rights contained in the first eight Amendments. See, *e.g., Gideon v. Wainwright*, 372 U.S. 335, 341 (1963). * * *

The decisions during this time abandoned three of the previously noted characteristics of the earlier period. * * * The Court made it clear that the governing standard is not whether *any* "civilized system [can] be imagined that would not accord the particular protection." *Duncan*, 391 U.S., at 149 n.14. Instead, the Court inquired whether a particular Bill of Rights guarantee is fundamental to *our* scheme of ordered liberty and system of justice. Id.; see also id. at 148 (referring to those "fundamental principles of liberty and justice which lie at the base of all *our* civil and political institutions" (emphasis added; internal quotation marks omitted)).

The Court also shed any reluctance to hold that rights guaranteed by the Bill of Rights met the requirements for protection under the Due Process Clause. The Court eventually incorporated almost all of the provisions of the Bill of Rights. Only a handful of the Bill of Rights protections remain unincorporated.

Finally, the Court abandoned "the notion that the Fourteenth Amendment applies to the States only a watered-down, subjective version of the individual guarantees of the Bill of Rights," stating that it would be "incongruous" to apply different standards "depending on whether the claim was asserted in a state or federal court." *Malloy v. Hogan*, 378 U.S. 1, 10–11 (1964). * * *. Instead, the Court decisively held that incorporated Bill of Rights protections "are all to be enforced against the States under the Fourteenth Amendment according to the same standards that protect those personal rights against federal encroachment." Id. at 10. * * *

Employing this approach, the Court overruled earlier decisions in which it had held that particular Bill of Rights guarantees or remedies did not apply to the States.

Current State of Incorporation Doctrine

Thus, today, only a few core criminal procedural rights—the Fifth Amendment's right to grand jury indictment, the Sixth Amendment's right to unanimity in a jury verdict, and the Eighth Amendment's prohibition against excessive fines clause—have not been incorporated to apply to the states.[2]

It is important to keep in mind that criminal procedural rights found in the federal constitution represent only the "floor" for rights to which a state criminal defendant is entitled. State constitutions, statutes, and rules can—and often do—provide more protection for criminal defendants than do the federal safeguards.

---

[2] In *McDonald*, the Court seemed to conclude in a footnote that the Excessive Bail Clause of the Eighth Amendment already had been incorporated, *see id.* at 3035 n.12 (citing *Schilb v. Kuebel*, 404 U.S. 357 (1971)), although many believed that the relevant language in *Schilb* was dicta and that the right had not been incorporated previously.

IV. CRIMINAL JURISDICTION

Just as you learned in Civil Procedure, a federal court cannot act in the absence of subject matter jurisdiction. This applies in the criminal context as well. The power of federal courts to hear criminal cases can be found in Article III, Section 2 of the Constitution:

> **The judicial Power shall extend to all Cases**, in Law and Equity, **arising under** this Constitution, **the Laws of the United States**, and Treaties made, or which shall be made, under their Authority;—to all Cases affecting Ambassadors, other public ministers and Consuls;—to all Cases of admiralty and maritime Jurisdiction;—**to Controversies to which the United States shall be a Party** . . .

Congress has vested this authority in federal district courts under Title 18, Section 3231, of the United States Code:

> The **district courts** of the United States shall have **original jurisdiction, exclusive of the courts of the States**, of **all offenses against the laws of the United States**.

As will be discussed in Chapter 7, *infra*, despite the federal rules' generally strict deadlines for the filing of motions, a motion alleging that a charging document fails to invoke the court's jurisdiction can be made at any time during the pendency of a criminal case.

V. FEDERAL RULES OF CRIMINAL PROCEDURE

Before the Federal Rules of Criminal Procedure (FRCP) were promulgated, the state of criminal procedure at the federal level was in disarray. The author describes elsewhere this pre-FRCP state of affairs:

> Despite the more general procedural reform efforts of the early twentieth century, by the end of the 1930s federal criminal procedure was still "in a somewhat amorphous and disorganized state." * * * Prior to the promulgation of the Federal Rules of Criminal Procedure, the procedure guiding criminal matters in federal courts was a hodge-podge gleaned from the common law, federal statutes "sporadically enacted at different times in regard to isolated points," * * * and the law of the forum state "to which the Federal courts conform in respect to many matters which are not governed by Federal statutes." * * *
>
> On June 29, 1940, Congress authorized the Supreme Court to promulgate rules governing federal criminal procedure, just as it had in previous years for civil procedure and for appellate procedure in criminal cases. * * * The Court appointed an Advisory Committee to draft the new rules. * * *

> The seventeen member Committee, chaired by Arthur T. Vanderbilt, a former president of the American Bar Association, was comprised of prominent practitioners and academics, learned in the criminal law and drawn from across the United States. * * * Some of the nation's foremost advocates of criminal law reform served on the Committee, including George H. Dession of Yale Law School and Sheldon Glueck of Harvard Law School, both advocates of integrating social considerations into criminal processes.

Roger A. Fairfax, Jr., *The Jurisdictional Heritage of the Grand Jury Clause*, 91 MINNESOTA L. REV. 398 (2006). After much deliberation and consultation with the bench, bar, and academy, this august body ultimately promulgated a set of rules which went into effect in 1946.

As Rule 1 states, "[t]hese rules govern the procedure in all criminal proceedings in the United States district courts, the United States courts of appeals, and the Supreme Court of the United States." Fed. R. Crim. P. 1(a)(1). The Rules are divided among nine subject-matter titles addressing: (1) applicability of the rules; (2) preliminary proceedings; (3) the grand jury, the indictment, and the information; (4) arraignment and preparation for trial; (5) venue; (6) trial; (7) post-conviction procedures; (8) supplementary and special proceedings; and (9) general provisions.

FRCP

Proposed amendments to the Rules are initially vetted by an Advisory Committee on Criminal Rules, consisting of federal judges, practitioners, and academics. These individuals are appointed by the Chief Justice for the purpose of advising the Judicial Conference of the United States Committee on Rules of Practice and Procedure ("Standing Committee"). With approval of the Standing Committee, the Advisory Committee may publish for comment proposed amendments to the FRCP. After considering the solicited feedback on the proposed rules amendment, the Advisory Committee may decide to recommend the change to the Standing Committee, which, in turn, considers the proposed amendment and may make a recommendation to the full Judicial Conference. If the Judicial Conference recommends the proposed rule amendment to the Supreme Court, the Court considers it and has until May 1st to issue an order promulgating the new rule. Each year, new changes to the Rules go into effect on December 1st, absent contrary Congressional action.

The broad purpose behind the rules can be found in the current Rule 2, which prescribes interpretation of the rules "to provide for the just determination of every criminal proceeding, to secure simplicity in procedure and fairness in administration, and to eliminate unjustifiable expense and delay." Fed. R. Crim. P. 2. As you consider the materials throughout this textbook, consider how the adjudicatory criminal procedure doctrines and rules you study advance or hinder the process values articulated in Rule 2—accuracy, simplicity, fairness, and efficiency.

NOTE ON STATE PRACTICE

Throughout this book, you will be asked to compare federal practice to that in your home state or the state where you intend to practice. Take a moment now to find out where the rules governing criminal procedure in that state can be found. Is there a separately promulgated set of rules, or are the rules contained in a set of statutes, or both? *See, e.g.,* Md. Crim. Proc. Code. Annotated (2013); Md. Rules Title 4 (Criminal Causes) (2013).

CHAPTER 2

PRELIMINARY PROCEEDINGS

I. THE PROBABLE CAUSE HEARING

The Fourth Amendment requires that the seizure of a person must be supported by probable cause, or evidence "sufficient to warrant a prudent man in believing that" a crime was committed and that the person sought to be seized committed it, *Beck v. Ohio*, 379 U.S. 89, 91 (1964). When law enforcement obtains a valid warrant prior to effecting an arrest, it means that the issuing judicial officer was satisfied that probable cause existed to justify the arrest. However, when the police effect a warrantless arrest of an individual, there has been no probable cause determination by anyone other than the arresting officer. As the Court makes clear in the following case, an arrestee in this situation is entitled to have a neutral judicial officer determine whether his continued detention is supported by probable cause.

Gerstein v. Pugh

Supreme Court of United States, 1975
420 U.S. 103

■ MR. JUSTICE POWELL delivered the opinion of the Court.

The issue in this case is whether a person arrested and held for trial under a prosecutor's information is constitutionally entitled to a judicial determination of probable cause for pretrial restraint of liberty.

I

In March 1971 respondents Pugh and Henderson were arrested in Dade County, Fla. Each was charged with several offenses under a prosecutor's information. Pugh was denied bail because one of the charges against him carried a potential life sentence, and Henderson remained in custody because he was unable to post a $4,500 bond.

In Florida, indictments are required only for prosecution of capital offenses. Prosecutors may charge all other crimes by information, without a prior preliminary hearing and without obtaining leave of court. * * * At the time respondents were arrested, a Florida rule seemed to authorize adversary preliminary hearings to test probable cause for detention in all cases. * * * But the Florida courts had held that the filing of an information foreclosed the suspect's right to a preliminary hearing. * * * They had also held that habeas corpus could not be used, except perhaps in exceptional circumstances, to test the probable cause for detention under an information. * * * The only possible methods for obtaining a judicial determination of probable cause were a special statute allowing a preliminary hearing after 30 days, * * * and arraignment, which the District Court found was often delayed a month or more after arrest. * * * As a result, a person charged by information could be detained for a substantial period solely on the decision of a prosecutor.

Respondents Pugh and Henderson filed a class action against Dade County officials in the Federal District Court, claiming a constitutional right to a judicial hearing on the issue of probable cause and requesting declaratory and injunctive relief. * * * The court certified the case as a class action under Fed.Rule Civ.Proc. 23(b)(2), and held that the Fourth and Fourteenth Amendments give all arrested persons charged by information a right to a judicial hearing on the question of probable cause. The District Court ordered the Dade County defendants to give the named plaintiffs an immediate preliminary hearing to determine probable cause for further detention. It also ordered them to submit a plan providing preliminary hearings in all cases instituted by information. * * * State Attorney Gerstein petitioned for review, and we granted certiorari because of the importance of the issue. * * * We affirm in part and reverse in part.

II

As framed by the proceedings below, this case presents two issues: whether a person arrested and held for trial on an information is entitled to a judicial determination of probable cause for detention, and if so, whether the adversary hearing ordered by the District Court and approved by the Court of Appeals is required by the Constitution.

A

Both the standards and procedures for arrest and detention have been derived from the Fourth Amendment and its common-law antecedents. * * * The standard for arrest is probable cause, defined in terms of facts and circumstances 'sufficient to warrant a prudent man in believing that the (suspect) had committed or was committing an offense.' *Beck v. Ohio*, 379 U.S. 89, 91, 85 S.Ct. 223, 225, 13 L.Ed.2d 142 (1964). * * * This standard, like those for searches and seizures, represents a necessary accommodation between the individual's right to liberty and the State's duty to control crime. 'These long-prevailing standards seek to safeguard citizens from rash and unreasonable interferences with privacy and from unfounded charges of crime. They also seek to give fair leeway for enforcing the law in the community's protection. Because many situations which confront officers in the course of executing their duties are more or less ambiguous, room must be allowed for some mistakes on their part. But the mistakes must be those of reasonable men, acting on facts leading sensibly to their conclusions of probability.

The rule of probable cause is a practical, nontechnical conception affording the best compromise that has been found for accommodating these often opposing interests. Requiring more would unduly hamper law enforcement. To allow less would be to leave law-abiding citizens at the mercy of the officers' whim or caprice.' Id., at 176, 69 S.Ct. at 1311.

To implement the Fourth Amendment's protection against unfounded invasions of liberty and privacy, the Court has required that the existence of probable cause be decided by a neutral and detached magistrate whenever possible. The classic statement of this principle appears in *Johnson v. United States*, 333 U.S. 10, 13–14 (1948):

> 'The point of the Fourth Amendment, which often is not grasped by zealous officers, is not that it denies law enforcement the support of the usual inferences which reasonable men draw from evidence. Its protection consists in requiring that those inferences be drawn by a neutral and detached magistrate instead of being judged by the officer engaged in the often competitive enterprise of ferreting out crime.'

See also *Terry v. Ohio*, 392 U.S. 1, 20–22, 88 S.Ct. 1868, 1879–1880, 20 L.Ed.2d 889 (1968).

Maximum protection of individual rights could be assured by requiring a magistrate's review of the factual justification prior to any arrest, but such a requirement would constitute an intolerable handicap for legitimate law enforcement. Thus, while the Court has expressed a preference for the use of arrest warrants when feasible, *Beck v. Ohio*, supra, 379 U.S. at 96, 85 S.Ct., at 228; *Wong Sun v. United States*, 371 U.S. 471, 479–482, 83 S.Ct. 407, 412–414, 9 L.Ed.2d 441 (1963), it has never invalidated an arrest supported by probable cause solely because the officers failed to secure a warrant. See *Ker v. California*, 374 U.S. 23, 83 S.Ct. 1623, 10 L.Ed.2d 726 (1963); *Draper v. United States*, 358 U.S. 307, 79 S.Ct. 329, 3 L.Ed.2d 327 (1959); *Trupiano v. United States*, 334 U.S. 699, 705, 68 S.Ct. 1229, 1232, 92 L.Ed. 1663 (1948).

Under this practical compromise, a policeman's on-the-scene assessment of probable cause provides legal justification for arresting a person suspected of crime, and for a brief period of detention to take the administrative steps incident to arrest. Once the suspect is in custody, however, the reasons that justify dispensing with the magistrate's neutral judgment evaporate. There no longer is any danger that the suspect will escape or commit further crimes while the police submit their evidence to a magistrate. And, while the State's reasons for taking summary action subside, the suspect's need for a neutral determination of probable cause increases significantly. The consequences of prolonged detention may be more serious than the interference occasioned by arrest. Pretrial confinement may imperil the suspect's job, interrupt his source of income, and impair his family relationships. See R. Goldfarb, Ransom 32–91 (1965); L. Katz, Justice Is the Crime 51–62 (1972). Even pretrial release may be accompanied by burdensome conditions that effect a significant restraint of liberty. See, e.g., 18 U.S.C. §§ 3146(a)(2), (5). When the stakes are this high, the detached judgment of a neutral magistrate is essential if the Fourth Amendment is to furnish meaningful protection from unfounded interference with liberty. Accordingly, we hold that the Fourth Amendment requires a judicial determination of probable cause as a prerequisite to extended restraint of liberty following arrest.

* * *

B

Under the Florida procedures challenged here, a person arrested without a warrant and charged by information may be jailed or subjected to other restraints pending trial without any opportunity for a probable cause determination. Petitioner defends this practice on the ground that the prosecutor's decision to file an information is itself a determination of probable cause that furnishes sufficient reason to detain a defendant pending trial. Although a conscientious decision that the evidence warrants prosecution affords a measure of protection against unfounded detention, we do not think prosecutorial judgment standing alone meets the requirements of the Fourth Amendment. Indeed, we think the Court's previous decisions compel disapproval of the Florida procedure. In *Albrecht v. United States*, 273 U.S. 1, 5, 47 S.Ct. 250, 251, 71 L.Ed. 505 (1927), the Court held that an arrest warrant issued solely upon a United States Attorney's information was invalid because the accompanying affidavits were defective. Although the Court's opinion did not explicitly state that the prosecutor's official oath could not furnish probable cause, that conclusion was implicit in the judgment that the arrest was illegal under the Fourth Amendment.[19]

More recently, in *Coolidge v. New Hampshire*, 403 U.S. 443, 449–453, 91 S.Ct. 2022, 2029–2031, 29 L.Ed.2d 564 (1971), the Court held that a prosecutor's responsibility to law enforcement is inconsistent with the constitutional role of a neutral and detached magistrate. We reaffirmed

---

[19] By contrast, the Court has held that an indictment, 'fair upon its face,' and returned by a 'properly constituted grand jury,' conclusively determines the existence of probable cause and requires issuance of an arrest warrant without further inquiry. *Ex parte United States*, 287 U.S. 241, 250, 53 S.Ct. 129, 131, 77 L.Ed. 283 (1932). See also *Giordenello v. United States*, 357 U.S. 480, 487, 78 S.Ct. 1245, 1250, 2 L.Ed.2d 1503 (1958). The willingness to let a grand jury's judgment substitute for that of a neutral and detached magistrate is attributable to the grand jury's relationship to the courts and its historical role of protecting individuals from unjust prosecution. See *United States v. Calandra*, 414 U.S. 338, 342–346, 94 S.Ct. 613, 617–619, 38 L.Ed.2d 561 (1974).

that principle in *Shadwick v. City of Tampa*, 407 U.S. 345, 92 S.Ct. 2119, 32 L.Ed.2d 783 (1972), and held that probable cause for the issuance of an arrest warrant must be determined by someone independent of police and prosecution. See also *United States v. United States District Court*, 407 U.S. 297, 317, 92 S.Ct. 2125, 2136, 32 L.Ed.2d 752 (1972). The reason for this separation of functions was expressed by Mr. Justice Frankfurter in a similar context:

> 'A democratic society, in which respect for the dignity of all men is central, naturally guards against the misuse of the law enforcement process. Zeal in tracking down crime is not in itself an assurance of soberness of judgment.

> Disinterestedness in law enforcement does not alone prevent disregard of cherished liberties. Experience has therefore counseled that safeguards must be provided against the dangers of the overzealous as well as the despotic. The awful instruments of the criminal law cannot be entrusted to a single functionary. The complicated process of criminal justice is therefore divided into different parts, responsibility for which is separately vested in the various participants upon whom the criminal law relies for its vindication.' *McNabb v. United States*, 318 U.S. 332, 343, 63 S.Ct. 608, 614, 87 L.Ed. 819 (1943).

In holding that the prosecutor's assessment of probable cause is not sufficient alone to justify restraint of liberty pending trial, we do not imply that the accused is entitled to judicial oversight or review of the decision to prosecute. Instead, we adhere to the Court's prior holding that a judicial hearing is not prerequisite to prosecution by information. *Beck v. Washington*, 369 U.S. 541, 545, 82 S.Ct. 955, 957, 8 L.Ed.2d 98 (1962); *Lem Woon v. Oregon*, 229 U.S. 586, 33 S.Ct. 783, 57 L.Ed. 1340 (1913). Nor do we retreat from the established rule that illegal arrest or detention does not void a subsequent conviction. *Frisbie v. Collins*, 342 U.S. 519, 72 S.Ct. 509, 96 L.Ed. 541 (1952); *Ker v. Illinois*, 119 U.S. 436, 7 S.Ct. 225, 30 L.Ed. 421 (1886). Thus, as the Court of Appeals noted below, although a suspect who is presently detained may challenge the probable cause for that confinement, a conviction will not be vacated on the ground that the defendant was detained pending trial without a determination of probable cause.

* * *

III

Both the District Court and the Court of Appeals held that the determination of probable cause must be accompanied by the full panoply of adversary safeguards-counsel, confrontation, cross-examination, and compulsory process for witnesses. A full preliminary hearing of this sort is modeled after the procedure used in many States to determine whether the evidence justifies going to trial under an information or presenting the case to a grand jury. See *Coleman v. Alabama*, 399 U.S. 1, 90 S.Ct. 1999, 26 L.Ed.2d 387 (1970) * * *. The standard of proof required of the prosecution is usually referred to as 'probable cause,' but in some jurisdictions it may approach a prima facie case of guilt. ALI, Model Code of Pre-arraignment Procedure, Commentary on Art. 330, pp. 90–91 (Tent. Draft No. 5, 1972). When the hearing takes this form, adversary procedures are customarily employed. The importance of the issue to both the State and the accused justifies the presentation of witnesses and full exploration of their testimony on cross-examination.

This kind of hearing also requires appointment of counsel for indigent defendants. *Coleman v. Alabama*, supra. And, as the hearing assumes increased importance and the procedures become more complex, the likelihood that it can be held promptly after arrest diminishes. See ALI, Model Code of Pre-arraignment Procedure, supra, at 33–34.

These adversary safeguards are not essential for the probable cause determination required by the Fourth Amendment. The sole issue is whether there is probable cause for detaining the arrested person pending further proceedings. This issue can be determined reliably without an adversary hearing. The standard is the same as that for arrest.[21] That standard-probable cause to believe the suspect has committed a crime-traditionally has been decided by a magistrate in a nonadversary proceeding on hearsay and written testimony, and the Court has approved these informal modes of proof.

> 'Guilt in a criminal case must be proved beyond a reasonable doubt and by evidence confined to that which long experience in the common-law tradition, to some extent embodied in the Constitution, has crystallized into rules of evidence consistent with that standard. These rules are historically grounded rights of our system, developed to safeguard men from dubious and unjust convictions, with resulting forfeitures of life, liberty and property.
>
> 'In dealing with probable cause, however, as the very name implies, we deal with probabilities. These are not technical; they are the factual and practical considerations of everyday life on which reasonable and prudent men, not legal technicians, act. The standard of proof is accordingly

---

[21] Because the standards are identical, ordinarily there is no need for further investigation before the probable cause determination can be made. 'Presumably, whomever the police arrest they must arrest on 'probable cause.' It is not the function of the police to arrest, as it were, at large and to use an interrogating process at police headquarters in order to determine whom they should charge before a committing magistrate on 'probable cause." *Mallory v. United States*, 354 U.S. 449, 456, 77 S.Ct. 1356, 1360, 1 L.Ed.2d 1479 (1957).

> correlative to what must be proved.' *Brinegar v. United States*,
> 338 U.S., at 174–175. * * *

The use of an informal procedure is justified not only by the lesser consequences of a probable cause determination but also by the nature of the determination itself. It does not require the fine resolution of conflicting evidence that a reasonable-doubt or even a preponderance standard demands, and credibility determinations are seldom crucial in deciding whether the evidence supports a reasonable belief in guilt. See F. Miller, Prosecution: The Decision to Charge a Suspect with a Crime 64–109 (1969). This is not to say that confrontation and cross-examination might not enhance the reliability of probable cause determinations in some cases. In most cases, however, their value would be too slight to justify holding, as a matter of constitutional principle, that these formalities and safeguards designed for trial must also be employed in making the Fourth Amendment determination of probable cause.

Because of its limited function and its nonadversary character, the probable cause determination is not a 'critical stage' in the prosecution that would require appointed counsel. The Court has identified as 'critical stages' those pretrial procedures that would impair defense on the merits if the accused is required to proceed without counsel. *Coleman v. Alabama*, 399 U.S. 1, 90 S.Ct. 1999, 26 L.Ed.2d 387 (1970); *United States v. Wade*, 388 U.S. 218, 226–227, 87 S.Ct. 1926, 1931–1932, 18 L.Ed.2d 1149 (1967). In *Coleman v. Alabama*, where the Court held that a preliminary hearing was a critical stage of an Alabama prosecution, the majority and concurring opinions identified two critical factors that distinguish the Alabama preliminary hearing from the probable cause determination required by the Fourth Amendment. First, under Alabama law the function of the preliminary hearing was to determine whether the evidence justified charging the suspect with an offense. A finding of no probable cause could mean that he would not be tried at all. The Fourth Amendment probable cause determination is addressed only to pretrial custody. To be sure, pretrial custody may affect to some extent the defendant's ability to assist in preparation of his defense, but this does not present the high probability of substantial harm identified as controlling in Wade and Coleman. Second, Alabama allowed the suspect to confront and cross-examine prosecution witnesses at the preliminary hearing. The Court noted that the suspect's defense on the merits could be compromised if he had no legal assistance for exploring or preserving the witnesses' testimony. This consideration does not apply when the prosecution is not required to produce witnesses for cross-examination.

Although we conclude that the Constitution does not require an adversary determination of probable cause, we recognize that state systems of criminal procedure vary widely. There is no single preferred pretrial procedure, and the nature of the probable cause determination usually will be shaped to accord with a State's pretrial procedure viewed as a whole. While we limit our holding to the precise requirement of the Fourth Amendment, we recognize the desirability of flexibility and experimentation by the States. It may be found desirable, for example, to make the probable cause determination at the suspect's first appearance before a judicial officer, see *McNabb v. United States*, 318 U.S., at 342–344, 63 S.Ct., at 613–614, or the determination may be incorporated into the procedure for setting bail or fixing other conditions of pretrial release. In some States, existing procedures may satisfy the requirement of the Fourth Amendment. Others may require only minor adjustment, such as acceleration of existing preliminary hearings. Current proposals for criminal procedure reform suggest other ways of testing probable cause for detention. Whatever procedure a State may adopt, it must provide a fair and reliable determination of probable cause as a condition for any significant pretrial restraint of liberty, and this determination must be made by a judicial officer either before or promptly after arrest.

IV

We agree with the Court of Appeals that the Fourth Amendment requires a timely judicial determination of probable cause as a prerequisite to detention, and we accordingly affirm that much of the judgment. As we do not agree that the Fourth Amendment requires the adversary hearing outlined in the District Court's decree, we reverse in part and remand to the Court of Appeals for further proceedings consistent with this opinion.

It is so ordered.

Affirmed in part, reversed in part, and remanded.

Gerstein *Takeaways*

In addition to its core holding that a warrantless arrestee is entitled to a judicial determination promptly after arrest, *Gerstein* reaffirmed some important principles discussed later in this chapter. First, a probable cause hearing does not need to be an adversarial hearing. Second, although a defendant may challenge her detention due to the lack of the requisite probable cause finding, she cannot challenge her *conviction* solely because of an illegal detention. Third, the *Gerstein* probable cause hearing is wholly distinct from the preliminary hearing discussed below. Finally, a defendant is not entitled to counsel at a *Gerstein* hearing, in contrast to the preliminary hearing discussed *infra*, which is a critical stage of the criminal proceedings and to which the right to counsel attaches. (Re-read the discussion of *Coleman v. Alabama* in Part III of the *Gerstein* opinion.)

Gerstein *Hearings in Federal Court?*

As discussed in the last chapter, all of the criminal procedural protections of the Bill of Rights constrain the federal government (and most of the protections constrain the states as well). Therefore, the Fourth Amendment's requirement of a prompt probable cause determination would seem to apply to the federal criminal process. However, there is no provision for such a probable cause hearing in the Federal Rules of Criminal Procedure, and *Gerstein* hearings are not held in federal courts as a matter of course. Why?

The answer can be found in the design of the federal rules. Federal Rule of Criminal Procedure 5(b) provides:

> **Arrest Without a Warrant.** If a defendant is arrested without a warrant, a complaint meeting Rule 4(a)'s requirement of probable cause must be promptly filed in the district where the offense was allegedly committed.

Under this provision, if there is a warrantless arrest, the government must obtain and promptly file a complaint supported by probable cause. As will be discussed *infra*, a complaint is supported by facts establishing probable cause and is sworn under oath before a judicial officer. Therefore, in every federal criminal case, either: (1) a pre-arrest complaint and warrant will be obtained after a judicial officer is satisfied that probable cause exists; or (2) a complaint issued by a judicial officer will be obtained and filed promptly after a warrantless arrest. In both cases, there will have been a timely probable cause determination by a judicial officer.

How Prompt Is "Prompt"?

The *Gerstein* Court held that "the Fourth Amendment requires a timely judicial determination of probable cause," and that "this determination must be made by a judicial officer either before or promptly after arrest." If the judicial determination does not take place until after arrest, what is prompt? Is there a time cutoff after which the Fourth Amendment has been violated? If so, does a jurisdiction which unnecessarily postpones the hearing until very late in—but still within—the allowed time frame still violate the Constitution? The Court grappled with these questions in the next case.

County of Riverside v. McLaughlin

Supreme Court of United States, 1991
500 U.S. 44

■ JUSTICE O'CONNOR delivered the opinion of the Court.

In *Gerstein v. Pugh*, 420 U.S. 103, 95 S.Ct. 854, 43 L.Ed.2d 54 (1975), this Court held that the Fourth Amendment requires a prompt judicial determination of probable cause as a prerequisite to an extended pretrial detention following a warrantless arrest. This case requires us to define what is "prompt" under Gerstein.

I

This is a class action brought under 42 U.S.C. § 1983 challenging the manner in which the County of Riverside, California (County), provides probable cause determinations to persons arrested without a warrant. At issue is the County's policy of combining probable cause determinations with its arraignment procedures. Under County policy, * * * arraignments must be conducted without unnecessary delay and, in any event, within two days of arrest. This 2-day requirement excludes from computation weekends and holidays. Thus, an individual arrested without a warrant late in the week may in some cases be held for as long as five days before receiving a probable cause determination. Over the Thanksgiving holiday, a 7-day delay is possible.

* * *

In March 1989, plaintiffs asked the District Court to issue a preliminary injunction requiring the County to provide all persons arrested without a warrant a judicial determination of probable cause within 36 hours of arrest. * * * The District Court issued the injunction, holding that the County's existing practice violated this Court's decision in Gerstein. * * *

[T]he Court of Appeals affirmed the order granting the preliminary injunction against Riverside County.

The court * * * determined that the County's policy of providing probable cause determinations at arraignment within 48 hours was "not in accord with Gerstein's requirement of a determination 'promptly after arrest'" because no more than 36 hours were needed "to complete the administrative steps incident to arrest." * * *

The Ninth Circuit thus joined the Fourth and Seventh Circuits in interpreting Gerstein as requiring a probable cause determination immediately following completion of the administrative procedures incident to arrest. *Llaguno v. Mingey*, 763 F.2d 1560, 1567–1568 (CA7 1985) (en banc); *Fisher v. Washington Metropolitan Area Transit Authority*, 690 F.2d 1133, 1139–1141 (CA4 1982). By contrast, the Second Circuit understands Gerstein to "stres[s] the need for flexibility" and to permit States to combine probable cause determinations with other pretrial proceedings. *Williams v. Ward*, 845 F.2d 374, 386 (1988), cert. denied, 488 U.S. 1020, 109 S.Ct. 818, 102 L.Ed.2d 807 (1989). We granted certiorari to resolve this conflict among the Circuits as to what constitutes a "prompt" probable cause determination under Gerstein.

II

[The Court disposes of petitioner's standing argument.]

* * *

III

A

In Gerstein, this Court held unconstitutional Florida procedures under which persons arrested without a warrant could remain in police custody for 30 days or more without a judicial determination of probable cause. In reaching this conclusion we attempted to reconcile important competing interests. On the one hand, States have a strong interest in protecting public safety by taking into custody those persons who are reasonably suspected of having engaged in criminal activity, even where there has been no opportunity for a prior judicial determination of probable cause. 420 U.S., at 112, 95 S.Ct., at 862. On the other hand, prolonged detention based on incorrect or unfounded suspicion may unjustly "imperil [a] suspect's job, interrupt his source of income, and impair his family relationships." Id., at 114, 95 S.Ct., at 863. We sought to balance these competing concerns by holding that States "must provide a fair and reliable determination of probable cause as a condition for any significant pretrial restraint of liberty, and this determination must be made by a judicial officer either before or promptly after arrest." Id., at 125, 95 S.Ct., at 868–869 (emphasis added).

The Court thus established a "practical compromise" between the rights of individuals and the realities of law enforcement. Id., at 113, 95 S.Ct., at 863. Under Gerstein, warrantless arrests are permitted but persons arrested without a warrant must promptly be brought before a neutral magistrate for a judicial determination of probable cause. Id., at 114, 95 S.Ct., at 863. Significantly, the Court stopped short of holding that jurisdictions were constitutionally compelled to provide a probable cause hearing immediately upon taking a suspect into custody and completing booking procedures. We acknowledged the burden that proliferation of pretrial proceedings places on the criminal justice system and recognized that the interests of everyone involved, including those persons who are arrested, might be disserved by introducing further procedural complexity into an already intricate system. Id., at 119–123, 95 S.Ct., at 865–868. Accordingly, we left it to the individual

States to integrate prompt probable cause determinations into their differing systems of pretrial procedures. Id., at 123–124, 95 S.Ct., at 867–868.

In so doing, we gave proper deference to the demands of federalism. We recognized that "state systems of criminal procedure vary widely" in the nature and number of pretrial procedures they provide, and we noted that there is no single "preferred" approach. Id., at 123, 95 S.Ct., at 868. We explained further that "flexibility and experimentation by the States" with respect to integrating probable cause determinations was desirable and that each State should settle upon an approach "to accord with [the] State's pretrial procedure viewed as a whole." Ibid. Our purpose in Gerstein was to make clear that the Fourth Amendment requires every State to provide prompt determinations of probable cause, but that the Constitution does not impose on the States a rigid procedural framework. Rather, individual States may choose to comply in different ways.

Inherent in Gerstein's invitation to the States to experiment and adapt was the recognition that the Fourth Amendment does not compel an immediate determination of probable cause upon completing the administrative steps incident to arrest. Plainly, if a probable cause hearing is constitutionally compelled the moment a suspect is finished being "booked," there is no room whatsoever for "flexibility and experimentation by the States." Ibid. Incorporating probable cause determinations "into the procedure for setting bail or fixing other conditions of pretrial release"—which Gerstein explicitly contemplated, id., at 124, 95 S.Ct., at 868—would be impossible. Waiting even a few hours so that a bail hearing or arraignment could take place at the same time as the probable cause determination would amount to a constitutional violation. Clearly, Gerstein is not that inflexible.

Notwithstanding Gerstein's discussion of flexibility, the Court of Appeals for the Ninth Circuit held that no flexibility was permitted. It construed Gerstein as "requir[ing] a probable cause determination to be made as soon as the administrative steps incident to arrest were completed, and that such steps should require only a brief period." 888 F.2d, at 1278 (emphasis added) (internal quotation marks omitted). This same reading is advanced by the dissents. See post, at 1671 (opinion of MARSHALL, J.); post at 1672–1673, 1674 (opinion of SCALIA, J.). The foregoing discussion readily demonstrates the error of this approach. Gerstein held that probable cause determinations must be prompt—not immediate. The Court explained that "flexibility and experimentation" were "desirab[le]"; that "[t]here is no single preferred pretrial procedure"; and that "the nature of the probable cause determination usually will be shaped to accord with a State's pretrial procedure viewed as a whole." 420 U.S., at 123, 95 S.Ct., at 868. The

Court of Appeals and Justice SCALIA disregard these statements, relying instead on selective quotations from the Court's opinion. As we have explained, Gerstein struck a balance between competing interests; a proper understanding of the decision is possible only if one takes into account both sides of the equation.

Justice SCALIA claims to find support for his approach in the common law. He points to several statements from the early 1800's to the effect that an arresting officer must bring a person arrested without a warrant before a judicial officer " 'as soon as he reasonably can.' " Post, at 1672 (emphasis in original). This vague admonition offers no more support for the dissent's inflexible standard than does Gerstein's statement that a hearing follow "promptly after arrest." 420 U.S., at 125, 95 S.Ct., at 869. As mentioned at the outset, the question before us today is what is "prompt" under Gerstein. We answer that question by recognizing that Gerstein struck a balance between competing interests.

B

Given that Gerstein permits jurisdictions to incorporate probable cause determinations into other pretrial procedures, some delays are inevitable. For example, where, as in Riverside County, the probable cause determination is combined with arraignment, there will be delays caused by paperwork and logistical problems. Records will have to be reviewed, charging documents drafted, appearance of counsel arranged, and appropriate bail determined. On weekends, when the number of arrests is often higher and available resources tend to be limited, arraignments may get pushed back even further. In our view, the Fourth Amendment permits a reasonable postponement of a probable cause determination while the police cope with the everyday problems of processing suspects through an overly burdened criminal justice system.

But flexibility has its limits; Gerstein is not a blank check. A State has no legitimate interest in detaining for extended periods individuals who have been arrested without probable cause. The Court recognized in Gerstein that a person arrested without a warrant is entitled to a fair and reliable determination of probable cause and that this determination must be made promptly.

Unfortunately, as lower court decisions applying Gerstein have demonstrated, it is not enough to say that probable cause determinations must be "prompt." This vague standard simply has not provided sufficient guidance. Instead, it has led to a flurry of systemic challenges to city and county practices, putting federal judges in the role of making legislative judgments and overseeing local jailhouse operations. * * *

Our task in this case is to articulate more clearly the boundaries of what is permissible under the Fourth Amendment. Although we hesitate to announce that the Constitution compels a specific time limit, it is important to provide some degree of certainty so that States and counties may establish procedures with confidence that they fall within constitutional bounds. Taking into account the competing interests articulated in Gerstein, we believe that a jurisdiction that provides judicial determinations of probable cause within 48 hours of arrest will, as a general matter, comply with the promptness requirement of Gerstein. For this reason, such jurisdictions will be immune from systemic challenges.

This is not to say that the probable cause determination in a particular case passes constitutional muster simply because it is provided within 48 hours. Such a hearing may nonetheless violate Gerstein if the arrested individual can prove that his or her probable cause determination was delayed unreasonably. Examples of unreasonable delay are delays for the purpose of gathering additional evidence to justify the arrest, a delay motivated by ill will against the arrested individual, or delay for delay's sake. In evaluating whether the delay in a particular case is unreasonable, however, courts must allow a substantial degree of flexibility. Courts cannot ignore the often unavoidable delays in transporting arrested persons from one facility to another, handling late-night bookings where no magistrate is readily available, obtaining the presence of an arresting officer who may be busy processing other suspects or securing the premises of an arrest, and other practical realities.

Where an arrested individual does not receive a probable cause determination within 48 hours, the calculus changes. In such a case, the arrested individual does not bear the burden of proving an unreasonable delay. Rather, the burden shifts to the government to demonstrate the existence of a bona fide emergency or other extraordinary circumstance. The fact that in a particular case it may take longer than 48 hours to consolidate pretrial proceedings does not qualify as an extraordinary circumstance. Nor, for that matter, do intervening weekends. A jurisdiction that chooses to offer combined proceedings must do so as soon as is reasonably feasible, but in no event later than 48 hours after arrest.

Justice SCALIA urges that 24 hours is a more appropriate outer boundary for providing probable cause determinations. See post, at 9. In arguing that any delay in probable cause hearings beyond completing the administrative steps incident to arrest and arranging for a magistrate is unconstitutional, Justice SCALIA, in effect, adopts the view of the Court of Appeals. Yet he ignores entirely the Court of Appeals' determination of the time required to complete those procedures. That court, better situated than this one, concluded that it takes 36 hours to process arrested persons in Riverside County. 888 F.2d, at 1278. In advocating a 24-hour rule, Justice SCALIA would compel Riverside County—and countless others across the Nation—to speed up its criminal justice mechanisms substantially, presumably by allotting local tax dollars to hire additional police officers and magistrates. There may be times when the Constitution compels such direct interference with local control, but this is not one. As we have explained, Gerstein clearly contemplated a reasonable accommodation between legitimate competing concerns. We do no more than recognize that such accommodation can take place without running afoul of the Fourth Amendment.

Everyone agrees that the police should make every attempt to minimize the time a presumptively innocent individual spends in jail. One way to do so is to provide a judicial determination of probable cause immediately upon completing the administrative steps incident to arrest—i.e., as soon as the suspect has been booked, photographed, and fingerprinted. As Justice SCALIA explains, several States, laudably, have adopted this approach. The Constitution does not compel so rigid a schedule, however. Under Gerstein, jurisdictions may choose to combine probable cause determinations with other pretrial proceedings, so long as they do so promptly. This necessarily means that only certain proceedings are candidates for combination. Only those proceedings that arise very early in the pretrial process—such as bail hearings and arraignments—may be chosen. Even then, every effort must be made to expedite the combined proceedings. See 420 U.S., at 124, 95 S.Ct., at 868.

IV

For the reasons we have articulated, we conclude that Riverside County is entitled to combine probable cause determinations with arraignments. The record indicates, however, that the County's current policy and practice do not comport fully with the principles we have outlined. The County's current policy is to offer combined proceedings within two days, exclusive of Saturdays, Sundays, or holidays. As a result, persons arrested on Thursdays may have to wait until the following Monday before they receive a probable cause determination. The delay is even longer if there is an intervening holiday. Thus, the County's regular practice exceeds the 48-hour period we deem constitutionally permissible, meaning that the County is not immune from systemic challenges, such as this class action.

As to arrests that occur early in the week, the County's practice is that "arraignment[s] usually tak[e] place on the last day" possible. * * * There may well be legitimate reasons for this practice; alternatively, this may constitute delay for delay's sake. We leave it to the Court of Appeals and the District Court, on remand, to make this determination.

The judgment of the Court of Appeals is vacated, and the case is remanded for further proceedings consistent with this opinion.

It is so ordered.

■ JUSTICE MARSHALL, with whom JUSTICE BLACKMUN and JUSTICE STEVENS join, dissenting.

In *Gerstein v. Pugh*, 420 U.S. 103, 95 S.Ct. 854, 43 L.Ed.2d 54 (1975), this Court held that an individual detained following a warrantless arrest is entitled to a "prompt" judicial determination of probable cause as a prerequisite to any further restraint on his liberty. See id., at 114–116, 125, 95 S.Ct., at 863–864, 868. I agree with Justice SCALIA that a probable-cause hearing is sufficiently "prompt" under Gerstein only when provided immediately upon completion of the "administrative steps incident to arrest," id., at 114, 95 S.Ct., at 863. See post, at 1673. Because the Court of Appeals correctly held that the County of Riverside must provide probable-cause hearings as soon as it completes the administrative steps incident to arrest, see 888 F.2d 1276, 1278 (CA9 1989), I would affirm the judgment of the Court of Appeals. Accordingly, I dissent.

Impermissible Reasons for Delaying Gerstein *Hearing*

The *McLaughlin* majority opinion spent quite a bit of time responding to Justice Scalia's dissent, which advanced the view that:

> absent extraordinary circumstances, it is an 'unreasonable seizure' within the meaning of the Fourth Amendment for the police, having arrested a suspect without a warrant, to delay a determination of probable cause for the arrest either (1) for reasons unrelated to arrangement of the probable-cause determination or completion of the steps incident to arrest, or (2) beyond 24 hours after the arrest.

McLaughlin, 500 U.S., at 70 (SCALIA, J., dissenting).

Although the Court did not share Justice's Scalia's view that a 24-hour benchmark was the appropriate compromise, it did make clear that staying within a 48-hour window did not guarantee that a jurisdiction would be in compliance with the Fourth Amendment. Importantly, if the probable cause hearing is delayed for impermissible reasons—such as gathering evidence or out of a desire to punish the detainee—the detention may violate the Fourth Amendment even if it is less than 48 hours in duration. Why is it problematic to allow jurisdictions to delay the hearing in order to gather additional evidence within the 48-hour window?

Manuel v. City of Joliet *and Pretrial Detention After the Start of Legal Process*

In *Manuel v. City of Joliet*, 580 U.S. ___, 137 S.Ct. 911 (2017), the U.S. Supreme Court made clear that the Fourth Amendment controlled the question of whether pretrial detention was lawful—even after an initial *Gerstein* judicial determination of probable cause. In *Manuel*, the petitioner brought suit against the city because he was detained for 48 days despite the fact there was no probable cause to believe the vitamin bottle found during a search contained an illegal substance. In fact, a field test, an evidence technician test at the police station, and a subsequent police laboratory test found no controlled substances. Nevertheless, Manuel was detained following a judge's determination of probable cause, based solely upon fabricated evidence of controlled substances as presented in the law enforcement complaint. The city argued that pretrial detention after legal process had begun (e.g., the Gerstein hearing) could not trigger a claim under the Fourth Amendment. The Court held that the *Gerstein* determination of probable cause (relying on fabricated evidence) did not extinguish the Fourth Amendment claim of the petitioner, and that a cause of action for unlawful pretrial detention—even after the start of legal process— was available to petitioner.

Variations in Procedural Posture in Criminal Procedure Cases

You may note that *Gerstein, McLaughlin,* and *Manuel* all derived from civil suits that came out of criminal cases. In *Gerstein*, the plaintiffs (respondents) filed a civil class action suit for declaratory and injunctive relief associated with their claim that the Constitution guaranteed a timely judicial assessment of probable cause. In *McLaughlin*, also a civil class action case, the plaintiffs (respondents) challenged Riverside County's practice of combining proceedings. The cause of action, also at issue in *Manuel*, was 42 U.S.C. § 1983, also known as a "constitutional tort" suit. This statute permits suit on the basis that the plaintiff's constitutional rights were violated by someone acting under the color of state law. *See* 42 U.S.C. § 1983; *Imbler v. Pachtman*, 424 U.S. 409, 417 (1976).

You will encounter other instances in this textbook in which the core criminal procedure issue has been addressed by the reviewing court not in the context of an appeal from the lower court decision in a *criminal* case, but in the context of an appeal from the lower court decision in a *civil* case.

NOTE ON STATE PRACTICE

Take a moment to find out where the rules governing probable cause hearings for warrantless arrests can be found in your home state or the state where you intend to practice. What is the deadline set by your state? 48 hours? 24 hours? What is the consequence for failure to meet the deadline? Does the jurisdiction combine the probable cause hearing with a bail or pretrial release determination, a subject covered in Chapter 3, infra? Which judicial officer typically makes the determination—a judge, a magistrate, a bail commissioner? *See, e.g.,* Maryland Rule 4–212(f) ("When a defendant is arrested without a warrant, the defendant shall be taken before a judicial officer of the District Court without unnecessary delay and in no event later than 24 hours after the arrest."); 4–216(a).

II. COMPLAINT

Rule 3. The Complaint

The complaint is a written statement of the essential facts constituting the offense charged. Except as provided in Rule 4.1, it must be made under oath before a magistrate judge or, if none is reasonably available, before a state or local judicial officer.

> ### Criminal Complaint Form
> http://www.uscourts.gov/sites/default/files/ao091.pdf

The criminal complaint is a form setting out the basic charge(s) against the defendant, and is often the first formal document filed in many criminal cases. The complaint typically is accompanied by an affidavit alleging facts establishing probable cause to believe the named defendant committed an offense. Often, the affidavit supporting a criminal complaint is drafted by the prosecutor with the assistance of the affiant, usually a case agent. The affiant swears to the truthfulness of the facts in the complaint and supporting affidavit(s) in the presence of the reviewing judicial officer, perhaps informally in chambers.

Under the federal rules, the complaint is typically filed either in support of an arrest warrant or summons, or after a warrantless arrest. In cases involving felony charges, an information or indictment will be filed subsequently, as only misdemeanors may proceed to trial on a complaint. *See* Fed. R. Crim. P. 7, 58. Aside from the need to comply with the Fifth Amendment Grand Jury Clause and Federal Rule of Criminal Procedure 7, a subsequent indictment (or information) also may be filed for the purpose of bringing additional charges not contained in the original complaint.

Of course, some cases will begin instead with the filing of a grand jury indictment or a criminal information, as discussed in Chapter 5, infra, thus obviating the need for a criminal complaint. However, the criminal complaint is frequently utilized in cases where there is a need to charge an offense in order to provide the basis for the immediate arrest of a defendant, or to otherwise commence criminal proceedings.

III. ARREST AND SUMMONS

Rule 4(a) provides that "[i]f the complaint or one or more affidavits with the complaint establish probable cause to believe that an offense has been committed and that the defendant committed it, the judge must issue an arrest warrant to an officer authorized to execute it." Fed. R. Crim. P. 4(a). Note that the rule uses the term "must" to describe the court's duty to issue an arrest warrant. The court has no discretion in this regard. However, the court must instead issue a summons rather than an arrest warrant if the attorney for the government requests it. See *id*.

Rule 4(b) governs the form the warrant and summons must take, and Rule 4(c) provides for the method of execution (and return) of the warrant or service (and return) of the summons. Rule 4(d) and the relatively new Rule 4.1 relate to the issuance of a complaint, warrant, or summons by telephone or "other reliable electronic means."

Arrest Warrant Form

http://www.uscourts.gov/sites/default/files/ao442.pdf

Summons Form

http://www.uscourts.gov/sites/default/files/ao083.pdf

**COUNSEL EXERCISE 1: Complaint and Warrant
(Prosecution)**

Draft for your case agent a complaint and an affidavit demonstrating probable cause to support a criminal complaint against the defendant. You should consult Title 18 of the United States Code to select one offense to charge, and ensure that the factual allegations satisfy every element of the charged offense. In addition, prepare an arrest warrant for execution by your case agent. All three of these documents will be presented to a magistrate judge for approval.

IV. THE INITIAL APPEARANCE

When a defendant is arrested or summonsed in the federal system, she must be brought "without unnecessary delay" before a judicial officer for an initial appearance. Fed. R. Crim. P. 5(a)(1). To be sure, the initial appearance is *not* a *Gerstein* hearing. As discussed above, the *Gerstein* requirement of a probable cause finding is satisfied in a federal case by either the pre-arrest warrant (or summons) filing of a complaint, or the prompt filing of a complaint following a warrantless arrest under Fed. R. Crim. P. 5(b).

Rather, a "Rule 5 hearing" is for the purpose of ensuring that a defendant is afforded the rights that attach once formal criminal proceedings are commenced. Importantly, the defendant is produced before a judicial officer who can visually assess his or her physical condition.[3] Although you may often hear this initial appearance referred to as an "arraignment," in the federal system, the term "arraignment" attaches to a later proceeding, governed by Fed. R. Crim. P. 10.

After setting the district in which the defendant must receive the Rule 5 hearing (depending upon where the arrest took place), *see* Fed. R. Crim. P. 5(c), the Rule sets out the particular procedures that must be followed when the defendant has been charged with a felony.[4]

Rule 5. Initial Appearance

. . .

(d) Procedure in a Felony Case.

(1) *Advice.* If the defendant is charged with a felony, the judge must inform the defendant of the following:

(A) the complaint against the defendant, and any affidavit filed with it;

(B) the defendant's right to retain counsel or to request that counsel be appointed if the defendant cannot obtain counsel;

(C) the circumstances, if any, under which the defendant may secure pretrial release;

(D) any right to a preliminary hearing; and

---

[3] However, the initial appearance may take place by video teleconferencing with the consent of the defendant. *See* Fed. R. Crim. P. 5(f).

[4] If the charge(s) against the defendant are limited to misdemeanor(s), the judicial officer advises the defendant under Rule 58(b)(2).

(E) the defendant's right not to make a statement, and that any statement made may be used against the defendant.

Thus, the judicial officer is required to give the defendant notice of the complaint and supporting affidavits containing the basic allegations against him. The defendant also must be informed of his right to retain private counsel or be appointed counsel if he is unable to do so. (*See* discussion of Fed. R. Crim. P. 44, *infra*.) The judicial officer also must inform the defendant how he might be released from custody prior to trial, (*see* discussion of Fed. R. Crim. P. 46, in Chapter 3, *infra*),[5] and any right to a Rule 5.1 Preliminary Hearing. (*See* discussion of Fed. R. Crim. P. 5.1, *infra*.) Finally, the defendant is entitled to a warning that he has the right to remain silent and that any statement made may be used adversely.

NOTE ON STATE PRACTICE

What is the judicial officer in your state required to communicate to an accused upon his or her first appearance? *See, e.g.,* Fla. R. Crim. P. 3.130(a).

The Federal Right to Counsel

As was mentioned in *Gerstein, supra*, the right to counsel in criminal pretrial proceedings is limited to "critical stages in the proceedings." In holding that the *Gerstein* probable cause hearing was not such a 'critical stage,' the Court said that it had "identified as 'critical stages' those pretrial procedures that would impair defense on the merits if the accused is required to proceed without counsel." *Gerstein, supra* (citing *Coleman v. Alabama*, 399 U.S. 1 (1970)).

Rule 5(d)(2) makes clear that, at the initial appearance, the defendant must be given the opportunity to consult with counsel, and Rule 5(d)(1)(B) provides that the defendant must be informed of her right to retain counsel or have counsel appointed if she is financially unable to do so. Indeed, under Rule 44, a federal defendant has the right to appointed counsel at *every* stage of the criminal proceeding.

Rule 44. Right to and Appointment of Counsel

(a) Right to Appointed Counsel. A defendant who is unable to obtain counsel is entitled to have counsel appointed to represent the defendant at every stage of the proceeding

---

5   Rule 5(d)(3) provides that "[t]he judge must detain or release the defendant as provided by statute or these rules." If the court does not release the defendant at the Rule 5 hearing, a temporary detainer is placed on the defendant until the detention hearing is scheduled. [Order Scheduling a Detention Hearing http://www.uscourts.gov/sites/default/files/ao470.pdf] The subject of pretrial release is taken up in Chapter 3, *infra*.

from initial appearance through appeal, unless the defendant waives this right.

As Rule 44(b) sets out, "[f]ederal law and local court rules govern the procedure for implementing the right to counsel." Fed. R. Crim. P. 44(b). The standards for the appointment of counsel can be found at 18 U.S.C. 3006A(a). The constitutional right to counsel is explored more fully in Chapter 9, *infra*.

NOTE ON STATE PRACTICE

For what stages of a criminal case does your state provide counsel? *See, e.g.,* Fla. R. Crim. P. 3.111 (providing that a person "shall have counsel appointed when he is formally charged with an offense, or as soon as feasible after custodial restraint or upon his first appearance before a committing magistrate, whichever occurs earliest").

V. PRELIMINARY HEARING

As is discussed in Chapter 4, *infra*, many jurisdictions do not require a grand jury indictment; rather, they permit the prosecutor to file criminal charges by "information." An information is essentially a charging document containing the bare allegations of the prosecutor without any prior scrutiny by a neutral judicial officer. However, in most of these jurisdictions, the allegations in the information are subject to a preliminary hearing in which a judicial officer determines whether the charges are supported by probable cause. But, does the Constitution *require* such a hearing? If so, *which* constitutional provision mandates the preliminary hearing? The next case explores these questions.

Albright v. Oliver
Supreme Court of United States, 1994
510 U.S. 266

■ CHIEF JUSTICE REHNQUIST announced the judgment of the Court and delivered an opinion, in which JUSTICE O'CONNOR, JUSTICE SCALIA, and JUSTICE GINSBURG join.

A warrant was issued for petitioner's arrest by Illinois authorities, and upon learning of it he surrendered and was released on bail. The prosecution was later dismissed on the ground that the charge did not state an offense under Illinois law. Petitioner asks us to recognize a substantive right under the Due Process Clause of the Fourteenth Amendment to be free from criminal prosecution except upon probable cause. We decline to do so.

Illinois authorities issued an arrest warrant for petitioner Kevin Albright, charging him on the basis of a previously filed criminal information with the sale of a substance which looked like an illegal drug. When he learned of the outstanding warrant, petitioner surrendered to respondent, Roger Oliver, a police detective employed by the city of Macomb, but denied his guilt of such an offense. He was released after posting bond, one of the conditions of which was that he not leave the State without permission of the court.

At a preliminary hearing, respondent Oliver testified that petitioner sold the look-alike substance to Moore, and the court found probable cause to bind petitioner over for trial. At a later pretrial hearing, the court dismissed the criminal action against petitioner on the ground that the charge did not state an offense under Illinois law.

Albright then instituted this action under Rev.Stat. § 1979, 42 U.S.C. § 1983, against Detective Oliver in his individual and official capacities, alleging that Oliver deprived him of substantive due process under the Fourteenth Amendment—his "liberty interest"—to be free from criminal prosecution except upon probable cause. The District Court granted respondent's motion to dismiss under Rule 12(b)(6) on the ground that the complaint did not state a claim under § 1983. The Court of Appeals for the Seventh Circuit affirmed, * * * [holding] that prosecution without probable cause is a constitutional tort actionable under § 1983 only if accompanied by incarceration or loss of employment or some other "palpable consequenc[e]." * * * The panel of the Seventh Circuit reasoned that "just as in the garden-variety public-officer defamation case that does not result in exclusion from an occupation, state tort remedies should be adequate and the heavy weaponry of constitutional litigation can be left at rest." * * * We granted certiorari, * * *, and while we affirm the judgment below, we do so on different grounds. We hold that it is the Fourth Amendment, and not substantive due process, under which petitioner Albright's claim must be judged.

Section 1983 "is not itself a source of substantive rights," but merely provides "a method for vindicating federal rights elsewhere conferred." *Baker v. McCollan,* 443 U.S. 137, 144, n. 3, 99 S.Ct. 2689, 2694, n. 3, 61 L.Ed.2d 433 (1979). The first step in any such claim is to identify the specific constitutional right allegedly infringed. *Graham v. Connor*, 490 U.S. 386, 394, 109 S.Ct. 1865, 1870, 104 L.Ed.2d 443 (1989); and *Baker v. McCollan, supra,* 443 U.S., at 140, 99 S.Ct., at 2692.

Petitioner's claim before this Court is a very limited one. He claims that the action of respondents infringed his substantive due process right to be free of prosecution without probable cause. He does not claim that Illinois denied him the procedural due process guaranteed by the Fourteenth Amendment. Nor does he claim a violation of his Fourth Amendment rights, notwithstanding the fact that his surrender to the State's show of authority constituted a seizure for purposes of the

Fourth Amendment. *Terry v. Ohio,* 392 U.S. 1, 19, 88 S.Ct. 1868, 1878, 20 L.Ed.2d 889 (1968); *Brower v. County of Inyo,* 489 U.S. 593, 596, 109 S.Ct. 1378, 1381, 103 L.Ed.2d 628 (1989).

We begin analysis of petitioner's claim by repeating our observation in *Collins v. Harker Heights,* 503 U.S. 115, 125, 112 S.Ct. 1061, 1068, 117 L.Ed.2d 261 (1992). "As a general matter, the Court has always been reluctant to expand the concept of substantive due process because the guideposts for responsible decisionmaking in this unchartered area are scarce and open-ended." The protections of substantive due process have for the most part been accorded to matters relating to marriage, family, procreation, and the right to bodily integrity. See, *e.g., Planned Parenthood of Southeastern Pa. v. Casey,* 505 U.S. 833, 847–849, 112 S.Ct. 2791, 2804–2806, 120 L.Ed.2d 674 (1992). (describing cases in which substantive due process rights have been recognized). Petitioner's claim to be free from prosecution except on the basis of probable cause is markedly different from *those recognized in this group of* cases.

Petitioner relies on our observations in cases such as *United States v. Salerno,* 481 U.S. 739, 746, 107 S.Ct. 2095, 2101, 95 L.Ed.2d 697 (1987), and *Daniels v. Williams,* 474 U.S. 327, 331, 106 S.Ct. 662, 664, 88 L.Ed.2d 662 (1986), that the Due Process Clause of the Fourteenth Amendment confers both substantive and procedural rights. This is undoubtedly true, but it sheds little light on the scope of substantive due process. Petitioner points in particular to language from *Hurtado v. California,* 110 U.S. 516, 527, 4 S.Ct. 111, 116, 28 L.Ed. 232 (1884), later quoted in *Daniels, supra,* stating that the words "by the law of the land" from the Magna Carta were " 'intended to secure the individual from the arbitrary exercise of the powers of government.' " This, too, may be freely conceded, but it does not follow that, in all of the various aspects of a criminal prosecution, the only inquiry mandated by the Constitution is whether, in the view of the Court, the governmental action in question was "arbitrary."

Hurtado held that the Due Process Clause did not make applicable to the States the Fifth Amendment's requirement that all prosecutions for an infamous crime be instituted by the indictment of a grand jury. In the more than 100 years which have elapsed since *Hurtado* was decided, the Court has concluded that a number of the procedural protections contained in the Bill of Rights were made applicable to the States by the Fourteenth Amendment. See *Mapp v. Ohio,* 367 U.S. 643, 81 S.Ct. 1684, 6 L.Ed.2d 1081 (1961), overruling *Wolf v. Colorado,* 338 U.S. 25, 69 S.Ct. 1359, 93 L.Ed. 1782 (1949), and holding the Fourth Amendment's exclusionary rule applicable to the States; *Malloy v. Hogan,* 378 U.S. 1, 84 S.Ct. 1489, 12 L.Ed.2d 653 (1964), overruling *Twining v. New Jersey,* 211 U.S. 78, 29 S.Ct. 14, 53 L.Ed. 97 (1908), and holding the Fifth Amendment's privilege against self-incrimination applicable to the States; *Benton v. Maryland,* 395 U.S. 784, 89 S.Ct. 2056, 23 L.Ed.2d 707 (1969), overruling *Palko v. Connecticut,* 302 U.S. 319, 58 S.Ct. 149, 82 L.Ed. 288 (1937), and holding the Double Jeopardy Clause of the Fifth Amendment applicable to the States; *Gideon v. Wainwright,* 372 U.S. 335, 83 S.Ct. 792, 9 L.Ed.2d 799 (1963), overruling *Betts v. Brady,* 316 U.S. 455, 62 S.Ct. 1252, 86 L.Ed. 1595 (1942), and holding that the Sixth Amendment's right to counsel was applicable to the States. See also *Klopfer v. North Carolina,* 386 U.S. 213, 87 S.Ct. 988, 18 L.Ed.2d 1 (1967) (Sixth Amendment speedy trial right applicable to the States); *Washington v. Texas,* 388 U.S. 14, 87 S.Ct. 1920, 18 L.Ed.2d 1019 (1967) (Sixth Amendment right to compulsory process applicable to the States); *Duncan v. Louisiana,* 391 U.S. 145, 88 S.Ct. 1444, 20 L.Ed.2d 491 (1968) (Sixth Amendment right to jury trial applicable to the States).

This course of decision has substituted, in these areas of criminal procedure, the specific guarantees of the various provisions of the Bill of Rights embodied in the first 10 Amendments to the Constitution for the more generalized language contained in the earlier cases construing the Fourteenth Amendment. It was through these provisions of the Bill of Rights that their Framers sought to restrict the exercise of arbitrary authority by the Government in particular situations. Where a particular Amendment "provides an explicit textual source of constitutional protection" against a particular sort of government behavior, "that Amendment, not the more generalized notion of 'substantive due process,' must be the guide for analyzing these claims." *Graham v. Connor, supra,* 490 U.S., at 395, 109 S.Ct., at 1871.

We think this principle is likewise applicable here. The Framers considered the matter of pretrial deprivations of liberty and drafted the Fourth Amendment to address it. The Fourth Amendment provides:

> "The right of the people to be secure in their persons, houses, papers, and effects, against unreasonable searches and seizures, shall not be violated, and no Warrants shall issue, but upon probable cause, supported by Oath or affirmation, and particularly describing the place to be searched, and the persons or things to be seized."

We have in the past noted the Fourth Amendment's relevance to the deprivations of liberty that go hand in hand with criminal prosecutions. See *Gerstein v. Pugh,* 420 U.S. 103, 114, 95 S.Ct. 854, 862, 43 L.Ed.2d 54 (1975) (holding that the Fourth Amendment requires a judicial determination of probable cause as a prerequisite to any extended restraint on liberty following an arrest). We have said that the accused is not "entitled to judicial oversight or review of the decision to prosecute." *Id.,* at 118–119, 95 S.Ct., at 865–866. See also *Beck v. Washington,* 369 U.S. 541, 545, 82 S.Ct. 955, 957, 8 L.Ed.2d 98 (1962);

Lem Woon v. Oregon, 229 U.S. 586, 33 S.Ct. 783, 57 L.Ed. 1340 (1913). But here petitioner was not merely charged; he submitted himself to arrest.

We express no view as to whether petitioner's claim would succeed under the Fourth Amendment, since he has not presented that question in his petition for certiorari. We do hold that substantive due process, with its "scarce and open-ended" "guideposts," *Collins v. Harker Heights,* 503 U.S., at 125, 112 S.Ct., at 1068, can afford him no relief.

The judgment of the Court of Appeals is therefore

Affirmed.

―――――――――――

No Constitutional Right to a Preliminary Hearing

The *Albright* Court reminded, as had the *Gerstein* Court, that a defendant is not "entitled to judicial oversight or review of the decision to prosecute." This restriction on the pretrial rights of the accused originates from a 100-year old decision, *Lem Woon v. Oregon*, 229 U.S. 586 (1913), in which the Court held that the Fourteenth Amendment's Due Process Clause did not prohibit the state from instituting a prosecution on serious criminal charges without judicial scrutiny for probable cause. In combination with the earlier decision in *Hurtado v. California*, 110 U.S. 516 (1884), *Lem Woon* means that one is entitled to neither a grand jury indictment (except in the federal system), nor a judge's review of a prosecutor's allegations in an information. In this sense, *Lem Woon* "doubled down" on the power of the prosecution to bring charges without independent review of whether they might be meritless. Scrutiny of the allegations can be deferred fully to the fact-finder at trial. Can you think of pretrial burdens a criminal defendant might suffer even if she is ultimately vindicated by the fact-finder's rejection of weak charges at trial? Even if the charges against the defendant are dismissed before trial?

The Federal Rule 5.1 Preliminary Hearing

Despite the fact that the Constitution does not require a preliminary hearing, the court, in the federal system, *must* conduct a preliminary hearing for a defendant charged with a felony or non-petty misdemeanor, absent one of the circumstances described in Rule 5.1(a). The Rule 5.1 preliminary hearing is an adversarial hearing, at which the defendant may cross-examine witnesses and introduce evidence. *See* Rule 5.1(e). However, the defendant may not object (at this stage) to any of the government's evidence on the ground that it was acquired illegally. *See id.* All testimony is recorded, and the basic trial rules regarding disclosure of prior statements of witnesses apply to the hearing. *See* Rule 5.1(g), (h).

If, at the conclusion of the hearing, the court finds probable cause to believe that an offense was committed and that the defendant committed it, the criminal case against the defendant is permitted to move forward. On the other hand, if the court does not find such probable cause, the complaint is dismissed without prejudice (meaning that the prosecutor is permitted to re-file the charges later) and the defendant is discharged. *See* Rule 5.1(f).

Strategic Considerations Related to Rule 5.1 Hearings

With its requirement that government offer testimony and evidence sufficient to establish probable cause, there can be significant advantages to the defendant who receives a preliminary hearing. The hearing forces the government to tip its hand as to its theory of the case very early in the proceedings. Good defense attorneys will use the Rule 5.1 hearing as an opportunity for fact discovery they otherwise would not have had at this stage of the case. Also, because the proceedings are on the record, the Rule 5.1 hearing "locks in" the testimony of the testifying case agent or other important fact witness for the government. Thus, the early testimony can serve as the basis for impeachment if the witness's testimony at trial strays from that given at the Rule 5.1 hearing in the beginning stages of the case.

Prosecutors often will try to limit the scope of testimony of preliminary hearing witnesses in hopes of limiting the scope of cross examination by defense counsel. They also typically favor putting on the stand an experienced case agent who can give summarizing hearsay testimony (which is permitted in Rule 5.1 hearings) rather than open up the lay fact witnesses to scrutiny at this stage.

However, given the many potential pitfalls for the government, many prosecutors simply try to avoid Rule 5.1 hearings altogether when possible. Rule 5.1(a) provides the circumstances when a preliminary hearing is *not* required.

Rule 5.1 Preliminary Hearing

(a) **In General.** If a defendant is charged with an offense other than a petty offense, a magistrate judge must conduct a preliminary hearing unless:

    (1) the defendant waives the hearing;

    (2) the defendant is indicted;

    (3) the government files an information under Rule 7(b) charging the defendant with a felony;

    (4) the government files an information charging the defendant with a misdemeanor; or

(5) the defendant is charged with a misdemeanor and consents to trial before a magistrate judge.

Rule 5.1(a)(1) and (a)(3) relate to situations when the defendant either waives the right to a preliminary hearing, or waives the right to a grand jury indictment and permits the government to proceed against him on an information (usually in the context of a guilty plea). Rule 5.1 (a)(5) relates to the defendant's decision to consent to trial on a misdemeanor before a magistrate judge, which cuts off the right to a preliminary hearing.

However, the other two provisions of Rule 5.1(a) give the government the power to remove the defendant's entitlement to a preliminary hearing. Under Rule 5.1(a)(4), the government can cut off the defendant's right to a preliminary hearing simply by filing an information against her charging a misdemeanor. This essentially commits the government to pursuing less serious misdemeanor charges in the case.

In a case in which the prosecutor plans to file felony charges, the defendant's right to a Rule 5.1 hearing can be cut off simply by obtaining a grand jury indictment. *See* Rule 5.1(a)(2). This is because, even with serious charges, the probable cause finding by the grand jury necessary to secure an indictment obviates the need for any other finding of probable cause. The grand jury indictment is, in a way, treated by the rule as the "gold standard" of probable cause findings, and, thus, there is no need for the court to scrutinize the evidence further. *See, Kaley v. United States*, 134 S.Ct. 1090, 1098 (2014) ("The grand jury gets to say—without any review, oversight, or second-guessing—whether probable cause exists to think a person committed a crime.").

Nevertheless, there are deadlines that the prosecutor must meet if the Rule 5.1 hearing is to be avoided. Rule 5.1(c) mandates that the magistrate judge "hold the preliminary hearing within a reasonable time, but no later than 14 days after the [Rule 5] initial appearance if the defendant is in custody and no later than 21 days if not in custody." Therefore, there can be significant time pressure placed on the prosecutor to present the case to a grand jury and obtain an indictment before the Rule 5.1 hearing clock runs.

NOTE ON STATE PRACTICE

Does your state provide a preliminary hearing to the accused? If so, under what circumstances? *See, e.g.,* Mass. R. Crim. P. 3(f).

COUNSEL EXERCISE 2A: Preliminary Hearing (Prosecution)

Prepare questions for a direct examination of the case agent who swore out the complaint and affidavit in support. You should be sure that the witness testimony satisfies every element of the charged offense and you should take care to keep the direct examination as narrow as possible so as to limit the scope of cross examination. Be sure to have the witness identify the defendant for the record.

COUNSEL EXERCISE 2B: Preliminary Hearing (Defense)

Prepare questions for a cross examination of the case agent who will testify in support of government's criminal complaint against your client. You should try to weaken the government's evidence establishing the various elements of the offense, and you should seek to obtain "free discovery" by finding out about the theory of the government's case and probing its potential weaknesses. In addition, you may use this opportunity to lock the government's witness, who is under oath, into certain statements.

VI. PETTY OFFENSE AND MISDEMEANORS

The adjudication of petty offenses and misdemeanors is governed by Rule 58 of the Federal Rules of Criminal Procedure. Although the procedural approach is very similar to that used for felony cases, there are certain variations, including the ability to use a citation or violation notice as the charging document in a case involving a petty offense. *See* Fed. R. Crim P. 7(a)(2), 58(b)(1). In addition, the right to have a criminal case disposed of by a district judge (as opposed to a magistrate judge) and the right to a jury trial do not extend to petty offenses. *See* 18 U.S.C. § 3401(b); Fed. R. Crim. P. 58(b)(2)(E), (F).

So, what is a petty offense? Whether an offense is considered petty (as defined in Title 18 of the United States Code at Section 19) is determined largely by the nature of the crime, and the statutory maximum fine and term of imprisonment. Infractions (maximum five days imprisonment), or Class B (maximum six months imprisonment) misdemeanors not resulting in death, or Class C misdemeanors (maximum thirty days imprisonment) not resulting in death are defined in Title 18 as petty offenses, unless the maximum statutory fine exceeds

$5000.00 for an individual or $10,000.00 for an organization. 18 U.S.C. § 19; 18 U.S.C. §§ 3559, 3571.

Non-petty offenses (including Class A misdemeanors and all classes of felony offenses) trigger the right to jury trial before a district judge. 18 U.S.C. § 3401. However, any matter "that does not dispose of a charge or defense" may be referred by a district judge for determination by a magistrate judge. Fed. R. Crim. P. 59(a). Indeed, dispositive matters also may be referred to a magistrate judge, although the magistrate judge's recommended disposition, findings of fact, and record of proceedings are subject to objection by the parties, and mandatory *de novo* review by a district judge. Fed. R. Crim. P. 59(b). In any event, before a case involving a non-petty offense is referred to a magistrate judge for trial, judgment, or sentencing, the defendant must consent. 18 U.S.C. § 3401; Fed. R. Crim. P. 58(b)(2)(E).

What Is a Magistrate Judge?

In these early chapters, reference has been made to "magistrate" and "magistrate judge." Although, in criminal procedure, the term "magistrate" can refer to non-lawyers who review arrest and search warrant applications for probable cause, magistrates in the federal system enjoy an elevated status. Indeed, in the Judicial Improvements Act of 1990, Congress changed the title from "magistrate" to "magistrate judge," in part to reflect this status. *See, e.g.,* Ruth Dapper, *A Judge by Any Other Name: Mistitling of the United States Magistrate Judge,* 9 FED. CTS. L. REV. 1 (2015). *See also* Hon. Lisa Margaret Smith, *Top 10 Things You Probably Never Knew About Magistrate Judges,* THE FEDERAL LAWYER, May/June 2014, at 38 ("The title of the position is 'U.S. Magistrate Judge.' ... The proper and preferred address is Magistrate Judge, or Judge, or Your Honor. Paraphrasing from Judge Randolph in [the film] *A Few Good Men,* we are quite certain that we have earned such a title.").

The duties and responsibilities of U.S. Magistrate Judges are outlined in Title 28 of the United States Code, at Sections 631–639. Absent a judicial emergency, U.S. Magistrate Judges must be members in good standing of a state bar for at least five years and cannot hold outside government employment. They do not have life tenure, are subject to removal for cause, and are appointed to an initial eight-year term, with eligibility for renewal. U.S. Magistrate Judges are appointed by the active district judges in a given district.

U.S. Magistrate Judges may oversee all manner of criminal matters, including initial appearances, detention hearings, arraignments, and pretrial motions, among others. Given the large criminal caseloads in many federal judicial districts, magistrate judges are indispensable to the efficient administration of justice. In fact, many federal criminal defendants will have their cases disposed of without encountering any judicial officer other than a magistrate judge. However, to be sure, as Rule 1(c) makes clear, "[w]hen these rules authorize a magistrate judge to act, any other federal judge may also act."

For an overview of the evolution of the role of federal magistrate judges, *see* Hon. Philip M. Pro, *United States Magistrate Judges: Present but Unaccounted For*, 16 NEV. L. J. 783 (2016); Hon. Dennis M. Cavanaugh, *Magistrate Judges Are Effective, Flexible Judiciary Resource*, THE THIRD BRANCH (Oct. 2008); Tim A. Baker, *The Expanding Role of Magistrate Judges in the Federal Courts*, 39 VALPARAISO U. L. REV. 661 (2005).

NOTE ON STATE PRACTICE

Does your state utilize magistrates or "commissioners" in criminal cases? If so, how are they appointed and compensated? Is there a requirement that they be a member of the state bar? Are they required to be attorneys at all? *See, e.g.,* MD. DEPT. LEG. SVCS., THE DISTRICT COURT COMMISSIONER 10–34 (2013) (50-state survey of functions and qualifications of magistrates and commissioners).

CHAPTER 3

BAIL AND PRETRIAL RELEASE

I. INTRODUCTION

When criminal charges are lodged against a defendant, the state and the public have an interest in ensuring that the individual facing criminal charges is present to answer those charges. Detention obviously performs that function. Detention before trial may also help to ensure the safety of the public if the detainee is prone to violence, and pretrial detention can help protect the well-being of individual victims or witnesses in the case. Indeed, detention might also help to protect the detainee from harming himself or harm at the hands of another.

On the other side of the ledger, however, a whole host of interests are implicated when one is detained in connection with pending or anticipated criminal charges. First and foremost is the detainee's liberty interest in being free from state custody. It is important to remember that a pretrial detainee is innocent until proven guilty and, therefore, is not properly the subject of criminal punishment.

Aside from the pure liberty interest are the detainee's interests in health and safety—being able to obtain proper medical care for conditions the individual might have or develop, and to be free from the intimidation or violence at the hands of fellow detainees.

The fact of the person's detention may burden economic interests as well. While the person is detained they cannot go to work or oversee their business operations, which could result in the loss of a job or income. Indeed, such income may be necessary to fund the person's legal defense. The detained individual may also be hindered from assisting in her own defense against the criminal charges being brought by the state. Detained individuals often do not have the ability to have full and free conversations with counsel, and cannot move about freely to help track down evidence or leads. Also, there is the burden on the detained individual's ability to review discovery materials—especially electronic discovery requiring a computer and internet access. These conditions *could* contribute to the greater likelihood of conviction for detained defendants. *See* BUREAU OF JUSTICE STATISTICS, FELONY DEFENDANTS IN LARGE URBAN COUNTIES 24 (2000) ("Seventy-seven percent of the defendants who were detained until case disposition were actually convicted of some offense, compared to 55% of those released pending disposition.")

Furthermore, the detention may keep the individual away from his or her familial obligations and relationships. Although it is clear that children and spouses of individuals who are detained may suffer, many detained individuals, such as volunteers and coaches, may have extra-familial caregiver responsibilities that go untended during their period of detention. Also, it should be remembered that a detainee may be housed a significant distance from his or her home, and some detention facilities impose severe restrictions on visits, such as limiting visits to immediate family members and permitting minors to visit only if accompanied by an adult. This would mean, for example, that if a detainee's fiancée, girlfriend, or boyfriend does not qualify for the visitation list, a detainee may not be able to have visits with his or her own children. Finally, there might also be a stigma associated with being locked up—even for those who ultimately may be vindicated—and, thus, a disruption of the detainee's social networks.

Balancing these interests—in justice and safety on the one hand, and the detainee's myriad interests on the other—can be a difficult task, to say the least. Often, the judge has quite limited information about the defendant and the evidence in the case. Also, judicial officers who are charged with the duty to make these decisions sometimes do so under the glare of intense public scrutiny. There can be tremendous pressure on a judge to deny release of someone accused of a heinous crime, regardless of the likelihood that the accused is a flight or safety risk. When judges make the decision to release an individual (or permit their release by setting bail), there is always the chance that the person will successfully flee and escape justice, obstruct justice, or, worse, will commit another crime or otherwise harm a member of the community. Most judges in this position would rather avoid such a situation occurring, particularly those many judges who are not life-tenured and are required to stand for reelection or reappointment at periodic intervals.

II. MECHANICS OF PRETRIAL DETENTION AND RELEASE

A. RELEASE ON PERSONAL RECOGNIZANCE/CONDITIONS

An individual charged with a crime can simply be released on his or her own personal recognizance. Once released in this manner, the person suffers no restrictions on freedom of movement or activity other than the requirement that they appear for subsequent proceedings in the case. A judge, however, may choose to impose conditions upon someone who is released on personal recognizance. Examples of such conditions might include submission to periodic testing for alcohol or illegal narcotics, relinquishment of a passport or restriction on travel out of the jurisdiction, a prohibition on coming in close proximity to a particular person or a place, the requirement that the individual attend school or seek employment, or a requirement that the individual not commit another criminal offense while on release. The violation of such conditions may cause the judicial officer to revoke the individual's release on personal recognizance. Electronic monitoring might also be a condition imposed to increase the likelihood of appearance at subsequent proceedings. See, e.g., Samuel R. Wiseman, *Pretrial Detention and the Right to Be Monitored*, 123 YALE L.J. 1344 (2014).

ADVOCACY POINT

It often is helpful to be able to present to the court information about support systems that will be in place while the defendant is released pending trial. For example, if the defendant has suffered from narcotics addiction, identifying a particular in-patient or out-patient drug treatment placement for the defendant may help to sway the court in favor of release. Likewise, ensuring that a responsible adult or agency will supervise a youthful defendant could persuade the court to release the defendant into the custody of that third party. Although, in many criminal defense practice contexts, there will be little time to track down such information or commitments prior to the detention hearing, it is worth the effort initially and later in the process if the client is afforded bail review.

B. RELEASE ON BAIL

Sometimes a judicial officer will not be convinced that the individual will return for subsequent proceedings without a financial incentive to do so. When a judge sets bail, she requires the defendant— in exchange for release from custody—to deposit a certain amount of money with the court as "insurance." If the defendant fails to appear, the deposited funds are forfeited, and the person is considered a fugitive.

Obviously, the concept of bail rests upon the assumption that the amount posted represents a sufficient incentive to the defendant. If the amount is too low, the person may be willing to sacrifice the funds in order to flee and avoid future appearances in court. On the other hand, if the amount is set too high, a defendant may be unable to raise the funds and may simply languish in detention until his or her case goes to trial or otherwise reaches disposition. Some may be compelled to plead guilty to crimes they did not commit in order to avoid lengthy detention. For too many defendants in the United States, the period of pretrial detention can exceed the amount of incarceration the sentencing judge likely would have imposed. In some instances, defendants in this posture end up serving more time than the sentencing judge ultimately would have been *authorized* by statute to impose. *See, e.g.*, JUSTICE POLICY INSTITUTE, BAIL FAIL: WHY THE U.S. SHOULD END THE PRACTICE OF USING MONEY FOR BAIL (2012); Jocelyn Simonson, *Bail Nullification*, 115 MICH. L. REV. 585 (2017) (proposing community bail funds as a response to the cash bail problem); Shaila Dewan, *When Bail is Out of Defendant's Reach, Other Costs Mount*, N.Y. TIMES, June 10, 2015; *see also* Alysia Santo, *No Bail, Less Hope: The Death of Kalief Browder*, THE MARSHALL PROJECT, June 9, 2015 (recounting the tragic death of a young man who had spent three years as a teenager in pretrial detention on a charge of theft of a backpack because he could not afford the $3,000 bail).

When defendants are unable to marshal enough funds to post bail, they often must turn to private bail bondsmen, who advance the required bail money to the court in exchange for a non-refundable percentage (usually 10 percent) of that amount from the defendant or her delegate—typically referred to as "bond.". Given that the bondsman has significant financial exposure, sometimes collateral—such as the deed to a house or the title to an automobile—may be required to cover the potential loss of the bond amount.

In addition, bondsmen typically will keep track the whereabouts of the defendant and will take extraordinary measures to ensure that the defendant appears at the required hearing. Such "extraordinary measures," depicted, for example, in popular reality television series "Dog the Bounty Hunter" and "Family Bonds," can sometimes lead to activities that would have been violative of the defendant's rights had the bondsmen been a state actor. However, although bondsmen and bounty hunters are subject to the laws of the jurisdictions in which they work, courts have generally treated them as private actors and outside of the reach of constitutional restrictions on state actors. *See, e.g.*, Rebecca B. Fisher, *The History of American Bounty Hunting as a Study in Stunted Legal Growth*, 33 N.Y.U. REV. L. SOC. CHANGE 199 (2009).

III. CONSTITUTIONAL ASPECTS OF BAIL AND PRETRIAL DETENTION

There is no right to bail under the United States Constitution; absent some statutory mandate, an individual can be held in custody pending trial. However, courts that do impose bail must undertake an individualized approach when determining the amount, and such amount must be rationally related to the purposes of bail. *See Stack v. Boyle*, 342 U.S. 1 (1951). Also, bail, if it is granted, cannot be excessive. *See* U.S. Const., Amend. VIII ("Excessive bail shall not be required . . . .")

Furthermore, as the person who is detained prior to trial still enjoys the presumption of innocence, the state has certain heightened duties to ensure that what initially might have been pretrial detention for legitimate reasons does not become punishment without due process. However, it can be difficult to determine when conditions of confinement prior to trial should be considered punishment, as the next case explores.

Bell v. Wolfish

Supreme Court of the United States, 1979
441 U.S. 520

■ MR. JUSTICE REHNQUIST delivered the opinion of the Court.

Over the past five Terms, this Court has in several decisions considered constitutional challenges to prison conditions or practices by convicted prisoners. This case requires us to examine the constitutional rights of pretrial detainees-those persons who have been charged with a crime but who have not yet been tried on the charge. The parties concede that to ensure their presence at trial, these persons legitimately may be incarcerated by the Government prior to a determination of their guilt or innocence, see 18 U.S.C. §§ 3146, 3148, and it is the scope of their rights during this period of confinement prior to trial that is the primary focus of this case.

This lawsuit was brought as a class action in the United States District Court for the Southern District of New York to challenge numerous conditions of confinement and practices at the Metropolitan Correctional Center (MCC), a federally operated short-term custodial facility in New York City designed primarily to house pretrial detainees. The District Court, in the words of the Court of Appeals for the Second Circuit, "intervened broadly into almost every facet of the institution" and enjoined no fewer than 20 MCC practices on constitutional and statutory grounds. The Court of Appeals largely affirmed the District Court's constitutional rulings and in the process held that under the Due Process Clause of the Fifth Amendment, pretrial detainees may "be subjected to only those 'restrictions and privations' which 'inhere in their confinement itself or which are justified by compelling necessities of jail administration.'" * * * We granted certiorari to consider the important constitutional questions raised by these decisions and to resolve an apparent conflict among the Circuits. We now reverse.

I

The MCC was constructed in 1975 to replace the converted waterfront garage on West Street that had served as New York City's federal jail since 1928. It is located adjacent to the Foley Square federal courthouse and has as its primary objective the housing of persons who are being detained in custody prior to trial for federal criminal offenses in the United States District Courts for the Southern and Eastern Districts of New York and for the District of New Jersey. Under the Bail Reform Act, 18 U.S.C. § 3146, a person in the federal system is committed to a detention facility only because no other less drastic means can reasonably ensure his presence at trial. In addition to pretrial detainees, the MCC also houses some convicted inmates who are awaiting sentencing or transportation to federal prison or who are serving generally relatively short sentences in a service capacity at the MCC, convicted prisoners who have been lodged at the facility under writs of habeas corpus *ad prosequendum* or *ad testificandum* issued to ensure their presence at upcoming trials, witnesses in protective custody, and persons incarcerated for contempt.

* * *

When the MCC opened in August 1975, the planned capacity was 449 inmates, an increase of 50% over the former West Street facility. Despite some dormitory accommodations, the MCC was designed primarily to house these inmates in 389 rooms, which originally were intended for single occupancy. While the MCC was under construction, however, the number of persons committed to pretrial detention began to rise at an "unprecedented" rate. The Bureau of Prisons took several steps to accommodate this unexpected flow of persons assigned to the facility, but despite these efforts, the inmate population at the MCC rose above its planned capacity within a short time after its opening. To provide sleeping space for this increased population, the MCC replaced the single bunks in many of the individual rooms and dormitories with double bunks. Also, each week some newly arrived inmates had to sleep on cots in the common areas until they could be transferred to residential rooms as space became available.

On November 28, 1975, less than four months after the MCC had opened, the named respondents initiated this action by filing in the District Court a petition for a writ of habeas corpus. The District Court certified the case as a class action on behalf of all persons confined at the MCC, pretrial detainees and sentenced prisoners alike. The petition served up a veritable potpourri of complaints that implicated virtually every facet of the institution's conditions and practices. Respondents charged, *inter alia*, that they had been deprived of their statutory and constitutional rights because of overcrowded conditions, undue length of confinement, improper searches, inadequate recreational, educational, and employment opportunities, insufficient staff, and objectionable restrictions on the purchase and receipt of personal items and books.

In two opinions and a series of orders, the District Court enjoined numerous MCC practices and conditions. With respect to pretrial detainees, the court held that because they are "presumed to be innocent and held only to ensure their presence at trial, 'any deprivation or restriction of * * * rights beyond those which are necessary for confinement alone, must be justified by a compelling necessity.' " And while acknowledging that the rights of sentenced inmates are to be measured by the different standard of the Eighth Amendment, the court declared that to house "an inferior minority of persons . . . in ways found unconstitutional for the rest" would amount to cruel and unusual punishment.

Applying these standards on cross-motions for partial summary judgment, the District Court enjoined the practice of housing two inmates in the individual rooms and prohibited enforcement of the so-called "publisher-only" rule, which at the time of the court's ruling prohibited the receipt of all books and magazines mailed from outside the MCC except those sent directly from a publisher or a book club. After a trial on the remaining issues, the District Court enjoined, *inter alia*, the doubling of capacity in the dormitory areas, the use of the common rooms to provide temporary sleeping accommodations, the prohibition against inmates' receipt of packages containing food and items of personal property, and the practice of requiring inmates to expose their body cavities for visual inspection following contact visits. The court also granted relief in favor of pretrial detainees, but not convicted inmates, with respect to the requirement that detainees remain outside their rooms during routine inspections by MCC officials.

The Court of Appeals largely affirmed the District Court's rulings . . . .

* * *

B

3

In evaluating the constitutionality of conditions or restrictions of pretrial detention that implicate only the protection against deprivation of liberty without due process of law, we think that the proper inquiry is whether those conditions amount to punishment of the detainee. For under the Due Process Clause, a detainee may not be punished prior to an adjudication of guilt in accordance with due process of law. A person lawfully committed to pretrial detention has not been adjudged guilty of any crime. He has had only a "judicial determination of probable cause as a prerequisite to [the] extended restraint of [his] liberty following arrest." And, if he is detained for a suspected violation of a federal law, he also has had a bail hearing. See 18 U.S.C. §§ 3146, 3148. Under such circumstances, the Government concededly may detain him to ensure his presence at trial and may subject him to the restrictions and conditions of the detention facility so long as those conditions and restrictions do not amount to punishment, or otherwise violate the Constitution.

Not every disability imposed during pretrial detention amounts to "punishment" in the constitutional sense, however. Once the Government has exercised its conceded authority to detain a person pending trial, it obviously is entitled to employ devices that are calculated to effectuate this detention. Traditionally, this has meant confinement in a facility which, no matter how modern or how antiquated, results in restricting the movement of a detainee in a manner in which he would not be restricted if he simply were free to walk the streets pending trial. Whether it be called a jail, a prison, or a custodial center, the purpose of the facility is to detain. Loss of freedom of choice and privacy are inherent incidents of confinement in such a facility. And the fact that such detention interferes with the detainee's understandable desire to live as comfortably as possible and with as little restraint as possible during confinement does not convert the conditions or restrictions of detention into "punishment."

This Court has recognized a distinction between punitive measures that may not constitutionally be imposed prior to a determination of guilt and regulatory restraints that may. See, *e. g., Kennedy v. Mendoza-Martinez, supra,* 372 U.S., at 168, 83 S.Ct., at 567. In *Kennedy v. Mendoza-Martinez, supra,* the Court ... described the tests traditionally applied to determine whether a governmental act is punitive in nature:

> "Whether the sanction involves an affirmative disability or restraint, whether it has historically been regarded as a punishment, whether it comes into play only on a finding of *scienter,* whether its operation will promote the traditional aims of punishment-retribution and deterrence, whether the behavior to which it applies is already a crime, whether an alternative purpose to which it may rationally be connected is assignable for it, and whether it appears excessive in relation to the alternative purpose assigned are all relevant to the inquiry, and may often point in differing directions."

* * *

4

The factors identified in *Mendoza-Martinez* provide useful guideposts in determining whether particular restrictions and conditions accompanying pretrial detention amount to punishment in the constitutional sense of that word. A court must decide whether the disability is imposed for the purpose of punishment or whether it is but an incident of some other legitimate governmental purpose.

Absent a showing of an expressed intent to punish on the part of detention facility officials, that determination generally will turn on "whether an alternative purpose to which [the restriction] may rationally be connected is assignable for it, and whether it appears excessive in relation to the alternative purpose assigned [to it]." Thus, if a particular condition or restriction of pretrial detention is reasonably related to a legitimate governmental objective, it does not, without more, amount to "punishment." Conversely, if a restriction or condition is not reasonably related to a legitimate goal-if it is arbitrary or purposeless-a court permissibly may infer that the purpose of the governmental action is punishment that may not constitutionally be inflicted upon detainees *qua* detainees. Courts must be mindful that these inquiries spring from constitutional requirements and that judicial answers to them must reflect that fact rather than a court's idea of how best to operate a detention facility.

5

One further point requires discussion. The petitioners assert, and respondents concede, that the "essential objective of pretrial confinement is to insure the detainees' presence at trial." While this interest undoubtedly justifies the original decision to confine an individual in some manner, we do not accept respondents' argument that the Government's interest in ensuring a detainee's presence at trial is the *only* objective that may justify restraints and conditions once the decision is lawfully made to confine a person. "If the government could confine or otherwise infringe the liberty of detainees only to the extent necessary to ensure their presence at trial, house arrest would in the end be the only constitutionally justified form of detention."

The Government also has legitimate interests that stem from its need to manage the facility in which the individual is detained. These legitimate operational concerns may require administrative measures that go beyond those that are, strictly speaking, necessary to ensure that the detainee shows up at trial. For example, the Government must be able to take steps to maintain security and order at the institution and make certain no weapons or illicit drugs reach detainees. Restraints that are reasonably related to the institution's interest in maintaining jail security do not, without more, constitute unconstitutional punishment, even if they are discomforting and are restrictions that the detainee would not have experienced had he been released while awaiting trial. We need not here attempt to detail the precise extent of the legitimate governmental interests that may justify conditions or restrictions of pretrial detention. It is enough simply to recognize that in addition to ensuring the detainees' presence at trial, the effective management of the detention facility once the individual is confined is a valid objective that may justify imposition of conditions and restrictions of pretrial detention and dispel any inference that such restrictions are intended as punishment.

_____

Strip Searches and the Eighth Amendment

The U.S. Supreme Court, in *Florence v. Board of Chosen Freeholders of County of Burlington*, 566 U.S. 318 (2012), upheld the constitutionality of strip searches for pretrial detainees entering a jail facility's general population. Justice Kennedy, writing for the majority, noted: "Correctional officials have a legitimate interest, indeed a responsibility, to ensure that jails are not made less secure by reason of what new detainees may carry in on their bodies. Facility personnel, other inmates, and the new detainee himself or herself may be in danger if these threats are introduced into the jail population." *Id.* at 322. In *Florence*, the search for weapons and contraband included, *inter alia*, a visual examination of the area under the detainee's genitals. Justice Kennedy concluded that the search procedures "struck a reasonable balance between inmate privacy and the needs of the institutions." *Id.* at 339.

Some facilities utilize technology to minimize the invasion of inmate privacy and the chance of prisoner humiliation and abuse during the intake search process. A chair, branded as the "B.O.S.S." ("Body Orifice Security Scanner") by one manufacturer, uses technology to perform a body scan of the inmate, who simply sits in a chair-shaped scanning device while the search for contraband is performed. *See, e.g.,* Dan Morse, *Maryland Using Body Scanner to Find Contraband in Prisons*, WASH. POST, Nov. 5, 2009.

IV. THE FEDERAL BAIL REFORM ACT OF 1984 AND FED. R. CRIM. P. 46

The Bail Reform Act of 1984 governs pretrial detention and release in the federal system. In *United States v. Salerno*, 481 U.S. 739 (1987), the U.S. Supreme Court upheld the statute against constitutional challenge on due process and Eighth Amendment grounds. The following excerpt from that case gives some historical background and general procedural framework of the statute:

> The Bail Reform Act of 1984 (Act) allows a federal court to detain an arrestee pending trial if the Government demonstrates by clear and convincing evidence after an adversary hearing that no release conditions "will reasonably assure . . . the safety of any other person and the community." The United States Court of Appeals for the Second Circuit struck down this provision of the Act as facially

unconstitutional, because, in that court's words, this type of pretrial detention violates "substantive due process." We granted certiorari because of a conflict among the Courts of Appeals regarding the validity of the Act.1 479 U.S. 929, 107 S.Ct. 397, 93 L.Ed.2d 351 (1986). We hold that, as against the facial attack mounted by these respondents, the Act fully comports with constitutional requirements. We therefore reverse.

I

Responding to "the alarming problem of crimes committed by persons on release," S.Rep. No. 98–225, p. 3 (1983), U.S. Code Cong. & Admin. News 1984, pp. 3182, 3185 Congress formulated the Bail Reform Act of 1984, 18 U.S.C. § 3141 *et seq.* (1982 ed., Supp. III), as the solution to a bail crisis in the federal courts. The Act represents the National Legislature's considered response to numerous perceived deficiencies in the federal bail process. By providing for sweeping changes in both the way federal courts consider bail applications and the circumstances under which bail is granted, Congress hoped to "give the courts adequate authority to make release decisions that give appropriate recognition to the danger a person may pose to others if released." S.Rep. No. 98–225, at 3, U.S. Code Cong. & Admin. News 1984, p. 3185.

To this end, § 3141(a) of the Act requires a judicial officer to determine whether an arrestee shall be detained. Section 3142(e) provides that "[i]f, after a hearing pursuant to the provisions of subsection (f), the judicial officer finds that no condition or combination of conditions will reasonably assure the appearance of the person as required and the safety of any other person and the community, he shall order the detention of the person prior to trial." Section 3142(f) provides the arrestee with a number of procedural safeguards. He may request the presence of counsel at the detention hearing, he may testify and present witnesses in his behalf, as well as proffer evidence, and he may cross-examine other witnesses appearing at the hearing. If the judicial officer finds that no conditions of pretrial release can reasonably assure the safety of other persons and the community, he must state his findings of fact in writing, § 3142(i), and support his conclusion with "clear and convincing evidence," § 3142(f).

The judicial officer is not given unbridled discretion in making the detention determination. Congress has specified the considerations relevant to that decision. These factors include the nature and seriousness of the charges, the substantiality of the Government's evidence against the arrestee, the arrestee's background and characteristics, and the nature and seriousness of the danger posed by the suspect's release. § 3142(g). Should a judicial officer order detention, the detainee is entitled to expedited appellate review of the detention order. §§ 3145(b), (c).

Below are excerpts of key provisions of the statute. It is an intricate, but important, law. Take the time to work through the language.

§ 3141. Release and detention authority generally

(a) Pending trial.—A judicial officer authorized to order the arrest of a person under section 3041 of this title before whom an arrested person is brought shall order that such person be released or detained, pending judicial proceedings, under this chapter.

(b) Pending sentence or appeal.—A judicial officer of a court of original jurisdiction over an offense, or a judicial officer of a Federal appellate court, shall order that, pending imposition or execution of sentence, or pending appeal of conviction or sentence, a person be released or detained under this chapter.

§ 3142. Release or detention of a defendant pending trial

(a) In general.—Upon the appearance before a judicial officer of a person charged with an offense, the judicial officer shall issue an order that, pending trial, the person be—

(1) released on personal recognizance or upon execution of an unsecured appearance bond, under subsection (b) of this section;

(2) released on a condition or combination of conditions under subsection (c) of this section;

(3) temporarily detained to permit revocation of conditional release, deportation, or exclusion under subsection (d) of this section; or

(4) detained under subsection (e) of this section.

(b) Release on personal recognizance or unsecured appearance bond.—The judicial officer shall order the pretrial release of the person on personal recognizance, or upon execution of an unsecured appearance bond in an amount specified by the court, subject to the condition that the person not commit a Federal, State, or local crime during the period of release and subject to the condition that the person cooperate in the collection of a DNA sample from the person if the collection of such a sample is authorized pursuant to section 3 of the DNA Analysis Backlog Elimination Act of 2000 (42 U.S.C. 14135a), unless the judicial officer determines that such release will not reasonably assure the appearance of the person as required or will endanger the safety of any other person or the community.

(c) Release on conditions.—(1) If the judicial officer determines that the release described in subsection (b) of this section will not reasonably assure the appearance of the person as required or will endanger the safety of any other person or the community, such judicial officer shall order the pretrial release of the person—

(A) subject to the condition that the person not commit a Federal, State, or local crime during the period of release and subject to the condition that the person cooperate in the collection of a DNA sample from the person if the collection of such a sample is authorized pursuant to section 3 of the DNA Analysis Backlog Elimination Act of 2000 (42 U.S.C. 14135a); and

(B) subject to the least restrictive further condition, or combination of conditions, that such judicial officer determines will reasonably assure the appearance of the person as required and the safety of any other person and the community, which may include the condition that the person—

(i) remain in the custody of a designated person, who agrees to assume supervision and to report any violation of a release condition to the court, if the designated person is able reasonably to assure the judicial officer that the person will appear as required and will not pose a danger to the safety of any other person or the community;

(ii) maintain employment, or, if unemployed, actively seek employment;

(iii) maintain or commence an educational program;

(iv) abide by specified restrictions on personal associations, place of abode, or travel;

(v) avoid all contact with an alleged victim of the crime and with a potential witness who may testify concerning the offense;

(vi) report on a regular basis to a designated law enforcement agency, pretrial services agency, or other agency;

(vii) comply with a specified curfew;

(viii) refrain from possessing a firearm, destructive device, or other dangerous weapon;

(ix) refrain from excessive use of alcohol, or any use of a narcotic drug or other controlled substance, as defined in section 102 of the Controlled Substances Act (21 U.S.C. 802), without a prescription by a licensed medical practitioner;

(x) undergo available medical, psychological, or psychiatric treatment, including treatment for drug or alcohol dependency, and remain in a specified institution if required for that purpose;

(xi) execute an agreement to forfeit upon failing to appear as required, property of a sufficient unencumbered value, including money, as is reasonably necessary to assure the appearance of the person as required, and shall provide the court with proof of ownership and the value of the property along with information regarding existing encumbrances as the judicial office may require;

(xii) execute a bail bond with solvent sureties; who will execute an agreement to forfeit in such amount as is reasonably necessary to assure appearance of the person as required and shall provide the court with information regarding the value of the assets and liabilities of the surety if other than an approved surety and the nature and extent of encumbrances against the surety's property; such surety shall have a net worth which shall have sufficient unencumbered value to pay the amount of the bail bond;

(xiii) return to custody for specified hours following release for employment, schooling, or other limited purposes; and

(xiv) satisfy any other condition that is reasonably necessary to assure the appearance of the person as required and to assure the safety of any other person and the community.

In any case that involves a minor victim under [various sections] of this title, or a failure to register offense under section 2250 of this title, any release order shall contain, at a minimum, a condition of electronic monitoring and each of the conditions specified at subparagraphs (iv), (v), (vi), (vii), and (viii).

(2) The judicial officer may not impose a financial condition that results in the pretrial detention of the person.

(3) The judicial officer may at any time amend the order to impose additional or different conditions of release.

(d) Temporary detention to permit revocation of conditional release, deportation, or exclusion.—If the judicial officer determines that—

(1) such person—

(A) is, and was at the time the offense was committed, on—

(i) release pending trial for a felony under Federal, State, or local law;

(ii) release pending imposition or execution of sentence, appeal of sentence or conviction, or completion of sentence, for any offense under Federal, State, or local law; or

(iii) probation or parole for any offense under Federal, State, or local law; or

(B) is not a citizen of the United States or lawfully admitted for permanent residence, as defined in section 101(a)(20) of the Immigration and Nationality Act (8 U.S.C. 1101(a)(20))); and

(2) such person may flee or pose a danger to any other person or the community;

such judicial officer shall order the detention of such person, for a period of not more than ten days, excluding Saturdays, Sundays, and holidays, and direct the attorney for the Government to notify the appropriate court, probation or parole official, or State or local law enforcement official, or the appropriate official of the Immigration and Naturalization Service. If the official fails or declines to take such person into custody during that period, such person shall be treated in accordance with the other provisions of this section, notwithstanding the applicability of other provisions of law governing release pending trial or deportation or exclusion proceedings. If temporary detention is sought under paragraph (1)(B) of this subsection, such person has the burden of proving to the court such person's United States citizenship or lawful admission for permanent residence.

(e) Detention.—**(1)** If, after a hearing pursuant to the provisions of subsection (f) of this section, the judicial officer finds that no condition or combination of conditions will reasonably assure the appearance of the person as required and the safety of any other person and the community, such judicial officer shall order the detention of the person before trial.

(2) In a case described in subsection (f)(1) of this section, a rebuttable presumption arises that no condition or combination of conditions will reasonably assure the safety of any other person and the community if such judicial officer finds that—

(A) the person has been convicted of a Federal offense that is described in subsection (f)(1) of this section, or of a State or local offense that would have been an offense described in subsection (f)(1) of this section if a circumstance giving rise to Federal jurisdiction had existed;

(B) the offense described in subparagraph (A) was committed while the person was on release pending trial for a Federal, State, or local offense; and

(C) a period of not more than five years has elapsed since the date of conviction, or the release of the person from imprisonment, for the offense described in subparagraph (A), whichever is later.

(3) Subject to rebuttal by the person, it shall be presumed that no condition or combination of conditions will reasonably assure the appearance of the person as required and the safety of the community if the judicial officer finds that there is probable cause to believe that the person committed—

(A) an offense for which a maximum term of imprisonment of ten years or more is prescribed in the Controlled Substances Act (21 U.S.C. 801 et seq.), the Controlled Substances Import and Export Act (21 U.S.C. 951 et seq.), or chapter 705 of title 46;

(B) an offense under section 924(c), 956(a), or 2332b of this title;

(C) an offense listed in section 2332b(g)(5)(B) of title 18, United States Code, for which a maximum term of imprisonment of 10 years or more is prescribed;

(D) an offense under chapter 77 of this title for which a maximum term of imprisonment of 20 years or more is prescribed; or

(E) an offense involving a minor victim under [various sections] of this title.

(f) Detention hearing.—The judicial officer shall hold a hearing to determine whether any condition or combination of conditions set forth in subsection (c) of this section will reasonably assure the appearance of such person as required and the safety of any other person and the community—

(1) upon motion of the attorney for the Government, in a case that involves—

(A) a crime of violence, a violation of section 1591, or an offense listed in section 2332b(g)(5)(B) for which a maximum term of imprisonment of 10 years or more is prescribed;

(B) an offense for which the maximum sentence is life imprisonment or death;

(C) an offense for which a maximum term of imprisonment of ten years or more is prescribed in the Controlled Substances Act (21 U.S.C. 801 et seq.), the Controlled Substances Import and Export Act (21 U.S.C. 951 et seq.), or chapter 705 of title 46;

(D) any felony if such person has been convicted of two or more offenses described in subparagraphs (A) through (C) of this paragraph, or two or more State or local offenses that would have been offenses described in subparagraphs (A) through (C) of this paragraph if a circumstance giving rise to Federal jurisdiction had existed, or a combination of such offenses; or

(E) any felony that is not otherwise a crime of violence that involves a minor victim or that involves the possession or use of a firearm or destructive device (as those terms are defined in section 921), or any other dangerous weapon, or involves a failure to register under section 2250 of title 18, United States Code; or

(2) Upon motion of the attorney for the Government or upon the judicial officer's own motion, in a case that involves—

(A) a serious risk that such person will flee; or

(B) a serious risk that such person will obstruct or attempt to obstruct justice, or threaten, injure, or intimidate, or attempt to threaten, injure, or intimidate, a prospective witness or juror.

The hearing shall be held immediately upon the person's first appearance before the judicial officer unless that person, or the attorney for the Government, seeks a continuance. Except for good cause, a continuance on motion of such person may not exceed five days (not including any intermediate Saturday, Sunday, or legal holiday), and a continuance on motion of the attorney for the Government may not exceed three days (not including any intermediate Saturday, Sunday, or legal holiday). During a continuance, such person shall be detained, and the judicial officer, on motion of the attorney for the Government or sua sponte, may order that, while in custody, a person who appears to be a narcotics addict receive a medical examination to determine whether such person is an addict. At the hearing, such person has the right to be represented by counsel, and, if financially unable to obtain adequate representation, to have counsel appointed. The person shall be afforded an opportunity to testify, to present witnesses, to cross-examine witnesses who appear at the hearing, and to present information by proffer or otherwise. The rules concerning admissibility of evidence in criminal trials do not apply to the presentation and consideration of information at the hearing. The facts the judicial officer uses to support a finding pursuant to subsection (e) that no condition or combination of conditions will reasonably assure the safety of any other person and the community shall be supported by clear and convincing evidence. The person may be detained pending completion of the hearing. The hearing may be reopened, before or after a determination by the judicial officer, at any time before trial if the judicial officer finds that information exists that was not known to the movant at the time of the hearing and that has a material bearing on the issue whether there are conditions of release that will reasonably assure the appearance of such person as required and the safety of any other person and the community.

(g) Factors to be considered.—The judicial officer shall, in determining whether there are conditions of release that will reasonably assure the appearance of the person as required and the safety of any other person and the community, take into account the available information concerning—

(1) the nature and circumstances of the offense charged, including whether the offense is a crime of violence, a violation of section 1591, a

Federal crime of terrorism, or involves a minor victim or a controlled substance, firearm, explosive, or destructive device;

(2) the weight of the evidence against the person;

(3) the history and characteristics of the person, including—

(A) the person's character, physical and mental condition, family ties, employment, financial resources, length of residence in the community, community ties, past conduct, history relating to drug or alcohol abuse, criminal history, and record concerning appearance at court proceedings; and

(B) whether, at the time of the current offense or arrest, the person was on probation, on parole, or on other release pending trial, sentencing, appeal, or completion of sentence for an offense under Federal, State, or local law; and

(4) the nature and seriousness of the danger to any person or the community that would be posed by the person's release. In considering the conditions of release described in subsection (c)(1)(B)(xi) or (c)(1)(B)(xii) of this section, the judicial officer may upon his own motion, or shall upon the motion of the Government, conduct an inquiry into the source of the property to be designated for potential forfeiture or offered as collateral to secure a bond, and shall decline to accept the designation, or the use as collateral, of property that, because of its source, will not reasonably assure the appearance of the person as required.

(h) Contents of release order.—In a release order issued under subsection (b) or (c) of this section, the judicial officer shall—

(1) include a written statement that sets forth all the conditions to which the release is subject, in a manner sufficiently clear and specific to serve as a guide for the person's conduct; and

(2) advise the person of—

(A) the penalties for violating a condition of release, including the penalties for committing an offense while on pretrial release;

(B) the consequences of violating a condition of release, including the immediate issuance of a warrant for the person's arrest; and

(C) sections 1503 of this title (relating to intimidation of witnesses, jurors, and officers of the court), 1510 (relating to obstruction of criminal investigations), 1512 (tampering with a witness, victim, or an informant), and 1513 (retaliating against a witness, victim, or an informant).

(i) Contents of detention order.—In a detention order issued under subsection (e) of this section, the judicial officer shall—

(1) include written findings of fact and a written statement of the reasons for the detention;

(2) direct that the person be committed to the custody of the Attorney General for confinement in a corrections facility separate, to the extent practicable, from persons awaiting or serving sentences or being held in custody pending appeal;

(3) direct that the person be afforded reasonable opportunity for private consultation with counsel; and

(4) direct that, on order of a court of the United States or on request of an attorney for the Government, the person in charge of the corrections facility in which the person is confined deliver the person to a United States marshal for the purpose of an appearance in connection with a court proceeding.

The judicial officer may, by subsequent order, permit the temporary release of the person, in the custody of a United States marshal or another appropriate person, to the extent that the judicial officer determines such release to be necessary for preparation of the person's defense or for another compelling reason.

(j) Presumption of innocence.—Nothing in this section shall be construed as modifying or limiting the presumption of innocence.

There are other provisions of the Bail Reform Act dealing with release or detention of a defendant pending sentence or appeal (18 U.S.C. § 3143), and detention of material witnesses. (18 U.S.C. s. 3144). The United States Attorney's Manual has a particularly granular analysis of the Bail Reform Act and the federal prosecutor's obligations under the law. *See* United States Attorney's Manual, Criminal Resource Manual, Title 9, Chapter 26 ("Release and Detention Pending Detention Proceedings").

Federal Rule of Criminal Procedure 46

Rule 46 of the Federal Rules of Criminal Procedure helps to implement the requirements set out in the Federal Bail Reform Act. It provides guidance on the standards to be applied to detention and release decisions made before trial, during, trial, pending sentencing or appeal, and pending a hearing on a violation of probation or supervised release. The rule also provides procedures for the court's consideration of whether a surety for a defendant's bond is appropriate and standards for the forfeiture of bail if the defendant breaches a condition of the bond. Finally, the rule contains provisions governing the court's supervision of detained individuals, the forfeiture of property as disposition of an offense, and the production of witness statements in connection with the detention hearing.

Appearance Bond

http://www.uscourts.gov/sites/default/files/ao098.pdf

Order Scheduling Detention Hearing

http://www.uscourts.gov/sites/default/files/ao470.pdf

Order Setting Conditions of Release

http://www.uscourts.gov/sites/default/files/ao199a.pdf

Additional Conditions of Release

http://www.uscourts.gov/sites/default/files/ao199b.pdf

Advice of Penalties and Sanctions

http://www.uscourts.gov/sites/default/files/ao199c.pdf

Order of Detention Pending Trial

http://www.uscourts.gov/sites/default/files/ao472.pdf

http://www.uscourts.gov/sites/default/files/ao472.pdf

Current Bail Reform Efforts at the Federal and State Levels

Spurred by a number of high-profile cases, there has been an increase in activity around reforming bail practices in the United States. Perhaps the most heartbreaking of these cases involved the pretrial detention of 16 year-old Kalief Browder, who, in 2010, was accused of stealing a backpack, arrested, and—unable to make the $3,000 bail—sat in the infamous Riker's Island for three years awaiting trial and maintaining his innocence. Browder's time on Riker's Island was harsh; when he was not in the midst of lengthy stretches of solitary confinement, he suffered assaults at the hands of prison staff and fellow inmates. During his confinement, Browder tried to take his life more than once. After Browder, still insisting that he was innocent, turned down a plea offer that would have released him immediately on time served, the charges eventually were dropped, and Browder's story became emblematic of the injustice posed by a system that conditions liberty on the ability to marshal the financial resources to make bail. His story prompted celebrities, such as Rosie O'Donnell and Jay-Z to draw attention to the problems with the current bail system—among them the lack of reliance on reasonable risk assessment tools in determining the need for pretrial detention. In 2015, Browder took his own life at the age of 22. For more on the tragic story of Kalief Browder and the shortcomings of the criminal justice system that failed him, *see, e.g.,* Jennifer Gonnerman, *Three Years on Rikers Without Trial*, THE NEW YORKER, October 6, 2014; Jennifer Gonnerman, *Kalief Browder, 1993–2015*, THE NEW YORKER, June 7, 2015; Ta-Nehisi Coates, *The Brief and Tragic Life of Kalief Browder*, THE ATLANTIC, June 8, 2015. At the time of publication of this edition, bipartisan bail reform legislation, co-sponsored by Republican Senator Rand Paul and Democratic Senator Kamala Harris is pending in the United States Senate, in the 115th Congress. *See* Pretrial Safety and Integrity Act of 2017, S. 1593, 115th Cong. (2017) ("The purpose of this Act is to provide States and Indian tribes to reform their criminal justice system to encourage the replacement of the use of payment of money bail as a condition of pretrial release in criminal cases."); Kamala Harris & Rand Paul, *To Shrink Jails, Let's Reform Bail*, N.Y. TIMES, July 20, 2017.

V. RIGHT TO COUNSEL IN DETENTION HEARINGS

There is no general federal constitutional right to counsel associated with the bail or pretrial release hearing. *See* Douglas L. Colbert, *Connecting Theory and Reality: Teaching Gideon and Indigent Defendants' Non-Right to Counsel at Bail*, 4 Ohio St. J. Crim. L. 167 (2006). However, state constitutions or statutes may provide counsel to defendants at the detention stage of criminal proceedings. *See DeWolfe v. Richmond*, 76 A.3d 1019 (Md. 2013).

Although there are compelling and obvious reasons defendants *should* enjoy representation when courts determine whether their liberty will be impaired pending trial, there can be practical impediments to the provision of counsel at this stage. The detention hearing may take place before the defendant has had the opportunity to retain counsel. Any effort of the part of the defendant to do so may be frustrated by the fact that he or she is in custody and cannot easily explore options for hiring a lawyer.

If the defendant does not have resources to retain counsel, there must be a determination whether he or she qualifies as indigent—a process that may take too long given the defendant's desire to obtain release as soon as possible. Also, many arrests take place after hours or on the weekend, at times when there are fewer lawyers available to consult with the defendant in custody and appear at a bail hearing. Having attorneys on duty to handle these bail hearings may be expensive and resource-intensive. Certain jurisdictions have permitted detention hearings via teleconference to alleviate some of these problems.

While there are policy and resource allocation issues that jurisdictions must resolve in determining whether they will provide counsel at the bail hearing stage, Congress has made clear that federal criminal defendants are entitled to counsel at every stage of the criminal process, including the detention hearing. *See* Fed. R. Crim. P. 44 ("A defendant who is unable to obtain counsel is entitled to have counsel appointed to represent the defendant at every stage of the proceeding from initial appearance through appeal, unless the defendant waives this right.")

NOTE ON STATE PRACTICE

Does your state provide counsel to the accused at the hearing on pretrial release? Are there mechanisms in place for a defendant to obtain review of an earlier decision to detain pretrial? Does the jurisdiction allow for video conferencing of detention hearings? *See, e.g.,* Kyle Rohrer, *Why Has the Bail Reform Act Not Been Adopted by the State Systems?*, 95 OR. L. REV. 517 (2017).

COUNSEL EXERCISE 3A: Detention Hearing (Prosecution)

Prepare to conduct a detention hearing under Federal Rule of Criminal Procedure 46 and 18 U.S.C. 3142(f). You should read the statute (18 U.S.C. 3142) carefully in preparation for the hearing, and plan to be asked about presumptions and other provisions in the statute. Using the information you have (including the complaint, affidavit, and, possibly, a Pretrial Services Report), you should marshal arguments in favor of detention. Prior to the hearing, you should prepare and print for submission to the court (with an additional copy for opposing counsel) a proposed Detention Order Pending Trial.

COUNSEL EXERCISE 3B: Detention Hearing
(Defense)

Prepare to conduct a detention hearing under Federal Rule of Criminal Procedure 46 and 18 U.S.C. 3142(f). You should read the statute (18 U.S.C. 3142) carefully in preparation for the hearing, and plan to be asked about presumptions and other provisions in the statute. Using the information you have (including the complaint, affidavit, and, possibly, a Pretrial Services Report), you should marshal arguments against detention. Prior to the hearing, you should prepare and print for submission to the court (with an additional copy for opposing counsel) a draft Order Setting Conditions of Release and Additional Conditions of Release.

CHAPTER 4

THE GRAND JURY

I. INTRODUCTION

The grand jury is a group of laypeople who, in certain circumstances, determine whether there is sufficient basis for criminal charges to proceed to trial. As discussed in Chapter One, supra, the Fifth Amendment to the Constitution guarantees to a federal criminal defendant the right to a grand jury indictment before serious criminal charges may be brought against him or her. However, the U.S. Supreme Court, in *Hurtado*, supra, decided that the grand jury right has not been incorporated to apply to the states. As such, only about half of the states require grand jury indictment as a prerequisite to criminal prosecution.

While relegating the indictment right to the category of those few criminal procedural rights that do not merit incorporation, the Supreme Court, has described the grand jury's special place within the federal constitutional structure, calling it "a constitutional fixture" and "a buffer or referee between the Government and the people." *United States v. Williams*, 504 U.S. 36 (1992).

So, what is the grand jury and what is its purpose? Where did the grand jury originate? How does it function? Is it still useful today? Why does it seem to be both dismissed and celebrated in American law? These and other questions are addressed below.

II. HISTORY OF THE GRAND JURY

Professor Fairfax, in *The Jurisdictional Heritage of the Grand Jury*, 91 MINN. L. REV. 398 (2006), provides some historical background on the grand jury:

> The right to grand jury indictment in federal felony criminal prosecutions flows from the Grand Jury Clause of the Fifth Amendment to the Constitution. However, the grand jury itself, "rooted in long centuries of Anglo-American history," is "an ancient institution of the common law," the heritage of which may go back as far as Athens, but safely can be traced back to the fourteenth century reign of Edward III, when "the modern practice of returning a panel of twenty-four men to inquire for the county was established and the body then received the name 'le graunde inquest.' "

During the first three centuries of the grand jury's use in England, it served largely the interests of the monarchy, although by the seventeenth century English grand juries had begun to stand between the Crown and accused subjects as a protection against unwarranted accusation. Eventually, the law required a valid indictment by a grand jury before a court could try a defendant for certain classes of crime. English history demonstrates that the grand jury was transformed from merely an arm of the Crown into a protector of individual liberty. Absent a grand jury indictment, English courts were powerless to try a defendant for certain serious crimes, irrespective of the wishes of the Crown.

The grand jury institution followed the English common law to the American colonies and quickly established itself as a buffer between the colonists and the King. The grand jury indictment was not only a prerequisite to serious criminal charges in many colonies, but the grand jury was woven into the fabric of everyday colonial life. Colonial grand juries also played a part in expressing colonists' dissatisfaction with the exercise of monarchical power by nullifying attempted prosecutions of critics of the Crown and aggressively issuing "angry and well-publicized presentments and indictments" against representatives of the Crown. The role of the grand jury in the colonies gave it "enhanced prestige" and special respect among American colonists during the pre-Revolution period.

After the Revolution, the colonists remained aware of the power and potential threat posed by any central governing authority. As a result, the right to indictment by grand jury was a topic of discussion among states deliberating the ratification of the Constitution. Ratifying conventions from such influential states as Massachusetts, New York, and New Hampshire considered amendments to the newly drafted Constitution that would have established the right to grand jury indictment. The Constitution as originally ratified, however, made no mention of grand juries.[52] Not until the ratification of the Fifth Amendment in 1791 as part of the Bill of Rights was the grand jury enshrined in the Constitution: "No person shall be held to answer for a capital, or otherwise infamous crime, unless on a presentment or indictment of a Grand Jury, except in cases arising in the land or naval forces,

---

[52] There was a mention of indictment in Article I, which explained that individuals whose conduct would subject them to impeachment might also otherwise be subject to criminal prosecution which, it was contemplated, would be initiated by grand jury indictment. *See* U.S. Const. art. I, s. 3, cl. 7.

or in the Militia, when in actual service in time of [W]ar or public danger . . . ." * * *

The grand jury played a prominent role in many of the significant controversies that faced the young nation following the ratification of the Constitution. For example, judges regularly used their charging messages to grand juries to sway popular opinion for political issues of the day, and grand juries were central to efforts to frustrate the Alien and Sedition Acts, Fugitive Slave Act, and civil rights laws passed during Reconstruction. *See* Roger A. Fairfax, Jr., *Grand Jury Discretion and Constitutional Design*, 93 CORNELL L. REV. 703 (2008).

Grand juries also were integral to the early 20th century efforts to combat public corruption, enforcement of civil rights laws in the 1950s and 1960s, and the investigation of the Watergate political scandal in the 1970s. Nevertheless, the grand jury suffers from a fairly low reputation within the American legal culture, as Judge Michael Daly Hawkins explains in *United States v. Navarro-Vargas*, 408 F.3d 1184, 1195–96 (9th Cir. 2005):

> By the twentieth century, dramatic confrontations between prosecutors and jurors in grand jury proceedings had become rare. Currently, grand jurors no longer perform any other function but to investigate crimes and screen indictments, and they tend to indict in the overwhelming number of cases brought by prosecutors. Because of this, many criticize the modern grand jury as no more than a "rubber stamp" for the prosecutor. * * * "Day in and day out, the grand jury affirms what the prosecutor calls upon it to affirm—investigating as it is led, ignoring what it is never advised to notice, failing to indict or indicting as the prosecutor 'submits' that it should." * * * Or, as the Supreme Court of New York so colorfully put it: "[M]any lawyers and judges have expressed skepticism concerning the power of the Grand Jury. This skepticism was best summarized by the Chief Judge of this state in 1985 when he publicly stated that a Grand Jury would indict a 'ham sandwich.'" * * *

> As the grand jury's tendency to indict has become more pronounced, some commentators claim that the modern grand jury has lost its independence. * * *

> Against this criticism, the Supreme Court has steadfastly insisted that the grand jury remains as a shield against unfounded prosecutions. *See Williams,* 504 U.S. at 47, 112 S.Ct. 1735 (the Grand jury "serv[es] as a kind of buffer or referee between the Government and the people"); *Mandujano,* 425 U.S. at 571, 96 S.Ct. 1768 (plurality opinion) ("the grand

jury continues to function as a barrier to reckless or unfounded charges"); *Wood,* 370 U.S. at 390, 82 S.Ct. 1364 (describing the grand jury as a "primary security to the innocent against hasty, malicious and oppressive persecution" as it stands "between the accuser and the accused . . . to determine whether a charge is founded upon reason or . . . dictated by an intimidating power by malice and personal ill will[ ]"); *Stirone v. United States,* 361 U.S. 212, 218, 80 S.Ct. 270, 4 L.Ed.2d 252 (1960); *Hale v. Henkel,* 201 U.S. 43, 61, 26 S.Ct. 370, 50 L.Ed. 652 (1906). *See also Branzburg v. Hayes,* 408 U.S. 665, 686–87, 92 S.Ct. 2646, 33 L.Ed.2d 626 (1972) (recognizing the dual function of the grand jury "of determining if there is probable cause to believe that a crime has been committed and of protecting citizens against unfounded criminal prosecutions."). *But see Dionisio,* 410 U.S. at 17, 93 S.Ct. 764 ("The grand jury may not always serve its historic role as a protective bulwark standing solidly between the ordinary citizen and an overzealous prosecutor . . . .").

III. THE GRAND JURY'S SCREENING FUNCTION

The grand jury determines whether there is probable cause to believe that the defendant committed a criminal offense. As discussed in Chapter 2, supra, the grand jury's determination of probable cause is the "gold standard." In other words, a grand jury's probable cause determination has conclusive effect for a number of purposes in the criminal process. The Supreme Court made this clear in *Kaley v. United States,* 134 S.Ct. 1090 (2014), when it held that there is no right to judicial review of a grand jury's probable cause determination used as the basis for the pretrial freezing of a defendant's assets made subject to a potential criminal forfeiture.

This Court has often recognized the grand jury's singular role in finding the probable cause necessary to initiate a prosecution for a serious crime. *See, e.g., Costello v. United States,* 350 U.S. 359, 362, 76 S.Ct. 406, 100 L.Ed. 397 (1956). "[A]n indictment 'fair upon its face,' and returned by a 'properly constituted grand jury,'" we have explained, "conclusively determines the existence of probable cause" to believe the defendant perpetrated the offense alleged. *Gerstein v. Pugh,* 420 U.S. 103, 117, n. 19, 95 S.Ct. 854, 43 L.Ed.2d 54 (1975) (quoting Ex parte United States, 287 U.S. 241, 250, 53 S.Ct. 129, 77 L.Ed. 283 (1932)). And "conclusively" has meant, case in and case out, just that. We have found no "authority for looking into and revising the judgment of the grand jury upon the evidence, for the purpose of determining whether or not the finding was founded upon sufficient proof." *Costello,* 350 U.S., at 362–363, 76 S.Ct. 406 (quoting *United States v. Reed,* 27 F.Cas. 727, 738 (No. 16,134) (C.C.N.D.N.Y.1852) (Nelson, J.)). To the contrary, "the whole history of the grand jury institution" demonstrates that "a challenge to the reliability or competence of the evidence" supporting a grand jury's finding of probable cause "will not be heard." *United States v. Williams,* 504 U.S. 36, 54, 112 S.Ct. 1735, 118 L.Ed.2d 352 (1992) (quoting *Costello,* 350 U.S., at 364, 76 S.Ct. 406, and *Bank of Nova Scotia v. United States,* 487 U.S. 250, 261, 108 S.Ct. 2369, 101 L.Ed.2d 228 (1988)). The grand jury gets to say—without any review, oversight, or second-guessing—whether probable cause exists to think that a person committed a crime.

And that inviolable grand jury finding, we have decided, may do more than commence a criminal proceeding (with all the economic, reputational, and personal harm that entails); the determination may also serve the purpose of immediately depriving the accused of her freedom. If the person charged is not yet in custody, an indictment triggers "issuance of an arrest warrant without further inquiry" into the case's strength. *Gerstein,* 420 U.S., at 117, n. 19, 95 S.Ct. 854; see *Kalina v. Fletcher,* 522 U.S. 118, 129, 118 S.Ct. 502, 139 L.Ed.2d 471 (1997). Alternatively, if the person was arrested without a warrant, an indictment eliminates her Fourth Amendment right to a prompt judicial assessment of probable cause to support any detention. See *Gerstein,* 420 U.S., at 114, 117, n. 19, 95 S.Ct. 854. In either situation, this Court—relying on the grand jury's "historical role of protecting individuals from unjust persecution"—has "let [that body's] judgment substitute for that of a neutral and detached magistrate." *Ibid.* The grand jury, all on its own, may effect a pretrial restraint on a person's liberty by finding probable cause to support a criminal charge. *Id.* at 1098.

Grand Jury Discretion?

Although the grand jury is tasked with determining whether probable cause exists to support the charges contemplated by the prosecutor, some have queried whether the grand jury has a more profound role to play in the bringing of criminal of criminal charges— that is, whether the grand jury is equipped to decide whether particular charges *should* be pursued, even if there is sufficient evidence to support an indictment. *See, e.g.,* Roger A. Fairfax, Jr., *Grand Jury Discretion and Constitutional Design,* 93 CORNELL L. REV. 703 (2008);

Niki Kuckes, *The Democratic Prosecutor: Explaining the Constitutional Function of the Federal Grand Jury*, 94 GEO. L.J. 1265 (2006).

The Model Grand Jury Charge approved by the Judicial Conference of the United States, the Benchbook for U.S. District Court Judges, and the Handbook for Federal Grand Jurors all refer to the duty of grand jurors to indict if the government presents evidence sufficient to establish probable cause. *See* JUDICIAL CONFERENCE OF THE UNITED STATES, MODEL GRAND JURY CHARGE (March 2005) ("[Y]ou should vote to indict where the evidence presented to you is sufficiently strong . . ."); FEDERAL JUDICIAL CENTER, BENCHBOOK FOR U.S. DISTRICT COURT JUDGES (March 2013) ("purpose of the grand jury is to determine whether there is sufficient evidence to justify a formal accusation . . ."); ADMINISTRATIVE OFFICE OF THE U.S. COURTS, HANDBOOK FOR FEDERAL GRAND JURORS (April 2012) ("If the grand jury finds that probable cause exists . . . then it will return . . . an 'indictment.'").

Some defendants have argued unsuccessfully that instructions to grand jurors that they "shall" or "must" or "will" indict (rather than "may" or even "should" indict) if they find probable cause deprive the defendant of their Fifth Amendment right to grand jury indictment by removing the grand jurors' discretion. *See, e.g., United States v. Navarro-Vargas*, 408 F.3d 1184 (9th Cir. 2005). Do you think the grand jury should take into account anything other than whether the government has presented enough evidence to establish probable cause when deciding whether to return an indictment? If a grand jury finds sufficient evidence to establish probable cause but declines to indict because the grand jurors disagree with the wisdom of the law or its application to a particular defendant, does this constitute grand jury nullification? If so, does it differ from petit jury nullification? *See* Chapter 15, *infra*.

IV. GRAND JURY OPERATION

Rule 6 of the Federal Rules of Criminal Procedure (set out below) sets out the basic features of the federal grand jury's operation.

Rule 6. The Grand Jury

(a) Summoning a Grand Jury.

(1) *In General.* When the public interest so requires, the court must order that one or more grand juries be summoned. A grand jury must have 16 to 23 members, and the court must order that enough legally qualified persons be summoned to meet this requirement.

(2) *Alternate Jurors.* When a grand jury is selected, the court may also select alternate jurors.

Alternate jurors must have the same qualifications and be selected in the same manner as any other juror. Alternate jurors replace jurors in the same sequence in which the alternates were selected. An alternate juror who replaces a juror is subject to the same challenges, takes the same oath, and has the same authority as the other jurors.

Rule 6(a) provides the basic procedure for summoning federal grand juries. You should keep in mind that in busy, urban districts, there are often multiple grand juries sitting at any given time. On the other hand, in sparsely-populated districts, grand juries do not sit as a matter of course, and are empaneled on an as-needed basis.

(b) Objection to the Grand Jury or to a Grand Juror

    (1) *Challenges*. Either the government or a defendant may challenge the grand jury on the ground that it was not lawfully drawn, summoned, or selected, and may challenge an individual juror on the ground that the juror is not legally qualified.

    (2) *Motion to Dismiss an Indictment.* A party may move to dismiss the indictment based on an objection to the grand jury or on an individual juror's lack of legal qualification, unless the court has previously ruled on the same objection under Rule 6(b)(1). The motion to dismiss is governed by 28 U.S.C. § 1867 (e). The court must not dismiss the indictment on the ground that a grand juror was not legally qualified if the record shows that at least 12 qualified jurors concurred in the indictment.

Challenges to the grand jury under Rule 6(b) are very difficult to mount. Although racial discrimination in the selection of grand jurors is violative of the Equal Protection Clause and constitutes grounds for reversal of a criminal conviction, such claims are notoriously difficult to prove. *See, e.g., Rose v. Mitchell*, 443 U.S. 545 (1979); Roger A. Fairfax, Jr., *Batson*'s Grand Jury DNA, 97 IOWA L. REV. 1511 (2012). Even more run-of-the-mill challenges to the legal qualifications of a grand juror often are frustrated by the inability of the defendant to obtain access to information about grand jurors given the secrecy requirements.

(c) Foreperson and Deputy Foreperson. The court will appoint one juror as the foreperson and another as the deputy foreperson. In the foreperson's absence, the deputy foreperson will act as the foreperson. The foreperson may administer

oaths and affirmations and will sign all indictments. The
foreperson—or another juror designated by the foreperson—
will record the number of jurors concurring in every indictment
and will file the record with the clerk, but the record may not
be made public unless the court so orders.

As described in Rule 6(c), the foreperson of the grand jury plays a
relatively ministerial role. The limited role of the foreperson was the
rationale for the Supreme Court's rejection, in *Hobby v. United States*,
468 U.S. 339 (1984), of the argument that racial discrimination in the
selection of a grand jury foreperson from among grand jurors (as
distinct from discrimination in the selection of grand jurors in the first
instance) was grounds under the Due Process Clause for reversal of a
conviction:

> As Rule 6(c) illustrates, the responsibilities of a federal grand
> jury foreman are essentially clerical in nature: administering
> oaths, maintaining records, and signing indictments. The
> secrecy imperative in grand jury proceedings demands that
> someone "mind the store," just as a secretary or clerk would
> keep records of other sorts of proceedings. But the ministerial
> trappings of the post carry with them no special powers or
> duties that meaningfully affect the rights of persons that the
> grand jury charges with a crime, beyond those possessed by
> every member of that body. The foreman has no authority
> apart from that of the grand jury as a whole to act in a manner
> that determines or influences whether an individual is to be
> prosecuted. Even the foreman's duty to sign the indictment is a
> formality, for the absence of the foreman's signature is a mere
> technical irregularity that is not necessarily fatal to the
> indictment. * * * As the Court of Appeals noted, the impact of a
> federal grand jury foreman upon the criminal justice system
> and the rights of persons charged with crime is "minimal and
> incidental at best."

(d) Who May Be Present.

(1) *While the Grand Jury Is in Session.* The
following persons may be present while the grand jury is
in session: attorneys for the government, the witness
being questioned, interpreters when needed, and a court
reporter or an operator of a recording device.

(2) *During Deliberations and Voting.* No person
other than the jurors, and any interpreter needed to assist
a hearing-impaired or speech-impaired juror, may be
present while the grand jury is deliberating or voting.

Rule 6(d) provides the exclusive list of who may be present at different phases of the grand jury process. Notice that the list does not include interns, administrative assistants, marshals to control the witness, or a case agent not testifying. *See United States v. Mechanik*, 475 U.S. 66 (1986) (finding violation of Rule 6(d) when two agents testified in tandem before the grand jury, but determining that the error was rendered harmless by the subsequent jury verdict on proof beyond a reasonable doubt).

Notice that Rule 6(d) also excludes counsel for either the witness being questioned or the target of the grand jury investigation. The Supreme Court has made clear that a grand jury witness has no constitutional right to counsel in the grand jury room. *See United States v. Mandujano*, 425 U.S. 564, 581 (1976) (citing *In re Groban*, 352 U.S. 330, 333 (1957)); *see also Conn v. Gabbert*, 526 U.S. 286 (1999). Even in those rare instances in federal grand jury proceedings in which targets of grand jury investigations testify before the grand jury, Rule 6(d) prohibits counsel to be present. Instead, the witness must consult with counsel outside of the grand jury room, sometimes even between questions.

NOTE ON STATE PRACTICE

Although FED. R. CRIM. P. 6(d) excludes attorneys for witnesses from the grand jury room, states may have different approaches. What are the rules in the jurisdiction in which you plan to practice? *See, e.g.,* N.Y. Crim Proc. L. §§ 190.25, 190.52.

(e) Recording and Disclosing the Proceedings.

(1) *Recording the Proceedings.* Except while the grand jury is deliberating or voting, all proceedings must be recorded by a court reporter or by a suitable recording device. But the validity of a prosecution is not affected by the unintentional failure to make a recording. Unless the court orders otherwise, an attorney for the government will retain control of the recording, the reporter's notes, and any transcript prepared from those notes.

(2) *Secrecy.*

(A) No obligation of secrecy may be imposed on any person except in accordance with Rule 6(e)(2)(B).

(B) Unless these rules provide otherwise, the following persons must not disclose a matter occurring before the grand jury:

(i) a grand juror;

(ii) an interpreter;

(iii) a court reporter;

(iv) an operator of a recording device;

(v) a person who transcribes recorded testimony;

(vi) an attorney for the government; or

(vii) a person to whom disclosure is made under Rule 6(e)(3)(A)(ii) or (iii).

(3) *Exceptions.*

(A) Disclosure of a grand-jury matter—other than the grand jury's deliberations or any grand juror's vote—may be made to:

(i) an attorney for the government for use in performing that attorney's duty;

(ii) any government personnel—including those of a state, state subdivision, Indian tribe, or foreign government—that an attorney for the government considers necessary to assist in performing that attorney's duty to enforce federal criminal law; or

(iii) a person authorized by 18 U.S.C. § 3322.

(B) A person to whom information is disclosed under Rule 6(e)(3)(A)(ii) may use that information only to assist an attorney for the government in performing that attorney's duty to enforce federal criminal law. An attorney for the government must promptly provide the court that impaneled the grand jury with the names of all persons to whom a disclosure has been made, and must certify that the attorney has advised those persons of their obligation of secrecy under this rule.

(C) An attorney for the government may disclose any grand-jury matter to another federal grand jury.

(D) An attorney for the government may disclose any grand-jury matter involving foreign intelligence, counterintelligence (as defined in 50 U.S.C. § 3003), or foreign intelligence information (as defined in Rule 6(e)(3)(D)(iii)) to any federal law enforcement, intelligence, protective, immigration, national defense, or national security official to assist the official receiving the information in the performance of that official's duties. An attorney for the government may also disclose any grand-jury matter involving, within the United States or elsewhere, a threat of attack or other grave hostile acts of a foreign power or its agent, a threat of domestic or international sabotage or terrorism, or clandestine intelligence gathering activities by an intelligence service or network of a foreign power or by its agent, to any appropriate federal, state, state subdivision, Indian tribal, or foreign government official, for the purpose of preventing or responding to such threat or activities.

(i) Any official who receives information under Rule 6(e)(3)(D) may use the information only as necessary in the conduct of that person's official duties subject to any limitations on the unauthorized disclosure of such information. Any state, state subdivision, Indian tribal, or foreign government official who receives information under Rule 6(e)(3)(D) may use the information only in a manner consistent with any guidelines issued by the Attorney General and the Director of National Intelligence.

(ii) Within a reasonable time after disclosure is made under Rule 6(e)(3)(D), an attorney for the government must file, under seal, a notice with the court in the district where the grand jury convened stating that such information was disclosed and the departments, agencies, or entities to which the disclosure was made.

(iii) As used in Rule 6(e)(3)(D), the term "foreign intelligence information" means:

(a) information, whether or not it concerns a United States person, that relates to the ability of the United States to protect against—

- actual or potential attack or other grave hostile acts of a foreign power or its agent;

- sabotage or international terrorism by a foreign power or its agent; or

- clandestine intelligence activities by an intelligence service or network of a foreign power or by its agent; or

(b) information, whether or not it concerns a United States person, with respect to a foreign power or foreign territory that relates to—

- the national defense or the security of the United States; or

- the conduct of the foreign affairs of the United States.

(E) The court may authorize disclosure—at a time, in a manner, and subject to any other conditions that it directs—of a grand-jury matter:

(i) preliminarily to or in connection with a judicial proceeding;

(ii) at the request of a defendant who shows that a ground may exist to dismiss the indictment because of a matter that occurred before the grand jury;

(iii) at the request of the government, when sought by a foreign court or prosecutor for use in an official criminal investigation;

(iv) at the request of the government if it shows that the matter may disclose a violation of State, Indian tribal, or foreign criminal law, as long as the disclosure is to an appropriate state, state-subdivision, Indian tribal, or foreign government official for the purpose of enforcing that law; or

(v) at the request of the government if it shows that the matter may disclose a violation of military criminal law under the Uniform Code of Military Justice, as long as the disclosure is to an appropriate military official for the purpose of enforcing that law.

(F) A petition to disclose a grand-jury matter under Rule 6(e)(3)(E)(i) must be filed in the district where the grand jury convened. Unless the hearing is ex parte—as it may be when the government is the petitioner—the petitioner must serve the petition on, and the court must afford a reasonable opportunity to appear and be heard to:

(i) an attorney for the government;

(ii) the parties to the judicial proceeding; and

(iii) any other person whom the court may designate.

(G) If the petition to disclose arises out of a judicial proceeding in another district, the petitioned court must transfer the petition to the other court unless the petitioned court can reasonably determine whether disclosure is proper. If the petitioned court decides to transfer, it must send to the transferee court the material sought to be disclosed, if feasible, and a written evaluation of the need for continued grand-jury secrecy. The transferee court must afford those persons identified in Rule 6(e)(3)(F) a reasonable opportunity to appear and be heard.

(4) *Sealed Indictment.* The magistrate judge to whom an indictment is returned may direct that the indictment be kept secret until the defendant is in custody or has been released pending trial. The clerk must then seal the indictment, and no person may disclose the indictment's existence except as necessary to issue or execute a warrant or summons.

(5) *Closed Hearing.* Subject to any right to an open hearing in a contempt proceeding, the court must close any hearing to the extent necessary to prevent disclosure of a matter occurring before a grand jury.

(6) *Sealed Records.* Records, orders, and subpoenas relating to grand-jury proceedings must be kept under seal to the extent and as long as necessary to prevent the unauthorized disclosure of a matter occurring before a grand jury.

(7) *Contempt.* A knowing violation of Rule 6, or of any guidelines jointly issued by the Attorney General and the Director of National Intelligence under Rule 6, may be punished as a contempt of court.

Rule 6(e) is among the most important provisions in the entire Federal Rules of Criminal Procedure because it anchors the all-important grand jury secrecy requirement.

As you read, Rule 6(e)(1) requires recording of grand jury proceedings, except during the grand jurors' deliberations and voting, which remain secret. Rule 6(e)(2) imposes a secrecy requirement upon the grand jurors themselves, interpreters, court reporters, operators of the recording device and those who transcribe the recorded testimony, the attorney for the government, and individuals who receive grand jury information under certain of the Rule 6(e)(3) exceptions. Note that there is no requirement of secrecy imposed upon *witnesses* before the grand jury.

Rule 6(e)(3)(A)(ii) does permit disclosure of certain grand jury matter to, for example, state or foreign prosecutors cooperating in a federal criminal investigation. However, those individuals can only use the information to assist in the federal criminal investigation, and the federal prosecutor must maintain for the court a list—often referred to as a "6(e) list"—of those who have received disclosure and must certify that these individuals have been informed of their secrecy obligations. *See* Fed. R. Crim. P. 6(e)(3)(B). A similar process is followed under Rule 6(e)(3)(D) for disclosure to authorized personnel in intelligence and national security matters.

Although federal grand jury matters can be disclosed to another federal grand jury, Rule 6(e)(3)(C), the court must authorize disclosure of grand jury material for other reasons, including for purposes of using it in a different judicial proceeding, in a state or foreign criminal proceeding, or to determine whether an irregularity in the grand jury process warrants dismissal of the indictment. *See* Fed. R. Crim. P. 6(e)(3)(E).

Other provisions of Rule 6(e) provide for sealing of the indictment and other records related to the grand jury, and the closing of hearings, in order to protect the secrecy of the grand jury. Rule 6(e)(4), 6(e)(5), 6(e)(6). Finally, as Rule 6(e)(7) provides, the contempt power of court can be used to punish violations of Rule 6(e). *See also* 18 U.S.C. § 401; Fed. R. Crim. P. 42.

> **(f) Indictment and Return.** A grand jury may indict only if at least 12 jurors concur. The grand jury—or its foreperson or deputy foreperson—must return the indictment to a magistrate judge in open court. To avoid unnecessary cost or delay, the magistrate judge may take the return by video teleconference from the court where the grand jury sits. If a complaint or information is pending against the defendant and 12 jurors do not concur in the indictment, the foreperson must promptly and in writing report the lack of concurrence to the magistrate judge.

Although 23 grand jurors are empaneled, 16 members of the grand jury need to be present in order for the grand jury to conduct business. As Rule 6(f) provides, it takes 12 to vote in favor of an indictment for the grand jury to return a "true bill."

> ## Record of the Number of Grand Jurors Concurring in an Indictment
>
> http://www.uscourts.gov/sites/default/files/ao190.pdf
>
> ## Report of a Grand Jury's Failure to Concur in an Indictment
>
> http://www.uscourts.gov/sites/default/files/ao191.pdf

Rarity of Grand Jury Declinations

It is exceedingly rare for a grand jury to vote not to indict in a given case. *See* Bureau of Justice Statistics, U.S. Dep't of Justice, Federal Justice Statistics 2010—Statistical Tables 12 (December 2013) (reflecting that federal grand juries declined to indict in only eleven of more than 160,000 cases in 2010). When one observes numbers this stark, it is tempting to conclude that the grand jury has no impact on whether a criminal case is brought. However, there are some potential explanations for why prosecutors have such a high rate of success when submitting indictments to the grand jury to a vote. Aside from the fact that the grand jury applies a probable cause standard, not the more exacting proof beyond a reasonable doubt standard, the grand jury process is unburdened by rules of evidence and other constraints on the presentation of proof. *See, e.g., Costello v. United States*, 350 U.S. 359 (1956). Additionally, and perhaps more importantly, the prosecutor can survey the grand jury on the strength of the government's case before requesting a vote on the indictment. Thus, flawed cases can be shored up with additional evidence before a grand jury vote, and cases that cannot be strengthened with additional evidence or advocacy simply may be scuttled and not submitted for a vote. Viewed in light of these realities of grand jury practice, the statistics may not be as damning as they might seem. *See, e.g.,* Roger A. Fairfax, Jr., *Grand Jury 2.0: Toward a Functional Makeover of the Ancient Bulwark of Liberty*, 19 WM. & MARY BILL OF RTS. L.J. 339, 342–43 (2010).

(g) Discharging the Grand Jury. A grand jury must serve until the court discharges it, but it may serve more than 18 months only if the court, having determined that an extension is in the public interest, extends the grand jury's service. An extension may be granted for no more than 6 months, except as otherwise provided by statute.

(h) Excusing a Juror. At any time, for good cause, the court may excuse a juror either temporarily or permanently, and if permanently, the court may impanel an alternate juror in place of the excused juror.

(i) "Indian Tribe" Defined. "Indian tribe" means an Indian tribe recognized by the Secretary of the Interior on a list published in the Federal Register under 25 U.S.C. § 479a–1.

V. GRAND JURY SUBPOENA POWER

The grand jury's power to compel the production of evidence and testimony is tremendously broad and robust. As the Supreme Court famously reiterated in *Branzburg v. Hayes*, 408 U.S. 665 (1972), the grand jury has a right to "every man's relevant evidence." *Id.* at 737. This subpoena power reaches virtually anyone—including the President of the United States—and anything, subject only to valid constitutional, statutory, and common law privileges.

In keeping with this broad power, grand jury subpoenas do not need to meet the thresholds set forth for trial subpoenas in *United States v. Nixon*, 418 U.S. 683 (1974) (requiring showing that evidence sought is relevant, admissible, and specific). Instead, grand jury subpoenas are subject to quash only if the subpoena meets the extremely high standard of being "unreasonable or oppressive." *United States v. R. Enterprises, Inc.*, 498 U.S. 292, 299 (1991) (quoting FED. R. CRIM. P. 17(C)).

There are, however, limits on the use of the grand jury for certain purposes. For example, the grand jury's subpoena power is not properly used to compel evidence for the purpose of using it in civil proceedings, or to continue to gather evidence after indictment in order to prepare for trial. Additionally, the Department of Justice has adopted the policy that the grand jury subpoena power should not be used for the purpose of locating fugitives. *See* UNITED STATES ATTORNEY'S MANUAL 9–11.120.

Subpoena to Testify Before Grand Jury

http://www.uscourts.gov/sites/default/files/ao110.pdf

VI. RIGHTS, PRIVILEGES, AND OBLIGATIONS OF GRAND JURY WITNESSES

As discussed above, in the absence of a valid privilege, grand jury witnesses are obligated to testify and produce evidence requested in a subpoena. A recalcitrant witness may be subject to either civil or criminal contempt and could be jailed for refusing to testify before the grand jury. In certain circumstances, the term of incarceration could extend for the duration of the grand jury's term. *See* 18 U.S.C. § 1826.

Contempt actions or even criminal prosecution for perjury might also be brought against a witness who testifies falsely before the grand jury. *See* 18 U.S.C. § 1623.

In addition to certain constitutional privileges (such as the Fifth Amendment privilege against self-incrimination)* and statutory privileges (such as the federal wiretap statute's exclusion of illegally-obtained electronic surveillance evidence), the common law evidentiary privileges recognized in federal court apply to grand jury proceedings. *See* Fed. R. Evid. 501. Among these are the spousal privilege, the clergy privilege, and the attorney-client privilege.

Advice of Rights to Grand Jury Witnesses

It is the custom of the U.S. Department of Justice to issue warnings to all witnesses before the grand jury, and the policy to do for any "target" or "subject" of a grand jury investigation. *See* UNITED STATES ATTORNEY'S MANUAL § 9–11.151. These warnings are typically included with the grand jury subpoena itself and given by the prosecutor in the record before the witness testifies. Below are excerpts of the prescribed warnings contained in the United States Attorney's Manual.

United States Attorney's Manual

9–11.151 Advice of "Rights" of Grand Jury Witnesses

Advice of Rights

- The grand jury is conducting an investigation of possible violations of Federal criminal laws involving: (State here the general subject matter of inquiry, e.g., conducting an illegal gambling business in violation of 18 U.S.C. § 1955).

- You may refuse to answer any question if a truthful answer to the question would tend to incriminate you.

- Anything that you do say may be used against you by the grand jury or in a subsequent legal proceeding.

- If you have retained counsel, the grand jury will permit you a reasonable opportunity to step outside the grand jury room to consult with counsel if you so desire.

Additional Advice to be Given to Targets: If the witness is a target, the above advice should also contain a supplemental warning that the witness's conduct is being investigated for possible violation of federal criminal law.

---

 * A refusal to comply with a grand jury subpoena based upon the Fifth Amendment's privilege against self-incrimination may be defeated with a grant of immunity to the witness. For an explanation of "the intersection of the grand jury's subpoena power and the Fifth Amendment rights of those subpoenaed," *see* Sara Sun Beale and James E. Felman, *The Fifth Amendment and the Grand Jury*, CRIMINAL JUSTICE (Spring 2007).

VII.   GRAND JURY REFORM OR ABOLITION?

In light of the various critiques of the grand jury mentioned earlier in the chapter, should we consider changing the structure of grand jury, or even scrapping the grand jury in favor of another system? Professor Fairfax, in *Grand Jury Innovation: Toward a Functional Makeover of the Ancient Bulwark of Liberty*, 19 WM & MARY BILL OF RIGHTS J. 339 (2010), considers some of the leading critiques of the grand jury.

> Why retain the grand jury? Given the low esteem in which the grand jury is held in American legal culture, it is surprising that we have not followed the lead of our English forbearers and abolished the whole enterprise. Complaints about the grand jury run the gamut from assertions that it imposes unnecessary costs on the system, to the allegation that it is the complete captive of the prosecution.

1.   Costliness

> Critics since Jeremy Bentham have made the argument that the grand jury is far too costly for whatever benefit it provides. During the debate in Congress over the utility of the grand jury in the early twentieth century, some lawmakers insisted that the costliness of maintaining the grand jury militated in favor of discarding it in the vast majority of cases. Despite these concerns, there is scant evidence of significant direct economic costs incurred as the result of retaining the grand jury. Of course, there needs to be physical space to house the grand jury, and the marginal cost of lighting and heating the grand jury room, often in the courthouse. Perhaps the courthouse budget must account for the price of refreshments for the grand jurors and per diem payments to grand jurors. Furthermore, there may be deputy marshals or other security personnel specifically assigned to protecting the grand jurors and certain administrative costs associated with the summoning and selection of grand jurors. Even with these various expenses, it is difficult to argue that the financial costs of the grand jury are more than nominal at best. However, even if the costs of the grand jury are not very significant, critics might respond that no amount of cost is justified by a weak or ineffective filter. Ironically, some of the same grand jury critics inclined to bemoan the manner in which the grand jury places unnecessary obstacles in the way of expedient prosecution also complain, as is discussed below, that the grand jury is an overly-compliant rubber stamp of the prosecutor, willing to indict on command.

2.   Ineffectiveness (Over-Compliance)

Another common gripe against the grand jury is that it is an ineffective filter for meritless criminal charges. Critics bemoan the fact that grand juries return a true bill in over ninety percent of cases presented by prosecutors. A grand jury, the famous saying goes, will "indict a 'ham sandwich.'" However, there may have been probable cause to believe the ham sandwich committed the crime. Statistics show that in over ninety-five percent of cases indicted by federal grand juries, a conviction follows. If a petit jury convicts on (or a judge overseeing a guilty plea is convinced that there exists) proof beyond a reasonable doubt, why should it be troubling that a grand jury found probable cause? Indeed, that petit juries overwhelmingly confirm grand juries' earlier probable cause determinations should not be surprising. First, because of stigma associated with the failure to obtain a true bill from a grand jury, many prosecutors work hard to ensure that the case has more than enough evidence to satisfy the probable cause standard employed by grand juries. In fact, federal prosecutors are instructed not to pursue criminal charges until they have obtained or believe they will obtain proof sufficient to survive a motion for judgment of acquittal at trial (proof beyond a reasonable doubt), a much more exacting standard than that required for grand jury indictment.

Furthermore, because the grand jury process is fluid, prosecutors often have the opportunity to poll grand jurors regarding weaknesses in the case. Given that a prosecutor can take another "bite at the apple" with regard to evidence presentation before the grand jury votes whether to indict, cases before the grand jury are strengthened and surprises at the voting stage can be kept to a minimum. Despite the common lore regarding the grand jury, even the grand jury's harshest critics must concede that, in the broad run of cases, weak or meritless charges largely are screened out by the grand jury.

3.   Redundancy

Cast as an antiquated filter for meritless criminal allegations in a modern criminal justice system replete with professional prosecutors, vigilant judges, near-universal criminal defense representation, and a watchful media, the grand jury is often characterized as redundant. When the grand jury operated in the nineteenth century, there were virtually no public prosecutors. Victims—either represented by counsel or otherwise—were able to bring their own allegations to trial, subject to the approval of the grand jury. As a result, the grand jury was tasked with making decisions whether and what to charge. Therefore, the grand jury helped to protect against abuse of the criminal process by private citizens seeking revenge or concession through the filing of criminal charges. Furthermore, the lack of a public police force meant that the grand jury played a substantial role in identifying individuals for criminal accusation. Also, the lack of right to counsel in that era meant that the grand jury was the only protection many putative criminal defendants were likely to enjoy.

In the modern criminal justice system, these functions are performed by public prosecutors, public police, and court-appointed defense attorneys. Moreover, in the absence of a grand jury, a judicial officer often will pass upon the accusations to ensure that they are supported by probable cause. Thus, the argument goes, there is no longer a need for the grand jury to perform these various roles played by modern institutional players.

However, such critiques fail to recognize that not all probable cause determinations are created equal. In the same way that a magistrate's probable cause determination is given more weight and deference than a police officer's, so too does a grand jury's probable cause determination enjoy greater respect. The reason for this is that the grand jury is not a governmental entity, but the community's representative. As such, it serves as a check on government officials (a judge and a prosecutor) who conceivably could collaborate to bring meritless charges against a defendant. The grand jury's added value rebuts the charge of redundancy critics often advance.

———————

A number of leading legal organizations, such as the American Bar Association and the National Association of Criminal Defense Lawyers, have advocated for reform of the grand jury. Among the leading reform suggestions include presence of defense counsel in the grand jury room, prohibition on presentation of inadmissible evidence, and the requirement that prosecutors present exculpatory evidence to the grand jury. The Commission to Reform the Federal Grand Jury, a non-governmental group of prominent attorneys and law professors, published in 2000 its "Bill of Rights for the Federal Grand Jury."

Federal Grand Jury Bill of Rights

1.   A witness before the grand jury who has not received immunity shall have the right to be accompanied by counsel in his or her appearance before the grand jury. Such counsel shall

be allowed to be present in the grand jury room only during the questioning of the witness and shall be allowed to advise the witness. Such counsel shall not be permitted to address the grand jurors, stop the proceedings, object to questions, stop the witness from answering a question, nor otherwise take an active part in proceedings before the grand jury. The court shall have the power to remove from the grand jury room, or otherwise sanction counsel for conduct inconsistent with this principle.

2.   No prosecutor shall knowingly fail to disclose to the federal grand jury evidence in the prosecutor's possession which exonerates the target or subject of the offense. Such disclosure obligations shall not include an obligation to disclose matters that affect credibility such as prior inconsistent statements or Giglio materials.

3.   The prosecutor shall not present to the federal grand jury evidence which he or she knows to be constitutionally inadmissible at trial because of a court ruling on the matter.

4.   A target or subject of a grand jury investigation shall have the right to testify before the grand jury. Prosecutors shall notify such targets or subjects of their opportunity to testify, unless notification may result in flight, endanger other persons or obstruct justice, or unless the prosecutor is unable to notify said persons with reasonable diligence. A target or subject of the grand jury may also submit to the court, to be made available to the foreperson, an offer, in writing, to provide information or evidence to the grand jury.

5.   Witnesses should have the right to receive a transcript of their federal grand jury testimony.

6.   The federal grand jury shall not name a person in an indictment as an unindicted co-conspirator to a criminal conspiracy. Nothing herein shall prevent the prosecutor from supplying such names in a bill of particulars.

7.   All non- immunized subjects or targets called before a federal grand jury shall be given a Miranda warning by the prosecutor before being questioned.

8.   All subpoenas for witnesses called before a federal grand jury shall be issued at least 72 hours before the date of appearance, not to include weekends and holidays, unless good cause is shown for an exemption.

9.   The federal grand jurors shall be given meaningful jury instructions, on the record, regarding their duties and

powers as grand jurors, and the charges they are to consider. All instructions, recommendations and commentary to grand jurors by the prosecution shall be recorded and shall be made available to the accused after an indictment, during pretrial discovery, and the court shall have discretion to dismiss an indictment, with or without prejudice, in the event of prosecutorial impropriety reflected in the transcript.

10. No prosecutor shall call before the federal grand jury any subject or target who has stated personally or through his attorney that he intends to invoke the constitutional privilege against self-incrimination.

COMMISSION TO REFORM THE GRAND JURY, FEDERAL GRAND JURY BILL OF RIGHTS (2000).

Which of these proposals would make the most significant improvement in the role and function of the grand jury? Would any change the fundamental nature of the grand jury?

Police Killings of Unarmed Civilians and Grand Jury Reform

The many high-profile cases (e.g., Michael Brown, Eric Garner, and Tamir Rice) in which grand juries have declined to indict police officers responsible for killing unarmed civilians—mostly African American males—have led to calls for the abolition of the grand jury. *See, e.g.,* James C. Harrington, *Abolish Grand Jury System*, SAN ANTONIO EXPRESS-NEWS, December 21, 2014; LaDoris Hazzard Cordell, *Grand Juries Should Be Abolished*, SLATE, December 9, 2014. Others have suggested that the grand jury is not solely to blame in these cases in which many have been dismayed by the outcome of grand jury proceedings. *See, e.g.,* Roger A. Fairfax, Jr., *Evidence Shows System Needs Mending Not Ending*, ORLANDO SENTINEL, December 26, 2014.

In any event, a number of grand jury reform proposals have arisen in the wake of these tragic events. *See, e.g.,* Lauren-Brooke Eisen, *What is on the Horizon for Grand Jury Reform?* HUFF. POST, January 23, 2015. For an analysis of some of the leading reform proposals related to these police killing cases, *see* Roger A. Fairfax, Jr., *The Grand Jury's Role in the Prosecution on Unjustified Police Killings—Challenges and Solutions*, 52 HARV. CIV. RTS.-CIV. LIB. L. REV. 397 (2017); Roger A. Fairfax, Jr., *Should the American Grand Jury Survive Ferguson?* 58 HOW. L.J. 825 (2015).

NOTE ON STATE PRACTICE

Recall that, although the Fifth Amendment's Grand Jury Clause has not been incorporated to apply to the states, about half of the states do in fact require grand jury indictment for many criminal offenses. Is grand jury indictment required in the state in which you plan to practice? Does the prosecutor have a choice whether to proceed by grand jury indictment? How many grand jurors serve on a typical grand jury? What is the duration of the grand jury's term? For more on state grand jury practices, *see* BUREAU OF JUSTICE STATISTICS, STATE COURT ORGANIZATION, 2004: PART VI, THE JURY (state-by-state information on grand jury structure and function).

COUNSEL EXERCISE 4: Grand Jury Indictment (Prosecution)

Prepare to conduct a grand jury proceeding. You should read Federal Rule of Criminal Procedure 6 carefully in preparation for the hearing. Using the information you have (including the complaint, affidavit, and prosecution memorandum), you should consider the strengths and weaknesses of the case and select the charges to include in the indictment. Assume that your case agent has testified to the same facts established in the preliminary hearing. Prior to the grand jury hearing, you should prepare a draft indictment.

CHAPTER 5

PROSECUTORIAL DISCRETION AND CHARGING DOCUMENTS

I. INTRODUCTION

The prosecutorial decision whether and what to charge is the most fundamental of the many choices made by criminal justice actors throughout the criminal process. *See, e.g.,* William J. Stuntz, *The Pathological Politics of Criminal Law*, 100 MICH. L. REV. 505 (2001). The following excerpt from Professor Fairfax's *Grand Jury Discretion and Constitutional Design*, 93 CORNELL L. REV. 703 (2008), provides an overview of some of the discretion underpinning the administration of criminal justice:

A. Inventorying Discretion in Criminal Justice

Discretion is the backbone of the criminal justice system. The administration of criminal justice is not wooden and mechanical—there are far too many criminal laws and far too many offenders for society's limited police, prosecutorial, judicial, and penological resources. Therefore, actors in the criminal justice system must exercise some discretion in deciding which individuals to arrest, prosecute, convict, and punish.

* * *

1. Executive Criminal Enforcement Policymaking

The Executive exercises tremendous discretion in setting policy regarding enforcement priorities. This takes two forms. First, the Executive may set policy on the criminalization of a certain type of conduct and work to persuade the Legislature to proscribe that conduct. Second, the Executive—from both a law enforcement and a prosecutorial standpoint—determines which criminal laws to enforce. For instance, a presidential administration hostile to laissez-faire approaches to market regulation might vigorously enforce antitrust laws to the detriment of other enforcement priorities. Likewise, an Executive with a strong gun-control position might exercise discretion to focus enforcement and prosecutorial resources on gun crimes.

2.   Law Enforcement Discretion

Although investigating certain types of criminal activity involves collaboration between law enforcement officials and prosecutors, prosecutors will often be unaware of potentially criminal conduct until law enforcement officials bring it to their attention after an investigation is underway or even complete. Law enforcement personnel, therefore, exercise tremendous discretion to determine whether to investigate an individual or entity in the first place and, if they discover criminal conduct, whether to bring it to the prosecutor for a charging decision. Any criminal procedure hornbook recounts the discretion law enforcement officers wield in determining who to stop and frisk, question, or ask for consent to conduct more invasive searches. Although the Constitution and statutes highly regulate the manner in which law enforcement personnel conduct investigations, the decision to investigate an individual in the first instance is unchecked.

Once law enforcement personnel have investigated a person of interest, they must decide whether to detain and/or seek charges against that person. This exercise of discretion has perhaps the most profound impact on a putative defendant because it comes at the point when the person will or will not be entered into the "system." Even where other actors exercise discretion later in the criminal justice process in the individual's favor, the stigma of the investigation and arrest, many times memorialized in an arrest record, can have lasting effects. And while indications of possible criminal conduct— enough to satisfy the probable cause standard—will often determine whether law enforcement will present a case to a prosecutor for a charging decision, other factors unrelated to the sufficiency of the evidence might drive this discretion. These factors include whether the individual might be a valuable asset to other investigatory activity, whether the individual is a prominent member of society, whether litigating the case would expose unconstitutional officer conduct to scrutiny, whether the case would advance the career of the investigating officer, and whether the case has received publicity. These and any number of other nonevidentiary factors, legitimate and illegitimate, may guide the virtually unfettered and unreviewable discretion of law enforcement officials.

3.   Prosecutorial Discretion

Perhaps the broadest exercise of discretion occurs at the crucial charging stage. Prosecutors in individual cases exercise discretion when deciding whether to charge a defendant in the first instance, and such discretion is virtually unfettered. The prosecutor can decide whether to charge an individual on any number of grounds. Often whether there is, or will likely be, enough admissible evidence to obtain a conviction will factor prominently in the prosecutor's decision to charge. For example, the resolve of a whistleblower or complaining witness, the credibility of the investigating law enforcement officer, or the availability of documentary, forensic, or other physical evidence will drive the prosecutor's discretion.

However, prosecutors just as often will decide whether to charge based on factors other than the sufficiency of the evidence. In exercising discretion whether to charge a defendant, a prosecutor might ask a host of nonevidentiary questions including whether the defendant is a recidivist or is likely to offend again, whether the prosecutor has a heavy caseload at the time, whether the type of case is career advancing, whether the case has received publicity, whether the victim is vocal and empowered, whether the investigating law enforcement agency is pleasant to work with, whether the case has jury appeal, whether a matter is more appropriately prosecuted by a different sovereign or handled as a civil matter, and whether the criminal conduct is a priority area for the prosecutor's superiors. While some of these bases seem more legitimate than others, all are typical grounds for prosecutors' exercise of their unfettered charging discretion.

Beyond that initial decision whether to charge, prosecutors make many other important discretionary judgments. Obviously, where a defendant's conduct implicates multiple criminal statutes, a prosecutor must decide which crimes to charge. And once the prosecutor charges the defendant with those crimes, it is within the discretion of the prosecutor to decide whether to dismiss some or all of the charges previously lodged. As with the decision to charge, each of these later prosecutorial decisions is marked by discretion that is, in most instances, unreviewable.

What would be the alternative to providing prosecutors such broad discretion? Would we expect prosecutors to prosecute every provable criminal violation of which they become aware? Professor Fairfax explores this question in the following excerpt from *Prosecutorial Nullification*, 52 B.C. L. REV. 1243 (2011):

Imagine a spectrum along which varying assessments of the appropriate scope of a prosecutor's discretion are plotted. At one end of the spectrum is the "full enforcement" model, in which it is urged that a prosecutor has the duty to prosecute every meritorious case that comes across her desk. Where a credible allegation is supported by sufficient admissible evidence, the prosecutor must pursue the charges. Any failure to do so—for whatever reason—is a breach of that duty. At the other end of the spectrum is the "complete discretion" model, which assumes that a prosecutor has plenary discretion to bring charges in only those cases that she deems appropriate and to decline to prosecute those cases that she does not. Under this view, a prosecutor's decision not to charge in a given case—for any reason at all—is deemed an appropriate exercise of discretion.

* * *

Certainly, given the realities of modern criminal justice, few, if any, would lay claim to a vision of prosecutorial discretion residing at either extreme. Both the full enforcement model and the complete discretion model carry negative consequences most would be unwilling to accept. Full enforcement of the law would be deemed by most as too inflexible and resource intensive to be workable in our society. Likewise, complete and unfettered discretion might too easily lead to the sort of arbitrary or improperly discriminatory criminal law enforcement our legal culture has shunned as a normative and constitutional matter. Thus, as we move away from either extreme, we find common articulations of the scope of prosecutorial discretion.

* * *

Many considerations impact the exercise of prosecutorial discretion. Given that most prosecutors in the United States are elected (and those who are not elected typically are appointed by elected officials), politics can come into play—for better or worse. *See* Ronald F. Wright, *Beyond Prosecutor Elections*, 67 S.M.U. L. REV. 593 (2014); Ronald F. Wright, *How Prosecutor Elections Fail Us*, 6 OH. ST. J. CRIM. L. 581 (2009). Some have argued that discussions of prosecutorial priorities need to go beyond the prosecution of crime and should take account of the role that a prosecutor's decisions have on the rate and cost of incarceration in a jurisdiction. *See* Russell Gold, *Promoting Democracy in Prosecution*, 86 WASH. L. REV. 69 (2011); *see also* R. Michael Cassidy, *(Ad)ministering Justice: A Prosecutor's Ethical Duty to Support Sentencing Reform*, 45 LOYOLA U. CHI. L.J. 981 (2014). What do you think should shape the enforcement priorities of a prosecutor's office? For more on the role of the prosecutor and the exercise of discretion, *see* ANGELA J. DAVIS, ARBITRARY JUSTICE: THE POWER OF THE AMERICAN PROSECUTOR (2007).

II. STANDARDS GUIDING PROSECUTORIAL DISCRETION

Although the prosecutor has broad—often described as plenary—discretion, that discretion must be guided appropriately so that it is consistent with enforcement priorities and ethical standards governing prosecutors. For example, the United States Attorney's Manual provides guidance for federal prosecutors in the exercise of their discretion whether to charge in a criminal case.

United States Attorney's Manual

9–27.220 Grounds for Commencing or Declining Prosecution

A. The attorney for the government should commence or recommend Federal prosecution if he/she believes that the person's conduct constitutes a Federal offense and that the admissible evidence will probably be sufficient to obtain and sustain a conviction, unless, in his/her judgment, prosecution should be declined because:

1. No substantial Federal interest would be served by prosecution;

2. The person is subject to effective prosecution in another jurisdiction; or

3. There exists an adequate non-criminal alternative to prosecution.

B. Comment. USAM 9–27.220 expresses the principle that, ordinarily, the attorney for the government should initiate or recommend Federal prosecution if he/she believes that the person's conduct constitutes a Federal offense and that the admissible evidence probably will be sufficient to obtain and sustain a conviction. Evidence sufficient to sustain a conviction is required under Rule 29(a), Fed. R. Crim. P., to avoid a judgment of acquittal. Moreover, both as a matter of fundamental fairness and in the interest of the efficient administration of justice, no prosecution should be initiated against any person unless the government believes that the person probably will be found guilty by an unbiased trier of fact. In this connection, it should be noted that, when deciding whether to prosecute, the government attorney need not have in hand all the evidence upon which he/she intends to rely at trial: it is sufficient that he/she have a reasonable belief that such evidence will be available and admissible at the time of trial. Thus, for example, it would be proper to commence a prosecution though a key witness is out of the country, so long as the witness's presence at trial could be expected with reasonable certainty.

The potential that—despite the law and the facts that create a sound, prosecutable case—the factfinder is likely to acquit the defendant because of the unpopularity of some factor involved in the prosecution or because of the overwhelming popularity of the defendant or his/her cause, is not a factor prohibiting prosecution. For example, in a civil rights case or a case involving an extremely popular political figure, it might be clear that the evidence of guilt—viewed objectively by an unbiased factfinder—would be sufficient to obtain and sustain a conviction, yet the prosecutor might reasonably doubt whether the jury would convict. In such a case, despite his/her negative assessment of the likelihood of a guilty verdict (based on factors extraneous to an objective view of the law and the facts), the prosecutor may properly conclude that it is necessary and desirable to commence or recommend prosecution and allow the criminal process to operate in accordance with its principles.

Merely because the attorney for the government believes that a person's conduct constitutes a Federal offense and that the admissible evidence will be sufficient to obtain and sustain a conviction, does not mean that he/she necessarily should initiate or recommend prosecution: USAM 9–27.220 notes three situations in which the prosecutor may properly decline to take action nonetheless: when no substantial Federal interest would be served by prosecution; when the person is subject to effective prosecution in another jurisdiction; and when there exists an adequate non-criminal alternative to prosecution. It is left to the judgment of the attorney for the government whether such a situation exists. In exercising that judgment, the attorney for the government should consult USAM 9–27.230, 9–27.240, or 9–27.250, as appropriate.

It should be noted that these and other charging standards in the United States Attorney's Manual (see USAM §§ 9–27.230, 9–27.250, 9–27.260, and 9–27.300) are for internal use and do not create a cause of action or basis for relief for defendants who might complain that they were not followed.

Non-Criminal Alternatives to Prosecution

Note that one of the grounds for declination highlighted in USAM § 9–27.220 is that "[t]here exists an adequate non-criminal alternative to prosecution." One such possible non-criminal alternative is the pursuit of civil relief against the would-be defendant. This could entail either the government or the victim pursuing civil sanctions or remedies. Another non-criminal alternative might be the use alternative dispute resolution tool such as criminal mediation. In these mediations, both the accused and the complainant submit to mediation, usually without counsel present. Although frequently used in property crime cases, criminal mediation has been utilized in all manner of contexts, including assaultive felonies. These mediations, which enjoy a high rate of satisfaction among participants, often result in an agreement that addresses the root cause of the dispute or other issues that led to the criminal complaint in the first instance. Once the agreement is reached and both parties have upheld their obligations, the original criminal charges are dismissed. For more on criminal mediation, *see* Roger A. Fairfax, Jr., *Criminal Mediation*, in AMERICAN BAR ASS'N, STATE OF CRIMINAL JUSTICE (2014).

The American Bar Association Criminal Justice Standards (Prosecution Function) also offer guidance to prosecutors for exercising their discretion in criminal cases.

ABA Criminal Justice Standards (Prosecution Function)

Standard 3–4.2 Decisions to Charge Are the Prosecutor's

(a) While the decision to arrest is often the responsibility of law enforcement personnel, the decision to institute formal criminal proceedings is the responsibility of the prosecutor. Where the law permits a law enforcement officer or other person to initiate proceedings by complaining directly to a judicial officer or the grand jury, the complainant should be required to present the complaint for prior review by the prosecutor, and the prosecutor's recommendation regarding the complaint should be communicated to the judicial officer or grand jury.

(b) The prosecutor's office should establish standards and procedures for evaluating complaints to determine whether formal criminal proceedings should be instituted.

(c) In determining whether formal criminal charges should be filed, prosecutors should consider whether further investigation should be undertaken. After charges are filed the prosecutor should oversee law enforcement investigative activity related to the case.

(d) If the defendant is not in custody when charged, the prosecutor should consider whether a voluntary appearance rather than a custodial arrest would suffice to protect the public and ensure the defendant's presence at court proceedings.

Standard 3–4.3 Minimum Requirements for Filing and Maintaining Criminal Charges

(a) A prosecutor should seek or file criminal charges only if the prosecutor reasonably believes that the charges are supported by probable cause, that admissible evidence will be sufficient to support conviction beyond a reasonable doubt, and that the decision to charge is in the interests of justice.

(b) After criminal charges are filed, a prosecutor should maintain them only if the prosecutor continues to reasonably believe that probable cause exists and that admissible evidence will be sufficient to support conviction beyond a reasonable doubt.

(c) If a prosecutor has significant doubt about the guilt of the accused or the quality, truthfulness, or sufficiency of the evidence in any criminal case assigned to the prosecutor, the prosecutor should disclose those doubts to supervisory staff. The prosecutor's office should then determine whether it is appropriate to proceed with the case.

(d) A prosecutor's office should not file or maintain charges if it believes the defendant is innocent, no matter what the state of the evidence.

Standard 3–4.4 Discretion in Filing, Declining, Maintaining, and Dismissing Criminal Charges

(a) In order to fully implement the prosecutor's functions and duties, including the obligation to enforce the law while exercising sound discretion, the prosecutor is not obliged to file or maintain all criminal charges which the evidence might support. Among the factors which the prosecutor may properly consider in exercising discretion to initiate, decline, or dismiss a criminal charge, even though it meets the requirements of Standard 3–4.3, are:

(i)   the strength of the case;

(ii)   the prosecutor's doubt that the accused is in fact guilty;

(iii) the extent or absence of harm caused by the offense;

(iv) the impact of prosecution or non-prosecution on the public welfare;

(v)   the background and characteristics of the offender, including any voluntary restitution or efforts at rehabilitation;

(vi) whether the authorized or likely punishment or collateral consequences are disproportionate in relation to the particular offense or the offender;

(vii) the views and motives of the victim or complainant;

(viii) any improper conduct by law enforcement;

(ix) unwarranted disparate treatment of similarly situated persons;

(x) potential collateral impact on third parties, including witnesses or victims;

(xi) cooperation of the offender in the apprehension or conviction of others;

(xii) the possible influence of any cultural, ethnic, socioeconomic or other improper biases;

(xiii) changes in law or policy;

(xiv) the fair and efficient distribution of limited prosecutorial resources;

(xv) the likelihood of prosecution by another jurisdiction; and

(xvi) whether the public's interests in the matter might be appropriately vindicated by available civil, regulatory, administrative, or private remedies.

(b) In exercising discretion to file and maintain charges, the prosecutor should not consider:

(i) partisan or other improper political or personal considerations;

(ii) hostility or personal animus towards a potential subject, or any other improper motive of the prosecutor; or

(iii) the impermissible criteria described in Standard 1.6 above.

(c) A prosecutor may file and maintain charges even if juries in the jurisdiction have tended to acquit persons accused of the particular kind of criminal act in question.

(d) The prosecutor should not file or maintain charges greater in number or degree than can reasonably be supported with evidence at trial and are necessary to fairly reflect the gravity of the offense or deter similar conduct.

(e) A prosecutor may condition a dismissal of charges, *nolle prosequi*, or similar action on the accused's relinquishment of a right to seek civil redress only if the accused has given informed consent, and such consent is disclosed to the court. A prosecutor should not use a civil waiver to avoid a bona fide claim of improper law enforcement actions, and a decision not to file criminal charges should be made on its merits and not for the purpose of obtaining a civil waiver.

(f) The prosecutor should consider the possibility of a noncriminal disposition, formal or informal, or a deferred prosecution or other diversionary disposition, when deciding whether to initiate or prosecute criminal charges. The prosecutor should be familiar with the services and resources of other agencies, public or private, that might assist in the evaluation of cases for diversion or deferral from the criminal process.

Do the ABA standards comport with the ABA Model Rules of Professional Conduct, which prohibit a prosecutor "from prosecuting a charge [she] knows is not supported by probable cause"? *See* ABA MODEL RULES OF PROFESSIONAL CONDUCT 3.8(a).

Remedying Abuse of Prosecutorial Discretion

Given that these standards are aspirational and unenforceable by criminal defendants, is there any remedy for the abuse of prosecutorial discretion? There is an Equal Protection Clause constraint on prosecutorial decisions that constitute selective enforcement, but those claims are extremely difficult to prove. *See United States v. Armstrong*, 517 U.S. 456 (1996). In response to concerns of prosecutorial misconduct and overreaching, Congress passed a law, often referred to as the "Hyde Amendment," (Pub.L.No. 105–119, § 617, 111 Stat. 2440, 2519, reprinted in 18 U.S.C.A. § 3006A (Historical and Statutory Notes)), that created a cause of action for federal criminal defendants to sue for attorney's fees in certain circumstances if they are vindicated:

> "During fiscal year 1998 and in any fiscal year thereafter, the court, in any criminal case (other than a case in which the defendant is represented by assigned counsel paid for by the public) pending on or after the date of the enactment of this Act [Nov. 26, 1997], may award to a prevailing party, other than the United States, a reasonable attorney's fee and other litigation expenses, where the court finds that the position of the United States was vexatious, frivolous, or in bad faith, unless the court finds that special circumstances make such an award unjust. Such awards shall be granted pursuant to the procedures and limitations (but not the burden of proof) provided for an award under section 2412 of title 28, United States Code. To determine whether or not to award fees and costs under this section, the court, for good cause shown, may receive evidence ex parte and in camera (which shall include the submission of classified evidence or evidence that reveals or might reveal the identity of an informant or undercover agent or matters occurring before a grand jury) and evidence or testimony so received shall be kept under seal. Fees and other expenses awarded under this provision to a party shall be paid by the agency over which the party prevails from any funds made available to the agency by appropriation. No new appropriations shall be made as a result of this provision."

In addition, a statute, 28 U.S.C. § 530B, imposes upon federal prosecutors the same ethical rules and regulations applicable to other attorneys practicing in a jurisdiction:

§ 530B. Ethical standards for attorneys for the Government

(a) An attorney for the Government shall be subject to State laws and rules, and local Federal court rules, governing attorneys in each State where such attorney engages in that attorney's duties, to the same extent and in the same manner as other attorneys in that State.

(b) The Attorney General shall make and amend rules of the Department of Justice to assure compliance with this section.

(c) As used in this section, the term "attorney for the Government" includes any attorney described in section 77.2(a) of part 77 of title 28 of the Code of Federal Regulations and also includes any independent counsel, or employee of such a counsel, appointed under chapter 40.

See also Lawrence Judson Welle, *Power, Policy and the Hyde Amendment: Ensuring Sound Judicial Interpretation of the Criminal Attorney's Fees Law*, 41 WM & MARY L. REV. 333 (1999).

III. CHARGING DOCUMENTS

Rule 7 of the Federal Rules of Criminal Procedure sets out the basic requirements of the two core charging documents in federal criminal practice—the indictment and the information. As discussed in Chapter Two, *supra*, a "complaint is a written statement of the essential facts constituting the offense charged." Fed. R. Crim. P. 3. Although the complaint typically is the first pleading in a criminal case, Rule 7 often requires either an information or a grand jury indictment in order to proceed with criminal charges. Simply put, the indictment and information are documents containing a statement of the allegations against the defendant, including the statutes or regulations allegedly violated and the essential facts constituting the offenses. Rule 7 provides detail on the purpose and contents of the indictment and the information.

Rule 7. The Indictment and the Information

(a) When Used.

(1) Felony. An offense (other than criminal contempt) must be prosecuted by an indictment if it is punishable:

(A) by death; or

(B) by imprisonment for more than one year.

(2) Misdemeanor. An offense punishable by imprisonment for one year or less may be prosecuted in accordance with Rule 58(b)(1).

* * *

This provision of Rule 7 implements the constitutional requirement found in the Fifth Amendment's Grand Jury Clause—"[n]o person shall be held to answer for a capital, or otherwise infamous crime, unless on a presentment or indictment of a grand jury." U.S. CONST. AMEND V. As discussed in Chapter Two, *supra*, petty offenses and misdemeanors may be disposed of under Rule 58.

* * *

(b) Waiving Indictment. An offense punishable by imprisonment for more than one year may be prosecuted by information if the defendant—in open court and after being advised of the nature of the charge and of the defendant's rights—waives prosecution by indictment.

* * *

Rule 7(b) permits the waiver of grand jury indictment when the defendant has been informed of the rights he or she is relinquishing. Waiver of grand jury indictment typically takes place in the context of guilty pleas. Note that the provision does not permit waiver of grand jury indictment in a capital case.

* * *

(c) Nature and Contents.

(1) In General. The indictment or information must be a plain, concise, and definite written statement of the essential facts constituting the offense charged and must be signed by an attorney for the government. It need not contain a formal introduction or conclusion. A count may incorporate by reference an allegation made in another count. A count may allege that the means by which the defendant committed the offense are unknown or that the defendant committed it by one or more specified means. For each count, the indictment or information must give the official or customary citation of the statute, rule, regulation, or other provision of law that the defendant is alleged to have violated. For purposes of an indictment referred to in section 3282 of title 18, United States Code, for which the identity of the defendant is unknown, it shall be sufficient for the indictment to describe the defendant as an individual whose name is unknown, but who has a particular DNA profile, as that term is defined in section 3282.

(2) Citation Error. Unless the defendant was misled and thereby prejudiced, neither an error in a citation nor a citation's omission is a ground to dismiss the indictment or information or to reverse a conviction.

* * *

Rule 7(c)(1) contains the central requirements for what must be contained in the indictment or information. Note that, in addition to the requirement of a "plain, concise, definite written statement of the essential facts constituting the offense charged," the rule requires that the prosecutor sign the charging document.

* * *

(d) Surplusage. Upon the defendant's motion, the court may strike surplusage from the indictment or information.

(e) Amending an Information. Unless an additional or different offense is charged or a substantial right of the defendant is prejudiced, the court may permit an information to be amended at any time before the verdict or finding.

(f) Bill of Particulars. The court may direct the government to file a bill of particulars. The defendant may move for a bill of particulars before or within 14 days after arraignment or at a later time if the court permits. The government may amend a bill of particulars subject to such conditions as justice requires.

* * *

Like Rule 7(c), Rule 7(f) implements the Sixth Amendment's requirement of notice. The provisions serve the defendant's right to trial and due process by providing the specific allegations against which she might mount a defense. They also serve the double jeopardy right by permitting the defendant to clearly articulate which offenses are precluded by prior prosecution.

Amendments and Variances

Once an indictment has been returned by a grand jury, the allegations in that indictment may not be changed in a material way. Such a change—or amendment—to the indictment is *per se* prejudicial to the defendant and will result in the reversal of a conviction. But what happens when the evidence presented at trial differs from the allegations in the charging document? This is characterized as a variance, which may or may not be prejudicial depending upon the context. A difference between the indictment allegations and the trial evidence may be deemed harmless error. However, when the variance between the allegations in the indictment and the evidence presented by the government (or the jury instructions given by the court) at trial is too great, it may be considered a constructive amendment and, therefore, *per se* prejudicial. *See Stirone v. United States*, 361 U.S, 212 (1960).

Judicial Review of Information Not Constitutionally Required

Recall that there is no constitutional requirement that an information be reviewed for probable cause as a prerequisite to prosecution. *See Gerstein v. Pugh*, Chapter 2, *infra*. What are the concerns with prosecutors having the power to force a defendant to defend allegations at trial without ever having a grand jury or judicial officer review those allegations to determine whether they are meritless?

Sample Grand Jury Indictment

https://www.justice.gov/usao-sdny/file/762376/download

Sample Criminal Information

https://www.justice.gov/usao-sdny/file/762616/download

ADVOCACY POINT

A Bill of Particulars is essentially a more detailed articulation of the factual allegations supporting the criminal charges outlined in the information or indictment. Defense counsel will often want to consider moving for a Bill of Particulars in order to obtain greater clarity on allegations related to matters such as dates of the alleged offense, names of alleged confederates or co-conspirators, or specific locations where the alleged criminal conduct took place. Such information could be helpful to defense counsel in developing a defense, including providing investigative leads, establishing an alibi, or pleading double jeopardy or an expired statute of limitations.

COUNSEL EXERCISE 5A:
Prosecution Memorandum

Draft a "prosecution memorandum," which outlines the facts and evidence in the case and proposes the possible charges along with the likelihood of conviction for each charge. The prosecution memorandum is usually prepared by the line prosecutor for consideration by a supervisor, or a committee of peer and supervisory prosecutors, and it is the line prosecutor's analysis of the case. Based on the consideration of the prosecution memorandum, the office will decide whether to charge the defendant and what crimes to charge.

COUNSEL EXERCISE 5B: "Sit Down" Memorandum

Prepare for a "sit-down" with the prosecutors to try to persuade them not to indict/prosecute your client. You should anticipate the offenses the prosecutors might plan to bring, and develop arguments why they should decline to do so. You will produce a talking points memo you can use as guidance when you make an oral presentation to the government during your meeting with them (the "sit-down"). You may mention likelihood of success on the merits, your client's lack of culpability, role in the offense, remorse, promise, community work, or anything else you think might be relevant to the prosecutor's exercise of discretion.

CHAPTER 6

Plea Bargaining and the Guilty Plea Process

I. Introduction

Although we study in this course many of the key legal rules and doctrines governing the criminal *trial* process, nearly all criminal convictions in the United States come as the result of a guilty plea. The Supreme Court took note of the ubiquity of guilty pleas in *Missouri v. Frye*, 566 U.S. 134 (2012), which, along with its companion case, *Lafler v. Cooper*, 566 U.S. 156 (2012), made clear that defendants engaged in the plea bargaining process enjoy the Sixth Amendment right to effective assistance of counsel—a topic taken up in Chapter Nine, *infra*.

> Ninety-seven percent of federal convictions and ninety-four percent of state convictions are the result of guilty pleas. *See* Dept. of Justice, Bureau of Justice Statistics, Sourcebook of Criminal Justice Statistics Online, Table 5.22.2009, http://www.albany.edu/sourcebook/pdf/t5222009.pdf (all Internet materials as visited Mar. 1, 2012, and available in Clerk of Court's case file); Dept. of Justice, Bureau of Justice Statistics, S. Rosenmerkel, M. Durose, & D. Farole, Felony Sentences in State Courts, 2006—Statistical Tables, p. 1 (NCJ226846, rev. Nov. 2010), http://bjs.ojp.usdoj.gov/content/pub/pdf/fssc06st.pdf; *Padilla, supra,* at ___, 130 S.Ct., at 1485–1486 (recognizing pleas account for nearly 95% of all criminal convictions). The reality is that plea bargains have become so central to the administration of the criminal justice system that defense counsel have responsibilities in the plea bargain process, responsibilities that must be met to render the adequate assistance of counsel that the Sixth Amendment requires in the criminal process at critical stages. Because ours "is for the most part a system of pleas, not a system of trials," *Lafler, post,* at 1388, 132 S.Ct. 1376, it is insufficient simply to point to the guarantee of a fair trial as a backstop that inoculates any errors in the pretrial process. "To a large extent . . . horse trading [between prosecutor and defense counsel] determines who goes to jail and for how long. That is what plea bargaining is. It is not some adjunct to the criminal justice system; it *is* the criminal justice system." Scott & Stuntz, *Plea Bargaining as Contract*, 101 YALE L. J. 1909, 1912 (1992). See also Barkow, *Separation of Powers and the Criminal Law*, 58

STAN. L. REV. 989, 1034 (2006) ("[Defendants] who do take their case to trial and lose receive longer sentences than even Congress or the prosecutor might think appropriate, because the longer sentences exist on the books largely for bargaining purposes. This often results in individuals who accept a plea bargain receiving shorter sentences than other individuals who are less morally culpable but take a chance and go to trial" (footnote omitted)). In today's criminal justice system, therefore, the negotiation of a plea bargain, rather than the unfolding of a trial, is almost always the critical point for a defendant.

So, is the fact that the vast majority of criminal cases are disposed of by way of guilty plea an indictment of our criminal justice system? The Court in *Frye* does not seem to think so: "To note the prevalence of plea bargaining is not to criticize it. The potential to conserve valuable prosecutorial resources and for defendants to admit their crimes and receive more favorable terms at sentencing means that a plea agreement can benefit both parties." *Frye*, at 1407–08.

II. PLEA BARGAINING

A. THE MECHANICS OF PLEA BARGAINING

A plea bargain is an agreement between the prosecutor and defendant on a particular disposition, or a range of potential dispositions. A typical plea bargain involves the defendant's concession of guilt for a certain offense or offenses in exchange for the dismissal or reduction of other, often more serious, offenses. In addition, a plea bargain may involve a guilty plea in exchange for a specific lesser sentence, or the prosecutor's recommendation for a particular sentence, or some agreed-upon limitation on the severity of sentence the court may impose on the defendant. In some cases, the defendant could plead guilty in exchange for some later benefit, such as dismissal of the charges following a period of probation or pretrial diversion, or after the defendant cooperates in the investigation or prosecution of another defendant.

Either the prosecutor or defense counsel may initiate plea negotiation by making an offer or proposal. These discussions are usually had informally, although some prosecutor's offices regularly communicate plea offers through formal letters to defense counsel. Prosecutors' plea offers may be accompanied by a deadline for acceptance. As it is in the interest of prosecutors' offices to maintain a strong negotiating position with the bar, these "exploding" plea offers are typically withdrawn once they lapse, with prosecutors reluctant to extend them again unless they are made less attractive. Defense counsel is obligated to communicate all plea offers to the defendant, and failure to do so is deemed ineffective assistance of counsel under the Sixth Amendment. *See Missouri v. Frye*, 566 U.S. 134 (2012).

B. PLEA BARGAINING AND THE WAIVER OF CONSTITUTIONAL RIGHTS

When a criminal defendant pleads guilty, she waives her right to trial, the privilege against self-incrimination, the right to confrontation of witnesses against her, the right to compulsory process, and the right to testify on her own behalf, among others. *See, e.g.,* FED. R. CRIM P. 11(a)(1)(B)–(F). Additionally, in the context of a pre-indictment guilty plea, she also may waive the right to grand jury indictment in an effort to expedite the guilty plea process. Many plea agreements also include the waiver of the right to appeal the conviction or sentence or key legal or factual issues underpinning both.

Are the benefits of plea bargaining cited by the Supreme Court in *Frye*—namely prosecutorial (and perhaps systemic) efficiency and the advantages to defendants—sufficient rationales for bypassing these important protections contained in the Bill of Rights? There are fair arguments that plea bargaining undermines justice in a number of ways, including promoting innocent defendants to plead guilty out of expediency or a sense of inevitability.[6] Can you name any other benefits of, or problems with, plea bargaining?

III. GUILTY PLEAS

The guilty plea process in federal courts is governed by Rule 11. Given that most convictions derive from defendants' decision to plead guilty, Rule 11 is central to the administration of federal criminal justice.

Rule 11. Pleas

   (a) Entering a Plea.

      (1) In General. A defendant may plead not guilty, guilty, or (with the court's consent) nolo contendere.

      (2) Conditional Plea. With the consent of the court and the government, a defendant may enter a conditional plea of guilty or nolo contendere, reserving in writing the right to have an appellate court review an adverse

---

[6] One commentator has encouraged criminal defendants to engage in mass protest by refusing to take guilty pleas in an effort to bring the criminal justice system to a halt in order to prompt substantive criminal justice reform. *See* Michelle Alexander, *Go to Trial: Crash the Justice System*, N.Y. TIMES, March 10, 2012.

determination of a specified pretrial motion. A defendant who prevails on appeal may then withdraw the plea.

(3) Nolo Contendere Plea. Before accepting a plea of nolo contendere, the court must consider the parties' views and the public interest in the effective administration of justice.

(4) Failure to Enter a Plea. If a defendant refuses to enter a plea or if a defendant organization fails to appear, the court must enter a plea of not guilty.

* * *

Rule 7(a) sets out the basic pleas a defendant may enter. Rule 10(a) requires that a defendant enter a plea at the arraignment on the information or indictment. Unless there has been a pre-arranged guilty plea, most defendants will simply plead not guilty at the arraignment. If a plea bargain is struck prior to trial, the court will accept the substitute plea of guilty (or nolo contendere) at what is referred to in federal court as a "change of plea" hearing under Rule 11.

Conditional pleas, under Rule 11(a)(2), permit the pleading defendant to reserve the right to challenge a previous ruling on appeal, and then withdraw the plea if the defendant prevails. However, are there certain issues, such as the constitutionality of the statute defining the crime to which the defendant is pleading guilty, that do not need to be expressly preserved for challenge in the plea agreement? In Class v. United States, No. 16–424, the Supreme Court is considering the issue whether a guilty plea inherently waives the defendant's right to challenge the constitutionality of the statute of conviction.

* * *

(b) Considering and Accepting a Guilty or Nolo Contendere Plea.

(1) Advising and Questioning the Defendant. Before the court accepts a plea of guilty or nolo contendere, the defendant may be placed under oath, and the court must address the defendant personally in open court. During this address, the court must inform the defendant of, and determine that the defendant understands, the following:

> **(A)** the government's right, in a prosecution for perjury or false statement, to use against the defendant any statement that the defendant gives under oath;

(B) the right to plead not guilty, or having already so pleaded, to persist in that plea;

(C) the right to a jury trial;

(D) the right to be represented by counsel—and if necessary have the court appoint counsel—at trial and at every other stage of the proceeding;

(E) the right at trial to confront and cross-examine adverse witnesses, to be protected from compelled self-incrimination, to testify and present evidence, and to compel the attendance of witnesses;

(F) the defendant's waiver of these trial rights if the court accepts a plea of guilty or nolo contendere;

(G) the nature of each charge to which the defendant is pleading;

(H) any maximum possible penalty, including imprisonment, fine, and term of supervised release;

(I) any mandatory minimum penalty;

(J) any applicable forfeiture;

(K) the court's authority to order restitution;

(L) the court's obligation to impose a special assessment;

(M) in determining a sentence, the court's obligation to calculate the applicable sentencing-guideline range and to consider that range, possible departures under the Sentencing Guidelines, and other sentencing factors under 18 U.S.C. § 3553(a);

(N) the terms of any plea-agreement provision waiving the right to appeal or to collaterally attack the sentence; and

(O) that, if convicted, a defendant who is not a United States citizen may be removed from the United States, denied citizenship, and denied admission to the United States in the future.

(2) Ensuring That a Plea Is Voluntary. Before accepting a plea of guilty or nolo contendere, the court must address the defendant personally in open court and determine that the plea is voluntary and did not result from force, threats, or promises (other than promises in a plea agreement).

* * *

One of the central purposes of Rule 11 is to ensure that the guilty plea is voluntary. The Constitution requires the court—federal or state—to make a record showing that the guilty plea was intelligent and voluntary. *See Boykin v. Alabama*, 395 U.S. 238 (1963).

The following excerpt from the Model Guilty Plea Colloquy in the Benchbook for U.S. District Court Judges seeks to establish, on the record, that the plea is knowing, intelligent, and voluntary:

Ask the defendant:

1.   Do you understand that you are now under oath and if you answer any of my questions falsely, your answers may later be used against you in another prosecution for perjury or making a false statement? [See Fed. R. Crim. P. 11(b)(1)(A)]

2.   What is your full name?

3.   Where were you born? [If the answer is not the United States or one of its territories, ask if the defendant is a United States citizen.]

4.   How old are you?

5.   How far did you go in school?

6.   Have you been treated recently for any mental illness or addiction to narcotic drugs of any kind? [Note: If the answer to this question is yes, pursue the subject with the defendant and with counsel in order to determine whether the defendant is currently competent to plead.]

7.   Are you currently under the influence of any drug, medication, or alcoholic beverage of any kind? [Note: Again, if the answer is yes, pursue the subject with the defendant and with counsel to determine whether the defendant is currently competent to plead.]

8.   Have you received a copy of the indictment (information) pending against you—that is, the written charges made against you in this case—and have you fully discussed those charges, and the case in general, with Mr./Ms. _____ as your counsel?

9.   Are you fully satisfied with the counsel, representation, and advice given to you in this case by your attorney, Mr./Ms. _____?

If there is a plea agreement of any kind, ask the defendant:

1.   [If the agreement is written:] Did you have an opportunity to read and discuss the plea agreement with your lawyer before you signed it?

2.   Does the plea agreement represent in its entirety any understanding you have with the government?

3.   Do you understand the terms of the plea agreement?

4.   Has anyone made any promise or assurance that is not in the plea agreement to persuade you to accept this agreement? Has anyone threatened you in any way to persuade you to accept this agreement?

FEDERAL JUDICIAL CENTER, BENCHBOOK FOR U.S. DISTRICT COURT JUDGES (March 2013).

* * *

(3) Determining the Factual Basis for a Plea.
Before entering judgment on a guilty plea, the court must determine that there is a factual basis for the plea.

* * *

The court must make a determination that the conduct admitted by the defendant actually constitutes the offense charged (or a lesser included offense charged) in the indictment or the information. *See* Advisory Committee Note, Fed. R. Crim. P. 11(b)(3). This judicial determination of the factual basis for a guilty plea theoretically can help protect against innocent defendants pleading guilty to crimes they did not commit. *See, e.g.,* Hon. Jed S. Rakoff, *Why Innocent People Plead Guilty*, N.Y. REV. BOOKS, Nov. 20, 2014.

There is, however, a special type of plea referred to as an *Alford* plea. In *North Carolina v. Alford*, 400 U.S. 25 (1970), the Court held that it is constitutional for a court to accept a guilty plea from a defendant claiming actual innocence, but who knowingly and intelligently declares that it is in his best interest to plead guilty (such as when there is strong evidence of guilt and a guilty plea would limit the sentencing exposure). Despite the *Alford* decision clarifying that such pleas do not violate the Constitution, states may ban their acceptance in these circumstances, particularly when factual basis determination requirements exist, such as the one in Rule 11(b)(3).

* * *

(c) Plea Agreement Procedure.

(1) In General. An attorney for the government and
the defendant's attorney, or the defendant when

proceeding pro se, may discuss and reach a plea agreement. The court must not participate in these discussions. If the defendant pleads guilty or nolo contendere to either a charged offense or a lesser or related offense, the plea agreement may specify that an attorney for the government will:

(A) not bring, or will move to dismiss, other charges;

(B) recommend, or agree not to oppose the defendant's request, that a particular sentence or sentencing range is appropriate or that a particular provision of the Sentencing Guidelines, or policy statement, or sentencing factor does or does not apply (such a recommendation or request does not bind the court); or

(C) agree that a specific sentence or sentencing range is the appropriate disposition of the case, or that a particular provision of the Sentencing Guidelines, or policy statement, or sentencing factor does or does not apply (such a recommendation or request binds the court once the court accepts the plea agreement).

(2) Disclosing a Plea Agreement. The parties must disclose the plea agreement in open court when the plea is offered, unless the court for good cause allows the parties to disclose the plea agreement in camera.

(3) Judicial Consideration of a Plea Agreement.

(A) To the extent the plea agreement is of the type specified in Rule 11(c)(1)(A) or (C), the court may accept the agreement, reject it, or defer a decision until the court has reviewed the presentence report.

(B) To the extent the plea agreement is of the type specified in Rule 11(c)(1)(B), the court must advise the defendant that the defendant has no right to withdraw the plea if the court does not follow the recommendation or request.

(4) Accepting a Plea Agreement. If the court accepts the plea agreement, it must inform the defendant that to the extent the plea agreement is of the type specified in Rule 11(c)(1)(A) or (C), the agreed disposition will be included in the judgment.

(5) Rejecting a Plea Agreement. If the court rejects a plea agreement containing provisions of the type specified in Rule 11(c)(1)(A) or (C), the court must do the following on the record and in open court (or, for good cause, in camera):

> **(A)** inform the parties that the court rejects the plea agreement;

> **(B)** advise the defendant personally that the court is not required to follow the plea agreement and give the defendant an opportunity to withdraw the plea; and

> **(C)** advise the defendant personally that if the plea is not withdrawn, the court may dispose of the case less favorably toward the defendant than the plea agreement contemplated.

* * *

Depending upon the type of plea agreement—either Rule 11(c)(1)(A), (B), or (C)—the court has options or obligations with regard to the disposition of the guilty plea and plea agreement under Rule 11(c)(3), (4), and (5). For proposals to enhance the role of the court in considering plea agreements, *see* Daniel S. McConkie, *Judges as Framers of Plea Bargaining*, 26 STAN. L. & POL'Y REV. 61 (2015); *see also* Roger A. Fairfax, Jr., *Thinking Outside the Jury Box: Deploying the Grand Jury in the Guilty Plea Process*, 57 WILLIAM & MARY L. REV. 1395 (2016) (thought experiment utilizing grand jury to support judicial role in plea process).

* * *

(d) Withdrawing a Guilty or Nolo Contendere Plea. A defendant may withdraw a plea of guilty or nolo contendere:

> **(1)** before the court accepts the plea, for any reason or no reason; or

> **(2)** after the court accepts the plea, but before it imposes sentence if:

>> **(A)** the court rejects a plea agreement under Rule 11(c)(5); or

>> **(B)** the defendant can show a fair and just reason for requesting the withdrawal.

* * *

The Supreme Court has emphasized the plea agreements are to be treated like contracts and can be subject to specific performance on the part of the prosecutor. *See Santobello v. New York*, 404 U.S. 257 (1971).

* * *

(e) Finality of a Guilty or Nolo Contendere Plea. After the court imposes sentence, the defendant may not withdraw a plea of guilty or nolo contendere, and the plea may be set aside only on direct appeal or collateral attack.

(f) Admissibility or Inadmissibility of a Plea, Plea Discussions, and Related Statements. The admissibility or inadmissibility of a plea, a plea discussion, and any related statement is governed by Federal Rule of Evidence 410.

(g) Recording the Proceedings. The proceedings during which the defendant enters a plea must be recorded by a court reporter or by a suitable recording device. If there is a guilty plea or a nolo contendere plea, the record must include the inquiries and advice to the defendant required under **Rule 11**(b) and (c).

(h) Harmless Error. A variance from the requirements of this rule is harmless error if it does not affect substantial rights.

ADVOCACY POINT

It is important for attorneys participating in a Rule 11 hearing to ensure that every required finding is made and that the defendant receives all of the advice to which he is entitled. Ultimately, the prosecutor is responsible for making certain the guilty plea is entered properly and is not subsequently subject to collateral attack. Therefore, prosecutors may want to maintain a checklist containing all of the requirements of Rule 11. In addition, the prosecutor may ask the defendant to sign in advance of the Rule 11 hearing a "Statement of Facts" establishing the elements of the crime.

Role of Defense Counsel in Guilty Plea Hearings

Defense counsel has a number of obligations to the client who is pleading guilty. Counsel must communicate to the client all plea offers made by the government. *See Missouri v. Frye*, 132 S.Ct. 1399, 1408 (2012). Counsel also must provide competent legal advice so that the client may evaluate such plea offers. *See Lafler v. Cooper*, 132 S.Ct. 1376, 1383–86 (2012); *see also* Chapter 9, *infra*. In addition, defense counsel should also advise the client regarding collateral consequences of conviction, including immigration consequences. *See Padilla v. Kentucky*, 130 S.Ct. 1473, 1486 (2010). A useful resource for defense counsel seeking to ascertain the many types of consequences of conviction is the National Inventory of the Collateral Consequences of Conviction, which is a searchable database of the collateral consequences of convictions in all jurisdictions across the United States. *See* https://niccc.csgjusticecenter.org/ (last visited October 9, 2017).

NOTE ON STATE PRACTICE

Take a look at the criminal procedural rules governing guilty pleas in the jurisdiction in which you plan to practice. What role does the judge play in the negotiation of the plea? Do any provisions of the rule bind the judge to impose a specific sentence under certain types of guilty pleas?

COUNSEL EXERCISE 6A and 6B: Plea Agreement (Prosecution and Defense)

Negotiate and draft a plea agreement. You should agree upon which type of plea agreement you are signing—under either Rule 11(c)(1)(A), 11(c)(1)(B), or 11(c)(1)(C). In addition to the plea agreement itself, you should prepare an information, a waiver of indictment, and a statement of facts. All of these pleadings should be filed along with the plea agreement. Finally, you should prepare to participate in a Rule 11 hearing at which the court will consider whether to accept the guilty plea.

COUNSEL EXERCISE 6C: Rule 11 Hearing (Law Clerk)

Prepare to advise a federal judge during a Rule 11 hearing. Create a memorandum containing a checklist of the advice the court must give the defendant and any findings the court must make. You should read Federal Rule of Criminal Procedure 11 carefully in preparation for the hearing.

CHAPTER 7

PRETRIAL MOTIONS

I. INTRODUCTION

A motion is simply a request that the court take a specific action or to issue an order. *See* FED. R. CRIM. P. 47(A). As in civil cases, attorneys in criminal matters file motions for various reasons before, during, and after trial. Prior to trial, of course, a defense attorney may decide to ask the court to dismiss the case altogether—perhaps because the statute of limitations has run or because the case is not within the jurisdiction of the court.

Such dispositive motions aside, other types of pretrial motions might be directed towards ensuring that the proceedings that follow are fair to both sides. For example, a defense attorney or prosecutor might file a motion asking the court to clarify the other side's discovery obligations and to order the production of certain information. Also, a defense attorney might make a motion to exclude from evidence certain items that were seized by the government in violation of the Fourth Amendment. In some cases, the exclusion of evidence may, for all practical purposes, be dispositive—such as when the illegally-seized narcotics in a possession of narcotics case are suppressed.

Pretrial motions usually are made formally in writing, but can be made orally if the court allows. *See* FED. R. CRIM. P. 47(A). In federal courts, motions must be filed seven days before the hearing date, unless the court sets a different deadline. *See* FED. R. CRIM. P. 47(C). Sometimes, judges can dispose of motions relatively easily and in summary fashion, while some motions require substantial written briefing, affidavits, oral argument, and extended analysis and statement of reasoning by the court. Also, there can be important and complicated questions related to whether and when a court's ruling on a motion is appealable.

Often, lawyers will submit a motion accompanied by a proposed order to be issued by the court. Written motions and accompanying pleadings typically are required to be served on opposing counsel, confirmed by a certificate of service. *See* FED. R. CRIM. P. 49. Note, however, that in jurisdictions—such as in the federal system—with electronic case filing, pleadings may be filed online and opposing counsel will receive the filed pleading instantly.

ADVOCACY POINT

It is good practice to include a proposed order along with the motion and supporting pleadings. Although the presence of a proposed order may not necessarily influence whether the court will rule in favor of a party, it may help to shape the relief granted by the court.

II. FEDERAL RULE OF CRIMINAL PROCEDURE 12

Rule 12 of the Federal Rules governs pretrial motions in criminal cases.

Rule 12. Pleadings and Pretrial Motions

(a) Pleadings. The pleadings in a criminal proceeding are the indictment, the information, and the pleas of not guilty, guilty, and nolo contendere.

(b) Pretrial Motions.

(1) In General. A party may raise by pretrial motion any defense, objection, or request that the court can determine without a trial on the merits. Rule 47 applies to a pretrial motion.

(2) Motions That May Be Made at Any Time. A motion that the court lacks jurisdiction may be made at any time while the case is pending.

Rule 12(b)(2) provides that a motion challenging the court's jurisdiction can be made at any time. This makes sense given that, as discussed in Chapter One, *supra*, jurisdiction is the power or authority of the court to hear the matter.

* * *

(3) Motions That Must Be Made Before Trial. The following defenses, objections, and requests must be raised by pretrial motion if the basis for the motion is then reasonably available and the motion can be determined without a trial on the merits:

(A) a defect in instituting the prosecution, including:

(i)   improper venue;

(ii) preindictment delay;

(iii) a violation of the constitutional right to a speedy trial;

    (iv) selective or vindictive prosecution; and

    (v) an error in the grand-jury proceeding or preliminary hearing;

  (B) a defect in the indictment or information, including:

    (i) joining two or more offenses in the same count (duplicity);

    (ii) charging the same offense in more than one count (multiplicity);

    (iii) lack of specificity;

    (iv) improper joinder; and

    (v) failure to state an offense;

  (C) suppression of evidence;

  (D) severance of charges or defendants under Rule 14; and

  (E) discovery under Rule 16.

As you can see, Rule 12(b)(3) outlines the motions that *must* be made before trial in order to obtain relief. These motions deal with significant procedural issues, such as venue, speedy trial, prosecutorial misconduct, grand jury proceedings and indictment, joinder of offenses or defendants, charging flaws, suppression of evidence, and discovery. The rationale behind this "use or lose" rule requiring pretrial submission of these motions is that defendants should not be able to "sandbag" the government by raising issues for the first time at the trial stage.

It should be noted that there is a qualification in the rule; pretrial filing of the motion is required only "if the basis for the motion is then reasonably available." Of course, there could be issues in early proceedings that defendants might not reasonably be able to identify. For example, a procedural irregularity that took place behind the closed doors of the grand jury could go undetected until discovery is handed over during trial. In such a case, the court may consider a motion addressing the issue despite that fact that it was not filed prior to trial. In any event, the court may consider any motion—even if not timely filed—for good cause, under Rule 12(c)(3).

* * *

(4) Notice of the Government's Intent to Use Evidence.

(A) At the Government's Discretion. At the arraignment or as soon afterward as practicable, the government may notify the defendant of its intent to use specified evidence at trial in order to afford the defendant an opportunity to object before trial under Rule 12(b)(3)(C).

(B) At the Defendant's Request. At the arraignment or as soon afterward as practicable, the defendant may, in order to have an opportunity to move to suppress evidence under Rule 12(b)(3)(C), request notice of the government's intent to use (in its evidence-in-chief at trial) any evidence that the defendant may be entitled to discover under Rule 16.

(c) Deadline for a Pretrial Motion; Consequences of Not Making a Timely Motion.

(1) Setting the Deadline. The court may, at the arraignment or as soon afterward as practicable, set a deadline for the parties to make pretrial motions and may also schedule a motion hearing. If the court does not set one, the deadline is the start of trial.

(2) Extending or Resetting the Deadline. At any time before trial, the court may extend or reset the deadline for pretrial motions.

(3) Consequences of Not Making a Timely Motion Under Rule 12(b)(3). If a party does not meet the deadline for making a Rule 12(b)(3) motion, the motion is untimely. But a court may consider the defense, objection, or request if the party shows good cause.

(d) Ruling on a Motion. The court must decide every pretrial motion before trial unless it finds good cause to defer a ruling. The court must not defer ruling on a pretrial motion if the deferral will adversely affect a party's right to appeal. When factual issues are involved in deciding a motion, the court must state its essential findings on the record.

(e) [Reserved]

(f) Recording the Proceedings. All proceedings at a motion hearing, including any findings of fact and conclusions of law made orally by the court, must be recorded by a court reporter or a suitable recording device.

(g) Defendant's Continued Custody or Release Status. If the court grants a motion to dismiss based on a defect in instituting the prosecution, in the indictment, or in the information, it may order the defendant to be released or detained under 18 U.S.C. § 3142 for a specified time until a new indictment or information is filed. This rule does not affect any federal statutory period of limitations.

(h) Producing Statements at a Suppression Hearing. Rule 26.2 applies at a suppression hearing under Rule 12(b)(3)(C). At a suppression hearing, a law enforcement officer is considered a government witness.

III. JOINDER OF OFFENSES, DEFENDANTS, OR CASES

A. JOINDER OF OFFENSES

As discussed in Chapter Five, *supra*, an indictment or the information charges a violation of a criminal statute. In certain circumstances, it is appropriate for the government to charge a defendant with more than one offense in a single indictment or information. Under Rule 8(a), multiple offenses may be so charged "if the offenses charged—whether felonies or misdemeanors or both—are of the same or similar character, or are based on the same act or transaction, or are connected with or constitute parts of a common scheme or plan." Fed. R. Crim. P. 8(a).

Although it would be unfair to force a defendant to defend against multiple, unrelated charges in one indictment or information, more than one charge may be included where there is a nexus among them. For example, the offenses might be similar—a string of bank robberies, for instance. Alternatively, a defendant might be alleged to have committed a number of offenses in connection to one transaction, such as when one commits a carjacking to obtain a getaway car after an armed robbery with a firearm stolen during a burglary. Further, a defendant might be alleged to have engaged in a number of instances of securities fraud and tax evasion as part of a Ponzi scheme defrauding victims of funds. In all of these scenarios, it may be appropriate for the various alleged crimes to be joined together in one indictment or information under Rule 8(a).

B. JOINDER OF DEFENDANTS

In a similar vein, Rule 8(b) permits multiple defendants to be charged in a single indictment or information. The joinder of defendants is permitted where "they are alleged to have participated in the same act or transaction, or in the same series of acts or transactions, constituting an offense or offenses." Fed. R. Crim. P. 8(b). Co-

conspirators and accomplices are prime candidates for joinder. When defendants are joined in this manner, it is not necessary that all defendants are charged in all counts of the indictment or information. *See id.*

C. JOINT TRIAL OF SEPARATE CASES

Even when offenses or defendants were not joined together in a single indictment, "separate cases [may] be tried together as though brought in a single indictment or information if all offenses and all defendants could have been joined in a single indictment or information [under Rule 8]." Fed. R. Crim. P. 13. In other words, the court has discretion to try cases together if all of the offenses and all of the defendants originally could have been charged together in one indictment or information had the government chosen to do so. However, if any of the offenses or defendants would not have been properly joined in a single charging document under Rule 8, consolidation of the cases for trial would be improper.

D. RELIEF FROM PREJUDICIAL JOINDER

The rationale underlying joinder of offenses or defendants, or the joint trial of separate cases, is efficiency. It saves time and court and prosecutorial resources when cases can be consolidated. However, sometimes offenses or defendants are charged together in a single indictment or information when the standards set forth in Rule 8 are not satisfied. Charged offenses might be wholly unrelated to each other, or defendants might not have sufficient connection with each other. Likewise, separate cases might be consolidated for a single trial when they would not have been properly joined under Rule 8. *But see United States v. Lane*, 474 U.S. 438 (1986) (misjoinder under Fed. R. Crim. P. 8 may be treated as harmless error).

> The problem with improper joinder of offenses or defendants, or improper consolidation of separate cases for trial is that they can prejudice the defendant(s) and frustrate an effective defense against the charges. A defense attorney may request that the court sever the improperly joined counts or defendants into two or more separate trials. This is done by filing a pleading commonly referred to as a Rule 14 "motion to sever." This is one of the motions that, as mentioned above, must be made before trial. *See* FED. R. CRIM. P. 12(B)(3)(B).

Rule 14(a) provides the court with the discretion to give relief to a defendant who is aggrieved by the joinder or consolidation:

Rule 14: Relief from Prejudicial Joinder

(a) Relief. If the joinder of offenses or defendants in an indictment, an information, or a consolidation for trial appears to prejudice a defendant or the government, the court may order separate trials of counts, sever the defendants' trials, or provide any other relief that justice requires.

For example, when there are multiple defendants joined together in one case, there is the danger that the jury may assume guilt by association. Also, defendants may be forced to defend against both the allegations brought by the government, and the cross-allegations of co-defendants at trial. However, the Supreme Court has held that "[m]utually antagonistic defenses are not prejudicial *per se*. Moreover, Rule 14 does not require severance even if prejudice is shown; rather, it leaves the tailoring of the relief to be granted, if any, to the district court's sound discretion." *Zafiro v. United States*, 506 U.S. 534, 538–39 (1993). The U.S. Supreme Court has recognized the danger that the admission of evidence against one defendant could prejudice a co-defendant. *See Bruton v. United States*, 391 U.S. 123 (1968) (admission of confession of co-defendant implicating defendant violated Sixth Amendment Confrontation Clause rights of defendant). To avoid such prejudice, a trial court not inclined to hold separate trials for co-defendants might seek to redact the incriminating statements to excise the name of the prejudiced defendant.

With regard to the improper joinder of offenses, a defendant may have to develop and present multiple (and perhaps conflicting) defenses against unrelated charges. Additionally, the fact-finder may be influenced by the fact that multiple crimes are charged against a defendant and also may subconsciously consider evidence of one crime when assessing culpability for another. Furthermore, juries might infer from the government's presentation of evidence on one offense, a general criminal disposition on the part of the defendant, thus leading to an assumption of guilt on another offense.

When deciding whether the joinder of offenses might prejudice a defendant because the jury might infer a criminal disposition, courts often consider Federal Rule of Evidence ("FRE") 404(b):

Federal Rule of Evidence 404(b)

(b) Crimes, Wrongs, or Other Acts.

(1) Prohibited Uses. Evidence of a crime, wrong, or other act is not admissible to prove a person's character in order to show that on a particular occasion the person acted in accordance with the character.

(2) Permitted Uses; Notice in a Criminal Case.
This evidence may be admissible for another purpose, such
as proving motive, opportunity, intent, preparation, plan,
knowledge, identity, absence of mistake, or lack of
accident. * * *

Thus, "other crimes" evidence is admissible for the purposes set out in
FRE 404(b)(2). Indeed, prosecutors frequently file motions to include
other crimes evidence under 404(b). However, if there is a danger that
the joinder of offenses will lead to the prejudice sought to be avoided in
FRE 404(b)(1), the court will consider providing relief.

COUNSEL EXERCISE 7A: Motion to Sever (Defense)

The defense attorney should draft a motion to sever one of the
offenses from the other charges in the indictment under Fed. R.
Crim. P. 14. Included with the motion should be a supporting brief or
memorandum of law, a proposed order, and a certificate of service.

COUNSEL EXERCISE 7B: Motion to Sever (Prosecution)

The prosecutor should file a reply brief opposing the motion to sever
the offense under Fed. R. Crim. P. 14. Included with the motion
should be a supporting brief or memorandum of law, a proposed
order, and a certificate of service.

IV. VENUE

The United States Constitution, provides:

The trial of all crimes, except in cases of impeachment, shall be
by jury; and such trial shall be held in the state where the said
crimes shall have been committed; but when not committed
within any state, the trial shall be at such place or places as
the Congress may by law have directed. U.S. CONST., art. III,
§ 2.

Thus, the original Constitution specifically directed that criminal
trials take place in the state in which the crime was committed. The
Bill of Rights also spoke to the venue of criminal cases:

In all criminal prosecutions, the accused shall enjoy the right
to a speedy and public trial, by an impartial jury of the State

and district wherein the crime shall have been committed, which district shall have been previously ascertained by law. U.S. CONST., amend. VI

Why might the Framers have been so concerned with *where* the trial of federal crimes takes place? *See, e.g., United States v. Cabrales*, 524 U.S. 1, 6 (1998).

A. PLACE OF PROSECUTION AND TRIAL

Rule 18 implements the constitutional venue requirements by setting the venue for most criminal cases in the district in which the crime allegedly was committed:

Rule 18. Place of Prosecution and Trial

> Unless a statute or these rules permit otherwise, the government must prosecute an offense in a district where the offense was committed. The court must set the place of trial within the district with due regard for the convenience of the defendant, any victim, and the witnesses, and the prompt administration of justice.

There are certain statutes that fix the venue for prosecution and trial. *See* Fed. R. Crim. P. 18, adv. cmte. note 2. These statutes, which relate primarily to "continuing offenses and offenses consisting of several transactions occurring in different districts," trump Rule 18's command. *Id.*; see also 18 U.S.C. §§ 3232–3244.

B. TRANSFER OF VENUE FOR GUILTY PLEA AND SENTENCING

A defendant who intends to plead guilty to an offense may simply wish to transfer the matter from the district in which the case is pending to another district for the purpose of the plea. This is typically done for the sake of convenience. For example, if a defendant lives and works in Virginia and is indicted on federal charges in the Central District of California, and simply plans to plead guilty, he or she may prefer to have the matter disposed of in federal court in Virginia.

Rule 20 provides for such a transfer in certain circumstances:

Rule 20. Transfer for Plea and Sentence

> **(a) Consent to Transfer**. A prosecution may be transferred from the district where the indictment or information is pending, or from which a warrant on a complaint has been issued, to the district where the defendant is arrested, held, or present if:

(1) the defendant states in writing a wish to plead guilty or nolo contendere and to waive trial in the district where the indictment, information, or complaint is pending, consents in writing to the court's disposing of the case in the transferee district, and files the statement in the transferee district; and

(2) the United States attorneys in both districts approve the transfer in writing.

It should be noted that the defendant's consent is not sufficient to trigger a Rule 20 transfer. The prosecutors in both the transferring and transferee district must approve the transfer in writing. Note also that the rule requires the defendant to state in writing the intention to plead guilty and submit to disposition in the transferee district. Such a transfer is possible under the rule only if the defendant intends to plead guilty to the charges. If the defendant changes his or her plea to "not guilty" following a transfer under Rule 20, the case is returned to the original district. *See* Fed. R. Crim. P. 20(c).

C. TRANSFER OF VENUE FOR TRIAL

A defendant who plans to defend against criminal charges may nonetheless desire to have the case transferred to a district other than that in which the charges are filed. Rule 21 permits transfer of a case for trial in certain circumstances:

Rule 21. Transfer for Trial

(a) For Prejudice. Upon the defendant's motion, the court must transfer the proceeding against that defendant to another district if the court is satisfied that so great a prejudice against the defendant exists in the transferring district that the defendant cannot obtain a fair and impartial trial there.

(b) For Convenience. Upon the defendant's motion, the court may transfer the proceeding, or one or more counts, against that defendant to another district for the convenience of the parties, any victim, and the witnesses, and in the interest of justice.

(c) Proceedings on Transfer. When the court orders a transfer, the clerk must send to the transferee district the file, or a certified copy, and any bail taken. The prosecution will then continue in the transferee district.

(d) Time to File a Motion to Transfer. A motion to transfer may be made at or before arraignment or at any other time the court or these rules prescribe.

Note that Rule 21(b) gives the court discretion to transfer the entire proceeding (or certain counts in the proceeding), upon the defendant's motion, for the convenience of the parties, victims, or witnesses if such a transfer is in the interest of justice. If, however, the defendant would suffer prejudice in the original district so significant that he or she could not receive a fair and impartial trial, the court has no discretion; it *must* transfer the proceedings if the defendant requests it. As noted above, this motion to transfer venue must be made before trial. *See* Fed. R. Crim. P. 12(b)(3)(A)(i).

ADVOCACY POINT

Where there is a concern that a defendant may not be able to obtain a fair and impartial trial due to prejudice in the original district, there may be interim steps a court may take short of transferring the proceeding to a new district. For example, the court may grant a continuance in an effort to allow passions to cool in the district of prosecution. A prosecutor may wish to suggest to the court various ways to ensure the defendant a fair trial without having to move the proceeding.

COUNSEL EXERCISE 7C: Motion to Transfer Venue (Defense)

The defense attorney should draft a motion to transfer venue under Fed. R. Crim. P. 21. Included with the motion should be a supporting brief or memorandum of law, a proposed order, and a certificate of service.

COUNSEL EXERCISE 7D: Motion to Transfer Venue (Prosecution)

The prosecutor should file a reply brief opposing the motion to transfer venue under Fed. R. Crim. P. 21. Included with the motion should be a supporting brief or memorandum of law, a proposed order, and a certificate of service.

V. MOTIONS TO SUPPRESS

When a criminal defendant wishes to have evidence excluded from trial, he or she may make a motion to suppress under Rule 41(h). As noted above, this motion generally must be made before trial. *See* Fed. R. Crim. P. 12(b)(3)(C).

A. SUPPRESSION HEARINGS

The most common basis for suppression of evidence is the alleged violation of the Fourth Amendment to the Constitution. Perhaps a piece of evidence was seized during an arrest in the absence of probable cause, or from a defendant's home in the absence of a warrant or an exception. The Fourth Amendment and the exclusionary rule are important features of many criminal cases:

> The fourth amendment to the Constitution of the United States provides a "right of the people to be secure in their persons, houses, papers, and effects, against unreasonable searches and seizures . . . ." * * * Although the proscription against unreasonable searches was clear, the remedy for a violation of the fourth amendment was not specified. * * * In order to make the fourth amendment viable, the Court declared that evidence seized during an unconstitutional search must be excluded at the individual's criminal trial. The enunciation of this exclusionary rule has had a far-reaching and controversial effect on the law of search and seizure. * * *

Carolyn A. Yagla, *The Good Faith Exception to the Exclusionary Rule: The Latest Example of "New Federalism" in the States*, 71 MARQ. L. REV. 166, 167–72, 178–80 (1987).

It is typically in the interest of the defendant to challenge the government's seizure of key evidence through a motion to suppress. Often, the court will hold a hearing on the defendant's suppression motion. The following description of suppression hearings is taken from Elizabeth Phillips Marsh, *Does Evidence Law Matter in Criminal Suppression Hearings?*, 25 LOY. L.A. L. REV. 987 (1992):

> In criminal cases defendants often move to suppress evidence on the basis of an alleged constitutional violation. Commonly, defendants allege violations of their Fourth, Fifth or Sixth Amendment rights. Assuming that the movant has standing' and has made a sufficient preliminary showing, the trial judge will order that a hearing be held to adjudicate the suppression issue(s).
>
> Hearings on the admissibility of confessions must be held outside the presence of the jury and virtually all hearings on motions to suppress based on other grounds are decided by a judge alone. The rationale for this format is obvious. If the evidence in question should be suppressed, it would be improper for a jury to hear the evidence during the

preliminary determination. Once a jury has heard evidence that was later suppressed, it would be difficult to ascertain whether or not the jury considered it in its adjudication on the merits, even in the face of the most punctilious judicial instructions to disregard the evidence. It would be like asking the jury not to think of a pink elephant when reaching its decision.

In addition, by holding the hearing outside the presence of the jury, the defendant is given an option to testify as to the conditions governing admissibility without taking the stand in the case-in-chief. * * *

For our immediate purpose, let us focus on the Federal Rules of Evidence to determine the extent that they govern in hearings on motions to suppress in federal courts. * * * It is clear that if the Rules apply at all to hearings on motions to suppress, they are—at the very least—dramatically relaxed. * * *

In hearings on motions to suppress, as with most of the proceedings excluded from the operation of the Rules, the judge is the fact finder. Presumably, a judge is able to disregard irrelevant or prejudicial evidence and evidence that would tend to support a relaxation or elimination of the applicability of the Rules. The standards for judicial determination are not purely discretionary, but they certainly include a high degree of flexibility premised on factual resolution. * * *

Traditionally, hearsay is admissible at hearings on motions to suppress, making article 8 of the Federal Rules of Evidence inapplicable.

Typically, the court, during the arraignment, will set the deadline for motions to suppress. The burden of proof is on the government to show by a preponderance of the evidence that the evidence was obtained in a manner consistent with the Constitution. As discussed above, evidentiary rules generally do not apply. Also, a defendant may testify in support of a Fourth Amendment claim and this testimony may not be used against her in the government's case-in-chief. However, the testimony can be used to impeach the defendant if she were to take the stand.

If the defendant prevails on the motion to suppress, the government may appeal the court's decision on an interlocutory basis as long as the defendant has not yet been placed in jeopardy (i.e., the jury has not been sworn). *See* 18 U.S.C. § 3731. The defendant, however, must await conviction before appealing the denial of a motion to suppress.

NOTE ON STATE PRACTICE

Note that the federal constitution is a floor, not a ceiling. There may be state constitutional and statutory bases for a motion to suppress evidence.

ADVOCACY POINT

In addition to seeking the exclusion of evidence, defense counsel may use the suppression hearing to obtain discovery on the government's case. For instance, the hearing is an opportunity to question key government witnesses under oath, gathering information on the government's theory of the case and locking in the testimony of those witnesses for the purposes of impeachment at trial. In addition, defense counsel can obtain a better sense of the strength of the government's case, which can be helpful in informing counsel's (and the client's) plea bargaining position.

COUNSEL EXERCISE 7E: Motion to Suppress (Defense)

The defense attorney should draft a motion to suppress evidence under Fed. R. Crim. P. 41(h). Included with the motion should be a supporting brief or memorandum of law, a proposed order, and a certificate of service.

COUNSEL EXERCISE 7F: Motion to Suppress (Prosecution)

The prosecutor should file a reply brief opposing the motion to suppress evidence under Fed. R. Crim. P. 41(h). Included with the motion should be a supporting brief or memorandum of law, a proposed order, and a certificate of service.

CHAPTER 8

DISCOVERY

I. INTRODUCTION

As compelling as the classic legal television show depictions might be, the last-minute, bombshell introduction of a surprise witness or a case-breaking piece of evidence undermines the quality of justice and the truth-seeking function of criminal litigation. In order to avoid such surprises or the suppression of information necessary to ensure due process or a fair trial, our criminal justice system imposes "discovery" obligations on parties in criminal litigation.

However, as the Supreme Court has noted, "[t]here is no general constitutional right to discovery in a criminal case." *Weatherford v. Bursey*, 429 U.S. 545 (1977). Although criminal discovery may advance the constitutional values of due process and fair trial, often statutes or rules impose the specific obligations prosecutors and defense counsel must meet in the course of criminal litigation. These rules governing the information that must be exchanged between the government and the accused in the period leading to trial are designed to ensure fairness, accuracy, and efficiency—all process values underlying the Federal Rules of Criminal Procedure. *See* FED. R. CRIM. P. 2.

* * *

II. STATUTORY REGULATION OF DISCOVERY

A. PRETRIAL DISCOVERY

1. RULE 16: DISCOVERY AND INSPECTION

Rule 16 of the Federal Rules of Criminal Procedure is the primary source for discovery obligations of both prosecutors and defense attorneys. There are other important disclosure obligations, such as the duty to disclose to the defendant exculpatory evidence, that are grounded in constitutional due process and fair trial concerns. *See Brady v. Maryland*, 373 U.S. 83 (1963), *infra*. However, Rule 16 regulates much of criminal discovery in federal criminal cases.

Rule 16. Discovery and Inspection

(a) Government's Disclosure.

(1) Information Subject to Disclosure.

(A) Defendant's Oral Statement. Upon a defendant's request, the government must disclose to the defendant the substance of any relevant oral statement made by the defendant, before or after arrest, in response to interrogation by a person the defendant knew was a government agent if the government intends to use the statement at trial.

(B) Defendant's Written or Recorded Statement. Upon a defendant's request, the government must disclose to the defendant, and make available for inspection, copying, or photographing, all of the following:

(i) any relevant written or recorded statement by the defendant if:

- statement is within the government's possession, custody, or control; and

- the attorney for the government knows—or through due diligence could know—that the statement exists;

(ii) the portion of any written record containing the substance of any relevant oral statement made before or after arrest if the defendant made the statement in response to interrogation by a person the defendant knew was a government agent; and

(iii) the defendant's recorded testimony before a grand jury relating to the charged offense.

(C) Organizational Defendant. Upon a defendant's request, if the defendant is an organization, the government must disclose to the defendant any statement described in Rule 16(a)(1)(A) and (B) if the government contends that the person making the statement:

(i) was legally able to bind the defendant regarding the subject of the statement because of that person's position as the defendant's director, officer, employee, or agent; or

(ii) was personally involved in the alleged conduct constituting the offense and was legally able to bind the defendant regarding that conduct because of that person's position as the defendant's director, officer, employee, or agent.

(D) Defendant's Prior Record. Upon a defendant's request, the government must furnish the defendant with a copy of the defendant's prior criminal record that is within the government's possession, custody, or control if the attorney for the government knows—or through due diligence could know—that the record exists.

(E) Documents and Objects. Upon a defendant's request, the government must permit the defendant to inspect and to copy or photograph books, papers, documents, data, photographs, tangible objects, buildings or places, or copies or portions of any of these items, if the item is within the government's possession, custody, or control and:

    (i) the item is material to preparing the defense;

    (ii) the government intends to use the item in its case-in-chief at trial; or

    (iii) the item was obtained from or belongs to the defendant.

(F) Reports of Examinations and Tests. Upon a defendant's request, the government must permit a defendant to inspect and to copy or photograph the results or reports of any physical or mental examination and of any scientific test or experiment if:

    (i) the item is within the government's possession, custody, or control;

    (ii) the attorney for the government knows—or through due diligence could know—that the item exists; and

    (iii) the item is material to preparing the defense or the government intends to use the item in its case-in-chief at trial.

(G) Expert Witnesses. At the defendant's request, the government must give to the defendant a written summary of any testimony that the government intends to use under Rules 702, 703, or 705 of the Federal Rules of Evidence during its case-in-chief at trial. If the government requests discovery under subdivision (b)(1)(C)(ii) and the defendant complies, the government must, at the defendant's request, give to the defendant a written summary of testimony that the government intends to use under Rules 702, 703, or 705 of the Federal Rules of Evidence as evidence at trial on the issue of the defendant's mental condition. The summary provided under this subparagraph must describe the witness's opinions, the bases and reasons for those opinions, and the witness's qualifications.

(2) Information Not Subject to Disclosure. Except as permitted by Rule 16(a)(1)(A)-(D), (F), and (G), this rule does not authorize the discovery or inspection of reports, memoranda, or other internal government documents made by an attorney for the government or other government agent in connection with investigating or prosecuting the case. Nor does this rule authorize the discovery or inspection of statements made by prospective government witnesses except as provided in 18 U.S.C. § 3500.

(3) Grand Jury Transcripts. This rule does not apply to the discovery or inspection of a grand jury's recorded proceedings, except as provided in Rules 6, 12(h), 16(a)(1), and 26.2.

(b) Defendant's Disclosure.

(1) Information Subject to Disclosure.

(A) Documents and Objects. If a defendant requests disclosure under Rule 16(a)(1)(E) and the government complies, then the defendant must permit the government, upon request, to inspect and to copy or photograph books, papers, documents, data, photographs, tangible objects, buildings or places, or copies or portions of any of these items if:

(i) the item is within the defendant's possession, custody, or control; and

(ii) the defendant intends to use the item in the defendant's case-in-chief at trial.

(B) Reports of Examinations and Tests. If a defendant requests disclosure under Rule 16(a)(1)(F) and the government complies, the defendant must permit the government, upon request, to inspect and to copy or photograph the results or reports of any physical or mental examination and of any scientific test or experiment if:

(i) the item is within the defendant's possession, custody, or control; and

(ii) the defendant intends to use the item in the defendant's case-in-chief at trial, or intends to call the witness who prepared the report and the report relates to the witness's testimony.

(C) Expert Witnesses. The defendant must, at the government's request, give to the government a written summary of any testimony that the defendant intends to use under Rules 702, 703, or 705 of the Federal Rules of Evidence as evidence at trial, if—

(i) the defendant requests disclosure under subdivision (a)(1)(G) and the government complies; or

(ii) the defendant has given notice under Rule 12.2(b) of an intent to present expert testimony on the defendant's mental condition. This summary must describe the witness's opinions, the bases and reasons for those opinions, and the witness's qualifications[.]

(2) Information Not Subject to Disclosure. Except for scientific or medical reports, Rule 16(b)(1) does not authorize discovery or inspection of:

(A) reports, memoranda, or other documents made by the defendant, or the defendant's attorney or agent, during the case's investigation or defense; or

(B) a statement made to the defendant, or the defendant's attorney or agent, by:

(i) the defendant;

(ii) a government or defense witness; or

(iii) a prospective government or defense witness.

(c) Continuing Duty to Disclose. A party who discovers additional evidence or material before or during trial must promptly disclose its existence to the other party or the court if:

(1) the evidence or material is subject to discovery or inspection under this rule; and

(2) the other party previously requested, or the court ordered, its production.

(d) Regulating Discovery.

(1) Protective and Modifying Orders. At any time the court may, for good cause, deny, restrict, or defer discovery or inspection, or grant other appropriate relief. The court may permit a party to show good cause by a written statement that the court will inspect ex parte. If relief is granted, the court must preserve the entire text of the party's statement under seal.

(2) Failure to Comply. If a party fails to comply with this rule, the court may:

(A) order that party to permit the discovery or inspection; specify its time, place, and manner; and prescribe other just terms and conditions;

(B) grant a continuance;

(C) prohibit that party from introducing the undisclosed evidence; or

(D) enter any other order that is just under the circumstances.

2.   RULES 12.1–12.3: DEFENDANT'S NOTICE REQUIREMENTS

Under Federal Rules of Criminal Procedure 12.1, 12.2, and 12.3, the defendant may have notice requirements associated with certain defenses (alibi, insanity, and public authority defenses) that may be advanced at trial. Under these provisions, defense counsel will be required to provide the government with notice of the intention to raise these defenses.

3.   RULE 15: DEPOSITIONS

Under Federal Rule of Criminal Procedure 15, "[a] party may move that a prospective witness be deposed in order to preserve testimony for trial." The court has discretion to allow a deposition in "exceptional circumstances and in the interest of justice." It should be noted that depositions in federal criminal cases are not for the purpose of traditional discovery. Rather, they are for the purpose of preserving testimony of a witness who likely will not be available for trial—for example, because he or she is terminally ill or is in the military and will be deployed overseas at the time of trial.

In some state jurisdictions, however, depositions are used in criminal proceedings for discovery purposes beyond testimony preservation. For example, in Florida, a deposition may be taken of a witness in a criminal case even when the witness is expected to be available to testify at trial. *See* Fla. R. Crim P. 3.220.

4. RULE 17: SUBPOENAS

Federal Rule of Criminal Procedure 17 governs the issuance of subpoenas for testimony at trial. The subpoena, which is enforced through the contempt power of the court, *see* Fed. R. Crim. P. 17(g), can compel the witness to produce documents and tangible objects as well.

5. RULE 17.1: PRETRIAL CONFERENCE

Under Federal Rule of Criminal Procedure 17.1, the court may hold pretrial conferences to resolve discovery disputes and other matters.

Rule 17.1. Pretrial Conference

On its own, or on a party's motion, the court may hold one or more pretrial conferences to promote a fair and expeditious trial. When a conference ends, the court must prepare and file a memorandum of any matters agreed to during the conference. The government may not use any statement made during the conference by the defendant or the defendant's attorney unless it is in writing and is signed by the defendant and the defendant's attorney.

B. DISCOVERY DURING TRIAL

1. THE JENCKS ACT, 18 U.S.C. § 3500

Again, Rule 16 regulates discovery *before* trial. There are certain statutes regulating the discovery process during various stages of the trial. The first of these is 18 U.S.C. § 3500, popularly referred to as the "Jencks Act." The statute is known as such because Congress passed the statute in response to the Supreme Court's ruling in *Jencks v. United States*, 353 U.S. 657 (1957), regarding the government's obligation "to produce, for the accused's inspection and for admission in evidence, relevant statements or reports in its possession of government witnesses touching the subject matter of their testimony at the trial." *Id.* at 672. Congress passed the Jencks Act, which requires disclosure of the statements of government witnesses who testify at trial.

18 USC § 3500. Demands for Production of Statements and Reports of Witnesses

(a) In any criminal prosecution brought by the United States, no statement or report in the possession of the United States which was made by a Government witness or prospective Government witness (other than the defendant) shall be the subject of subpoena, discovery, or inspection until said witness has testified on direct examination in the trial of the case.

(b) After a witness called by the United States has testified on direct examination, the court shall, on motion of the defendant, order the United States to produce any statement (as hereinafter defined) of the witness in the possession of the United States which relates to the subject matter as to which the witness has testified. If the entire contents of any such statement relate to the subject matter of the testimony of the witness, the court shall order it to be delivered directly to the defendant for his examination and use.

(c) If the United States claims that any statement ordered to be produced under this section contains matter which does not relate to the subject matter of the testimony of the witness, the court shall order the United States to deliver such statement for the inspection of the court in camera. Upon such delivery the court shall excise the portions of such statement which do not relate to the subject matter of the testimony of the witness. With such material excised, the court shall then direct delivery of such statement to the defendant for his use. If, pursuant to such procedure, any portion of such statement is withheld from the defendant and the defendant objects to such withholding, and the trial is continued to an adjudication of the guilt of the defendant, the entire text of such statement shall be preserved by the United States and, in the event the defendant appeals, shall be made available to the appellate court for the purpose of determining the correctness of the ruling of the trial judge. Whenever any statement is delivered to a defendant pursuant to this section, the court in its discretion, upon application of said defendant, may recess proceedings in the trial for such time as it may determine to be reasonably required for the examination of such statement by said defendant and his preparation for its use in the trial.

(d) If the United States elects not to comply with an order of the court under subsection (b) or (c) hereof to deliver to the defendant any such statement, or such portion thereof as the court may direct, the court shall strike from the record the testimony of the witness, and the trial shall proceed unless the court in its discretion shall determine that the interests of justice require that a mistrial be declared.

(e) The term "statement", as used in subsections (b), (c), and (d) of this section in relation to any witness called by the United States, means—

(1) a written statement made by said witness and signed or otherwise adopted or approved by him;

(2) a stenographic, mechanical, electrical, or other recording, or a transcription thereof, which is a substantially verbatim recital of an oral statement made by said witness and recorded contemporaneously with the making of such oral statement; or

(3) a statement, however taken or recorded, or a transcription thereof, if any, made by said witness to a grand jury.

Note that the Jencks Act does not require disclosure of the witness's statement until after he or she has testified on direct examination. Thus, the government may choose to keep such a statement secret. As the Court in *Jencks* put it, the government burden is "to decide whether the public prejudice of allowing the crime to go unpunished is greater than that attendant upon the possible disclosure of state secrets and other confidential information in the Government's possession." *Id.* Once the government puts the witness on the stand, the previous statements of that witness must be disclosed to defense for use in cross-examination.

The Jencks Act is implemented through Federal Rule of Criminal Procedure 26.2, which also imposes the duty to disclose prior statements of testifying defense witnesses. Notwithstanding the statute and Rule 26.2, many local court rules require disclosure of the witness statement well before an anticipated government witness takes the stand. *See, e.g.,* Local Criminal Rule 26.2(E)(4), U.S. District Court, N. Dist. Fla. (requesting that Jencks material be made available to other party "sufficiently in advance so as to avoid any delays or interruptions at trial"). Accelerating disclosure in this way enhances fairness to the defendant by giving defense counsel a reasonable amount of time to prepare for cross-examination, and avoids unnecessary continuances in the trial.

ADVOCACY POINT

The Jencks Act and Rule 26.2 apply to written statements and statements made before the grand jury by a witness. These provisions also apply to "substantially verbatim, contemporaneously recorded recital[s]" of witness statements. Sometimes, prosecutors are present when potential witnesses are interviewed by investigating agents, and may be tempted to take notes of the witnesses' statements. However, prosecutors will often take great lengths to avoid writing verbatim accounts of witness statements, so as to not create "Jencks" material that must be disclosed to defense counsel.

2. Juror and Witness Lists

Although technically prior to the taking of testimony at trial, the disclosure of information related to jurors and witnesses is part and parcel of the trial stage discovery obligations in criminal cases. However, there can be restrictions on the information that is shared with the defense, particularly where there are concerns regarding witness or juror intimidation and obstruction of justice.

In capital cases, the interest in avoiding the obstruction of justice is balanced against the need for a defendant facing a capital conviction to have full and fair opportunity to vet potential jurors and prepare to confront witnesses. Title 18, Section 3432 of the United States Code attempts to strike that balance:

18 USC § 3432 Indictment and List of Jurors and Witnesses for Prisoner in Capital Cases

A person charged with treason or other capital offense shall at least three entire days before commencement of trial, excluding intermediate weekends and holidays, be furnished with a copy of the indictment and a list of the veniremen, and of the witnesses to be produced on the trial for proving the indictment, stating the place of abode of each venireman and witness, except that such list of the veniremen and witnesses need not be furnished if the court finds by a preponderance of the evidence that providing the list may jeopardize the life or safety of any person.

In addition, the U.S. Attorney's Manual provides guidance to federal prosecutors confronted with the question whether to disclose the identity of government witnesses prior to trial:

U.S. Attorney's Manual section 9–6.200: Pretrial Disclosure of Witness Identity

Insuring the safety and cooperativeness of prospective witnesses, and safeguarding the judicial process from undue influence, are among the highest priorities of federal prosecutors. *See* Victim and Witness Protection Act of 1982, P.L. 97–291, § 2, 96 Stat. 1248–9. The Attorney General Guidelines for Victim Witness Assistance 2000 provide that prosecutors should keep in mind that the names, addresses, and phone numbers of victims and witnesses are private and should reveal such information to the defense only pursuant to Federal Rule of Procedure 16, any local rules, customs or court orders, or special prosecutorial need.

Therefore, it is the Department's position that pretrial disclosure of a witness' identity or statement should not be made if there is, in the judgment of the prosecutor, any reason to believe that such disclosure would endanger the safety of the witness or any other person, or lead to efforts to obstruct justice. Factors relevant to the possibility of witness intimidation or obstruction of justice include, but are not limited to, the types of charges pending against the defendant, any record or information about the propensity of the defendant or the defendant's confederates to engage in witness intimidation or obstruction of justice, and any threats directed by the defendant or others against the witness. In addition, pretrial disclosure of a witness' identity or statements should not ordinarily be made against the known wishes of any witness.

However, pretrial disclosure of the identity or statements of a government witness may often promote the prompt and just resolution of the case. Such disclosure may enhance the prospects that the defendant will plead guilty or lead to the initiation of plea negotiations; in the event the defendant goes to trial, such disclosure may expedite the conduct of the trial by eliminating the need for a continuance.

Accordingly, with respect to prosecutions in federal court, a prosecutor should give careful consideration, as to each prospective witness, whether absent any indication of potential adverse consequences of the kind mentioned above reason exists to disclose such witness' identity prior to trial. It should be borne in mind that a decision by the prosecutor to disclose pretrial the identity of potential government witnesses may be conditioned upon the defendant's making reciprocal disclosure as to the identity of the potential defense witnesses. Similarly, when appropriate in light of the facts and circumstances of the case, a prosecutor may determine to disclose only the identity, but not the current address or whereabouts of a witness.

Prosecutors should be aware that they have the option of applying for a protective order if discovery of the private information may create a risk of harm to the victim or witness and the prosecutor may seek a temporary restraining order under 18 U.S.C. § 1514 prohibiting harassment of a victim or witness.

In sum, whether or not to disclose the identity of a witness prior to trial is committed to the discretion of the federal prosecutor, and that discretion should be exercised on a case-by-case, and witness-by-witness basis. Considerations of witness safety and willingness to cooperate, and the integrity of the judicial process are paramount.

III. CONSTITUTIONAL REGULATION OF DISCOVERY

A. THE *BRADY* RULE

The case of *Brady v. Maryland*, 373 U.S. 83 (1963) provides the framework for determining what due process of law requires when prosecutors withhold exculpatory evidence from the accused.

Brady v. Maryland

Supreme Court of the United States, 1963
373 U.S. 83

■ Opinion of the Court by MR. JUSTICE DOUGLAS, announced by MR. JUSTICE BRENNAN.

Petitioner and a companion, Boblit, were found guilty of murder in the first degree and were sentenced to death, their convictions being affirmed by the Court of Appeals of Maryland. 220 Md. 454, 154 A.2d 434. Their trials were separate, petitioner being tried first. At his trial Brady took the stand and admitted his participation in the crime, but he claimed that Boblit did the actual killing. And, in his summation to the jury, Brady's counsel conceded that Brady was guilty of murder in the first degree, asking only that the jury return that verdict 'without capital punishment.' Prior to the trial petitioner's counsel had requested the prosecution to allow him to examine Boblit's extrajudicial statements. Several of those statements were shown to him; but one dated July 9, 1958, in which Boblit admitted the actual homicide, was withheld by the prosecution and did not come to petitioner's notice until after he had been tried, convicted, and sentenced, and after his conviction had been affirmed.

Petitioner moved the trial court for a new trial based on the newly discovered evidence that had been suppressed by the prosecution. Petitioner's appeal from a denial of that motion was dismissed by the Court of Appeals without prejudice to relief under the Maryland Post Conviction Procedure Act. 222 Md. 442, 160 A.2d 912. The petition for post-conviction relief was dismissed by the trial court; and on appeal the Court of Appeals held that suppression of the evidence by the prosecution denied petitioner due process of law and remanded the case for a retrial of the question of punishment, not the question of guilt. 226 Md. 422, 174 A.2d 167. The case is here on certiorari, 371 U.S. 812, 83 S.Ct. 56, 9 L.Ed.2d 54.

The crime in question was murder committed in the perpetration of a robbery. Punishment for that crime in Maryland is life imprisonment or death, the jury being empowered to restrict the punishment to life by addition of the words 'without capital punishment.' 3 Md.Ann.Code, 1957, Art. 27, § 413. In Maryland, by reason of the state constitution, the jury in a criminal case are 'the Judges of Law, as well as of fact.' Art. XV, § 5. The question presented is whether petitioner was denied a federal right when the Court of Appeals restricted the new trial to the question of punishment.

We agree with the Court of Appeals that suppression of this confession was a violation of the Due Process Clause of the Fourteenth Amendment. The Court of Appeals relied in the main on two decisions from the Third Circuit Court of Appeals—*United States ex rel. Almeida v. Baldi*, 195 F.2d 815, 33 A.L.R.2d 1407, and *United States ex rel. Thompson v. Dye*, 221 F.2d 763—which, we agree, state the correct constitutional rule.

This ruling is an extension of *Mooney v. Holohan*, 294 U.S. 103, 112, 55 S.Ct. 340, 342, 79 L.Ed. 791, where the Court ruled on what nondisclosure by a prosecutor violates due process:

'It is a requirement that cannot be deemed to be satisfied by mere notice and hearing if a state has contrived a conviction through the pretense of a trial which in truth is but used as a means of depriving a defendant of liberty through a deliberate deception of court and jury by the presentation of testimony known to be perjured. Such a contrivance by a state to procure the conviction and imprisonment of a defendant is as inconsistent with the rudimentary demands of justice as is the obtaining of a like result by intimidation.'

In *Pyle v. Kansas*, 317 U.S. 213, 215–216, 63 S.Ct. 177, 178, 87 L.Ed. 214, we phrased the rule in broader terms:

'Petitioner's papers are inexpertly drawn, but they do set forth allegations that his imprisonment resulted from perjured testimony, knowingly used by the State authorities to obtain his conviction, and from the deliberate suppression by those same authorities of evidence favorable to him. These allegations sufficiently charge a deprivation of rights guaranteed by the Federal Constitution, and, if proven, would entitle petitioner to release from his present custody. *Mooney v. Holohan*, 294 U.S. 103, 55 S.Ct. 340, 79 L.Ed. 791.'

The Third Circuit in the Baldi case construed that statement in *Pyle v. Kansas* to mean that the 'suppression of evidence favorable' to the accused was itself sufficient to amount to a denial of due process. 195 F.2d, at 820. In *Napue v. Illinois,* 360 U.S. 264, 269, 79 S.Ct. 1173, 3 L.Ed.2d 1217, we extended the test formulated in *Mooney v. Holohan* when we said: 'The same result obtains when the State, although not soliciting false evidence, allows it to go uncorrected when it appears.' And see *Alcorta v. Texas*, 355 U.S. 28, 78 S.Ct. 103, 2 L.Ed.2d 9; *Wilde v. Wyoming*, 362 U.S. 607, 80 S.Ct. 900, 4 L.Ed.2d 985. Cf. *Durley v.*

Mayo, 351 U.S. 277, 285, 76 S.Ct. 806, 811, 100 L.Ed. 1178 (dissenting opinion).

We now hold that the suppression by the prosecution of evidence favorable to an accused upon request violates due process where the evidence is material either to guilt or to punishment, irrespective of the good faith or bad faith of the prosecution.

The principle of *Mooney v. Holohan* is not punishment of society for misdeeds of a prosecutor but avoidance of an unfair trial to the accused. Society wins not only when the guilty are convicted but when criminal trials are fair; our system of the administration of justice suffers when any accused is treated unfairly. An inscription on the walls of the Department of Justice states the proposition candidly for the federal domain: 'The United States wins its point whenever justice is done its citizens in the courts.' A prosecution that withholds evidence on demand of an accused which, if made available, would tend to exculpate him or reduce the penalty helps shape a trial that bears heavily on the defendant. That casts the prosecutor in the role of an architect of a proceeding that does not comport with standards of justice, even though, as in the present case, his action is not 'the result of guile,' to use the words of the Court of Appeals. 226 Md., at 427, 174 A.2d, at 169.

The question remains whether petitioner was denied a constitutional right when the Court of Appeals restricted his new trial to the question of punishment. In justification of that ruling the Court of Appeals stated:

> 'There is considerable doubt as to how much good Boblit's undisclosed confession would have done Brady if it had been before the jury. It clearly implicated Brady as being the one who wanted to strangle the victim, Brooks. Boblit, according to this statement, also favored killing him, but he wanted to do it by shooting. We cannot put ourselves in the place of the jury and assume what their views would have been as to whether it did or did not matter whether it was Brady's hands or Boblit's hands that twisted the shirt about the victim's neck. * * * (I)t would be 'too dogmatic' for us to say that the jury would not have attached any significance to this evidence in considering the punishment of the defendant Brady.

> 'Not without some doubt, we conclude that the withholding of this particular confession of Boblit's was prejudicial to the defendant Brady. * * *

> 'The appellant's sole claim of prejudice goes to the punishment imposed. If Boblit's withheld confession had been before the jury, nothing in it could have reduced the appellant Brady's

offense below murder in the first degree. We, therefore, see no
occasion to retry that issue.' 226 Md., at 429–430, 174 A.2d, at
171. (Italics added.)

If this were a jurisdiction where the jury was not the judge of the law, a
different question would be presented. But since it is, how can the
Maryland Court of Appeals state that nothing in the suppressed
confession could have reduced petitioner's offense 'below murder in the
first degree'? If, as a matter of Maryland law, juries in criminal cases
could determine the admissibility of such evidence on the issue of
innocence or guilt, the question would seem to be foreclosed.

But Maryland's constitutional provision making the jury in criminal
cases 'the Judges of Law' does not mean precisely what it seems to say.
The present status of that provision was reviewed recently in *Giles v.
State*, 229 Md. 370, 183 A.2d 359, appeal dismissed, 372 U.S. 767, 83
S.Ct. 1102, where the several exceptions, added by statute or carved out
by judicial construction, are reviewed. One of those exceptions, material
here, is that 'Trial courts have always passed and still pass upon the
admissibility of evidence the jury may consider on the issue of the
innocence or guilt of the accused.' 229 Md., at 383, 183 A.2d, at p. 365.
The cases cited make up a long line going back nearly a century.
Wheeler v. State, 42 Md. 563, 570, stated that instructions to the jury
were advisory only, 'except in regard to questions as to what shall be
considered as evidence.' And the court 'having such right, it follows of
course, that it also has the right to prevent counsel from arguing
against such an instruction.' *Bell v. State*, 57 Md. 108, 120. And see
Beard v. State, 71 Md. 275, 280, 17 A. 1044, 1045, 4 L.R.A. 675; *Dick v.
State*, 107 Md. 11, 21, 68 A. 286, 290. Cf. *Vogel v. State*, 163 Md. 267,
162 A. 705.

We usually walk on treacherous ground when we explore state law, for
state courts, state agencies, and state legislatures are its final
expositors under our federal regime. But, as we read the Maryland
decisions, it is the court, not the jury, that passes on the 'admissibility
of evidence' pertinent to 'the issue of the innocence or guilt of the
accused.' *Giles v. State*, supra. In the present case a unanimous Court of
Appeals has said that nothing in the suppressed confession 'could have
reduced the appellant Brady's offense below murder in the first degree.'
We read that statement as a ruling on the admissibility of the
confession on the issue of innocence or guilt. A sporting theory of justice
might assume that if the suppressed confession had been used at the
first trial, the judge's ruling that it was not admissible on the issue of
innocence or guilt might have been flouted by the jury just as might
have been done if the court had first admitted a confession and then
stricken it from the record. But we cannot raise that trial strategy to
the dignity of a constitutional right and say that the deprival of this

defendant of that sporting chance through the use of a bifurcated trial (cf. *Williams v. New York*, 337 U.S. 241, 69 S.Ct. 1079, 93 L.Ed. 1337) denies him due process or violates the Equal Protection Clause of the Fourteenth Amendment.

Affirmed.

'Materiality' Under the Brady *Rule*

Courts are often required to determine whether the information the prosecutor failed to disclose is deemed 'material' for purposes of applying the *Brady* rule. *See, e.g., Wearry v. Cain*, 577 U.S. ___, 136 S.Ct. 1002 (2016); *see also Overton v. United States, Turner v. United States*, No. 15–1504 (June 22, 2017). Materiality has been a relatively controversial issue. For critical views of how courts have performed in assessing materiality under the *Brady* doctrine, *see, e.g.*, TIFFANY M. JOSLYN ET AL., MATERIAL INDIFFERENCE: HOW COURTS ARE IMPEDING FAIR DISCLOSURE IN CRIMINAL CASES (2014); Daniel S. Medwed, Brady's *Bunch of Flaws*, 67 WASH & LEE L. REV. 1533 (2010).

Ethical Obligations of Prosecutors

It should be remembered that, in addition to the constitutional duty to disclose exculpatory evidence to the defendant, prosecutors also have ethical obligations to satisfy in this regard. *See, e.g.*, ABA MODEL RULES OF PROFESSIONAL CONDUCT 3.8; ABA MODEL CODE OF PROFESSIONAL RESPONSIBILITY, CANON 7; ABA STANDARDS ON CRIMINAL JUSTICE (PROSECUTION FUNCTION) 3–3.54 (Identification and Disclosure of Information and Evidence).

NOTE ON STATE PRACTICE

Check the ethical rules in the jurisdiction in which you plan to practice and find the provision related to the ethical obligation of prosecutors to disclose exculpatory evidence to the defense. *See, e.g.*, MASS. CRIM. P. R. 14(a)(1)(A)(iii).

B. EXTENSION OF THE *BRADY* RULE

In *Giglio v. United States*, 405 U.S. 150 (1972), the Supreme Court explored whether the Brady rule extended to the withholding of evidence that is not, strictly speaking, exculpatory, but that could be used to impeach government witnesses.

Giglio v. United States

Supreme Court of the United States, 1972
405 U.S. 150

■ MR. CHIEF JUSTICE BURGER delivered the opinion of the Court.

Petitioner was convicted of passing forged money orders and sentenced to five years' imprisonment. While appeal was pending in the Court of Appeals, defense counsel discovered new evidence indicating that the Government had failed to disclose an alleged promise made to its key witness that he would not be prosecuted if he testified for the Government. We granted certiorari to determine whether the evidence not disclosed was such as to require a new trial under the due process criteria of *Napue v. Illinois*, 360 U.S. 264, 79 S.Ct. 1173, 3 L.Ed.2d 1217 (1959), and *Brady v. Maryland*, 373 U.S. 83, 83 S.Ct. 1194, 10 L.Ed.2d 215 (1963).

The controversy in this case centers around the testimony of Robert Taliento, petitioner's alleged coconspirator in the offense and the only witness linking petitioner with the crime. The Government's evidence at trial showed that in June 1966 officials at the Manufacturers Hanover Trust Co. discovered that Taliento, as teller at the bank, had cashed several forged money orders. Upon questioning by FBI agents, he confessed supplying petitioner with one of the bank's customer signature cards used by Giglio to forge $2,300 in money orders; Taliento then processed these money orders through the regular channels of the bank. Taliento related this story to the grand jury and petitioner was indicted; thereafter, he was named as a coconspirator with petitioner but was not indicted.

Trial commenced two years after indictment. Taliento testified, identifying petitioner as the instigator of the scheme. Defense counsel vigorously cross-examined, seeking to discredit his testimony by revealing possible agreements or arrangements for prosecutorial leniency:

> '(Counsel.) Did anybody tell you at any time that if you implicated somebody else in this case that you yourself would not be prosecuted?
>
> '(Taliento.) Nobody told me I wouldn't be prosecuted.
>
> 'Q. They told you you might not be prosecuted?
>
> 'A. I believe I still could be prosecuted.
>
> . . . . . .
>
> 'Q. Were you ever arrested in this case or charged with anything in connection with these money orders that you testified to?

'A. Not at that particular time.

'Q. To this date, have you been charged with any crime?

'A. Not that I know of, unless they are still going to prosecute.'

In summation, the Government attorney stated, '(Taliento) received no promises that he would not be indicted.'

The issue now before the Court arose on petitioner's motion for new trial based on newly discovered evidence. An affidavit filed by the Government as part of its opposition to a new trial confirms petitioner's claim that a promise was made to Taliento by one assistant, DiPaola, that if he testified before the grand jury and at trial he would not be prosecuted. DiPaola presented the Government's case to the grand jury but did not try the case in the District Court, and Golden, the assistant who took over the case for trial, filed an affidavit stating that DiPaola assured him before the trial that no promises of immunity had been made to Taliento. The United States Attorney, Hoey, filed an affidavit stating that he had personally consulted with Taliento and his attorney shortly before trial to emphasize that Taliento would definitely be prosecuted if he did not testify and that if he did testify he would be obliged to rely on the 'good judgment and conscience of the Government' as to whether he would be prosecuted.

The District Court did not undertake to resolve the apparent conflict between the two Assistant United States Attorneys, DiPaola and Golden, but proceeded on the theory that even if a promise had been made by DiPaola it was not authorized and its disclosure to the jury would not have affected its verdict. We need not concern ourselves with the differing versions of the events as described by the two assistants in their affidavits. The heart of the matter is that one Assistant United States Attorney—the first one who dealt with Taliento—now states that he promised Taliento that he would not be prosecuted if he cooperated with the Government.

As long ago as *Mooney v. Holohan*, 294 U.S. 103, 112, 55 S.Ct. 340, 342, 79 L.Ed. 791 (1935), this Court made clear that deliberate deception of a court and jurors by the presentation of known false evidence is incompatible with 'rudimentary demands of justice.' This was reaffirmed in *Pyle v. Kansas*, 317 U.S. 213, 63 S.Ct. 177, 87 L.Ed. 214 (1942). In *Napue v. Illinois*, 360 U.S. 264, 79 S.Ct. 1173, 3 L.Ed.2d 1217 (1959), we said, '(t)he same result obtains when the State, although not soliciting false evidence, allows it to go uncorrected when it appears.' Id., at 269, 79 S.Ct., at 1177. Thereafter *Brady v. Maryland*, 373 U.S., at 87, 83 S.Ct., at 1197, held that suppression of material evidence justifies a new trial 'irrespective of the good faith or bad faith of the prosecution.' See American Bar Association, Project on Standards for

Criminal Justice, Prosecution Function and the Defense Function § 3.11(a). When the 'reliability of a given witness may well be determinative of guilt or innocence,' nondisclosure of evidence affecting credibility falls within this general rule. Napue, supra, at 269, 79 S.Ct., at 1177. We do not, however, automatically require a new trial whenever 'a combing of the prosecutors' files after the trial has disclosed evidence possibly useful to the defense but not likely to have changed the verdict . . . .' *United States v. Keogh*, 391 F.2d 138, 148 (CA2 1968). A finding of materiality of the evidence is required under Brady, supra, at 87, 83 S.Ct., at 1196, 10 L.Ed.2d 215. A new trial is required if 'the false testimony could . . . in any reasonable likelihood have affected the judgment of the jury . . .' Napue, supra, at 271, 79 S.Ct., at 1178.

In the circumstances shown by this record, neither DiPaola's authority nor his failure to inform his superiors or his associates is controlling. Moreover, whether the nondisclosure was a result of negligence or design, it is the responsibility of the prosecutor. The prosecutor's office is an entity and as such it is the spokesman for the Government. A promise made by one attorney must be attributed, for these purposes, to the Government. See Restatement (Second) of Agency § 272. See also American Bar Association, Project on Standards for Criminal Justice, Discovery and Procedure Before Trial § 2.1(d). To the extent this places a burden on the large prosecution offices, procedures and regulations can be established to carry that burden and to insure communication of all relevant information on each case to every lawyer who deals with it.

Here the Government's case depended almost entirely on Taliento's testimony; without it there could have been no indictment and no evidence to carry the case to the jury. Taliento's credibility as a witness was therefore an important issue in the case, and evidence of any understanding or agreement as to a future prosecution would be relevant to his credibility and the jury was entitled to know of it.

For these reasons, the due process requirements enunciated in Napue and the other cases cited earlier require a new trial, and the judgment of conviction is therefore reversed and the case is remanded for further proceedings consistent with this opinion.

Reversed and remanded.

ADVOCACY POINT

When a government agent is burdened by significant impeachment evidence—such as prior judicial finding of perjury or false testimony under oath, the agent is often described as being "Giglio-impaired." Prosecutors may, whenever possible, avoid relying on such a "Giglio-impaired" agent as a key witness at trial.

Exculpatory Evidence in the Guilty Plea Context

The Supreme Court, in *United States v. Ruiz*, 536 U.S. 622 (2002), held that a defendant pleading guilty to a criminal offense does not have a constitutional right to prosecutorial disclosure of impeachment evidence. However, the Court did not resolve whether the government has an obligation to disclose material evidence of the defendant's actual innocence prior to the guilty plea. For views on this issue, *see, e.g.*, Kevin C. McMunigal, *Guilty Pleas,* Brady *Disclosure, and Wrongful Convictions*, 57 CASE WESTERN L. REV. 651 (2007); Corrina B. Lain, *Accuracy Where it Matters: Brady v. Maryland in the Plea Bargaining Context*, 80 WASH. U. L. Q. 1 (2002).

COUNSEL EXERCISE 8: Discovery Motion
(Defense)

The defense counsel should draft a pretrial discovery motion requesting all of the disclosures to which the defendant is entitled under the Constitution, statutes, and Federal Rules of Criminal Procedure. Assume that the court has asked for this motion in advance of a Rule 17.1 Pretrial Conference. Also, if you believe you have an obligation to request or give notice of any anticipated defense under Rules 12.1–12.3, would like to request a deposition under Rule 15, or have any other discovery issue to bring to the attention of the court, such notices and requests also should be included in the motion. Included with the motion should be a supporting brief or memorandum of law, a proposed order, and a certificate of service.

CHAPTER 9

RIGHT TO EFFECTIVE ASSISTANCE OF COUNSEL

I. INTRODUCTION

"In all criminal prosecutions, the accused shall enjoy the right . . . to have the Assistance of Counsel for his defence."

U.S. CONST., amend. VI.

Many of the constitutional and procedural rights discussed throughout this book would be meaningless without counsel available to press those rights on behalf of the criminal defendant. Furthermore, "counsel" in this regard means more than a person licensed to practice law; it means someone with sufficient competence to protect the rights, privileges, and interests of the accused. This Chapter will examine the Sixth Amendment right to counsel, and what is expected of an effective advocate under the Constitution and other laws.

II. MINIMUM STANDARDS OF REPRESENTATION

Powell v. Alabama
Supreme Court of the United States, 1932
287 U.S. 45

■ MR. JUSTICE SUTHERLAND delivered the opinion of the Court.

These cases were argued together and submitted for decision as one case.

The petitioners, hereinafter referred to as defendants, are negroes charged with the crime of rape, committed upon the persons of two white girls. The crime is said to have been committed on March 25, 1931. The indictment was returned in a state court of first instance on March 31, and the record recites that on the same day the defendants were arraigned and entered pleas of not guilty. There is a further recital to the effect that upon the arraignment they were represented by counsel. But no counsel had been employed, and aside from a statement made by the trial judge several days later during a colloquy immediately preceding the trial, the record does not disclose when, or under what circumstances, an appointment of counsel was made, or who was appointed. During the colloquy referred to, the trial judge, in response to a question, said that he had appointed all the members of the bar for the purpose of arraigning the defendants and then of course anticipated that the members of the bar would continue to help the defendants if no counsel appeared. Upon the argument here both sides accepted that as a correct statement of the facts concerning the matter.

There was a severance upon the request of the state, and the defendants were tried in three several groups, as indicated above. As each of the three cases was called for trial, each defendant was arraigned, and, having the indictment read to him, entered a plea of not guilty. Whether the original arraignment and pleas were regarded as ineffective is not shown. Each of the three trials was completed within a single day.

Under the Alabama statute the punishment for rape is to be fixed by the jury, and in its discretion may be from ten years imprisonment to death. The juries found defendants guilty and imposed the death penalty upon all. The trial court overruled motions for new trials and sentenced the defendants in accordance with the verdicts. The judgments were affirmed by the state supreme court. Chief Justice Anderson thought the defendants had not been accorded a fair trial and strongly dissented. *Weems v. State*, 224 Ala. 524, 141 So. 215; *Patterson v. State*, 224 Ala. 531, 141 So. 195; *Powell v. State*, 224 Ala. 540, 141 So. 201.

In this court the judgments are assailed upon the grounds that the defendants, and each of them, were denied due process of law and the equal protection of the laws, in contravention of the Fourteenth Amendment, specifically as follows: (1) They were not given a fair, impartial, and deliberate trial; (2) they were denied the right of counsel, with the accustomed incidents of consultation and opportunity of preparation for trial; and (3) they were tried before juries from which qualified members of their own race were systematically excluded. These questions were properly raised and saved in the courts below.

The only one of the assignments which we shall consider is the second, in respect of the denial of counsel; and it becomes unnecessary to discuss the facts of the case or the circumstances surrounding the prosecution except in so far as they reflect light upon that question.

The record shows that on the day when the offense is said to have been committed, these defendants, together with a number of other negroes, were upon a freight train on its way through Alabama. On the same train were seven white boys and the two white girls. A fight took place between the negroes and the white boys, in the course of which the white boys, with the exception of one named Gilley, were thrown off the train. A message was sent ahead, reporting the fight and asking that every negro be gotten off the train. The participants in the fight, and the two girls, were in an open gondola car. The two girls testified that each of them was assaulted by six different negroes in turn, and they identified the seven defendants as having been among the number. None of the white boys was called to testify, with the exception of Gilley, who was called in rebuttal.

Before the train reached Scottsboro, Ala., a sheriff's posse seized the defendants and two other negroes. Both girls and the negroes then were taken to Scottsboro, the county seat. Word of their coming and of the alleged assault had preceded them, and they were met at Scottsboro by a large crowd. It does not sufficiently appear that the defendants were seriously threatened with, or that they were actually in danger of, mob violence; but it does appear that the attitude of the community was one of great hostility. The sheriff thought it necessary to call for the militia to assist in safeguarding the prisoners. Chief Justice Anderson pointed out in his opinion that every step taken from the arrest and arraignment to the sentence was accompanied by the military. Soldiers took the defendants to Gadsden for safe-keeping, brought them back to Scottsboro for arraignment, returned them to Gadsden for safe-keeping while awaiting trial, escorted them to Scottsboro for trial a few days later, and guarded the courthouse and grounds at every stage of the proceedings. It is perfectly apparent that the proceedings, from beginning to end, took place in an atmosphere of tense, hostile, and excited public sentiment. During the entire time, the defendants were closely confined or were under military guard. The record does not disclose their ages, except that one of them was nineteen; but the record clearly indicates that most, if not all, of them were youthful, and they are constantly referred to as 'the boys.' They were ignorant and illiterate. All of them were residents of other states, where alone members of their families or friends resided.

However guilty defendants, upon due inquiry, might prove to have been, they were, until convicted, presumed to be innocent. It was the duty of the court having their cases in charge to see that they were denied no necessary incident of a fair trial. With any error of the state court involving alleged contravention of the state statutes or Constitution we, of course, have nothing to do. The sole inquiry which we are permitted to make is whether the federal Constitution was contravened (*Rogers v. Peck*, 199 U.S. 425, 434, 26 S.Ct. 87, 50 L.Ed. 256; *Hebert v. State of Louisiana*, 272 U.S. 312, 316, 47 S.Ct. 103, 71 L.Ed. 270, 48 A.L.R. 1102); and as to that, we confine ourselves, as already suggested, to the inquiry whether the defendants were in substance denied the right of counsel, and if so, whether such denial infringes the due process clause of the Fourteenth Amendment.

First. The record shows that immediately upon the return of the indictment defendants were arraigned and pleaded not guilty. Apparently they were not asked whether they had, or were able to employ, counsel, or wished to have counsel appointed; or whether they had friends or relatives who might assist in that regard if communicated with. That it would not have been an idle ceremony to have given the defendants reasonable opportunity to communicate with their families and endeavor to obtain counsel is demonstrated by the fact that very soon after conviction, able counsel appeared in their behalf. This was pointed out by Chief Justice Anderson in the course of his dissenting opinion. 'They were nonresidents,' he said, 'and had little time or opportunity to get in touch with their families and friends who were scattered throughout two other states, and time has demonstrated that they could or would have been represented by able counsel had a better opportunity been given by a reasonable delay in the trial of the cases judging from the number and activity of counsel that appeared immediately or shortly after their conviction.' *Powell v. State*, 224 Ala. at pages 554, 555, 141 So. 201, 214.

It is hardly necessary to say that the right to counsel being conceded, a defendant should be afforded a fair opportunity to secure counsel of his own choice. Not only was that not done here, but such designation of counsel as was attempted was either so indefinite or so close upon the trial as to amount to a denial of effective and substantial aid in that regard. This will be amply demonstrated by a brief review of the record.

April 6, six days after indictment, the trials began. When the first case was called, the court inquired whether the parties were ready for trial. The state's attorney replied that he was ready to proceed. No one answered for the defendants or appeared to represent or defend them. Mr. Roddy, a Tennessee lawyer not a member of the local bar, addressed the court, saying that he had not been employed, but that people who were interested had spoken to him about the case. He was asked by the court whether he intended to appear for the defendants, and answered that he would like to appear along with counsel that the court might appoint. The record then proceeds:

> 'The Court: If you appear for these defendants, then I will not appoint counsel; if local counsel are willing to appear and assist you under the circumstances all right, but I will not appoint them.
>
> 'Mr. Roddy: Your Honor has appointed counsel, is that correct?
>
> 'The Court: I appointed all the members of the bar for the purpose of arraigning the defendants and then of course I anticipated them to continue to help them if no counsel appears.
>
> 'Mr. Roddy: Then I don't appear then as counsel but I do want to stay in and not be ruled out in this case.
>
> 'The Court: Of course I would not do that—

'Mr. Roddy: I just appear here through the courtesy of Your Honor.

'The Court: Of course I give you that right * * *.'

And then, apparently addressing all the lawyers present, the court inquired:

'* * * Well are you all willing to assist?

'Mr. Moody: Your Honor appointed us all and we have been proceeding along every line we know about it under Your Honor's appointment.

'The Court: The only thing I am trying to do is, if counsel appears for these defendants I don't want to impose on you all, but if you feel like counsel from Chattanooga—

'Mr. Moody: I see his situation of course and I have not run out of anything yet. Of course, if Your Honor purposes to appoint us, Mr. Parks, I am willing to go on with it. Most of the bar have been down and conferred with these defendants in this case; they did not know what else to do.

'The Court: The thing, I did not want to impose on the members of the bar if counsel unqualifiedly appears; if you all feel like Mr. Roddy is only interested in a limited way to assist, then I don't care to appoint—

'Mr. Parks: Your Honor, I don't feel like you ought to impose on any member of the local bar if the defendants are represented by counsel.

'The Court: That is what I was trying to ascertain, Mr. Parks.

'Mr. Parks: Of course if they have counsel, I don't see the necessity of the Court appointing anybody; if they haven't counsel, of course I think it is up to the Court to appoint counsel to represent them.

'The Court: I think you are right about it Mr. Parks and that is the reason I was trying to get an expression from Mr. Roddy.

'Mr. Roddy: I think Mr. Parks is entirely right about it, if I was paid down here and employed, it would be a different thing, but I have not prepared this case for trial and have only been called into it by people who are interested in these boys from Chattanooga. Now, they have not given me an opportunity to prepare the case and I am not familiar with the procedure in Alabama, but I merely came down here as a friend of the people who are interested and not as paid counsel, and certainly I haven't any money to pay them and nobody I am interested in had me to come down here has put up any fund of money to come down here and pay counsel. If they should do it I would be glad to turn it over—a counsel but I am merely here at the solicitation of people who have become interested in this case without any payment of fee and without any preparation for trial and I think the boys would be better off if I step entirely out of the case according to my way of looking at it and according to my lack of preparation for it and not being familiar with the procedure in Alabama * * *.'

Mr. Roddy later observed:

'If there is anything I can do to be of help to them, I will be glad to do it; I am interested to that extent.

'The Court: Well gentlemen, if Mr. Roddy only appears as assistant that way, I think it is proper that I appoint members of this bar to represent them, I expect that is right. If Mr. Roddy will appear, I wouldn't of course, I would not appoint anybody. I don't see, Mr. Roddy, how I can make a qualified appointment or a limited appointment. Of course, I don't mean to cut off your assistance in any way—Well gentlemen, I think you understand it.

'Mr. Moody: I am willing to go ahead and help Mr. Roddy in anything I can do about it, under the circumstances.

'The Court: All right, all the lawyers that will; of course I would not require a lawyer to appear if—

'Mr. Moody: I am willing to go ahead and help Mr. Roddy in anything I can do about it, under the circumstances.

'The Court: All right, all the lawyers that will, of course, I would not require a lawyer to appear if—

'Mr. Moody: I am willing to do that for him as a member of the bar; I will go ahead and help do anything I can do.

'The Court: All right.'

And in this casual fashion the matter of counsel in a capital case was disposed of.

It thus will be seen that until the very morning of the trial no lawyer had been named or definitely designated to represent the defendants. Prior to that time, the trial judge had 'appointed all the members of the bar' for the limited 'purpose of arraigning the defendants.' Whether they would represent the defendants thereafter, if no counsel appeared in their behalf, was a matter of speculation only, or, as the judge indicated, of mere anticipation on the part of the court. Such a designation, even if made for all purposes, would, in our opinion, have fallen far short of meeting, in any proper sense, a requirement for the appointment of counsel. How many lawyers were members of the bar does not appear; but, in the very nature of things, whether many or few, they would not, thus collectively named, have been given that clear appreciation of responsibility or impressed with that individual sense of duty which should and naturally would accompany the appointment of a selected member of the bar, specifically named and assigned.

That this action of the trial judge in respect of appointment of counsel was little more than an expansive gesture, imposing no substantial or definite obligation upon any one, is borne out by the fact that prior to the calling of the case for trial on April 6, a leading member of the local bar accepted employment on the side of the prosecution and actively participated in the trial. It is true that he said that before doing so he had understood Mr. Roddy would be employed as counsel for the defendants. This the lawyer is question, of his own accord, frankly stated to the court; and no doubt he acted with the utmost good faith. Probably other members of the bar had a like understanding. In any event, the circumstance lends emphasis to the conclusion that during perhaps the most critical period of the proceedings against these defendants, that is to say, from the time of their arraignment until the beginning of their trial, when consultation, thorough-going investigation and preparation were vitally important, the defendants did not have the aid of counsel in any real sense, although they were as much entitled to such aid during that period as at the trial itself. *People ex rel. Burgess v. Riseley*, 66 How.Pr.(N.Y.) 67; *Batchelor v. State*, 189 Ind. 69, 76, 125 N.E. 773.

Nor do we think the situation was helped by what occurred on the morning of the trial. At that time, as appears from the colloquy printed above, Mr. Roddy stated to the court that he did not appear as counsel, but that he would like to appear along with counsel that the court might appoint; that he had not been given an opportunity to prepare the case; that he was not familiar with the procedure in Alabama, but merely came down as a friend of the people who were interested; that he thought the boys would be better off if he should step entirely out of the case. Mr. Moody, a member of the local bar, expressed a willingness to help Mr. Roddy in anything he could do under the circumstances. To this the court responded: 'All right, all the lawyers that will; of course I would not require a lawyer to appear if—.' And Mr. Moody continued: 'I am willing to do that for him as a member of the bar; I will go ahead and help do anything I can do.' With this dubious understanding, the trials immediately proceeded. The defendants, young, ignorant, illiterate, surrounded by hostile sentiment, haled back and forth under guard of soldiers, charged with an atrocious crime regarded with especial horror in the community where they were to be tried, were thus put in peril of their lives within a few moments after counsel for the first time charged with any degree of responsibility began to represent them.

It is not enough to assume that counsel thus precipitated into the case thought there was no defense, and exercised their best judgment in proceeding to trial without preparation. Neither they nor the court could say what a prompt and thorough-going investigation might disclose as to the facts. No attempt was made to investigate. No opportunity to do so was given. Defendants were immediately hurried to trial. Chief Justice Anderson, after disclaiming any intention to criticize harshly counsel who attempted to represent defendants at the trials, said: '* * * The record indicates that the appearance was rather pro forma than zealous and active * * *.' Under the circumstances disclosed, we hold that defendants were not accorded the right of counsel in any substantial sense. To decide otherwise, would simply be to ignore actualities.

* * *

It is true that great and inexcusable delay in the enforcement of our criminal law is one of the grave evils of our time. Continuances are frequently granted for unnecessarily long periods of time, and delays incident to the disposition of motions for new trial and hearings upon appeal have come in many cases to be a distinct reproach to the administration of justice. The prompt disposition of criminal cases is to be commended and encouraged. But in reaching that result a defendant, charged with a serious crime, must not be stripped of his right to have sufficient time to advise with counsel and prepare his defense. To do that is not to proceed promptly in the calm spirit of regulated justice but to go forward with the haste of the mob.

[THE COURT explores its precedent on the inclusion of specifically enumerated rights in the concept of due process of law.]

* * *

In the light of the facts outlined in the forepart of this opinion—the ignorance and illiteracy of the defendants, their youth, the circumstances of public hostility, the imprisonment and the close surveillance of the defendants by the military forces, the fact that their friends and families were all in other states and communication with them necessarily difficult, and above all that they stood in deadly peril of their lives—we think the failure of the trial court to give them reasonable time and opportunity to secure counsel was a clear denial of due process.

But passing that, and assuming their inability, even if opportunity had been given, to employ counsel, as the trial court evidently did assume, we are of opinion that, under the circumstances just stated, the necessity of counsel was so vital and imperative that the failure of the trial court to make an effective appointment of counsel was likewise a denial of due process within the meaning of the Fourteenth Amendment. Whether this would be so in other criminal prosecutions, or under other circumstances, we need not determine. All that it is necessary now to decide, as we do decide, is that in a capital case, where the defendant is unable to employ counsel, and is incapable adequately of making his own defense because of ignorance, feeble-mindedness, illiteracy, or the like, it is the duty of the court, whether requested or not, to assign counsel for him as a necessary requisite of due process of law; and that duty is not discharged by an assignment at such a time or under such circumstances as to preclude the giving of effective aid in the preparation and trial of the case. To hold otherwise would be to ignore the fundamental postulate, already adverted to, 'that there are certain immutable principles of justice which inhere in the very idea of free government which no member of the Union may disregard.' *Holden v. Hardy*, supra. In a case such as this, whatever may be the rule in other cases, the right to have counsel appointed, when necessary, is a logical corollary from the constitutional right to be heard by counsel. Compare *Carpenter & Sprague v. Dane County*, 9 Wis. 274; *Dane County v. Smith*, 13 Wis. 585, 586, 80 Am.Dec. 754; *Hendryx v. State*, 130 Ind. 265, 268, 269, 29 N.E. 1131; *Cutts v. State*, 54 Fla. 21, 23, 45 So. 491; *People v. Goldenson*, 76 Cal. 328, 344, 19 P. 161; *Delk v. State*, 99 Ga. 667, 669, 670, 26 S.E. 752.

In *Hendryx v. State*, supra, there was no statute authorizing the assignment of an attorney to defend an indigent person accused of crime, but the court held that such an assignment was necessary to accomplish the ends of public justice, and that the court possessed the inherent power to make it. 'Where a prisoner,' the court said (page 269 of 130 Ind., 29 N.E. 1131, 1132), 'without legal knowledge is confined in jail, absent from his friends, without the aid of legal advice or the means of investigating the charge against him, it is impossible to conceive of a fair trial where he is compelled to conduct his cause in court, without the aid of counsel. * * * Such a trial is not far removed from an exparte proceeding.'

Let us suppose the extreme case of a prisoner charged with a capital offense, who is deaf and dumb, illiterate, and feeble-minded, unable to employ counsel, with the whole power of the state arrayed against him, prosecuted by counsel for the state without assignment of counsel for his defense, tried, convicted, and sentenced to death. Such a result, which, if carried into execution, would be little short of judicial murder, it cannot be doubted would be a gross violation of the guarantee of due process of law; and we venture to think that no appellate court, state or federal, would hesitate so to decide. See *Stephenson v. State*, 4 Ohio App. 128; *Williams v. State*, 163 Ark. 623, 628, 260 S.W. 721; *Grogan v. Commonwealth*, 222 Ky. 484, 485, 1 S.W.(2d) 779; *Mullen v. State*, 28 Okl.Cr. 218, 230, 230 P. 285; *Williams v. Commonwealth* (Ky.) 110 S.W. 339, 340. The duty of the trial court to appoint counsel under such circumstances is clear, as it is clear under circumstances such as are disclosed by the record here; and its power to do so, even in the absence of a statute, can not be questioned. Attorneys are officers of the court, and are bound to render service when required by such an appointment. See Cooley, Constitutional Limitations, supra, 700 and note.

The United States by statute and every state in the Union by express provision of law, or by the determination of its courts, make it the duty of the trial judge, where the accused is unable to employ counsel, to appoint counsel for him. In most states the rule applies broadly to all criminal prosecutions, in others it is limited to the more serious crimes, and in a very limited number, to capital cases. A rule adopted with such unanimous accord reflects, if it does not establish the inherent right to have counsel appointed at least in cases like the present, and lends convincing support to the conclusion we have reached as to the fundamental nature of that right.

The judgments must be reversed and the causes remanded for further proceedings not inconsistent with this opinion.

Judgments reversed.

The Scottsboro *Cases and the Supreme Court*

Powell v. Alabama was part of the long, tragic saga of these young African-American defendants often referred to as the "Scottsboro Boys." These Scottsboro cases not only produced the court's decision in *Powell*, which recognized that the Sixth Amendment and due process require minimum standards for representation in serious criminal cases, they also led to the Court's decision in *Norris v. Alabama*, 294 U.S. 587 (1935), in which the court held that evidence that no African-Americans ever had been called for grand jury service in Scottsboro established a prima facie case of systematic discrimination that violated the Equal Protection Clause. For more on the Scottsboro Cases, *see, e.g.*, JAMES GOODMAN, STORIES OF SCOTTSBORO (1995); DAN T. CARTER, SCOTTSBORO: A TRAGEDY OF THE AMERICAN SOUTH (1970).

Strickland v. Washington

Supreme Court of the United States, 1984
466 U.S. 668

■ JUSTICE O'CONNOR delivered the opinion of the Court.

This case requires us to consider the proper standards for judging a criminal defendant's contention that the Constitution requires a conviction or death sentence to be set aside because counsel's assistance at the trial or sentencing was ineffective.

I

A

During a 10-day period in September 1976, respondent planned and committed three groups of crimes, which included three brutal stabbing murders, torture, kidnaping, severe assaults, attempted murders, attempted extortion, and theft. After his two accomplices were arrested, respondent surrendered to police and voluntarily gave a lengthy statement confessing to the third of the criminal episodes. The State of Florida indicted respondent for kidnaping and murder and appointed an experienced criminal lawyer to represent him.

Counsel actively pursued pretrial motions and discovery. He cut his efforts short, however, and he experienced a sense of hopelessness about the case, when he learned that, against his specific advice, respondent had also confessed to the first two murders. By the date set for trial, respondent was subject to indictment for three counts of first-degree murder and multiple counts of robbery, kidnaping for ransom, breaking and entering and assault, attempted murder, and conspiracy to commit robbery. Respondent waived his right to a jury trial, again acting against counsel's advice, and pleaded guilty to all charges, including the three capital murder charges.

In the plea colloquy, respondent told the trial judge that, although he had committed a string of burglaries, he had no significant prior criminal record and that at the time of his criminal spree he was under extreme stress caused by his inability to support his family. App. 50–53. He also stated, however, that he accepted responsibility for the crimes. E.g., id., at 54, 57. The trial judge told respondent that he had "a great deal of respect for people who are willing to step forward and admit their responsibility" but that he was making no statement at all about his likely sentencing decision. Id., at 62.

Counsel advised respondent to invoke his right under Florida law to an advisory jury at his capital sentencing hearing. Respondent rejected the advice and waived the right. He chose instead to be sentenced by the trial judge without a jury recommendation.

In preparing for the sentencing hearing, counsel spoke with respondent about his background. He also spoke on the telephone with respondent's wife and mother, though he did not follow up on the one unsuccessful effort to meet with them. He did not otherwise seek out character witnesses for respondent. App. to Pet. for Cert. A265. Nor did he request a psychiatric examination, since his conversations with his client gave no indication that respondent had psychological problems. Id., at A266.

Counsel decided not to present and hence not to look further for evidence concerning respondent's character and emotional state. That decision reflected trial counsel's sense of hopelessness about overcoming the evidentiary effect of respondent's confessions to the gruesome crimes. See id., at A282. It also reflected the judgment that it was advisable to rely on the plea colloquy for evidence about respondent's background and about his claim of emotional stress: the plea colloquy communicated sufficient information about these subjects, and by forgoing the opportunity to present new evidence on these subjects, counsel prevented the State from cross-examining respondent on his claim and from putting on psychiatric evidence of its own. Id., at A223–A225.

Counsel also excluded from the sentencing hearing other evidence he thought was potentially damaging. He successfully moved to exclude respondent's "rap sheet." Id., at A227; App. 311. Because he judged that a presentence report might prove more detrimental than helpful, as it would have included respondent's criminal history and thereby would have undermined the claim of no significant history of criminal activity, he did not request that one be prepared. App. to Pet. for Cert. A227–A228, A265–A266.

At the sentencing hearing, counsel's strategy was based primarily on the trial judge's remarks at the plea colloquy as well as on his reputation as a sentencing judge who thought it important for a convicted defendant to own up to his crime. Counsel argued that respondent's remorse and acceptance of responsibility justified sparing him from the death penalty. Id., at A265–A266. Counsel also argued that respondent had no history of criminal activity and that respondent committed the crimes under extreme mental or emotional disturbance, thus coming within the statutory list of mitigating circumstances. He further argued that respondent should be spared death because he had surrendered, confessed, and offered to testify against a codefendant and because respondent was fundamentally a good person who had briefly gone badly wrong in extremely stressful circumstances. The State put on evidence and witnesses largely for the purpose of describing the details of the crimes. Counsel did not cross-examine the medical experts who testified about the manner of death of respondent's victims.

The trial judge found several aggravating circumstances with respect to each of the three murders. He found that all three murders were especially heinous, atrocious, and cruel, all involving repeated stabbings. All three murders were committed in the course of at least one other dangerous and violent felony, and since all involved robbery, the murders were for pecuniary gain. All three murders were committed to avoid arrest for the accompanying crimes and to hinder law enforcement. In the course of one of the murders, respondent knowingly subjected numerous persons to a grave risk of death by deliberately stabbing and shooting the murder victim's sisters-in-law, who sustained severe—in one case, ultimately fatal—injuries.

With respect to mitigating circumstances, the trial judge made the same findings for all three capital murders. First, although there was no admitted evidence of prior convictions, respondent had stated that he had engaged in a course of stealing. In any case, even if respondent had no significant history of criminal activity, the aggravating circumstances "would still clearly far outweigh" that mitigating factor. Second, the judge found that, during all three crimes, respondent was not suffering from extreme mental or emotional disturbance and could appreciate the criminality of his acts. Third, none of the victims was a participant in, or consented to, respondent's conduct. Fourth, respondent's participation in the crimes was neither minor nor the result of duress or domination by an accomplice. Finally, respondent's age (26) could not be considered a factor in mitigation, especially when viewed in light of respondent's planning of the crimes and disposition of the proceeds of the various accompanying thefts.

In short, the trial judge found numerous aggravating circumstances and no (or a single comparatively insignificant) mitigating circumstance. With respect to each of the three convictions for capital murder, the trial judge concluded: "A careful consideration of all matters presented to the court impels the conclusion that there are insufficient mitigating circumstances . . . to outweigh the aggravating circumstances." * * * He therefore sentenced respondent to death on each of the three counts of murder and to prison terms for the other crimes. The Florida Supreme Court upheld the convictions and sentences on direct appeal.

B

Respondent subsequently sought collateral relief in state court on numerous grounds, among them that counsel had rendered ineffective assistance at the sentencing proceeding. Respondent challenged counsel's assistance in six respects. He asserted that counsel was ineffective because he failed to move for a continuance to prepare for sentencing, to request a psychiatric report, to investigate and present character witnesses, to seek a presentence investigation report, to present meaningful arguments to the sentencing judge, and to investigate the medical examiner's reports or cross-examine the medical experts. In support of the claim, respondent submitted 14 affidavits from friends, neighbors, and relatives stating that they would have testified if asked to do so. He also submitted one psychiatric report and one psychological report stating that respondent, though not under the influence of extreme mental or emotional disturbance, was "chronically frustrated and depressed because of his economic dilemma" at the time of his crimes. App. 7; see also id., at 14.

The trial court denied relief without an evidentiary hearing, finding that the record evidence conclusively showed that the ineffectiveness claim was meritless. App. to Pet. for Cert. A206–A243. Four of the assertedly prejudicial errors required little discussion. First, there were no grounds to request a continuance, so there was no error in not requesting one when respondent pleaded guilty. Id., at A218–A220. Second, failure to request a presentence investigation was not a serious error because the trial judge had discretion not to grant such a request and because any presentence investigation would have resulted in admission of respondent's "rap sheet" and thus would have undermined his assertion of no significant history of criminal activity. Id., at A226–A228. Third, the argument and memorandum given to the sentencing judge were "admirable" in light of the overwhelming aggravating circumstances and absence of mitigating circumstances. Id., at A228. Fourth, there was no error in failure to examine the medical examiner's reports or to cross-examine the medical witnesses testifying on the manner of death of respondent's victims, since respondent admitted that the victims died in the ways shown by the unchallenged medical evidence. Id., at A229.

The trial court dealt at greater length with the two other bases for the ineffectiveness claim. The court pointed out that a psychiatric examination of respondent was conducted by state order soon after respondent's initial arraignment. That report states that there was no indication of major mental illness at the time of the crimes. Moreover, both the reports submitted in the collateral proceeding state that, although respondent was "chronically frustrated and depressed because of his economic dilemma," he was not under the influence of extreme mental or emotional disturbance. All three reports thus directly undermine the contention made at the sentencing hearing that respondent was suffering from extreme mental or emotional disturbance during his crime spree. Accordingly, counsel could reasonably decide not to seek psychiatric reports; indeed, by relying solely on the plea colloquy to support the emotional disturbance contention, counsel denied the State an opportunity to rebut his claim with psychiatric testimony. In any event, the aggravating circumstances were so overwhelming that no substantial prejudice resulted from the absence at sentencing of the psychiatric evidence offered in the collateral attack.

The court rejected the challenge to counsel's failure to develop and to present character evidence for much the same reasons. The affidavits submitted in the collateral proceeding showed nothing more than that certain persons would have testified that respondent was basically a good person who was worried about his family's financial problems. Respondent himself had already testified along those lines at the plea colloquy. Moreover, respondent's admission of a course of stealing rebutted many of the factual allegations in the affidavits. For those reasons, and because the sentencing judge had stated that the death sentence would be appropriate even if respondent had no significant prior criminal history, no substantial prejudice resulted from the absence at sentencing of the character evidence offered in the collateral attack.

Applying the standard for ineffectiveness claims articulated by the Florida Supreme Court in *Knight v. State*, 394 So.2d 997 (1981), the trial court concluded that respondent had not shown that counsel's assistance reflected any substantial and serious deficiency measurably below that of competent counsel that was likely to have affected the outcome of the sentencing proceeding. The court specifically found: "[A]s a matter of law, the record affirmatively demonstrates beyond any doubt that even if [counsel] had done each of the . . . things [that respondent alleged counsel had failed to do] at the time of sentencing, there is not even the remotest chance that the outcome would have been any different. The plain fact is that the aggravating circumstances proved in this case were completely overwhelming. . . ." App. to Pet. for Cert. A230.

The Florida Supreme Court affirmed the denial of relief. * * * For essentially the reasons given by the trial court, the State Supreme Court concluded that respondent had failed to make out a prima facie case of either "substantial deficiency or possible prejudice" and, indeed, had "failed to such a degree that we believe, to the point of a moral certainty, that he is entitled to no relief. . . ." Id., at 287. Respondent's claims were "shown conclusively to be without merit so as to obviate the need for an evidentiary hearing." Id., at 286.

C

Respondent next filed a petition for a writ of habeas corpus in the United States District Court for the Southern District of Florida. He advanced numerous grounds for relief, among them ineffective assistance of counsel based on the same errors, except for the failure to move for a continuance, as those he had identified in state court. The District Court held an evidentiary hearing to inquire into trial counsel's efforts to investigate and to present mitigating circumstances. Respondent offered the affidavits and reports he had submitted in the state collateral proceedings; he also called his trial counsel to testify. The State of Florida, over respondent's objection, called the trial judge to testify.

The District Court disputed none of the state court factual findings concerning trial counsel's assistance and made findings of its own that are consistent with the state court findings. The account of trial counsel's actions and decisions given above reflects the combined findings. On the legal issue of ineffectiveness, the District Court concluded that, although trial counsel made errors in judgment in failing to investigate nonstatutory mitigating evidence further than he did, no prejudice to respondent's sentence resulted from any such error in judgment. Relying in part on the trial judge's testimony but also on the same factors that led the state courts to find no prejudice, the District Court concluded that "there does not appear to be a likelihood, or even a significant possibility," that any errors of trial counsel had affected the outcome of the sentencing proceeding. App. to Pet. for Cert. A285–A286. The District Court went on to reject all of respondent's other grounds for relief, including one not exhausted in state court, which the District Court considered because, among other reasons, the State urged its consideration. Id., at A286–A292. The court accordingly denied the petition for a writ of habeas corpus.

On appeal, a panel of the United States Court of Appeals for the Fifth Circuit affirmed in part, vacated in part, and remanded with instructions to apply to the particular facts the framework for analyzing ineffectiveness claims that it developed in its opinion. 673 F.2d 879 (5th Cir.1982). The panel decision was itself vacated when Unit B of the former Fifth Circuit, now the Eleventh Circuit, decided to rehear the case en banc. 679 F.2d 23 (1982). The full Court of Appeals developed its own framework for analyzing ineffective assistance claims and reversed the judgment of the District Court and remanded the case for new factfinding under the newly announced standards. 693 F.2d 1243 (1982).

* * *

The Court of Appeals thus laid down the tests to be applied in the Eleventh Circuit in challenges to convictions on the ground of ineffectiveness of counsel.

* * *

D

Petitioners, who are officials of the State of Florida, filed a petition for a writ of certiorari seeking review of the decision of the Court of Appeals.

The petition presents a type of Sixth Amendment claim that this Court has not previously considered in any generality. The Court has considered Sixth Amendment claims based on actual or constructive denial of the assistance of counsel altogether, as well as claims based on state interference with the ability of counsel to render effective assistance to the accused. * * * [However,] the Court has never directly and fully addressed a claim of "actual ineffectiveness" of counsel's assistance in a case going to trial. * * *

* * *

For these reasons, we granted certiorari to consider the standards by which to judge a contention that the Constitution requires that a criminal judgment be overturned because of the actual ineffective assistance of counsel. 462 U.S. 1105, 103 S.Ct. 2451, 77 L.Ed.2d 1332 (1983). * * *

II

In a long line of cases that includes *Powell v. Alabama*, 287 U.S. 45, 53 S.Ct. 55, 77 L.Ed. 158 (1932), *Johnson v. Zerbst*, 304 U.S. 458, 58 S.Ct. 1019, 82 L.Ed. 1461 (1938), and *Gideon v. Wainwright*, 372 U.S. 335, 83 S.Ct. 792, 9 L.Ed.2d 799 (1963), this Court has recognized that the Sixth Amendment right to counsel exists, and is needed, in order to protect the fundamental right to a fair trial. The Constitution guarantees a fair trial through the Due Process Clauses, but it defines the basic elements of a fair trial largely through the several provisions of the Sixth Amendment, including the Counsel Clause:

> "In all criminal prosecutions, the accused shall enjoy the right to a speedy and public trial, by an impartial jury of the State and district wherein the crime shall have been committed, which district shall have been previously ascertained by law, and to be informed of the nature and cause of the accusation; to be confronted with the witnesses against him; to have compulsory process for obtaining witnesses in his favor, and to have the Assistance of Counsel for his defence."

Thus, a fair trial is one in which evidence subject to adversarial testing is presented to an impartial tribunal for resolution of issues defined in advance of the proceeding. The right to counsel plays a crucial role in the adversarial system embodied in the Sixth Amendment, since access to counsel's skill and knowledge is necessary to accord defendants the "ample opportunity to meet the case of the prosecution" to which they are entitled. * * *

Because of the vital importance of counsel's assistance, this Court has held that, with certain exceptions, a person accused of a federal or state crime has the right to have counsel appointed if retained counsel cannot be obtained. See *Argersinger v. Hamlin*, 407 U.S. 25, 92 S.Ct. 2006, 32 L.Ed.2d 530 (1972); *Gideon v. Wainwright*, supra; *Johnson v. Zerbst*, supra. That a person who happens to be a lawyer is present at trial alongside the accused, however, is not enough to satisfy the constitutional command. The Sixth Amendment recognizes the right to the assistance of counsel because it envisions counsel's playing a role that is critical to the ability of the adversarial system to produce just results. An accused is entitled to be assisted by an attorney, whether retained or appointed, who plays the role necessary to ensure that the trial is fair.

For that reason, the Court has recognized that "the right to counsel is the right to the effective assistance of counsel." *McMann v. Richardson*, 397 U.S. 759, 771, n. 14, 90 S.Ct. 1441, 1449, n. 14, 25 L.Ed.2d 763 (1970). Government violates the right to effective assistance when it interferes in certain ways with the ability of counsel to make independent decisions about how to conduct the defense. See, e.g., *Geders v. United States*, 425 U.S. 80, 96 S.Ct. 1330, 47 L.Ed.2d 592 (1976) (bar on attorney-client consultation during overnight recess); *Herring v. New York*, 422 U.S. 853, 95 S.Ct. 2550, 45 L.Ed.2d 593 (1975) (bar on summation at bench trial); *Brooks v. Tennessee*, 406 U.S. 605, 612–613, 92 S.Ct. 1891, 1895, 32 L.Ed.2d 358 (1972) (requirement that defendant be first defense witness); *Ferguson v. Georgia*, 365 U.S. 570, 593–596, 81 S.Ct. 756, 768–770, 5 L.Ed.2d 783 (1961) (bar on direct examination of defendant). Counsel, however, can also deprive a defendant of the right to effective assistance, simply by failing to render "adequate legal assistance," *Cuyler v. Sullivan*, 446 U.S., at 344, 100 S.Ct., at 1716. Id., at 345–350, 100 S.Ct., at 1716–1719 (actual conflict of interest adversely affecting lawyer's performance renders assistance ineffective).

The Court has not elaborated on the meaning of the constitutional requirement of effective assistance in the latter class of cases—that is, those presenting claims of "actual ineffectiveness." In giving meaning to the requirement, however, we must take its purpose—to ensure a fair trial—as the guide. The benchmark for judging any claim of ineffectiveness must be whether counsel's conduct so undermined the proper functioning of the adversarial process that the trial cannot be relied on as having produced a just result.

The same principle applies to a capital sentencing proceeding such as that provided by Florida law. We need not consider the role of counsel in an ordinary sentencing, which may involve informal proceedings and standardless discretion in the sentencer, and hence may require a different approach to the definition of constitutionally effective assistance. A capital sentencing proceeding like the one involved in this case, however, is sufficiently like a trial in its adversarial format and in the existence of standards for decision, see *Barclay v. Florida*, 463 U.S. 939, 952–954, 103 S.Ct. 3418, 3425, 77 L.Ed.2d 1134 (1983); *Bullington v. Missouri*, 451 U.S. 430, 101 S.Ct. 1852, 68 L.Ed.2d 270 (1981), that counsel's role in the proceeding is comparable to counsel's role at trial— to ensure that the adversarial testing process works to produce a just result under the standards governing decision. For purposes of describing counsel's duties, therefore, Florida's capital sentencing proceeding need not be distinguished from an ordinary trial.

III

A convicted defendant's claim that counsel's assistance was so defective as to require reversal of a conviction or death sentence has two components. First, the defendant must show that counsel's performance was deficient. This requires showing that counsel made errors so serious that counsel was not functioning as the "counsel" guaranteed the defendant by the Sixth Amendment. Second, the defendant must show that the deficient performance prejudiced the defense. This requires showing that counsel's errors were so serious as to deprive the defendant of a fair trial, a trial whose result is reliable. Unless a defendant makes both showings, it cannot be said that the conviction or death sentence resulted from a breakdown in the adversary process that renders the result unreliable.

A

As all the Federal Courts of Appeals have now held, the proper standard for attorney performance is that of reasonably effective assistance. * * * When a convicted defendant complains of the ineffectiveness of counsel's assistance, the defendant must show that counsel's representation fell below an objective standard of reasonableness.

More specific guidelines are not appropriate. The Sixth Amendment refers simply to "counsel," not specifying particular requirements of effective assistance. It relies instead on the legal profession's maintenance of standards sufficient to justify the law's presumption that counsel will fulfill the role in the adversary process that the Amendment envisions. * * * The proper measure of attorney performance remains simply reasonableness under prevailing professional norms.

Representation of a criminal defendant entails certain basic duties. Counsel's function is to assist the defendant, and hence counsel owes the client a duty of loyalty, a duty to avoid conflicts of interest.* * * From counsel's function as assistant to the defendant derive the overarching duty to advocate the defendant's cause and the more particular duties to consult with the defendant on important decisions and to keep the defendant informed of important developments in the course of the prosecution. Counsel also has a duty to bring to bear such skill and knowledge as will render the trial a reliable adversarial testing process. See *Powell v. Alabama*, 287 U.S., at 68–69, 53 S.Ct., at 63–64.

These basic duties neither exhaustively define the obligations of counsel nor form a checklist for judicial evaluation of attorney performance. In any case presenting an ineffectiveness claim, the performance inquiry must be whether counsel's assistance was reasonable considering all the circumstances. Prevailing norms of practice as reflected in American Bar Association standards and the like, e.g., ABA Standards for Criminal Justice 4–1.1 to 4–8.6 (2d ed. 1980) ("The Defense Function"), are guides to determining what is reasonable, but they are only guides. No particular set of detailed rules for counsel's conduct can satisfactorily take account of the variety of circumstances faced by defense counsel or the range of legitimate decisions regarding how best to represent a criminal defendant. Any such set of rules would interfere with the constitutionally protected independence of counsel and restrict the wide latitude counsel must have in making tactical decisions. * * * Indeed, the existence of detailed guidelines for representation could distract counsel from the overriding mission of vigorous advocacy of the defendant's cause. Moreover, the purpose of the effective assistance guarantee of the Sixth Amendment is not to improve the quality of legal representation, although that is a goal of considerable importance to the legal system. The purpose is simply to ensure that criminal defendants receive a fair trial.

Judicial scrutiny of counsel's performance must be highly deferential. It is all too tempting for a defendant to second-guess counsel's assistance after conviction or adverse sentence, and it is all too easy for a court, examining counsel's defense after it has proved unsuccessful, to conclude that a particular act or omission of counsel was unreasonable. * * * A fair assessment of attorney performance requires that every effort be made to eliminate the distorting effects of hindsight, to reconstruct the circumstances of counsel's challenged conduct, and to evaluate the conduct from counsel's perspective at the time. Because of the difficulties inherent in making the evaluation, a court must indulge a strong presumption that counsel's conduct falls within the wide range of reasonable professional assistance; that is, the defendant must overcome the presumption that, under the circumstances, the challenged action "might be considered sound trial strategy." * * * There are countless ways to provide effective assistance in any given case. Even the best criminal defense attorneys would not defend a particular client in the same way. * * *

The availability of intrusive post-trial inquiry into attorney performance or of detailed guidelines for its evaluation would encourage the proliferation of ineffectiveness challenges. Criminal trials resolved unfavorably to the defendant would increasingly come to be followed by a second trial, this one of counsel's unsuccessful defense. Counsel's performance and even willingness to serve could be adversely affected. Intensive scrutiny of counsel and rigid requirements for acceptable assistance could dampen the ardor and impair the independence of defense counsel, discourage the acceptance of assigned cases, and undermine the trust between attorney and client.

Thus, a court deciding an actual ineffectiveness claim must judge the reasonableness of counsel's challenged conduct on the facts of the particular case, viewed as of the time of counsel's conduct. A convicted defendant making a claim of ineffective assistance must identify the acts or omissions of counsel that are alleged not to have been the result of reasonable professional judgment. The court must then determine whether, in light of all the circumstances, the identified acts or omissions were outside the wide range of professionally competent assistance. In making that determination, the court should keep in mind that counsel's function, as elaborated in prevailing professional norms, is to make the adversarial testing process work in the particular case. At the same time, the court should recognize that counsel is strongly presumed to have rendered adequate assistance and made all significant decisions in the exercise of reasonable professional judgment.

These standards require no special amplification in order to define counsel's duty to investigate, the duty at issue in this case. As the Court of Appeals concluded, strategic choices made after thorough investigation of law and facts relevant to plausible options are virtually unchallengeable; and strategic choices made after less than complete investigation are reasonable precisely to the extent that reasonable professional judgments support the limitations on investigation. In other words, counsel has a duty to make reasonable investigations or to make a reasonable decision that makes particular investigations unnecessary. In any ineffectiveness case, a particular decision not to investigate must be directly assessed for reasonableness in all the circumstances, applying a heavy measure of deference to counsel's judgments.

The reasonableness of counsel's actions may be determined or substantially influenced by the defendant's own statements or actions. Counsel's actions are usually based, quite properly, on informed strategic choices made by the defendant and on information supplied by the defendant. In particular, what investigation decisions are reasonable depends critically on such information. For example, when the facts that support a certain potential line of defense are generally known to counsel because of what the defendant has said, the need for further investigation may be considerably diminished or eliminated altogether. And when a defendant has given counsel reason to believe that pursuing certain investigations would be fruitless or even harmful, counsel's failure to pursue those investigations may not later be challenged as unreasonable. In short, inquiry into counsel's conversations with the defendant may be critical to a proper assessment of counsel's investigation decisions, just as it may be critical to a proper assessment of counsel's other litigation decisions. * * *

B

An error by counsel, even if professionally unreasonable, does not warrant setting aside the judgment of a criminal proceeding if the error had no effect on the judgment. * * * The purpose of the Sixth Amendment guarantee of counsel is to ensure that a defendant has the assistance necessary to justify reliance on the outcome of the proceeding. Accordingly, any deficiencies in counsel's performance must be prejudicial to the defense in order to constitute ineffective assistance under the Constitution.

In certain Sixth Amendment contexts, prejudice is presumed. Actual or constructive denial of the assistance of counsel altogether is legally presumed to result in prejudice. So are various kinds of state interference with counsel's assistance.* * * Prejudice in these circumstances is so likely that case-by-case inquiry into prejudice is not worth the cost. * * * Moreover, such circumstances involve impairments of the Sixth Amendment right that are easy to identify and, for that reason and because the prosecution is directly responsible, easy for the government to prevent.

One type of actual ineffectiveness claim warrants a similar, though more limited, presumption of prejudice. In *Cuyler v. Sullivan*, 446 U.S., at 345–350, 100 S.Ct., at 1716–1719, the Court held that prejudice is presumed when counsel is burdened by an actual conflict of interest. In those circumstances, counsel breaches the duty of loyalty, perhaps the most basic of counsel's duties. Moreover, it is difficult to measure the precise effect on the defense of representation corrupted by conflicting interests. Given the obligation of counsel to avoid conflicts of interest and the ability of trial courts to make early inquiry in certain situations likely to give rise to conflicts, see, e.g., Fed.Rule Crim.Proc. 44(c), it is reasonable for the criminal justice system to maintain a fairly rigid rule of presumed prejudice for conflicts of interest. Even so, the rule is not quite the per se rule of prejudice that exists for the Sixth Amendment claims mentioned above. Prejudice is presumed only if the defendant demonstrates that counsel "actively represented conflicting interests" and that "an actual conflict of interest adversely affected his lawyer's performance." * * *

Conflict of interest claims aside, actual ineffectiveness claims alleging a deficiency in attorney performance are subject to a general requirement that the defendant affirmatively prove prejudice. The government is not responsible for, and hence not able to prevent, attorney errors that will result in reversal of a conviction or sentence. Attorney errors come in an infinite variety and are as likely to be utterly harmless in a particular case as they are to be prejudicial. They cannot be classified according to likelihood of causing prejudice. Nor can they be defined with sufficient precision to inform defense attorneys correctly just what conduct to avoid. Representation is an art, and an act or omission that is unprofessional in one case may be sound or even brilliant in another. Even if a defendant shows that particular errors of counsel were unreasonable, therefore, the defendant must show that they actually had an adverse effect on the defense.

It is not enough for the defendant to show that the errors had some conceivable effect on the outcome of the proceeding.

* * *

The defendant must show that there is a reasonable probability that, but for counsel's unprofessional errors, the result of the proceeding would have been different. A reasonable probability is a probability sufficient to undermine confidence in the outcome.

In making the determination whether the specified errors resulted in the required prejudice, a court should presume, absent challenge to the judgment on grounds of evidentiary insufficiency, that the judge or jury acted according to law. An assessment of the likelihood of a result more favorable to the defendant must exclude the possibility of arbitrariness, whimsy, caprice, "nullification," and the like. A defendant has no entitlement to the luck of a lawless decisionmaker, even if a lawless decision cannot be reviewed. The assessment of prejudice should proceed on the assumption that the decisionmaker is reasonably, conscientiously, and impartially applying the standards that govern the decision. It should not depend on the idiosyncracies of the particular decisionmaker, such as unusual propensities toward harshness or leniency. Although these factors may actually have entered into counsel's selection of strategies and, to that limited extent, may thus affect the performance inquiry, they are irrelevant to the prejudice inquiry. Thus, evidence about the actual process of decision, if not part of the record of the proceeding under review, and evidence about, for example, a particular judge's sentencing practices, should not be considered in the prejudice determination.

The governing legal standard plays a critical role in defining the question to be asked in assessing the prejudice from counsel's errors. When a defendant challenges a conviction, the question is whether there is a reasonable probability that, absent the errors, the factfinder would have had a reasonable doubt respecting guilt. When a defendant challenges a death sentence such as the one at issue in this case, the question is whether there is a reasonable probability that, absent the errors, the sentencer—including an appellate court, to the extent it independently reweighs the evidence—would have concluded that the balance of aggravating and mitigating circumstances did not warrant death.

In making this determination, a court hearing an ineffectiveness claim must consider the totality of the evidence before the judge or jury. Some of the factual findings will have been unaffected by the errors, and factual findings that were affected will have been affected in different ways. Some errors will have had a pervasive effect on the inferences to be drawn from the evidence, altering the entire evidentiary picture, and some will have had an isolated, trivial effect. Moreover, a verdict or conclusion only weakly supported by the record is more likely to have been affected by errors than one with overwhelming record support. Taking the unaffected findings as a given, and taking due account of the effect of the errors on the remaining findings, a court making the prejudice inquiry must ask if the defendant has met the burden of showing that the decision reached would reasonably likely have been different absent the errors.

IV

A number of practical considerations are important for the application of the standards we have outlined. Most important, in adjudicating a claim of actual ineffectiveness of counsel, a court should keep in mind that the principles we have stated do not establish mechanical rules. Although those principles should guide the process of decision, the ultimate focus of inquiry must be on the fundamental fairness of the proceeding whose result is being challenged. In every case the court should be concerned with whether, despite the strong presumption of reliability, the result of the particular proceeding is unreliable because of a breakdown in the adversarial process that our system counts on to produce just results.

* * *

Although we have discussed the performance component of an ineffectiveness claim prior to the prejudice component, there is no reason for a court deciding an ineffective assistance claim to approach the inquiry in the same order or even to address both components of the inquiry if the defendant makes an insufficient showing on one. In particular, a court need not determine whether counsel's performance was deficient before examining the prejudice suffered by the defendant as a result of the alleged deficiencies. The object of an ineffectiveness claim is not to grade counsel's performance. If it is easier to dispose of an ineffectiveness claim on the ground of lack of sufficient prejudice, which we expect will often be so, that course should be followed. Courts should strive to ensure that ineffectiveness claims not become so burdensome to defense counsel that the entire criminal justice system suffers as a result.

The principles governing ineffectiveness claims should apply in federal collateral proceedings as they do on direct appeal or in motions for a new trial. As indicated by the "cause and prejudice" test for overcoming procedural waivers of claims of error, the presumption that a criminal judgment is final is at its strongest in collateral attacks on that judgment. * * * An ineffectiveness claim, however, as our articulation of the standards that govern decision of such claims makes clear, is an attack on the fundamental fairness of the proceeding whose result is challenged. Since fundamental fairness is the central concern of the writ of habeas corpus, * * * no special standards ought to apply to ineffectiveness claims made in habeas proceedings.

V

Having articulated general standards for judging ineffectiveness claims, we think it useful to apply those standards to the facts of this case in order to illustrate the meaning of the general principles. * * *

Application of the governing principles is not difficult in this case. The facts as described above * * * make clear that the conduct of respondent's counsel at and before respondent's sentencing proceeding cannot be found unreasonable. They also make clear that, even assuming the challenged conduct of counsel was unreasonable, respondent suffered insufficient prejudice to warrant setting aside his death sentence.

With respect to the performance component, the record shows that respondent's counsel made a strategic choice to argue for the extreme emotional distress mitigating circumstance and to rely as fully as possible on respondent's acceptance of responsibility for his crimes. Although counsel understandably felt hopeless about respondent's prospects, * * * nothing in the record indicates, as one possible reading of the District Court's opinion suggests, * * * that counsel's sense of hopelessness distorted his professional judgment. Counsel's strategy choice was well within the range of professionally reasonable judgments, and the decision not to seek more character or psychological evidence than was already in hand was likewise reasonable.

The trial judge's views on the importance of owning up to one's crimes were well known to counsel. The aggravating circumstances were utterly overwhelming. Trial counsel could reasonably surmise from his conversations with respondent that character and psychological evidence would be of little help. Respondent had already been able to mention at the plea colloquy the substance of what there was to know about his financial and emotional troubles. Restricting testimony on respondent's character to what had come in at the plea colloquy ensured that contrary character and psychological evidence and respondent's criminal history, which counsel had successfully moved to exclude, would not come in. On these facts, there can be little question, even without application of the presumption of adequate performance, that trial counsel's defense, though unsuccessful, was the result of reasonable professional judgment.

With respect to the prejudice component, the lack of merit of respondent's claim is even more stark. The evidence that respondent says his trial counsel should have offered at the sentencing hearing would barely have altered the sentencing profile presented to the sentencing judge. As the state courts and District Court found, at most this evidence shows that numerous people who knew respondent thought he was generally a good person and that a psychiatrist and a psychologist believed he was under considerable emotional stress that did not rise to the level of extreme disturbance. Given the overwhelming aggravating factors, there is no reasonable probability that the omitted evidence would have changed the conclusion that the aggravating circumstances outweighed the mitigating circumstances and, hence, the sentence imposed. Indeed, admission of the evidence respondent now offers might even have been harmful to his case: his "rap sheet" would probably have been admitted into evidence, and the psychological reports would have directly contradicted respondent's claim that the mitigating circumstance of extreme emotional disturbance applied to his case.

Failure to make the required showing of either deficient performance or sufficient prejudice defeats the ineffectiveness claim. Here there is a double failure. More generally, respondent has made no showing that the justice of his sentence was rendered unreliable by a breakdown in the adversary process caused by deficiencies in counsel's assistance. Respondent's sentencing proceeding was not fundamentally unfair.

We conclude, therefore, that the District Court properly declined to issue a writ of habeas corpus. The judgment of the Court of Appeals is accordingly

Reversed.

* * *

■ JUSTICE MARSHALL, dissenting.

The Sixth and Fourteenth Amendments guarantee a person accused of a crime the right to the aid of a lawyer in preparing and presenting his defense. It has long been settled that "the right to counsel is the right to the effective assistance of counsel." *McMann v. Richardson*, 397 U.S. 759, 771, n. 14, 90 S.Ct. 1441, n. 14, 25 L.Ed.2d 763 (1970). The state and lower federal courts have developed standards for distinguishing effective from inadequate assistance. Today, for the first time, this Court attempts to synthesize and clarify those standards. For the most part, the majority's efforts are unhelpful. Neither of its two principal holdings seems to me likely to improve the adjudication of Sixth Amendment claims. And, in its zeal to survey comprehensively this field of doctrine, the majority makes many other generalizations and suggestions that I find unacceptable.

* * *

I

* * *

A

My objection to the performance standard adopted by the Court is that it is so malleable that, in practice, it will either have no grip at all or will yield excessive variation in the manner in which the Sixth Amendment is interpreted and applied by different courts. To tell lawyers and the lower courts that counsel for a criminal defendant must behave "reasonably" and must act like "a reasonably competent attorney," * * * is to tell them almost nothing. In essence, the majority has instructed judges called upon to assess claims of ineffective assistance of counsel to advert to their own intuitions regarding what constitutes "professional" representation, and has discouraged them from trying to develop more detailed standards governing the performance of defense counsel. In my view, the Court has thereby not only abdicated its own responsibility to interpret the Constitution, but also impaired the ability of the lower courts to exercise theirs.

The debilitating ambiguity of an "objective standard of reasonableness" in this context is illustrated by the majority's failure to address important issues concerning the quality of representation mandated by the Constitution. It is an unfortunate but undeniable fact that a person of means, by selecting a lawyer and paying him enough to ensure he prepares thoroughly, usually can obtain better representation than that available to an indigent defendant, who must rely on appointed counsel, who, in turn, has limited time and resources to devote to a given case. Is a "reasonably competent attorney" a reasonably competent adequately paid retained lawyer or a reasonably competent appointed attorney? It is also a fact that the quality of representation available to ordinary defendants in different parts of the country varies significantly. Should the standard of performance mandated by the Sixth Amendment vary by locale? The majority offers no clues as to the proper responses to these questions.

The majority defends its refusal to adopt more specific standards primarily on the ground that "[n]o particular set of detailed rules for counsel's conduct can satisfactorily take account of the variety of circumstances faced by defense counsel or the range of legitimate decisions regarding how best to represent a criminal defendant." * * * I agree that counsel must be afforded "wide latitude" when making "tactical decisions" regarding trial strategy, * * * but many aspects of the job of a criminal defense attorney are more amenable to judicial oversight. For example, much of the work involved in preparing for a trial, applying for bail, conferring with one's client, making timely objections to significant, arguably erroneous rulings of the trial judge, and filing a notice of appeal if there are colorable grounds therefor could profitably be made the subject of uniform standards.

* * *

B

I object to the prejudice standard adopted by the Court for two independent reasons. First, it is often very difficult to tell whether a defendant convicted after a trial in which he was ineffectively represented would have fared better if his lawyer had been competent. Seemingly impregnable cases can sometimes be dismantled by good defense counsel. On the basis of a cold record, it may be impossible for a reviewing court confidently to ascertain how the government's evidence and arguments would have stood up against rebuttal and cross-examination by a shrewd, well-prepared lawyer. The difficulties of estimating prejudice after the fact are exacerbated by the possibility that evidence of injury to the defendant may be missing from the record precisely because of the incompetence of defense counsel. In view of all these impediments to a fair evaluation of the probability that the outcome of a trial was affected by ineffectiveness of counsel, it seems to me senseless to impose on a defendant whose lawyer has been shown to have been incompetent the burden of demonstrating prejudice.

Second and more fundamentally, the assumption on which the Court's holding rests is that the only purpose of the constitutional guarantee of effective assistance of counsel is to reduce the chance that innocent persons will be convicted. In my view, the guarantee also functions to ensure that convictions are obtained only through fundamentally fair procedures. The majority contends that the Sixth Amendment is not violated when a manifestly guilty defendant is convicted after a trial in which he was represented by a manifestly ineffective attorney. I cannot agree. Every defendant is entitled to a trial in which his interests are vigorously and conscientiously advocated by an able lawyer. A proceeding in which the defendant does not receive meaningful assistance in meeting the forces of the State does not, in my opinion, constitute due process.

In *Chapman v. California,* 386 U.S. 18, 23, 87 S.Ct. 824, 827, 17 L.Ed.2d 705 (1967), we acknowledged that certain constitutional rights are "so basic to a fair trial that their infraction can never be treated as harmless error." Among these rights is the right to the assistance of counsel at trial. * * * In my view, the right to effective assistance of counsel is entailed by the right to counsel, and abridgment of the former is equivalent to abridgment of the latter. I would thus hold that a showing that the performance of a defendant's lawyer departed from constitutionally prescribed standards requires a new trial regardless of whether the defendant suffered demonstrable prejudice thereby.

* * *

I respectfully dissent.

Ethical Standards for Competent Representation of Criminal Defendants

The *Strickland* case excerpt above is lengthy—perhaps the lengthiest in the book. However, it is worth the space given the importance of the framework the case sets forth for determining when a lawyer has failed to meet constitutional standards for representation.

There is also another dimension to the quality of representation in criminal cases. In addition to the Sixth Amendment's constitutional standard, attorneys also must consider their obligations under ethical rules and standards. *See, e.g.,* AMERICAN BAR ASSOCIATION CRIMINAL JUSTICE STANDARDS (DEFENSE FUNCTION) 4–1.1 (noting that the Standards are "intended to provide guidance for the professional conduct and performance of defense counsel").

The crisis of indigent criminal defense in the United States and excessive public defender caseloads further complicate the challenge of ensuring effective assistance of counsel. *See, e.g.,* Eve Brensike Primus, *Culture as a Structural Problem in Indigent Defense*, 100 MINN. L. REV. 1769 (2016); Roger A. Fairfax, Jr., *Searching for Solutions to the Indigent Defense Crisis in the Broader Criminal Justice Reform Agenda*, 122 YALE L.J. 2316 (2013); Mary Sue Backus & Paul Marcus, *The Right to Counsel in Criminal Cases, A National Crisis*, 57 HASTINGS L.J. 1031, 1045–46 (2006); Charles J. Ogletree, Jr., *An Essay on the New Public Defender for the 21st Century*, 58 LAW & CONTEMP. PROBS. 81, 81 & n.2 (1995).

Fundamental Strategic Decisions of Counsel

Strickland gives fairly wide latitude to defense counsel who employ reasonable strategy in the representation of the defendant. This deference applies to relatively mundane matters such as how to frame a closing argument, *see, e.g., Yarborough v. Gentry*, 540 U.S. 1 (2003), to the actual concession of the client's guilt in a capital case, a matter addressed in the case excerpted below.

Florida v. Nixon

Supreme Court of the United States, 2004
543 U.S. 175

■ JUSTICE GINSBURG delivered the opinion of the Court.

This capital case concerns defense counsel's strategic decision to concede, at the guilt phase of the trial, the defendant's commission of murder, and to concentrate the defense on establishing, at the penalty phase, cause for sparing the defendant's life. Any concession of that order, the Florida Supreme Court held, made without the defendant's express consent-however gruesome the crime and despite the strength of the evidence of guilt-automatically ranks as prejudicial ineffective assistance of counsel necessitating a new trial. We reverse the Florida Supreme Court's judgment.

Defense counsel undoubtedly has a duty to discuss potential strategies with the defendant. See *Strickland v. Washington,* 466 U.S. 668, 688, 104 S.Ct. 2052, 80 L.Ed.2d 674 (1984). But when a defendant, informed by counsel, neither consents nor objects to the course counsel describes as the most promising means to avert a sentence of death, counsel is not automatically barred from pursuing that course. The reasonableness of counsel's performance, after consultation with the defendant yields no response, must be judged in accord with the inquiry generally applicable to ineffective-assistance-of-counsel claims: Did counsel's representation "f[a]ll below an objective standard of reasonableness"? *Id.,* at 688, 694, 104 S.Ct. 2052. The Florida Supreme Court erred in applying, instead, a presumption of deficient performance, as well as a presumption of prejudice; that latter presumption, we have instructed, is reserved for cases in which counsel fails meaningfully to oppose the prosecution's case. *United States v. Cronic,* 466 U.S. 648, 659, 104 S.Ct. 2039, 80 L.Ed.2d 657 (1984). A presumption of prejudice is not in order based solely on a defendant's failure to provide express consent to a tenable strategy counsel has adequately disclosed to and discussed with the defendant.

* * *

There are, however, certain decisions a defendant always retains. These include whether to plead guilty, whether to waive the right to a trial by jury, and whether to testify on his or her own behalf. *See* ABA MODEL RULES OF PROFESSIONAL CONDUCT 1.2; see also Erica J. Hashimoto, *Resurrecting Autonomy: The Criminal Defendant's Right to Control the Case*, 90 B.U. L. REV. 1147 (2010). In *Nixon*, supra, defense counsel chose the strategy of conceding guilt without consulting the client. But what if the client tells counsel explicitly that he or she does not want to concede guilt, but the attorney does so anyway? The U.S. Supreme Court is taking up this question in *McCoy v. Louisiana*, No. 16–8255.

Effective Assistance of Counsel in the Plea Bargaining Context

Lafler v. Cooper, 566 U.S. 156 (2012), and *Missouri v. Frye*, 566 U.S. 133 (2012), are two 5–4 opinions authored by Justice Kennedy in companion cases that broadened the application of the right to constitutionally competent counsel in the plea bargaining context. In *Lafler*, the respondent rejected a plea offer because of inaccurate legal advice from his attorney and was convicted at trial and given a much harsher sentence than the sentencing recommendation contemplated in the rejected plea deal. In *Frye*, the respondent was never told about a plea offer extended by the government to his attorney. After that plea offer lapsed, Frye accepted a second, less favorable plea offer leading to a much lengthier term of incarceration than he would have been exposed to under the original plea offer.

Of course, the Sixth Amendment right to effective assistance of counsel already had applied to the guilty plea stage, which is considered a critical stage of criminal proceedings. The Court had long ago applied the *Strickland* standard for assessing ineffective assistance of counsel claims to plea bargaining. The Court, in *Padilla v. Kentucky*, 559 U.S. 356 (2010), reinforced this a couple of years ago when it held that the *Strickland* standard applies to counsel's advice regarding immigration consequences of the guilty plea and resulting criminal conviction. *See also Lee v. United States*, No. 16–327 (erroneous advice leading to mandatory deportation of legal resident).

However, *Lafler* and *Frye* are significant because they make clear that defendants enjoy the right to effective assistance of counsel during the entire plea process—not just at the guilty plea, but throughout the plea negotiation stage as well. The coverage of the Sixth Amendment is extended to situations in which a defendant rejects (or loses the opportunity to accept) a plea offer because of ineffective assistance of counsel.

Just as importantly, the Court acknowledged that "criminal justice today is for the most part a system of pleas, not a system of trials." *Lafler*, 555 U.S. at 170. The decision to plead guilty pursuant to a plea agreement usually makes a tremendous difference in the defendant's exposure to punishment, and the negotiation of such a plea agreement is really the point at which the defendant's need for competent counsel is at its apex.

However, *Lafler* and *Frye* leave open a number of important questions. First, what is ineffective assistance of counsel in the plea bargaining context? *Frye* tells us that failure to communicate a plea offer to the client constitutes deficient performance, and we can assume that inaccurate legal advice inducing a client to reject a plea offer is also deficient performance. But what else is deficient performance? The Court acknowledged that bargaining and negotiation style will vary from lawyer to lawyer. How do we determine when plea bargaining tactics are constitutionally incompetent rather than simply quirky or unorthodox?

Also, how to determine prejudice? The Court made clear that in order to establish *Strickland* prejudice in the context of plea bargaining the defendant must show a reasonable probability not only that he would have accepted the earlier plea offer had he been afforded effective assistance of counsel, but that the prosecution would not have withdrawn or rescinded the plea offer, and that the court would not have rejected the proposed plea agreement. That involves a great deal of speculation and may prove difficult for defendants to establish on the ground.

Finally, what is the remedy? Even where a defendant is able to establish deficient performance on the part of her attorney and prejudice as a result, the question remains what remedy should attach. The Court acknowledged that a number of outcomes might be appropriate, including the lower court exercising discretion not to provide any remedy at all, which, as Justice Scalia argued in dissent, seems an odd position when addressing a constitutional violation.

Constructive Denial of the Right to Effective Assistance of Counsel

Not all denials of the right to effective assistance of counsel are caused by deficient performance on the part of the lawyer. For example, although actual denial of counsel is reversible error, a defendant could be constructively denied effective assistance of counsel if a detention center limits too severely meetings between the lawyer and client or otherwise burdens the attorney-client relationship. *See, e.g., Weatherford v. Bursey*, 429 U.S. 545 (1977); *Geders v. United States*, 425 U.S. 80 (1976). Also, if a defendant has the means to pay for, and desires to hire, a particular qualified lawyer, to deny that choice is reversible error. *See United States v. Gonzalez-Lopez*, 548 U.S. 140 (2006). Finally, burdens on the ability if defense counsel to perform core functions, such as giving a closing argument at trial, has been held to violate the Sixth Amendment. *See, e.g., Herring v. New York*, 422 U.S. 853 (1975); *see also Glebe v. Frost*, 135 S.Ct. 429 (2014).

CHAPTER 10

DEFENDANT'S RIGHT TO SELF-REPRESENTATION AND RIGHT TO BE PRESENT AT PROCEEDINGS

I. DEFENDANT'S RIGHT TO SELF-REPRESENTATION

"In all criminal prosecutions, the accused shall enjoy the right . . . to have the Assistance of Counsel for his defence."

U.S. CONST., amend. VI.

A close reading of the text of the Sixth Amendment quoted above reveals that what the right entails is the *assistance* of counsel. The accused is the principal and her attorney is simply her assistant. So, what happens when the accused does not desire to have the assistance of counsel? Is the right to assistance of counsel one that may be waived, even when doing so will do great damage to the legal interests of the accused? The Supreme Court addresses these questions in the following case:

Faretta v. California
Supreme Court of the United States, 1975
422 U.S. 806

■ MR. JUSTICE STEWART delivered the opinion of the Court.

The Sixth and Fourteenth Amendments of our Constitution guarantee that a person brought to trial in any state or federal court must be afforded the right to the assistance of counsel before he can be validly convicted and punished by imprisonment. This clear constitutional rule has emerged from a series of cases decided here over the last 50 years. The question before us now is whether a defendant in a state criminal trial has a constitutional right to proceed without counsel when he voluntarily and intelligently elects to do so. Stated another way, the question is whether a State may constitutionally hale a person into its criminal courts and there force a lawyer upon him, even when he insists that he wants to conduct his own defense. It is not an easy question, but we have concluded that a State may not constitutionally do so.

I

Anthony Faretta was charged with grand theft in an information filed in the Superior Court of Los Angeles County, Cal. At the arraignment, the Superior Court Judge assigned to preside at the trial appointed the public defender to represent Faretta. Well before the date of trial, however, Faretta requested that he be permitted to represent himself. Questioning by the judge revealed that Faretta had once represented himself in a criminal prosecution, that he had a high school education, and that he did not want to be represented by the public defender because he believed that that office was 'very loaded down with . . . a heavy case load.' The judge responded that he believed Faretta was 'making a mistake' and emphasized that in further proceedings Faretta would receive no special favors. Nevertheless, after establishing that Faretta wanted to represent himself and did not want a lawyer, the judge, in a 'preliminary ruling,' accepted Faretta's waiver of the assistance of counsel. The judge indicated, however, that he might reverse this ruling if it later appeared that Faretta was unable adequately to represent himself.

Several weeks thereafter, but still prior to trial, the judge sua sponte held a hearing to inquire into Faretta's ability to conduct his own defense, and questioned him specifically about both the hearsay rule and the state law governing the challenge of potential jurors. After consideration of Faretta's answers, and observation of his demeanor, the judge ruled that Faretta had not made an intelligent and knowing waiver of his right to the assistance of counsel, and also ruled that Faretta had no constitutional right to conduct his own defense. The judge, accordingly, reversed his earlier ruling permitting self-representation and again appointed the public defender to represent Faretta. Faretta's subsequent request for leave to act as co-counsel was rejected, as were his efforts to make certain motions on his own behalf. Throughout the subsequent trial, the judge required that Faretta's defense be conducted only through the appointed lawyer from the public defender's office. At the conclusion of the trial, the jury found Faretta guilty as charged, and the judge sentenced him to prison.

The California Court of Appeal, relying upon a then-recent California Supreme Court decision that had expressly decided the issue, affirmed the trial judge's ruling that Faretta had no federal or state constitutional right to represent himself. Accordingly, the appellate court affirmed Faretta's conviction. A petition for rehearing was denied without opinion, and the California Supreme Court denied review. We granted certiorari. 415 U.S. 975, 94 S.Ct. 1559, 39 L.Ed.2d 870.

II

In the federal courts, the right of self-representation has been protected by statute since the beginnings of our Nation. Section 35 of the Judiciary Act of 1789, 1 Stat. 73, 92, enacted by the First Congress and signed by President Washington one day before the Sixth Amendment was proposed, provided that 'in all the courts of the United States, the parties may plead and manage their own causes personally or by the assistance of such counsel . . . .' The right is currently codified in 28 U.S.C. § 1654.

With few exceptions, each of the several States also accords a defendant the right to represent himself in any criminal case. The constitutions of 36 States explicitly confer that right. Moreover, many state courts have expressed the view that the right is also supported by the Constitution of the United States.

This Court has more than once indicated the same view. In *Adams v. United States ex rel. McCann*, 317 U.S. 269, 279, 63 S.Ct. 236, 241, 87 L.Ed. 268, the Court recognized that the Sixth Amendment right to the assistance of counsel implicitly embodies a 'correlative right to dispense with a lawyer's help.' The defendant in that case, indicted for federal mail fraud violations, insisted on conducting his own defense without benefit of counsel. He also requested a bench trial and signed a waiver of his right to trial by jury. The prosecution consented to the waiver of a jury, and the waiver was accepted by the court. The defendant was convicted, but the Court of Appeals reversed the conviction on the ground that a person accused of a felony could not competently waive his right to trial by jury except upon the advice of a lawyer. This Court reversed and reinstated the conviction, holding that 'an accused, in the exercise of a free and intelligent choice, and with the considered approval of the court, may waive trial by jury, and so likewise may he competently and intelligently waive his Constitutional right to assistance of counsel.' Id., at 275, 63 S.Ct., at 240.

The Adams case does not, of course, necessarily resolve the issue before us. It held only that 'the Constitution does not force a lawyer upon a defendant.' Id., at 279, 63 S.Ct., at 242. Whether the Constitution forbids a State from forcing a lawyer upon a defendant is a different question. But the Court in Adams did recognize, albeit in dictum, an affirmative right of self-representation:

'The right to assistance of counsel and the correlative right to dispense with a lawyer's help are not legal formalisms. They rest on considerations that go to the substance of an accused's position before the law. . . .

'. . . What were contrived as protections for the accused should not be turned into fetters. . . . To deny an accused a choice of procedure in circumstances in which he, though a layman, is as capable as any lawyer of making an intelligent choice, is to impair the worth of great Constitutional safeguards by treating them as empty verbalisms.

'. . . When the administration of the criminal law . . . is hedged about as it is by the Constitutional safeguards for the protection of an accused, to deny him in the exercise of his free choice the right to dispense with some of these safeguards . . . is to imprison a man in his privileges and call it the Constitution.' Id., at 279–280, 63 S.Ct., at 241–242. (emphasis added).

In other settings as well, the Court has indicated that a defendant has a constitutionally protected right to represent himself in a criminal trial. For example, in *Snyder v. Massachusetts*, 291 U.S. 97, 54 S.Ct. 330, 78 L.Ed. 674, the Court held that the Confrontation Clause of the Sixth Amendment gives the accused a right to be present at all stages of the proceedings where fundamental fairness might be thwarted by his absence. This right to 'presence' was based upon the premise that the 'defense may be made easier if the accused is permitted to be present at the examination of jurors or the summing up of counsel, for it will be in his power, if present, to give advice or suggestion or even to supersede his lawyers altogether and conduct the trial himself.' Id., at 106, 54 S.Ct., at 332 (emphasis added). And in *Price v. Johnston*, 334 U.S. 266, 68 S.Ct. 1049, 92 L.Ed. 1356, the Court, in holding that a convicted person had no absolute right to argue his own appeal, said this holding was in 'sharp contrast' to his 'recognized privilege of conducting his own defense at the trial.' Id., at 285, 68 S.Ct., at 1060.

The United States Court of Appeals have repeatedly held that the right of self-representation is protected by the Bill of Rights. In *United States v. Plattner*, 330 F.2d 271, the Court of Appeals for the Second Circuit emphasized that the Sixth Amendment grants the accused the rights of confrontation, of compulsory process for witnesses in his favor, and of assistance of counsel as minimum procedural requirements in federal criminal prosecutions. The right to the assistance of counsel, the court concluded, was intended to supplement the other rights of the defendant, and not to impair 'the absolute and primary right to conduct one's own defense in propria persona.' Id., at 274. The court found support for its decision in the language of the 1789 federal statute; in the statutes and rules governing criminal procedure, see 28 U.S.C. § 1654, and Fed.Rule Crim.Proc. 44; in the many state constitutions that expressly guarantee self representations and in this Court's recognition of the right in Adams and Price. On these grounds, the Court of Appeals held that implicit in the Fifth Amendment's guarantee of due process of law, and implicit also in the Sixth Amendment's guarantee of a right to the assistance of counsel, is 'the right of the accused personally to manage and conduct his own defense in a criminal case.' 330 F.2d, at 274. See also *United States ex rel. Maldonado v. Denno*, 348 F.2d 12, 15 (CA2); *MacKenna v. Ellis*, 263 F.2d 35, 41 (CA5); *United States v. Sternman*, 415 F.2d 1165, 1169–1170 (CA6); *Lowe v. United States*, 418 F.2d 100, 103 (CA7); *United States v. Warner*, 428 F.2d 730, 733 (CA8); *Haslam v. United States*, 431 F.2d 362, 365 (CA9); compare *United States v. Dougherty*, 154 U.S.App.D.C. 76, 86, 473 F.2d 1113, 1123 (intimating right is constitutional but finding it unnecessary to reach issue) with *Brown v. United States*, 105 U.S.App.D.C. 77, 79–80, 264 F.2d 363, 365–366 (plurality opinion stating right is no more than statutory in nature).

This Court's past recognition of the right of self-representation, the federal-court authority holding the right to be of constitutional dimension, and the state constitutions pointing to the right's fundamental nature form a consensus not easily ignored. '(T)he mere fact that a path is a beaten one,' Mr. Justice Jackson once observed, 'is a persuasive reason for following it.' We confront here a nearly universal conviction, on the part of our people as well as our courts, that forcing a lawyer upon an unwilling defendant is contrary to his basic right to defend himself if he truly wants to do so.

III

This consensus is soundly premised. The right of self-representation finds support in the structure of the Sixth Amendment, as well as in the English and colonial jurisprudence from which the Amendment emerged.

A

The Sixth Amendment includes a compact statement of the rights necessary to a full defense:

'In all criminal prosecutions, the accused shall enjoy the right . . . to be informed of the nature and cause of the accusation; to be confronted with the witnesses against him; to have compulsory process for obtaining witnesses in his favor, and to have the Assistance of Counsel for his defence.'

Because these rights are basic to our adversary system of criminal justice, they are part of the 'due process of law' that is guaranteed by the Fourteenth Amendment to defendants in the criminal courts of the States. The rights to notice, confrontation, and compulsory process, when taken together, guarantee that a criminal charge may be answered in a manner now considered fundamental to the fair administration of American justice—through the calling and interrogation of favorable witnesses, the cross-examination of adverse witnesses, and the orderly introduction of evidence. In short, the

Amendment constitutionalizes the right in an adversary criminal trial to make a defense as we know it. See *California v. Green*, 399 U.S. 149, 176, 90 S.Ct. 1930, 1944, 26 L.Ed.2d 489 (Harlan, J., concurring).

The Sixth Amendment does not provide merely that a defense shall be made for the accused; it grants to the accused personally the right to make his defense. It is the accused, not counsel, who must be 'informed of the nature and cause of the accusation,' who must be 'confronted with the witnesses against him,' and who must be accorded 'compulsory process for obtaining witnesses in his favor.' Although not stated in the Amendment in so many words, the right to self-representation—to make one's own defense personally—is thus necessarily implied by the structure of the Amendment. The right to defend is given directly to the accused; for it is he who suffers the consequences if the defense fails.

The counsel provision supplements this design. It speaks of the 'assistance' of counsel, and an assistant, however expert, is still an assistant. The language and spirit of the Sixth Amendment contemplate that counsel, like the other defense tools guaranteed by the Amendment, shall be an aid to a willing defendant—not an organ of the State interposed between an unwilling defendant and his right to defend himself personally. To thrust counsel upon the accused, against his considered wish, thus violates the logic of the Amendment. In such a case, counsel is not an assistant, but a master; and the right to make a defense is stripped of the personal character upon which the Amendment insists. It is true that when a defendant chooses to have a lawyer manage and present his case, law and tradition may allocate to the counsel the power to make binding decisions of trial strategy in many areas. Cf. *Henry v. Mississippi*, 379 U.S. 443, 451, 85 S.Ct. 564, 569, 13 L.Ed.2d 408; *Brookhart v. Janis*, 384 U.S. 1, 7–8, 86 S.Ct. 1245, 1248–1249, 16 L.Ed.2d 314; *Fay v. Noia*, 372 U.S. 391, 439, 83 S.Ct. 822, 849, 9 L.Ed.2d 837. This allocation can only be justified, however, by the defendant's consent, at the outset, to accept counsel as his representative. An unwanted counsel 'represents' the defendant only through a tenuous and unacceptable legal fiction. Unless the accused has acquiesced in such representation, the defense presented is not the defense guaranteed him by the Constitution, for, in a very real sense, it is not his defense.

B

The Sixth Amendment, when naturally read, thus implies a right of self-representation. This reading is reinforced by the Amendment's roots in English legal history.

In the long history of British criminal jurisprudence, there was only one tribunal that ever adopted a practice of forcing counsel upon an unwilling defendant in a criminal proceeding. The tribunal was the Star

Chamber. That curious institution, which flourished in the late 16th and early 17th centuries, was of mixed executive and judicial character, and characteristically departed from common-law traditions. For those reasons, and because it specialized in trying 'political' defenses, the Star Chamber has for centuries symbolized disregard of basic individual rights. The Star Chamber not merely allowed but required defendants to have counsel. The defendant's answer to an indictment was not accepted unless it was signed by counsel. When counsel refused to sign the answer, for whatever reason, the defendant was considered to have confessed. Stephen commented on this procedure: 'There is something specially repugnant to justice in using rules of practice in such a manner as to debar a prisoner from defending himself, especially when the professed object of the rules so used is to provide for his defence.' 1 J. Stephen, A History of the Criminal Law of England 341–342 (1883). The Star Chamber was swept away in 1641 by the revolutionary fervor of the Long Parliament. The notion of obligatory counsel disappeared with it.

By the common law of that time, it was not representation by counsel but self-representation that was the practice in prosecutions for serious crime. At one time, every litigant was required to 'appear before the court in his own person and conduct his own cause in his own words.' While a right to counsel developed early in civil cases and in cases of misdemeanor, a prohibition against the assistance of counsel continued for centuries in prosecutions for felony or treason. Thus, in the 16th and 17th centuries the accused felon or traitor stood alone, with neither counsel nor the benefit of other rights—to notice, confrontation, and compulsory process—that we now associate with a genuinely fair adversary proceeding. The trial was merely a 'long argument between the prisoner and the counsel for the Crown.' As harsh as this now seems, at least 'the prisoner was allowed to make what statements he liked. . . . Obviously this public oral trial presented many more opportunities to a prisoner than the secret enquiry based on written depositions, which, on the continent, had taken the place of a trial. . . .'

With the Treason Act of 1695, there began a long and important era of reform in English criminal procedure. The 1695 statute granted to the accused traitor the rights to a copy of the indictment, to have his witnesses testify under oath, and 'to make . . . full Defence, by Counsel learned in the Law.' It also provided for court appointment of counsel, but only if the accused so desired. Thus, as new rights developed, the accused retained his established right 'to make what statements he liked.' The right to counsel was viewed as guaranteeing a choice between representation by counsel and the traditional practice of self-representation. The ban on counsel in felony cases, which had been substantially eroded in the courts, was finally eliminated by statute in

1836. In more recent years, Parliament has provided for court appointment of counsel in serious criminal cases, but only at the accused's request. At no point in this process of reform in England was counsel ever forced upon the defendant. The common-law rule, succinctly stated in *R. v. Woodward,* (1944) K.B. 118, 119 (1944) 1 All E.R. 159, 160, has evidently always been that 'no person charged with a criminal offence can have counsel forced upon him against his will.' See 3 Halsbury's Laws of England 1141, pp. 624–625 (4th ed. 1973); *R. v. Maybury*, 11 L.T.R.(n.s.) 566 (Q.B.1865).

In the American Colonies the insistence upon a right of self-representation was, if anything, more fervent than in England.

The colonists brought with them an appreciation of the virtues of self-reliance and a traditional distrust of law-years. When the Colonies were first settled, 'the lawyer was synonymous with the cringing Attorneys-General and Solicitors-General of the Crown and the arbitrary Justices of the King's Court, all bent on the conviction of those who opposed the King's prerogatives, and twisting the law to secure convictions.' This prejudice gained strength in the Colonies where 'distrust of lawyers became an institution.' Several Colonies prohibited pleading for hire in the 17th century. The prejudice persisted into the 18th century as 'the lower classes came to identify lawyers with the upper class.' The years of Revolution and Confederation saw an upsurge of antilawyer sentiment, a 'sudden revival, after the War of the Revolution, of the old dislike and distrust of lawyers as a class.' In the heat of these sentiments the Constitution was forged.

This is not to say that the Colonies were slow to recognize the value of counsel in criminal cases. Colonial judges soon departed from ancient English practice and allowed accused felons the aid of counsel for their defense. At the same time, however, the basic right of self-representation was never questioned. We have found no instance where a colonial court required a defendant in a criminal case to accept as his representative an unwanted lawyer. Indeed, even where counsel was permitted, the general practice continued to be self-representation.

The right of self-representation was guaranteed in many colonial charters and declarations of rights. These early documents establish that the 'right to counsel' meant to the colonists a right to choose between pleading through a lawyer and representing oneself. After the Declaration of Independence, the right of self-representation, along with other rights basic to the making of a defense, entered the new state constitutions in wholesale fashion. The right to counsel was clearly thought to supplement the primary right of the accused to defend himself, utilizing his personal rights to notice, confrontation, and compulsory process. And when the Colonies or newly independent States provided by statute rather than by constitution for court appointment of counsel in criminal cases, they also meticulously preserved the right of the accused to defend himself personally.

The recognition of the right of self-representation was not limited to the state lawmakers. As we have noted, § 35 of the Judiciary Act of 1789, signed one day before the Sixth Amendment was proposed, guaranteed in the federal courts the right of all parties to 'plead and manage their own causes personally or by the assistance of . . . counsel.' 1 Stat. 92. See 28 U.S.C. § 1654. At the time James Madison drafted the Sixth Amendment, some state constitutions guaranteed an accused the right to be heard 'by himself' and by counsel; others provided that an accused was to be 'allowed' counsel. The various state proposals for the Bill of Rights had similar variations in terminology. In each case, however, the counsel provision was embedded in a package of defense rights granted personally to the accused. There is no indication that the differences in phrasing about 'counsel' reflected any differences of principle about self-representation. No State or Colony had ever forced counsel upon an accused; no spokesman had ever suggested that such a practice would be tolerable, much less advisable. If anyone had thought that the Sixth Amendment, as drafted, failed to protect the long-respected right of self-representation, there would undoubtedly have been some debate or comment on the issue. But there was none.

In sum, there is no evidence that the colonists and the Framers ever doubted the right of self-representation, or imagined that this right might be considered inferior to the right of assistance of counsel. To the contrary, the colonists and the Framers, as well as their English ancestors, always conceived of the right to counsel as an 'assistance' for the accused, to be used at his option, in defending himself. The Framers selected in the Sixth Amendment a form of words that necessarily implies the right of self-representation. That conclusion is supported by centuries of consistent history.

IV

There can be no blinking the fact that the right of an accused to conduct his own defense seems to cut against the grain of this Court's decisions holding that the Constitution requires that no accused can be convicted and imprisoned unless he has been accorded the right to the assistance of counsel. See *Powell v. Alabama*, 287 U.S. 45, 53 S.Ct. 55, 77 L.Ed. 158; *Johnson v. Zerbst*, 304 U.S. 458, 58 S.Ct. 1019, 82 L.Ed. 1461; *Gideon v. Wainwright*, 372 U.S. 335, 83 S.Ct. 792, 9 L.Ed.2d 799; *Argersinger v. Hamlin*, 407 U.S. 25, 92 S.Ct. 2006, 32 L.Ed.2d 530. For it is surely true that the basic thesis of those decisions is that the help of a lawyer is essential to assure the defendant a fair trial. And a strong argument can surely be made that the whole thrust of those decisions must inevitably lead to the conclusion that a State may constitutionally impose a lawyer upon even an unwilling defendant.

But it is one thing to hold that every defendant, rich or poor, has the right to the assistance of counsel, and quite another to say that a State may compel a defendant to accept a lawyer he does not want. The value of state-appointed counsel was not unappreciated by the Founders, yet the notion of compulsory counsel was utterly foreign to them. And whatever else may be said of those who wrote the Bill of Rights, surely there can be no doubt that they understood the inestimable worth of free choice.

It is undeniable that in most criminal prosecutions defendants could better defend with counsel's guidance than by their own unskilled efforts. But where the defendant will not voluntarily accept representation by counsel, the potential advantage of a lawyer's training and experience can be realized, if at all, only imperfectly. To force a lawyer on a defendant can only lead him to believe that the law contrives against him. Moreover, it is not inconceivable that in some rare instances, the defendant might in fact present his case more effectively by conducting his own defense. Personal liberties are not rooted in the law of averages. The right to defend is personal. The defendant, and not his lawyer or the State, will bear the personal consequences of a conviction. It is the defendant, therefore, who must be free personally to decide whether in his particular case counsel is to his advantage. And although he may conduct his own defense ultimately to his own detriment, his choice must be honored out of 'that respect for the individual which is the lifeblood of the law.' *Illinois v. Allen*, 397 U.S. 337, 350–351, 90 S.Ct. 1057, 1064, 25 L.Ed.2d 353 (Brennan, J., concurring).

V

When an accused manages his own defense, he relinquishes, as a purely factual matter, many of the traditional benefits associated with the right to counsel. For this reason, in order to represent himself, the accused must 'knowingly and intelligently' forgo those relinquished benefits. *Johnson v. Zerbst*, 304 U.S., at 464–465, 58 S.Ct., at 1023. Cf. *Von Moltke v. Gillies*, 332 U.S. 708, 723–724, 68 S.Ct. 316, 323, 92 L.Ed. 309 (plurality opinion of Black, J.). Although a defendant need not himself have the skill and experience of a lawyer in order competently and intelligently to choose self-representation, he should be made aware of the dangers and disadvantages of self-representation, so that the record will establish that 'he knows what he is doing and his choice is made with eyes open.' *Adams v. United States ex rel. McCann*, 317 U.S., at 279, 63 S.Ct., at 242.

Here, weeks before trial, Faretta clearly and unequivocally declared to the trial judge that he wanted to represent himself and did not want counsel. The record affirmatively shows that Faretta was literate, competent, and understanding, and that he was voluntarily exercising his informed free will. The trial judge had warned Faretta that he thought it was a mistake not to accept the assistance of counsel, and that Faretta would be required to follow all the 'ground rules' of trial procedure. We need make no assessment of how well or poorly Faretta had mastered the intricacies of the hearsay rule and the California code provisions that govern challenges of potential jurors on voir dire. For his technical legal knowledge, as such, was not relevant to an assessment of his knowing exercise of the right to defend himself.

In forcing Faretta, under these circumstances, to accept against his will a state-appointed public defender, the California courts deprived him of his constitutional right to conduct his own defense. Accordingly, the judgment before us is vacated, and the case is remanded for further proceedings not inconsistent with this opinion.

It is so ordered.

Judgment vacated and case remanded.

The Right to Represent One's Own Self

The right to represent one's own self was first codified in the Judiciary Act of 1789. Today, it can be found at Title 28, United States Code, section 1654: "In all courts of the United States the parties may plead and conduct their own cases personally or by counsel as, by the rules of such courts, respectively, are permitted to manage and conduct causes therein." However, the Supreme Court has recognized the ability of states to place limits on the ability of defendants to proceed *pro se* at trial if they lack mental competency to do so—even if the defendant has been declared competent to stand trial. *See Indiana v. Edwards*, 554 U.S. 164 (2008); *see also Dusky v. United States*, 362 U.S. 402 (1960) (standard for competency to stand trial). For some views on legal and policy limits on self-representation, *see, e.g.,* Max S. Meckstroth, *The Case Against Self-Representation in Capital Proceedings*, 99 MINN. L. REV. 1935 (2015); William L. Nichol, *Criminal Law-Mental Competence and the Right to Self-Representation*, 78 MISS. L.J. 227 (2008).

In addition, there are other limits on the right. The court may deny the right if the *pro se* defendant is disruptive to the proceeding, refuses to respect the decorum of the courtroom, or poses a significant threat to witnesses on cross-examination (such as a young complaining witness in a sexual abuse prosecution). The court can also appoint standby counsel to replace a *pro se* defendant, *see Faretta, supra* at 834 n.46; *McKaskle v. Wiggins*, 465 U.S 168 (1984), and has discretion to appoint hybrid counsel to assist the *pro se* defendant. *See McKaskle*, 465 U.S. at 177–78. Interestingly, although a defendant has a right to represent herself at trial, she has no right to *pro se* representation on appeal. *See*

Martinez v. Court of Appeal of California, Fourth Appellate Dist., 528 U.S. 152 (2000). Why? Can you think of an extra-constitutional reason?

Model Colloquy for Faretta *Warning*

The following excerpt from the Benchbook for United States District Court Judges provides a flavor for how the *Faretta* colloquy often proceeds:

1.   Have you ever studied law?

2.   Have you ever represented yourself in a criminal action?

3.   Do you understand that you are charged with these crimes:

[state the crimes with which the defendant is charged]?

4.   Do you understand that if you are found guilty of the crime charged in Count I, the court must impose a special assessment of $100 and could sentence you to as many as ___ years in prison, impose a term of supervised release that follows imprisonment, fine you as much as $___, and direct you to pay restitution?

[Ask the defendant a similar question for each crime charged in the indictment or information.]

5.   Do you understand that if you are found guilty of more than one of these crimes, this court can order that the sentences be served consecutively, that is, one after another?

6.   Do you understand that there are advisory Sentencing Guidelines that may have an effect on your sentence if you are found guilty?

7.   Do you understand that if you represent yourself, you are on your own? I cannot tell you or even advise you how you should try your case.

8.   Are you familiar with the Federal Rules of Evidence?

9.   Do you understand that the rules of evidence govern what evidence may or may not be introduced at trial, that in representing yourself, you must abide by those very technical rules, and that they will not be relaxed for your benefit?

10. Are you familiar with the Federal Rules of Criminal Procedure?

11. Do you understand that those rules govern the way a criminal action is tried in federal court, that you are bound by those rules, and that they will not be relaxed for your benefit?

[Then say to the defendant something to this effect:]

12. I must advise you that in my opinion, a trained lawyer would defend you far better than you could defend yourself. I think it is unwise of you to try to represent yourself. You are not familiar with the law. You are not familiar with court procedure.

You are not familiar with the rules of evidence. I strongly urge you not to try to represent yourself.

13. Now, in light of the penalty that you might suffer if you are found guilty, and in light of all of the difficulties of representing yourself, do you still desire to represent yourself and to give up your right to be represented by a lawyer?

14. Is your decision entirely voluntary?

[If the answers to the two preceding questions are yes, say something to the following effect:]

15. I find that the defendant has knowingly and voluntarily waived the right to counsel. I will therefore permit the defendant to represent himself [herself].

BENCHBOOK FOR U.S. DISTRICT COURT JUDGES (March 2013) (Section 1.02: Assignment of counsel or pro se representation).

COUNSEL EXERCISE 10A: Pro Se Motion
(Prosecution)

Assume for purposes of this exercise that the defendant is asking the court's permission to represent himself or herself at his or her upcoming trial. The government should draft a memorandum of law in opposition to the defendant's motion. Defense counsel should draft a memorandum of law to support the opposition to the *pro se* motion.

* * *

II. DEFENDANT'S RIGHT TO BE PRESENT AT PROCEEDINGS

Given the defendant's right to a fair, speedy, and public trial, it should not be surprising that he or she also has the right to be present for the proceedings. Rule 43 of the Federal Rules of Criminal Procedure provides detailed guidance regarding how the defendant's right to be present is balanced against other important considerations—including the security of the courtroom and the decorum of the proceedings.

A. RULE 43—DEFENDANT'S PRESENCE

Rule 43. Defendant's Presence

(a) When Required. Unless this rule, Rule 5, or Rule 10 provides otherwise, the defendant must be present at:

    (1) the initial appearance, the initial arraignment, and the plea;

    (2) every trial stage, including jury impanelment and the return of the verdict; and

    (3) sentencing.

(b) When Not Required. A defendant need not be present under any of the following circumstances:

    (1) Organizational Defendant. The defendant is an organization represented by counsel who is present.

    (2) Misdemeanor Offense. The offense is punishable by fine or by imprisonment for not more than one year, or both, and with the defendant's written consent, the court permits arraignment, plea, trial, and sentencing to occur by video teleconferencing or in the defendant's absence.

    (3) Conference or Hearing on a Legal Question. The proceeding involves only a conference or hearing on a question of law.

    (4) Sentence Correction. The proceeding involves the correction or reduction of sentence under Rule 35 or 18 U.S.C. § 3582 (c).

(c) Waiving Continued Presence.

    (1) In General. A defendant who was initially present at trial, or who had pleaded guilty or nolo contendere, waives the right to be present under the following circumstances:

        (A) when the defendant is voluntarily absent after the trial has begun, regardless of whether the court informed the defendant of an obligation to remain during trial;

        (B) in a noncapital case, when the defendant is voluntarily absent during sentencing; or

        (C) when the court warns the defendant that it will remove the defendant from the courtroom for disruptive behavior, but the defendant persists in conduct that justifies removal from the courtroom.

(2) Waiver's Effect. If the defendant waives the right to be present, the trial may proceed to completion, including the verdict's return and sentencing, during the defendant's absence.

B. WAIVER OF THE RIGHT TO BE PRESENT

As you see in FED. R. CRIM. P. 43(c)(1)(A), "the trial may proceed to completion" in absentia if "the defendant is voluntarily absent after trial has begun." *Id.* But what happens when a defendant is present but is so disruptive to the proceedings that he or she must be removed? In *Illinois v. Allen*, 397 U.S. 335 (1970), the Court explored the question of when a defendant has waived the right to be present and what constitutionally permissible methods are available to a court in dealing with disruptive defendants.

Illinois v. Allen

Supreme Court of the United States, 1970
397 U.S. 337

■ MR. JUSTICE BLACK delivered the opinion of the Court.

The Confrontation Clause of the Sixth Amendment to the United States Constitution provides that: 'In all criminal prosecutions, the accused shall enjoy the right * * * to be confronted with the witnesses against him * * *.' We have held that the Fourteenth Amendment makes the guarantees of this clause obligatory upon the States. *Pointer v. Texas*, 380 U.S. 400, 85 S.Ct. 1065, 13 L.Ed.2d 923 (1965). One of the most basic of the rights guaranteed by the Confrontation Clause is the accused's right to be present in the courtroom at every stage of his trial. *Lewis v. United States*, 146 U.S. 370, 13 S.Ct. 136, 36 L.Ed. 1011 (1892). The question presented in this case is whether an accused can claim the benefit of this constitutional right to remain in the courtroom while at the same time he engages in speech and conduct which is so noisy, disorderly, and disruptive that it is exceedingly difficult or wholly impossible to carry on the trial.

The issue arose in the following way. The respondent, Allen, was convicted by an Illinois jury of armed robbery and was sentenced to serve 10 to 30 years in the Illinois State Penitentiary. The evidence against him showed that on August 12, 1956, he entered a tavern in Illinois and, after ordering a drink, took $200 from the bartender at gunpoint. The Supreme Court of Illinois affirmed his conviction, *People v. Allen*, 37 Ill.2d 167, 226 N.E.2d 1 (1967), and this Court denied certiorari. 389 U.S. 907, 88 S.Ct. 226, 19 L.Ed.2d 225 (1967). Later Allen filed a petition for a writ of habeas corpus in federal court alleging that he had been wrongfully deprived by the Illinois trial judge of his constitutional right to remain present throughout his trial. Finding no constitutional violation, the District Court declined to issue the writ. The Court of Appeals reversed, 413 F.2d 232 (1969), Judge Hastings dissenting.

The facts surrounding Allen's expulsion from the courtroom are set out in the Court of Appeals' opinion sustaining Allen's contention:

> 'After his indictment and during the pretrial stage, the petitioner (Allen) refused court-appointed counsel and indicated to the trial court on several occasions that he wished to conduct his own defense. After considerable argument by the petitioner, the trial judge told him, 'I'll let you be your own lawyer, but I'll ask Mr. Kelly (court-appointed counsel) (to) sit in and protect the record for you, insofar as possible.'

> 'The trial began on September 9, 1957. After the State's Attorney had accepted the first four jurors following their voir dire examination, the petitioner began examining the first juror and continued at great length. Finally, the trial judge interrupted the petitioner, requesting him to confine his questions solely to matters relating to the prospective juror's qualifications. At that point, the petitioner started to argue with the judge in a most abusive and disrespectful manner. At last, and seemingly in desperation, the judge asked appointed counsel to proceed with the examination of the jurors. The petitioner continued to talk, proclaiming that the appointed attorney was not going to act as his lawyer. He terminated his remarks by saying, 'When I go out for lunchtime, you're (the judge) going to be a corpse here.' At that point he tore the file which his attorney had and threw the papers on the floor. The trial judge thereupon stated to the petitioner, 'One more outbreak of that sort and I'll remove you from the courtroom.' This warning had no effect on the petitioner. He continued to talk back to the judge, saying, 'There's not going to be no trial, either. I'm going to sit here and you're going to talk and you can bring your shackles out and straight jacket and put them on me and tape my mouth, but it will do no good because there's not going to be no trial.' After more abusive remarks by the petitioner, the trial judge ordered the trial to proceed in the petitioner's absence. The petitioner was removed from the courtroom. The voir dire examination then continued and the jury was selected in the absence of the petitioner.

> 'After a noon recess and before the jury was brought into the courtroom, the petitioner, appearing before the judge, complained about the fairness of the trial and his appointed attorney. He also said he wanted to be present in the court

during his trial. In reply, the judge said that the petitioner would be permitted to remain in the courtroom if he 'behaved (himself) and (did) not interfere with the introduction of the case.' The jury was brought in and seated. Counsel for the petitioner then moved to exclude the witnesses from the courtroom. The (petitioner) protested this effort on the part of his attorney, saying: 'There is going to be no proceeding. I'm going to start talking and I'm going to keep on talking all through the trial. There's not going to be no trial like this. I want my sister and my friends here in court to testify for me.' The trial judge thereupon ordered the petitioner removed from the courtroom.' 413 F.2d, at 233–234.

After this second removal, Allen remained out of the courtroom during the presentation of the State's case-in-chief, except that he was brought in on several occasions for purposes of identification. During one of these latter appearances, Allen responded to one of the judge's questions with vile and abusive language. After the prosecution's case had been presented, the trial judge reiterated his promise to Allen that he could return to the courtroom whenever he agreed to conduct himself properly. Allen gave some assurances of proper conduct and was permitted to be present through the remainder of the trial, principally his defense, which was conducted by his appointed counsel.

The Court of Appeals went on to hold that the Supreme Court of Illinois was wrong in ruling that Allen had by his conduct relinquished his constitutional right to be present, declaring that:

> 'No conditions may be imposed on the absolute right of a criminal defendant to be present at all stages of the proceeding. The insistence of a defendant that he exercise this right under unreasonable conditions does not amount to a waiver. Such conditions, if insisted upon, should and must be dealt with in a manner that does not compel the relinquishment of his right.

> 'In light of the decision in *Hopt v. Utah*, 110 U.S. 574, 4 S.Ct. 202, 28 L.Ed. 262 (1884) and *Shields v. United States*, 273 U.S. 583, 47 S.Ct. 478, 71 L.Ed. 787 (1927), as well as the constitutional mandate of the sixth amendment, we are of the view that the defendant should not have been excluded from the courtroom during his trial despite his disruptive and disrespectful conduct. The proper course for the trial judge was to have restrained the defendant by whatever means necessary, even if those means included his being shackled and gagged.' 413 F.2d at 235.

The Court of Appeals felt that the defendant's Sixth Amendment right to be present at his own trial was so 'absolute' that, no matter how unruly or disruptive the defendant's conduct might be, he could never be held to have lost that right so long as he continued to insist upon it, as Allen clearly did. Therefore the Court of Appeals concluded that a trial judge could never expel a defendant from his own trial and that the judge's ultimate remedy when faced with an obstreperous defendant like Allen who determines to make his trial impossible is to bind and gag him. We cannot agree that the Sixth Amendment, the cases upon which the Court of Appeals relied, or any other cases of this Court so handicap a trial judge in conducting a criminal trial. The broad dicta in *Hopt v. Utah*, supra, and *Lewis v. United States*, 146 U.S. 370, 13 S.Ct. 136, 36 L.Ed. 1011 (1892), that a trial can never continue in the defendant's absence have been expressly rejected. *Diaz v. United States*, 223 U.S. 442, 32 S.Ct. 250, 56 L.Ed. 500 (1912). We accept instead the statement of Mr. Justice Cardozo who, speaking for the Court in *Snyder v. Massachusetts*, 291 U.S. 97, 106, 54 S.Ct. 330, 332, 78 L.Ed. 674 (1934), said: 'No doubt the privilege (of personally confronting witnesses) may be lost by consent or at times even by misconduct.' Although mindful that courts must indulge every reasonable presumption against the loss of constitutional rights, *Johnson v. Zerbst*, 304 U.S. 458, 464, 58 S.Ct. 1019, 1023, 82 L.Ed. 1461 (1938), we explicitly hold today that a defendant can lose his right to be present at trial if, after he has been warned by the judge that he will be removed if he continues his disruptive behavior, he nevertheless insists on conducting himself in a manner so disorderly, disruptive, and disrespectful of the court that his trial cannot be carried on with him in the courtroom. Once lost, the right to be present can, of course, be reclaimed as soon as the defendant is willing to conduct himself consistently with the decorum and respect inherent in the concept of courts and judicial proceedings.

It is essential to the proper administration of criminal justice that dignity, order, and decorum be the hallmarks of all court proceedings in our country. The flagrant disregard in the courtroom of elementary standards of proper conduct should not and cannot be tolerated. We believe trial judges confronted with disruptive, contumacious, stubbornly defiant defendants must be given sufficient discretion to meet the circumstances of each case. No one formula for maintaining the appropriate courtroom atmosphere will be best in all situations. We think there are at least three constitutionally permissible ways for a trial judge to handle an obstreperous defendant like Allen: (1) bind and gag him, thereby keeping him present; (2) cite him for contempt; (3) take him out of the courtroom until he promises to conduct himself properly.

I

Trying a defendant for a crime while he sits bound and gagged before the judge and jury would to an extent comply with that part of the Sixth Amendment's purposes that accords the defendant an opportunity to confront the witnesses at the trial. But even to contemplate such a technique, much less see it, arouses a feeling that no person should be tried while shackled and gagged except as a last resort. Not only is it possible that the sight of shackles and gags might have a significant effect on the jury's feelings about the defendant, but the use of this technique is itself something of an affront to the very dignity and decorum of judicial proceedings that the judge is seeking to uphold. Moreover, one of the defendant's primary advantages of being present at the trial, his ability to communicate with his counsel, is greatly reduced when the defendant is in a condition of total physical restraint. It is in part because of these inherent disadvantages and limitations in this method of dealing with disorderly defendants that we decline to hold with the Court of Appeals that a defendant cannot under any possible circumstances be deprived of his right to be present at trial. However, in some situations which we need not attempt to foresee, binding and gagging might possibly be the fairest and most reasonable way to handle a defendant who acts as Allen did here.

II

In a footnote the Court of Appeals suggested the possible availability of contempt of court as a remedy to make Allen behave in his robbery trial, and it is true that citing or threatening to cite a contumacious defendant for criminal contempt might in itself be sufficient to make a defendant stop interrupting a trial. If so, the problem would be solved easily, and the defendant could remain in the courtroom. Of course, if the defendant is determined to prevent any trial, then a court in attempting to try the defendant for contempt is still confronted with the identical dilemma that the Illinois court faced in this case. And criminal contempt has obvious limitations as a sanction when the defendant is charged with a crime so serious that a very severe sentence such as death or life imprisonment is likely to be imposed. In such a case the defendant might not be affected by a mere contempt sentence when he ultimately faces a far more serious sanction. Nevertheless, the contempt remedy should be borne in mind by a judge in the circumstances of this case.

Another aspect of the contempt remedy is the judge's power, when exercised consistently with state and federal law, to imprison an unruly defendant such as Allen for civil contempt and discontinue the trial until such time as the defendant promises to behave himself. This procedure is consistent with the defendant's right to be present at trial, and yet it avoids the serious shortcomings of the use of shackles and gags. It must be recognized, however, that a defendant might conceivably, as a matter of calculated strategy, elect to spend a prolonged period in confinement for contempt in the hope that adverse witnesses might be unavailable after a lapse of time. A court must guard against allowing a defendant to profit from his own wrong in this way.

III

The trial court in this case decided under the circumstances to remove the defendant from the courtroom and to continue his trial in his absence until and unless he promised to conduct himself in a manner befitting an American courtroom. As we said earlier, we find nothing unconstitutional about this procedure. Allen's behavior was clearly of such an extreme and aggravated nature as to justify either his removal from the courtroom or his total physical restraint. Prior to his removal he was repeatedly warned by the trial judge that he would be removed from the courtroom if he persisted in his unruly conduct, and, as Judge Hastings observed in his dissenting opinion, the record demonstrates that Allen would not have been at all dissuaded by the trial judge's use of his criminal contempt powers. Allen was constantly informed that he could return to the trial when he would agree to conduct himself in an orderly manner. Under these circumstances we hold that Allen lost his right guaranteed by the Sixth and Fourteenth Amendments to be present throughout his trial.

IV

It is not pleasant to hold that the respondent Allen was properly banished from the court for a part of his own trial. But our courts, palladiums of liberty as they are, cannot be treated disrespectfully with impunity. Nor can the accused be permitted by his disruptive conduct indefinitely to avoid being tried on the charges brought against him. It would degrade our country and our judicial system to permit our courts to be bullied, insulted, and humiliated and their orderly progress thwarted and obstructed by defendants brought before them charged with crimes. As guardians of the public welfare, our state and federal judicial systems strive to administer equal justice to the rich and the poor, the good and the bad, the native and foreign born of every race, nationality, and religion. Being manned by humans, the courts are not perfect and are bound to make some errors. But, if our courts are to remain what the Founders intended, the citadels of justice, their proceedings cannot and must not be infected with the sort of scurrilous, abusive language and conduct paraded before the Illinois trial judge in this case. The record shows that the Illinois judge at all times conducted himself with that dignity, decorum, and patience that befit a judge. Even in holding that the trial judge had erred, the Court of Appeals praised his 'commendable patience under severe provocation.'

We do not hold that removing this defendant from his own trial was the only way the Illinois judge could have constitutionally solved the problem he had. We do hold, however, that there is nothing whatever in this record to show that the judge did not act completely within his discretion. Deplorable as it is to remove a man from his own trial, even for a short time, we hold that the judge did not commit legal error in doing what he did.

The judgment of the Court of Appeals is reversed.

Reversed.

As the *Allen* case demonstrates, although judges are permitted to maintain decorum in their courtrooms, they must show some degree of patience with defendants. This is particularly true if the perceived misbehavior of a defendant relates to the individual's communication with counsel. *See, e.g., United States v. Ward*, 598 F.3d 1054 (8th Cir. 2010) (removal from courtroom for defying judge's order to stop talking to attorney was not harmless error); *see also* Sarah Podmaniczky, *Order in the Court: Decorum, Rambunctious Defendants, and the Right to Be Present at Trial*, 14 U. PA. J. CONST. L. 1283, 1286 (2012).

C. SAFETY AND SECURITY MEASURES

In *Deck v. Missouri*, 544 U.S. 622 (2005), the Supreme Court reaffirmed that courts cannot routinely place defendants in shackles (or other restraints) visible to the jury. *Deck* dealt with the shackling of a capital defendant during the sentencing phase of the trial.

> ### COUNSEL EXERCISE 10B: Proposed Order of Exclusion of Defendant from Proceedings (Defense)
>
> Assume that the defendant's trial is set to begin with jury selection. After the defendant's outbursts during a pretrial hearing, the court is planning to exclude the defendant from further proceedings, but has asked each party to opine on the proposed order before entering it. The defense should draft a memorandum of law in opposition to the proposed order. Included with the motion should be a supporting brief or memorandum of law, a proposed order, and a certificate of service.

COUNSEL EXERCISE 10C: Proposed Order of Exclusion of Defendant from Proceedings (Prosecution)

Assume that the defendant's trial is set to begin with jury selection. After the defendant's outbursts during a pretrial hearing, the court is planning to exclude the defendant from further proceedings, but has asked each party to opine on the proposed order before entering it. The government should draft a memorandum of law either in support of, or in opposition to (your choice), the proposed order. Included with the motion should be a supporting brief or memorandum of law, a proposed order, and a certificate of service.

CHAPTER 11

SPEEDY TRIAL

I. INTRODUCTION

"In all criminal prosecutions, the accused shall enjoy the right to a speedy and public trial."

U.S. CONST., amend. VI.

There are significant burdens visited upon someone who is accused of a criminal offense. The psychological burden of having one's legal status in limbo and the stigma associated with being prosecuted can be significant. For those defendants who suffer a pretrial restraint on liberty, there are many difficulties associated with such detention, including a diminished ability to help mount a defense. The passage of time will typically exacerbate the difficulties suffered by criminal defendants; the longer the delays in the process, the more burdensome the process. For these reasons, the right to speedy trial is a central protection in the Bill of Rights.

II. CONSTITUTIONAL SPEEDY TRIAL LIMITS

Klopfer v. State of North Carolina
Supreme Court of the United States, 1967
386 U.S. 213

■ MR. CHIEF JUSTICE WARREN delivered the opinion of the Court.

The question involved in this case is whether a State may indefinitely postpone prosecution on an indictment without stated justification over the objection of an accused who has been discharged from custody. It is presented in the context of an application of an unusual North Carolina criminal procedural device known as the 'nolle prosequi with leave.'

Under North Carolina criminal procedure, when the prosecuting attorney of a county, denominated the solicitor, determines that he does not desire to proceed further with a prosecution, he may take a nolle prosequi, thereby declaring 'that he will not, at that time, prosecute the suit further. Its effect is to put the defendant without day, that is, he is discharged and permitted to go whithersoever he will, without entering into a recognizance to appear at any other time.' *Wilkinson v. Wilkinson*, 159 N.C. 265, 266–267, 74 S.E. 740, 741, 39 L.R.A.,N.S., 1215 (1912). But the taking of the nolle prosequi does not permanently terminate proceedings on the indictment. On the contrary, 'When a nolle prosequi is entered, the case may be restored to the trial docket when ordered by the judge upon the solicitor's application.' *State v. Klopfer*, 266 N.C. 349, 350, 145 S.E.2d 909, 910 (1966). And if the solicitor petitions the court to nolle prosequi the case 'with leave,' the consent required to reinstate the prosecution at a future date is implied in the order 'and the solicitor (without further order) may have the case restored for trial.' Ibid. Since the indictment is not discharged by either a nolle prosequi or nolle prosequi with leave, the statute of limitations remains tolled. *State v. Williams*, 151 N.C. 660, 65 S.E. 908 (1909).

Although entry of a nolle prosequi is said to be 'usually and properly left to the discretion of the Solicitor,' *State v. Moody*, 69 N.C. 529, 531 (1873), early decisions indicate that the State was once aware that the trial judge would have to exercise control over the procedure to prevent oppression of defendants. See *State v. Smith*, 129 N.C. 546, 40 S.E. 1 (1901); *State v. Thornton*, 35 N.C. 256 (1852). But, in the present case, neither the court below nor the solicitor offers any reason why the case of petitioner should have been nolle prossed except for the suggestion of the Supreme Court that the solicitor, having tried the defendant once and having obtained only a mistrial, 'may have concluded that another go at it would not be worth the time and expense of another effort.' 266 N.C., at 350, 145 S.E.2d, at 910. In his brief in this Court, the Attorney General quotes this language from the opinion below in support of the judgment.

Whether this procedure is presently sustained by the North Carolina courts under a statute or under their conception of the common-law procedure is not indicated by the opinion of the court, the transcript or the briefs of the parties in the present case. The only statutory reference to a nolle prosequi is in § 15–175, General Statutes of North Carolina, which on its face does not apply to the facts of this case. Perhaps the procedure's genesis lies in early nineteenth century decisions of the State's Supreme Court approving the use of a nolle prosequi with leave to reinstate the indictment, although those early applications of the procedure were quite different from those of the period following enactment of § 15–175. Compare *State v. Thompson*, 10 N.C. 613 (1825), and *State v. Thornton*, 35 N.C. 256 (1852) (capias issued immediately after entry of the nolle prosequi with leave), with *State v. Smith, 170 N.C. 742, 87 S.E. 98 (1915)* (capias issued eight years after a nolle prosequi with leave was taken, even though the defendant had been available for trial in 1907).

The consequence of this extraordinary criminal procedure is made apparent by the case before the Court. A defendant indicted for a misdemeanor may be denied an opportunity to exonerate himself in the discretion of the solicitor and held subject to trial, over his objection, throughout the unlimited period in which the solicitor may restore the case to the calendar. During that period, there is no means by which he can obtain a dismissal or have the case restored to the calendar for trial. In spite of this result, both the Supreme Court and the Attorney General state as a fact, and rely upon it for affirmance in this case, that this procedure as applied to the petitioner placed no limitations upon him, and was in no way violative of his rights. With this we cannot agree.

This procedure was applied to the petitioner in the following circumstances:

> On February 24, 1964, petitioner was indicted by the grand jury of Orange County for the crime of criminal trespass, a misdemeanor punishable by fine and imprisonment in an amount and duration determined by the court in the exercise of its discretion. The bill charged that he entered a restaurant on January 3, 1964, and, 'after being ordered * * * to leave the said premises, wilfully and unlawfully refused to do so, knowing or having reason to know that he * * * had no license therefor * * *.' Prosecution on the indictment began with admirable promptness during the March 1964 Special Criminal Session of the Superior Court of Orange County; but, when the jury failed to reach a verdict, the trial judge declared a mistrial and ordered the case continued for the term.

> Several weeks prior to the April 1965 Criminal Session of the Superior Court, the State's solicitor informed petitioner of his intention to have a nolle prosequi with leave entered in the case. During the session, petitioner, through his attorney, opposed the entry of such an order in open court. The trespass charge, he contended, was abated by the Civil Rights Act of 1964 as construed in *Hamm v. City of Rock Hill*, 379 U.S. 306, 85 S.Ct. 384, 13 L.Ed.2d 300 (1964). In spite of petitioner's opposition, the court indicated that it would approve entry of a nolle prosequi with leave if requested to do so by the solicitor. But the solicitor declined to make a motion for a nolle prosequi with leave. Instead, he filed a motion with the court to continue the case for yet another term, which motion was granted.

> The calendar for the August 1965 Criminal Session of the court did not list Klopfer's case for trial. To ascertain the status on his case, petitioner filed a motion expressing his desire to have the charge pending against him 'permanently concluded in accordance with the applicable laws of the State of North Carolina and of the United States as soon as is reasonably possible.' Noting that some 18 months had elapsed since the indictment, petitioner, a professor of zoology at Duke University, contended that the pendency of the indictment

greatly interfered with his professional activities and with his travel here and abroad. 'Wherefore,' the motion concluded, 'the defendant * * * petitions the Court that the Court in the exercise of its general supervisory jurisdiction inquire into the trial status of the charge pending against the defendant and * * * ascertain the intention of the State in regard to the trial of said charge and as to when the defendant will be brought to trial.'

In response to the motion, the trial judge considered the status of petitioner's case in open court on Monday, August 9, 1965, at which time the solicitor moved the court that the State be permitted to take a nolle prosequi with leave. Even though no justification for the proposed entry was offered by the State, and, in spite of petitioner's objection to the order, the court granted the State's motion.

On appeal to the Supreme Court of North Carolina, petitioner contended that the entry of the nolle prosequi with leave order deprived him of his right to a speedy trial as required by the Fourteenth Amendment to the United States Constitution. Although the Supreme Court acknowledged that entry of the nolle prosequi with leave did not permanently discharge the indictment, it nevertheless affirmed. Its opinion concludes:

> 'Without question a defendant has the right to a speedy trial, if there is to be a trial. However, we do not understand the defendant has the right to compel the State to prosecute him if the state's prosecutor, in his discretion and with the court's approval, elects to take a nolle prosequi. In this case one jury seems to have been unable to agree. The solicitor may have concluded that another go at it would not be worth the time and expense of another effort.

> 'In this case the solicitor and the court, in entering the nolle prosequi with leave followed the customary procedure in such cases. Their discretion is not reviewable under the facts disclosed by this record. The order is affirmed.' 266 N.C., at 350–351, 145 S.E.2d, at 910.

The North Carolina Supreme Court's conclusion—that the right to a speedy trial does not afford affirmative protection against an unjustified postponement of trial for an accused discharged from custody—has been explicitly rejected by every other state court which has considered the question. That conclusion has also been implicitly rejected by the numerous courts which have held that a nolle prossed indictment may not be reinstated at a subsequent term.

We, too, believe that the position taken by the court below was erroneous. The petitioner is not relieved of the limitations placed upon his liberty by this prosecution merely because its suspension permits him to go 'whithersoever he will.' The pendency of the indictment may subject him to public scorn and deprive him of employment, and almost certainly will force curtailment of his speech, associations and participation in unpopular causes. By indefinitely prolonging this oppression, as well as the 'anxiety and concern accompanying public accusation,' the criminal procedure condoned in this case by the Supreme Court of North Carolina clearly denies the petitioner the right to a speedy trial which we hold is guaranteed to him by the Sixth Amendment of the Constitution of the United States.

While there has been a difference of opinion as to what provisions of this Amendment to the Constitution apply to the States through the Fourteenth Amendment, that question has been settled as to some of them in the recent cases of *Gideon v. Wainwright*, 372 U.S. 335, 83 S.Ct. 792, 9 L.Ed.2d 799 (1963), and *Pointer v. State of Texas*, 380 U.S. 400, 85 S.Ct. 1065, 13 L.Ed.2d 923 (1965). In the latter case, which dealt with the confrontation-of-witnesses provision, we said:

> 'In the light of Gideon, Malloy, and other cases cited in those opinions holding various provisions of the Bill of Rights applicable to the States by virtue of the Fourteenth Amendment, the statements made in West (*West v. State of Louisiana*, 194 U.S. 258, 24 S.Ct. 650, 48 L.Ed. 965) and similar cases generally declaring that the Sixth Amendment does not apply to the States can no longer be regarded as the law. We hold that petitioner was entitled to be tried in accordance with the protection of the confrontation guarantee of the Sixth Amendment, and that that guarantee, like the right against compelled self-incrimination, is 'to be enforced against the States under the Fourteenth Amendment according to the same standards that protect those personal rights against federal encroachment.' *Malloy v. Hogan*, supra, 378 U.S. (1), at 10, 84 S.Ct. (1489), at 1495 (12 L.Ed.2d 653).'

We hold here that the right to a speedy trial is as fundamental as any of the rights secured by the Sixth Amendment. That right has its roots at the very foundation of our English law heritage. Its first articulation in modern jurisprudence appears to have been made in Magna Carta (1215), wherein it was written, 'We will sell to no man, we will not deny or defer to any man either justice or right'; but evidence of recognition of the right to speedy justice in even earlier times is found in the Assize of Clarendon (1166). By the late thirteenth century, justices, armed with commissions of gaol delivery and/or oyer and terminer were visiting the countryside three times a year. These justices, Sir Edward Coke wrote in Part II of his Institutes, 'have not suffered the prisoner to be long detained, but at their next coming have given the prisoner full and speedy justice, * * * without detaining him long in prison.' To Coke, prolonged detention without trial would have been contrary to the law and custom of England; but he also believed that the delay in trial, by itself, would be an improper denial of justice. In his explication of Chapter 29 of the Magna Carta, he wrote that the words 'We will sell to no man, we will not deny or defer to any man either justice or right' had the following effect:

> 'And therefore, every subject of this realme, for injury done to him in bonis terris, vel persona, by any other subject, be he ecclesiasticall, or temporall, free, or bond, man, or woman, old, or young, or be he outlawed, excommunicated, or any other without exception, may take his remedy by the course of the law, and have justice, and right for the injury done to him, freely without sale, fully without any deniall, and speedily without delay.'

Coke's Institutes were read in the American Colonies by virtually every student of the law. Indeed, Thomas Jefferson wrote that at the time he studied law (1762–1767), 'Coke Lyttleton was the universal elementary book of law students.' And to John Rutledge of South Carolina, the Institutes seemed 'to be almost the foundation of our law.' To Coke, in turn, Magna Carta was one of the fundamental bases of English liberty. Thus, it is not surprising that when George Mason drafted the first of the colonial bills of rights, he set forth a principle of Magna Carta, using phraseology similar to that of Coke's explication: '(I)n all capital or criminal prosecutions,' the Virginia Declaration of Rights of 1776 provided, 'a man hath a right * * * to a speedy trial * * *.' That this right was considered fundamental at this early period in our history is evidenced by its guarantee in the constitutions of several of the States of the new nation, as well as by its prominent position in the Sixth Amendment. Today, each of the 50 States guarantees the right to a speedy trial to its citizens.

The history of the right to a speedy trial and its reception in this country clearly establish that it is one of the most basic rights preserved by our Constitution.

For the reasons stated above, the judgment must be reversed and remanded for proceedings not inconsistent with the opinion of the Court. It is so ordered.

Judgment reversed and case remanded.

■ MR. JUSTICE STEWART concurs in the result.

■ MR. JUSTICE HARLAN, concurring in the result.

While I entirely agree with the result reached by the Court, I am unable to subscribe to the constitutional premises upon which that result is based—quite evidently the viewpoint that the Fourteenth Amendment 'incorporates' or 'absorbs' as such all or some of the specific provisions of the Bill of Rights. I do not believe that this is sound constitutional doctrine. See my opinion concurring in the result in *Pointer v. State of Texas*, 380 U.S. 400, 408, 85 S.Ct. 1065, 1070, 13 L.Ed.2d 923.

I would rest decision of this case not on the 'speedy trial' provision of the Sixth Amendment, but on the ground that this unusual North Carolina procedure, which in effect allows state prosecuting officials to put a person under the cloud of an unliquidated criminal charge for an indeterminate period, violates the requirement of fundamental fairness assured by the Due Process Clause of the Fourteenth Amendment. To support that conclusion I need only refer to the traditional concepts of due process set forth in the opinion of THE CHIEF JUSTICE.

Burdens Associated with Pendency of Charges

The Court in *Klopfer* noted that "the pendency of the indictment may subject [the defendant] to public scorn and deprive him of employment, and almost certainly will force curtailment of his speech, associations and participation in unpopular causes." 386 U.S. at 222. *Klopfer* involved a civil rights protestor who may have been particularly vulnerable to prosecutorial misconduct designed to silence his advocacy, but you should see that the ability to hold charges over the head of a would-be defendant creates burdens for anyone subjected to such a situation.

Delays in Charging

The Supreme Court, in *Klopfer*, incorporated the Sixth Amendment's speedy trial right to apply to the states. As described in the case, the "nolle prosequi with leave" hung over the defendant's head, giving rise to some of the burdens associated with criminal accusation described above. But what if the state simply delays initiating prosecution in the first place? Does the Sixth Amendment provide a remedy when the government takes an extended period of time before bring criminal charges? The Court grappled with this question in the next case.

United States v. Marion
Supreme Court of the United States, 1971
404 U.S. 307

■ MR. JUSTICE WHITE delivered the opinion of the Court.

This appeal requires us to decide whether dismissal of a federal indictment was constitutionally required by reason of a period of three years between the occurrence of the alleged criminal acts and the filing of the indictment.

On April 21, 1970, the two appellees were indicted and charged in 19 counts with operating a business known as Allied Enterprises, Inc., which was engaged in the business of selling and installing home improvements such as intercom sets, fire control devices, and burglary detection systems. Allegedly, the business was fraudulently conducted and involved misrepresentations, alterations of documents, and deliberate nonperformance of contracts. The period covered by the indictment was March 15, 1965, to February 6, 1967; the earliest specific act alleged occurred on September 3, 1965, the latest on January 19, 1966.

On May 5, 1970, appellees filed a motion to dismiss the indictment 'for failure to commence prosecution of the alleged offenses charged therein within such time as to afford (them their) rights to due process of law and to a speedy trial under the Fifth and Sixth Amendments to the Constitution of the United States.' No evidence was submitted, but from the motion itself and the arguments of counsel at the hearing on the motion, it appears that Allied Enterprises had been subject to a Federal Trade Commission cease and desist order on February 6, 1967, and that a series of articles appeared in the Washington Post in October 1967, reporting the results of that newspaper's investigation of practices employed by home improvement firms such as Allied. The articles also contained purported statements of the then United States Attorney for the District of Columbia describing his office's investigation of these firms and predicting that indictments would soon be forthcoming. Although the statements attributed to the United States Attorney did not mention Allied specifically, that company was mentioned in the course of the newspaper stories. In the summer of 1968, at the request of the United States Attorney's office, Allied delivered certain of its records to that office, and in an interview there appellee Marion discussed his conduct as an officer of Allied Enterprises. The grand jury that indicted appellees was not impaneled until September 1969, appellees were not informed of the grand jury's concern with them until March 1970, and the indictment was finally handed down in April.

Appellees moved to dismiss because the indictment was returned 'an unreasonably oppressive and unjustifiable time after the alleged offenses.' They argued that the indictment required memory of many specific acts and conversations occurring several years before, and they contended that the delay was due to the negligence or indifference of the United States Attorney in investigating the case and presenting it to a grand jury. No specific prejudice was claimed or demonstrated. The District Court judge dismissed the indictment for 'lack of speedy prosecution' at the conclusion of the hearing and remarked that since the Government must have become aware of the relevant facts in 1967, the defense of the case 'is bound to have been seriously prejudiced by the delay of at least some three years in bringing the prosecution that should have been brought in 1967, or at the very latest early 1968.

The United States appealed directly to this Court pursuant to 18 U.S.C. § 3731 (1964 ed., Supp. V). We postponed consideration of the question of jurisdiction until the hearing on the merits of the case. We now hold that the Court has jurisdiction, and on the merits we reverse the judgment of the District Court.

I

Prior to its recent amendment, 18 U.S.C. § 3731 [1964 ed., Supp. V] authorized an appeal to this Court by the United States when in any criminal case a district court sustained 'a motion in bar, when the defendant has not been put in jeopardy.' It is plain to us that the appeal of the United States is within the purview of this section. Appellees had not been placed in jeopardy when the District Court rendered its judgment. The trial judge based his ruling on undue delay prior to indictment, a matter that was beyond the power of the Government to cure since re-indictment would not have been permissible under such a ruling. The motion to dismiss rested on grounds that had nothing to do with guilt or innocence or the truth of the allegations in the indictment but was, rather, a plea in the nature of confession and avoidance, that is, where the defendant does not deny that he has committed the acts alleged and that the acts were a crime but instead pleads that he cannot be prosecuted because of some extraneous factor, such as the running of the statute of limitations or the denial of a speedy trial. See *United States v. Weller*, 401 U.S. 254, 260, 91 S.Ct. 602, 606, 28 L.Ed.2d 26 (1971). The motion rested on constitutional grounds exclusively, and neither the motion, the arguments of counsel, the Court's oral opinion, nor its judgment mentioned Federal Rule of Criminal Procedure 48(b), as a ground for dismissal. Our jurisdiction to hear this appeal has been satisfactorily established.

II

Appellees do not claim that the Sixth Amendment was violated by the two-month delay between the return of the indictment and its dismissal. Instead, they claim that their rights to a speedy trial were violated by the period of approximately three years between the end of the criminal scheme charged and the return of the indictment; it is argued that this delay is so substantial and inherently prejudicial that the Sixth Amendment required the dismissal of the indictment. In our view, however, the Sixth Amendment speedy trial provision has no application until the putative defendant in some way becomes an 'accused,' an event that occurred in this case only when the appellees were indicted on April 21, 1970.

The Sixth Amendment provides that '[i]n all criminal prosecutions, the accused shall enjoy the right to a speedy and public trial . . . .' On its face, the protection of the Amendment is activated only when a criminal prosecution has begun and extends only to those persons who have been 'accused' in the course of that prosecution. These provisions would seem to afford no protection to those not yet accused, nor would they seem to require the Government to discover, investigate, and accuse any person within any particular period of time. The amendment would appear to guarantee to a criminal defendant that the Government will move with the dispatch that is appropriate to assure him an early and proper disposition of the charges against him. '(T)he essential ingredient is orderly expedition and not mere speed.' *Smith v. United States*, 360 U.S. 1, 10, 79 S.Ct. 991, 997, 3 L.Ed.2d 1041 (1959).

Our attention is called to nothing in the circumstances surrounding the adoption of the Amendment indicating that it does not mean what it appears to say, nor is there more than marginal support for the proposition that, at the time of the adoption of the Amendment, the prevailing rule was that prosecutions would not be permitted if there had been long delay in presenting a charge. The framers could hardly have selected less appropriate language if they had intended the speedy trial provision to protect against pre-accusation delay. No opinions of this Court intimate support for appellees' thesis, and the courts of appeals that have considered the question in constitutional terms have never reversed a conviction or dismissed an indictment solely on the basis of the Sixth Amendment's speedy trial provision where only pre-indictment delay was involved.

Legislative efforts to implement federal and state speedy trial provisions also plainly reveal the view that these guarantees are applicable only after a person has been accused of a crime. The Court has pointed out that '(a)t the common law, and in the absence of special statutes of limitations, the mere failure to find an indictment will not operate to discharge the accused from the offense nor will a nolle prosequi entered by the government, or the failure of the grand jury to indict.' *United States v. Cadarr*, 197 U.S. 475, 478, 25 S.Ct. 487, 488, 49 L.Ed. 842 (1905). Since it is 'doubtless true that in some cases the power of the government has been abused and charges have been kept hanging over the heads of citizens, and they have been committed for unreasonable periods, resulting in hardship,' the Court noted that many States '(w)ith a view to preventing such wrong to the citizen . . . (and) in aid of the constitutional provisions, national and state, intended to secure to the accused a speedy trial' had passed statutes limiting the time within which such trial must occur after charge or indictment.

Characteristically, these statutes to which the Court referred are triggered only when a citizen is charged or accused. The statutes vary greatly in substance, structure and interpretation, but a common denominator is that '(i)n no event ... (does) the right to speedy trial arise before there is some charge or arrest, even though the prosecuting authorities had knowledge of the offense long before this.' Note, The Right to a Speedy Trial, 57 Col.L.Rev. 846, 848 (1957).

No federal statute of general applicability has been enacted by Congress to enforce the speedy trial provision of the Sixth Amendment, but Federal Rule of Criminal Procedure 48(b), which has the force of law, authorizes dismissal of an indictment, information, or complaint '(i)f there is unnecessary delay in presenting the charge to a grand jury or in filing an information against a defendant who has been held to answer to the district court, or if there is unnecessary delay in bringing a defendant to trial ....' The rule clearly is limited to post-arrest situations.

Appellees' position is, therefore, at odds with longstanding legislative and judicial constructions of the speedy trial provisions in both national and state constitutions.

III

It is apparent also that very little support for appellees' position emerges from a consideration of the purposes of the Sixth Amendment's speedy trial provision, a guarantee that this Court has termed 'an important safeguard to prevent undue and oppressive incarceration prior to trial, to minimize anxiety and concern accompanying public accusation and to limit the possibilities that long delay will impair the ability of an accused to defend himself.' *United States v. Ewell*, 383 U.S. 116, 120, 86 S.Ct. 773, 776, 15 L.Ed.2d 627 (1966); see also *Klopfer v. North Carolina*, 386 U.S. 213, 221–226, 87 S.Ct. 988, 992–995, 18 L.Ed.2d 1 (1967); *Dickey v. Florida*, 398 U.S. 30, 37–38, 90 S.Ct. 1564, 1568–1569, 26 L.Ed.2d 26 (1970). Inordinate delay between arrest, indictment, and trial may impair a defendant's ability to present an effective defense. But the major evils protected against by the speedy trial guarantee exist quite apart from actual or possible prejudice to an accused's defense. To legally arrest and detain, the Government must assert probable cause to believe the arrestee has committed a crime. Arrest is a public act that may seriously interfere with the defendant's liberty, whether he is free on bail or not, and that may disrupt his employment, drain his financial resources, curtail his associations, subject him to public obloquy, and create anxiety in him, his family and his friends. These considerations were substantial underpinnings for the decision in *Klopfer v. North Carolina*, supra; see also *Smith v. Hooey*, 393 U.S. 374, 377–378, 89 S.Ct. 575, 576–577, 21 L.Ed.2d 607 (1969). So viewed, it is readily understandable that it is either a formal indictment or information or else the actual restraints imposed by arrest and holding to answer a criminal charge that engage the particular protections of the speedy trial provision of the Sixth Amendment.

Invocation of the speedy trial provision thus need not await indictment, information, or other formal charge. But we decline to extend that reach of the amendment to the period prior to arrest. Until this event occurs, a citizen suffers no restraints on his liberty and is not the subject of public accusation: his situation does not compare with that of a defendant who has been arrested and held to answer. Passage of time, whether before or after arrest, may impair memories, cause evidence to be lost, deprive the defendant of witnesses, and otherwise interfere with his ability to defend himself. But this possibility of prejudice at trial is not itself sufficient reason to wrench the Sixth Amendment from its proper context. Possible prejudice is inherent in any delay, however short; it may also weaken the Government's case.

The law has provided other mechanisms to guard against possible as distinguished from actual prejudice resulting from the passage of time between crime and arrest or charge. As we said in *United States v. Ewell*, supra, 386 U.S., at 122, 86 S.Ct., at 777, 'the applicable statute of limitations ... is ... the primary guarantee against bringing overly stale criminal charges.' Such statutes represent legislative assessments of relative interests of the State and the defendant in administering and receiving justice; they 'are made for the repose of society and the protection of those who may (during the limitation) ... have lost their means of defence.' *Public Schools v. Walker*, 9 Wall. 282, 288, 19 L.Ed. 576 (1870). These statutes provide predictability by specifying a limit beyond which there is an irrebuttable presumption that a defendant's right to a fair trial would be prejudiced. As this Court observed in *Toussie v. United States*, 397 U.S. 112, 114–115, 90 S.Ct. 858, 860, 25 L.Ed.2d 156 (1970):

> 'The purpose of a statute of limitations is to limit exposure to criminal prosecution to a certain fixed period of time following the occurrence of those acts the legislature has decided to punish by criminal sanctions. Such a limitation is designed to protect individuals from having to defend themselves against charges when the basic facts may have become obscured by the passage of time and to minimize the danger of official punishment because of acts in the far-distant past. Such a time limit may also have the salutary effect of encouraging law enforcement officials promptly to investigate suspected criminal activity.'

There is thus no need to press the Sixth Amendment into service to guard against the mere possibility that pre-accusation delays will prejudice the defense in a criminal case since statutes of limitation already perform that function.

Since appellees rely only on potential prejudice and the passage of time between the alleged crime and the indictment, see Part IV, infra, we perhaps need go no further to dispose of this case, for the indictment was the first official act designating appellees as accused individuals and that event occurred within the statute of limitations. Nevertheless, since a criminal trial is the likely consequence of our judgment and since appellees may claim actual prejudice to their defense, it is appropriate to note here that the statute of limitations does not fully define the appellees' rights with respect to the events occurring prior to indictment. Thus, the Government concedes that the Due Process Clause of the Fifth Amendment would require dismissal of the indictment if it were shown at trial that the pre-indictment delay in this case caused substantial prejudice to appellees' rights to a fair trial and that the delay was an intentional device to gain tactical advantage over the accused.16 Cf. *Brady v. Maryland*, 373 U.S. 83, 83 S.Ct. 1194, 10 L.Ed.2d 215 (1963); *Napue v. Illinois*, 360 U.S. 264, 79 S.Ct. 1173, 3 L.Ed.2d 1217 (1959). However, we need not, and could not now, determine when and in what circumstances actual prejudice resulting from pre-accusation delays requires the dismissal of the prosecution. Actual prejudice to the defense of a criminal case may result from the shortest and most necessary delay; and no one suggests that every delay-caused detriment to a defendant's case should abort a criminal prosecution. To accommodate the sound administration of justice to the rights of the defendant to a fair trial will necessarily involve a delicate judgment based on the circumstances of each case. It would be unwise at this juncture to attempt to forecast our decision in such cases.

IV

In the case before us, neither appellee was arrested, charged, or otherwise subjected to formal restraint prior to indictment. It was this event, therefore, that transformed the appellees into 'accused' defendants who are subject to the speedy trial protections of the Sixth Amendment.

The 38-month delay between the end of the scheme charged in the indictment and the date the defendants were indicted did not extend beyond the period of the applicable statute of limitations here. Appellees have not, of course, been able to claim undue delay pending trial, since the indictment was brought on April 21, 1970, and dismissed on June 8, 1970. Nor have appellees adequately demonstrated that the pre-indictment delay by the Government violated the Due Process Clause. No actual prejudice to the conduct of the defense is alleged or proved, and there is no showing that the Government intentionally delayed to gain some tactical advantage over appellees or to harass them. Appellees rely solely on the real possibility of prejudice inherent in any extended delay: that memories will dim, witnesses become inaccessible, and evidence be lost. In light of the applicable statute of limitations, however, these possibilities are not in themselves enough to demonstrate that appellees cannot receive a fair trial and to therefore justify the dismissal of the indictment. Events of the trial may demonstrate actual prejudice, but at the present time appellees' due process claims are speculative and premature.

Reversed.

***

Starting the Clock

What event starts the clock for purposes of speedy trial? The court has considered the deprivation of liberty as the key factor. Therefore, the arrest of the defendant starts the speedy trial clock. *See Dillingham v. United States*, 423 U.S. 64 (1975). Also, the speedy trial clock often stops in the interim period between the dropping of charges and their reinstatement, as long as the defendant is not detained. *See United Sates v. MacDonald*, 456 U.S. 1 (1982); *see also United States v. Loud Hawk*, 474 U.S. 302 (1986).

It should be noted that there is no duty of prosecutors to charge as soon as probable cause is achieved. *See United States v. Lovasco*, 431 U.S. 783 (1977). As noted in *Marion*, the statute of limitations is "the primary guarantee against bringing overly stale criminal charges." *Id.* What are some of the strongest policy reasons against imposing such a duty on prosecutors to file charges as expeditiously as possible?

Post-Conviction, Pre-Sentencing Delay

The U.S. Supreme Court held, in *Betterman v. Montana*, 136 S.Ct. 1609 (2016), that the Sixth Amendment's Speedy Trial Clause does not apply to post-conviction delay prior to sentencing. Writing for a unanimous court, Justice Ginsburg noted that criminal proceedings can be categorized into three phases—pre-charge, pre-conviction, and pre-sentencing. *See id.* The Speedy Trial Clause right attaches, Justice Ginsburg explained, only during the second phase. *See id.* (citing *Marion, supra*). Following conviction, Justice Ginsburg observed, the presumption of innocence rationale at the heart of the Speedy Trial Clause falls away. Justice Ginsburg did note that a defendant might find relief in rules or statutes that require the avoidance of delay in the sentencing process, but because the petitioner's claim was rooted in the Speedy Trial Clause and not due process, no relief was available. *See id.*

Guideposts for Assessing Speedy Trial Claims

What standards do courts apply when assessing claims that the speedy trial right has been violated by governmental delay? The next case illuminates how courts evaluate speedy trial claims.

Barker v. Wingo

Supreme Court of the United States, 1972
407 U.S. 514

■ MR. JUSTICE POWELL delivered the opinion of the Court.

Although a speedy trial is guaranteed the accused by the Sixth Amendment to the Constitution, this Court has dealt with that right on infrequent occasions. See *Beavers v. Haubert*, 198 U.S. 77, 25 S.Ct. 573, 49 L.Ed. 950 (1905); *Pollard v. United States*, 352 U.S. 354, 77 S.Ct. 481, 1 L.Ed.2d 393 (1957); *United States v. Ewell*, 383 U.S. 116, 86 S.Ct. 773, 15 L.Ed.2d 627 (1966); *United States v. Marion,* 404 U.S. 307, 92 S.Ct. 455, 30 L.Ed.2d 468 (1971). See also *United States v. Provoo*, 17 F.R.D. 183 (D.Md.), aff'd, 350 U.S. 857, 76 S.Ct. 101, 100 L.Ed. 761 (1955). The Court's opinion in *Klofper v. North Carolina*, 386 U.S. 213, 87 S.Ct. 988, 18 L.Ed.2d 1 (1967), established that the right to a speedy trial is 'fundamental' and is imposed by the Due Process Clause of the Fourteenth Amendment on the States. See *Smith v. Hooey*, 393 U.S. 374, 89 S.Ct. 575, 21 L.Ed.2d 607 (1969); *Dickey v. Florida*, 398 U.S. 30, 90 S.Ct. 1564, 26 L.Ed.2d 26 (1970). As Mr. Justice Brennan pointed out in his concurring opinion in Dickey, in none of these cases have we attempted to set out the criteria by which the speedy trial right is to be judged. 398 U.S., at 40–41, 90 S.Ct. at 1570. This case compels us to make such an attempt.

I

On July 20, 1958, in Christian County, Kentucky, an elderly couple was beaten to death by intruders wielding an iron tire tool. Two suspects, Silas Manning and Willie Barker, the petitioner, were arrested shortly thereafter. The grand jury indicted them on September 15. Counsel was appointed on September 17, and Barker's trial was set for October 21. The Commonwealth had a stronger case against Manning, and it believed that Barker could not be convicted unless Manning testified against him. Manning was naturally unwilling to incriminate himself. Accordingly, on October 23, the day Silas Manning was brought to trial, the Commonwealth sought and obtained the first of what was to be a series of 16 continuances of Barker's trial. Barker made no objection. By first convicting Manning, the Commonwealth would remove possible problems of self-incrimination and would be able to assure his testimony against Barker.

The Commonwealth encountered more than a few difficulties in its prosecution of Manning. The first trial ended in a hung jury. A second trial resulted in a conviction, but the Kentucky Court of Appeals reversed because of the admission of evidence obtained by an illegal search. *Manning v. Commonwealth*, 328 S.W.2d 421 (1959). At his third trial, Manning was again convicted, and the Court of Appeals again reversed because the trial court had not granted a change of venue. *Manning v. Commonwealth*, 346 S.W.2d 755 (1961). A fourth trial resulted in a hung jury. Finally, after five trials, Manning was convicted, in March 1962, of murdering one victim, and after a sixth trial, in December 1962, he was convicted of murdering the other.

The Christian County Circuit Court holds three terms each year—in February, June, and September. Barker's initial trial was to take place in the September term of 1958. The first continuance postponed it until the February 1959 term. The second continuance was granted for one month only. Every term thereafter for as long as the Manning prosecutions were in process, the Commonwealth routinely moved to continue Barker's case to the next term. When the case was continued from the June 1959 term until the following September, Barker, having spent 10 months in jail, obtained his release by posting a $5,000 bond. He thereafter remained free in the community until his trial. Barker made no objection, through his counsel, to the first 11 continuances.

When on February 12, 1962, the Commonwealth moved for the twelfth time to continue the case until the following term, Barker's counsel filed a motion to dismiss the indictment. The motion to dismiss was denied two weeks later, and the Commonwealth's motion for a continuance was granted. The Commonwealth was granted further continuances in June 1962 and September 1962, to which Barker did not object.

In February 1963, the first term of court following Manning's final conviction, the Commonwealth moved to set Barker's trial for March 19. But on the day scheduled for trial, it again moved for a continuance until the June term. It gave as its reason the illness of the ex-sheriff who was the chief investigating officer in the case. To this continuance, Barker objected unsuccessfully.

The witness was still unable to testify in June, and the trial, which had been set for June 19, was continued again until the September term over Barker's objection. This time the court announced that the case would be dismissed for lack of prosecution if it were not tried during the next term. The final trial date was set for October 9, 1963. On that date, Barker again moved to dismiss the indictment, and this time specified that his right to a speedy trial had been violated. The motion was denied; the trial commenced with Manning as the chief prosecution witness; Barker was convicted and given a life sentence.

Barker appealed his conviction to the Kentucky Court of Appeals, relying in part on his speedy trial claim. The court affirmed. *Barker v. Commonwealth,* 385 S.W.2d 671 (1964). In February 1970 Barker petitioned for habeas corpus in the United States District Court for the Western District of Kentucky. Although the District Court rejected the petition without holding a hearing, the court granted petitioner leave to appeal in forma pauperis and a certificate of probable cause to appeal. On appeal, the Court of Appeals for the Sixth Circuit affirmed the District Court. 442 F.2d 1141 (1971). It ruled that Barker had waived his speedy trial claim for the entire period before February 1963, the date on which the court believed he had first objected to the delay by filing a motion to dismiss. In this belief the court was mistaken, for the record reveals that the motion was filed in February 1962. The Commonwealth so conceded at oral argument before this Court. The court held further that the remaining period after the date on which Barker first raised his claim and before his trial—which it thought was only eight months but which was actually 20 months—was not unduly long. In addition, the court held that Barker had shown no resulting prejudice, and that the illness of the exsheriff was a valid justification for the delay. We granted Barker's petition for certiorari. 404 U.S. 1037, 92 S.Ct. 719, 30 L.Ed.2d 729 (1972).

II

The right to a speedy trial is generically different from any of the other rights enshrined in the Constitution for the protection of the accused. In addition to the general concern that all accused persons be treated according to decent and fair procedures, there is a societal interest in providing a speedy trial which exists separate from, and at times in opposition to, the interests of the accused. The inability of courts to provide a prompt trial has contributed to a large backlog of cases in urban courts which, among other things, enables defendants to negotiate more effectively for pleas of guilty to lesser offenses and otherwise manipulate the system. In addition, persons released on bond for lengthy periods awaiting trial have an opportunity to commit other crimes. It must be of little comfort to the residents of Christian County, Kentucky, to know that Barker was at large on bail for over four years while accused of a vicious and brutal murder of which he was ultimately convicted. Moreover, the longer an accused is free awaiting trial, the more tempting becomes his opportunity to jump bail and escape. Finally, delay between arrest and punishment may have a detrimental effect on rehabilitation.

If an accused cannot make bail, he is generally confined, as was Barker for 10 months, in a local jail. This contributes to the overcrowding and generally deplorable state of those institutions. Lengthy exposure to these conditions 'has a destructive effect on human character and makes the rehabilitation of the individual offender much more difficult.' At times the result may even be violent rioting. Finally, lengthy pretrial detention is costly. The cost of maintaining a prisoner in jail varies from $3 to $9 per day, and this amounts to millions across the Nation. In addition, society loses wages which might have been earned, and it must often support families of incarcerated breadwinners.

A second difference between the right to speedy trial and the accused's other constitutional rights is that deprivation of the right may work to the accused's advantage. Delay is not an uncommon defense tactic. As the time between the commission of the crime and trial lengthens, witnesses may become unavailable or their memories may fade. If the witnesses support the prosecution, its case will be weakened, sometimes seriously so. And it is the prosecution which carries the burden of proof. Thus, unlike the right to counsel or the right to be free from compelled self-in-crimination, deprivation of the right to speedy trial does not per se prejudice the accused's ability to defend himself.

Finally, and perhaps most importantly, the right to speedy trial is a more vague concept than other procedural rights. It is, for example, impossible to determine with precision when the right has been denied. We cannot definitely say how long is too long in a system where justice is supposed to be swift but deliberate. As a consequence, there is no fixed point in the criminal process when the State can put the defendant to the choice of either exercising or waiving the right to a speedy trial. If, for example, the State moves for a 60-day continuance, granting that continuance is not a violation of the right to speedy trial unless the circumstances of the case are such that further delay would endanger the values the right protects. It is impossible to do more than generalize about when those circumstances exist. There is nothing comparable to the point in the process when a defendant exercises or waives his right to counsel or his right to a jury trial. Thus, as we recognized in *Beavers v. Haubert*, supra, any inquiry into a speedy trial claim necessitates a functional analysis of the right in the particular context of the case:

> 'The right of a speedy trial is necessarily relative. It is consistent with delays and depends upon circumstances. It secures rights to a defendant. It does not preclude the rights of public justice.' 198 U.S., at 87, 25 S.Ct. at 576, 49 L.Ed. 950.

The amorphous quality of the right also leads to the unsatisfactorily severe remedy of dismissal of the indictment when the right has been deprived. This is indeed a serious consequence because it means that a defendant who may be guilty of a serious crime will go free, without having been tried. Such a remedy is more serious than an exclusionary rule or a reversal for a new trial, but it is the only possible remedy.

III

Perhaps because the speedy trial right is so slippery, two rigid approaches are urged upon us as ways of eliminating some of the uncertainty which courts experience in protecting the right. The first suggestion is that we hold that the Constitution requires a criminal defendant to be offered a trial within a specified time period. The result of such a ruling would have the virtue of clarifying when the right is infringed and of simplifying courts' application of it. Recognizing this, some legislatures have enacted laws, and some courts have adopted procedural rules which more narrowly define the right. The United States Court of Appeals for the Second Circuit has promulgated rules for the district courts in that Circuit establishing that the government must be ready for trial within six months of the date of arrest, except in unusual circumstances, or the charge will be dismissed. This type of rule is also recommended by the American Bar Association.

But such a result would require this Court to engage in legislative or rulemaking activity, rather than in the adjudicative process to which we should confine our efforts. We do not establish procedural rules for the States, except when mandated by the Constitution. We find no constitutional basis for holding that the speedy trial right can be quantified into a specified number of days or months. The States, of course, are free to prescribe a reasonable period consistent with constitutional standards, but our approach must be less precise.

The second suggested alternative would restrict consideration of the right to those cases in which the accused has demanded a speedy trial. Most States have recognized what is loosely referred to as the 'demand rule,' although eight States reject it. It is not clear, however, precisely what is meant by that term. Although every federal court of appeals that has considered the question has endorsed some kind of demand rule, some have regarded the rule within the concept of waiver, whereas others have viewed it as a factor to be weighed in assessing whether there has been a deprivation of the speedy trial right. We shall refer to the former approach as the demand-waiver doctrine. The demand-waiver doctrine provides that a defendant waives any consideration of his right to speedy trial for any period prior to which he has not demanded a trial. Under this rigid approach, a prior demand is a necessary condition to the consideration of the speedy trial right. This essentially was the approach the Sixth Circuit took below.

Such an approach, by presuming waiver of a fundamental right from inaction, is inconsistent with this Court's pronouncements on waiver of constitutional rights. The Court has defined waiver as 'an intentional relinquishment or abandonment of a known right or privilege.' *Johnson v. Zerbst*, 304 U.S. 458, 464, 58 S.Ct. 1019, 1023, 82 L.Ed. 1461 (1938). Courts should 'indulge every reasonable presumption against waiver,'

Aetna Ins. Co. v. Kennedy, 301 U.S. 389, 393, 57 S.Ct. 809, 812, 81 L.Ed. 1177 (1937), and they should 'not presume acquiescence in the loss of fundamental rights,' *Ohio Bell Tel. Co. v. Public Utilities Comm'n*, 301 U.S. 292, 307, 57 S.Ct. 724, 731, 81 L.Ed. 1093 (1937). In *Carnley v. Cochran*, 369 U.S. 506, 82 S.Ct. 884, 8 L.Ed.2d 70 (1962), we held:

> 'Presuming waiver from a silent record is impermissible. The record must show, or there must be an allegation and evidence which show, that an accused was offered counsel but intelligently and understandably rejected the offer. Anything less is not waiver.' Id., at 516, 82 S.Ct., at 890.

The Court has ruled similarly with respect to waiver of other rights designed to protect the accused. See, e.g., *Miranda v. Arizona*, 384 U.S. 436, 475–476, 86 S.Ct. 1602, 1628–1627, 16 L.Ed.2d 694 (1966); *Boykin v. Alabama*, 395 U.S. 238, 89 S.Ct. 1709, 23 L.Ed.2d 274 (1969).

In excepting the right to speedy trial from the rule of waiver we have applied to other fundamental rights, courts that have applied the demand-waiver rule have relied on the assumption that delay usually works for the benefit of the accused and on the absence of any readily ascertainable time in the criminal process for a defendant to be given the choice of exercising or waiving his right. But it is not necessarily true that delay benefits the defendant. There are cases in which delay appreciably harms the defendant's ability to defend himself. Moreover, a defendant confined to jail prior to trial is obviously disadvantaged by delay as is a defendant released on bail but unable to lead a normal life because of community suspicion and his own anxiety.

The nature of the speedy trial right does make it impossible to pinpoint a precise time in the process when the right must be asserted or waived, but that fact does not argue for placing the burden of protecting the right solely on defendants. A defendant has no duty to bring himself to trial; the State has that duty as well as the duty of insuring that the trial is consistent with due process. Moreover, for the reasons earlier expressed, society has a particular interest in bringing swift prosecutions, and society's representatives are the ones who should protect that interest.

It is also noteworthy that such a rigid view of the demand-waiver rule places defense counsel in an awkward position. Unless he demands a trial early and often, he is in danger of frustrating his client's right. If counsel is willing to tolerate some delay because he finds it reasonable and helpful in preparing his own case, he may be unable to obtain a speedy trial for his client at the end of that time. Since under the demand-waiver rule no time runs until the demand is made, the government will have whatever time is otherwise reasonable to bring the defendant to trial after a demand has been made. Thus, if the first demand is made three months after arrest in a jurisdiction which prescribes a six-month rule, the prosecution will have a total of nine months—which may be wholly unreasonable under the circumstances. The result in practice is likely to be either an automatic, pro forma demand made immediately after appointment of counsel or delays which, but for the demand-waiver rule, would not be tolerated. Such a result is not consistent with the interests of defendants, society, or the Constitution.

We reject, therefore, the rule that a defendant who fails to demand a speedy trial forever waives his right. This does not mean, however, that the defendant has no responsibility to assert his right. We think the better rule is that the defendant's assertion of or failure to assert his right to a speedy trial is one of the factors to be considered in an inquiry into the deprivation of the right. Such a formulation avoids the rigidities of the demand-waiver rule and the resulting possible unfairness in its application. It allows the trial court to exercise a judicial discretion based on the circumstances, including due consideration of any applicable formal procedural rule. It would permit, for example, a court to attach a different weight to a situation in which the defendant knowingly fails to object from a situation in which his attorney acquiesces in long delay without adequately informing his client, or from a situation in which no counsel is appointed. It would also allow a court to weigh the frequency and force of the objections as opposed to attaching significant weight to a purely pro forma objection.

In ruling that a defendant has some responsibility to assert a speedy trial claim, we do not depart from our holdings in other cases concerning the waiver of fundamental rights, in which we have placed the entire responsibility on the prosecution to show that the claimed waiver was knowingly and voluntarily made. Such cases have involved rights which must be exercised or waived at a specific time or under clearly identifiable circumstances, such as the rights to plead not guilty, to demand a jury trial, to exercise the privilege against self-incrimination, and to have the assistance of counsel. We have shown above that the right to a speedy trial is unique in its uncertainty as to when and under what circumstances it must be asserted or may be deemed waived. But the rule we announce today, which comports with constitutional principles, places the primary burden on the courts and the prosecutors to assure that cases are brought to trial. We hardly need add that if delay is attributable to the defendant, then his waiver may be given effect under standard waiver doctrine, the demand rule aside.

We, therefore, reject both of the inflexible approaches—the fixed-time period because it goes further than the Constitution requires; the demand-waiver rule because it is insensitive to a right which he have deemed fundamental. The approach we accept is a balancing test, in which the conduct of both the prosecution and the defendant are weighed.

IV

A balancing test necessarily compels courts to approach speedy trial cases on an ad hoc basis. We can do little more than identify some of the factors which courts should assess in determining whether a particular defendant has been deprived of his right. Though some might express them in different ways, we identify four such factors: Length of delay, the reason for the delay, the defendant's assertion of his right, and prejudice to the defendant.

The length of the delay is to some extent a triggering mechanism. Until there is some delay which is presumptively prejudicial, there is no necessity for inquiry into the other factors that go into the balance. Nevertheless, because of the imprecision of the right to speedy trial, the length of delay that will provoke such an inquiry is necessarily dependent upon the peculiar circumstances of the case. To take but one example, the delay that can be tolerated for an ordinary street crime is considerably less than for a serious, complex conspiracy charge.

Closely related to length of delay is the reason the government assigns to justify the delay. Here, too, different weights should be assigned to different reasons. A deliberate attempt to delay the trial in order to hamper the defense should be weighted heavily against the government. A more neutral reason such as negligence or overcrowded courts should be weighted less heavily but nevertheless should be considered since the ultimate responsibility for such circumstances must rest with the government rather than with the defendant. Finally, a valid reason, such as a missing witness, should serve to justify appropriate delay.

We have already discussed the third factor, the defendant's responsibility to assert his right. Whether and how a defendant asserts his right is closely related to the other factors we have mentioned. The strength of his efforts will be affected by the length of the delay, to some extent by the reason for the delay, and most particularly by the personal prejudice, which is not always readily identifiable, that he experiences. The more serious the deprivation, the more likely a defendant is to complain. The defendant's assertion of his speedy trial right, then, is entitled to strong evidentiary weight in determining whether the defendant is being deprived of the right. We emphasize that failure to assert the right will make it difficult for a defendant to prove that he was denied a speedy trial.

A fourth factor is prejudice to the defendant. Prejudice, of course, should be assessed in the light of the interests of defendants which the speedy trial right was designed to protect. This Court has identified three such interests: (i) to prevent oppressive pretrial incarceration; (ii) to minimize anxiety and concern of the accused; and (iii) to limit the possibility that the defense will be impaired. Of these, the most serious is the last, because the inability of a defendant adequately to prepare his case skews the fairness of the entire system. If witnesses die or disappear during a delay, the prejudice is obvious. There is also prejudice if defense witnesses are unable to recall accurately events of the distant past. Loss of memory, however, is not always reflected in the record because what has been forgotten can rarely be shown.

We have discussed previously the societal disadvantages of lengthy pretrial incarceration, but obviously the disadvantages for the accused who cannot obtain his release are even more serious. The time spent in jail awaiting trial has a detrimental impact on the individual. It often means loss of a job; it disrupts family life; and it enforces idleness. Most jails offer little or no recreational or rehabilitative programs. The time spent in jail is simply dead time. Moreover, if a defendant is locked up, he is hindered in his ability to gather evidence, contact witnesses, or otherwise prepare his defense. Imposing those consequences on anyone who has not yet been convicted is serious. It is especially unfortunate to impose them on those persons who are ultimately found to be innocent. Finally, even if an accused is not incarcerated prior to trial, he is still disadvantaged by restraints on his liberty and by living under a cloud of anxiety, suspicion, and often hostility. See cases cited in n. 33, supra.

We regard none of the four factors identified above as either a necessary or sufficient condition to the finding of a deprivation of the right of speedy trial. Rather, they are related factors and must be considered together with such other circumstances as may be relevant. In sum, these factors have no talismanic qualities; courts must still engage in a difficult and sensitive balancing process. But, because we are dealing with a fundamental right of the accused, this process must be carried out with full recognition that the accused's interest in a speedy trial is specifically affirmed in the Constitution.

V

The difficulty of the task of balancing these factors is illustrated by this case, which we consider to be close. It is clear that the length of delay between arrest and trial—well over five years—was extraordinary. Only seven months of that period can be attributed to a strong excuse, the illness of the exsheriff who was in charge of the investigation. Perhaps some delay would have been permissible under ordinary circumstances, so that Manning could be utilized as a witness in Barker's trial, but more than four years was too long a period, particularly since a good part of that period was attributable to the

Commonwealth's failure or inability to try Manning under circumstances that comported with due process.

Two counterbalancing factors, however, outweigh these deficiencies. The first is that prejudice was minimal. Of course, Barker was prejudiced to some extent by living for over four years under a cloud of suspicion and anxiety. Moreover, although he was released on bond for most of the period, he did spend 10 months in jail before trial. But there is no claim that any of Barker's witnesses died or otherwise became unavailable owing to the delay. The trial transcript indicates only two very minor lapses of memory—one on the part of a prosecution witness—which were in no way significant to the outcome.

More important than the absence of serious prejudice, is the fact that Barker did not want a speedy trial. Counsel was appointed for Barker immediately after his indictment and represented him throughout the period. No question is raised as to the competency of such counsel. Despite the fact that counsel had notice of the motions for continuances, the record shows no action whatever taken between October 21, 1958, and February 12, 1962, that could be construed as the assertion of the speedy trial right. On the latter date, in response to another motion for continuance, Barker moved to dismiss the indictment. The record does not show on what ground this motion was based, although it is clear that no alternative motion was made for an immediate trial. Instead the record strongly suggests that while he hoped to take advantage of the delay in which he had acquiesced, and thereby obtain a dismissal of the charges, he definitely did not want to be tried. Counsel conceded as much at oral argument:

> 'Your honor, I would concede that Willie Mae Barker probably—I don't know this for a fact—probably did not want to be tried. I don't think any man wants to be tried. And I don't consider this a liability on his behalf. I don't blame him.' Tr. of Oral Arg. 39.

The probable reason for Barker's attitude was that he was gambling on Manning's acquittal. The evidence was not very strong against Manning, as the reversals and hung juries suggest, and Barker undoubtedly thought that if Manning were acquitted, he would never be tried. Counsel also conceded this:

> 'Now, it's true that the reason for this delay was the Commonwealth of Kentucky's desire to secure the testimony of the accomplice, Silas Manning. And it's true that if Silas Manning were never convicted, Willie Mae Barker would never have been convicted. We concede this. Id., at 15.

That Barker was gambling on Manning's acquittal is also suggested by his failure, following the pro forma motion to dismiss filed in February

1962, to object to the Commonwealth's next two motions for continuances. Indeed, it was not until March 1963, after Manning's convictions were final, that Barker, having lost his gamble, began to object to further continuances. At that time, the Commonwealth's excuse was the illness of the ex-sheriff, which Barker has conceded justified the further delay.

We do not hold that there may never be a situation in which an indictment may be dismissed on speedy trial grounds where the defendant has failed to object to continuances. There may be a situation in which the defendant was represented by incompetent counsel, was severely prejudiced, or even cases in which the continuances were granted ex parte. But barring extraordinary circumstances, we would be reluctant indeed to rule that a defendant was denied this constitutional right on a record that strongly indicates, as does this one, that the defendant did not want a speedy trial. We hold, therefore, that Barker was not deprived of his due process right to a speedy trial.

The judgment of the Court of Appeals is affirmed.

Affirmed.

Remedy for Violation of the Constitutional Speedy Trial Right

The sole remedy for a violation of the speedy trial right is outright dismissal of the case. In other words, other remedies such as the reduction of the defendant's sentence, or the exclusion of certain government evidence are insufficient. The court *must* dismiss the case, and this dismissal *must* be with prejudice, meaning that the government cannot simply obtain a new indictment and start over. *See Strunk v. United States*, 412 U.S. 434 (1973). Is dismissal with prejudice too harsh of a remedy? What effect might this sanction have on courts' decision to find a constitutional speedy trial violation in the first place?

III. STATUTORY SPEEDY TRIAL LIMITS

The Speedy Trial Act of 1974, codified at 18 U.S.C. §§ 3161–3174, implements the speedy trial protection. As such, it is usually the primary touchstone for courts in ensuring that cases progress in a manner consistent with the spirit of the Speedy Trial Clause.

18 U.S.C. § 3161. Time limits and exclusions

(a) In any case involving a defendant charged with an offense, the appropriate judicial officer, at the earliest practicable time, shall, after consultation with the counsel for the defendant and the attorney for the

Government, set the case for trial on a day certain, or list it for trial on a weekly or other short-term trial calendar at a place within the judicial district, so as to assure a speedy trial.

(b)   Any information or indictment charging an individual with the commission of an offense shall be filed within thirty days from the date on which such individual was arrested or served with a summons in connection with such charges. If an individual has been charged with a felony in a district in which no grand jury has been in session during such thirty-day period, the period of time for filing of the indictment shall be extended an additional thirty days.

(c)(1)   In any case in which a plea of not guilty is entered, the trial of a defendant charged in an information or indictment with the commission of an offense shall commence within seventy days from the filing date (and making public) of the information or indictment, or from the date the defendant has appeared before a judicial officer of the court in which such charge is pending, whichever date last occurs. If a defendant consents in writing to be tried before a magistrate judge on a complaint, the trial shall commence within seventy days from the date of such consent.

(2)   Unless the defendant consents in writing to the contrary, the trial shall not commence less than thirty days from the date on which the defendant first appears through counsel or expressly waives counsel and elects to proceed pro se.

(d)(1)   If any indictment or information is dismissed upon motion of the defendant, or any charge contained in a complaint filed against an individual is dismissed or otherwise dropped, and thereafter a complaint is filed against such defendant or individual charging him with the same offense or an offense based on the same conduct or arising from the same criminal episode, or an information or indictment is filed charging such defendant with the same offense or an offense based on the same conduct or arising from the same criminal episode, the provisions of subsections (b) and (c) of this section shall be applicable with respect to such subsequent complaint, indictment, or information, as the case may be.

(2)   If the defendant is to be tried upon an indictment or information dismissed by a trial court and reinstated following an appeal, the trial shall commence within seventy days from the date the action occasioning the trial becomes final, except that the court retrying the case may extend the period for trial not to exceed one hundred and eighty days from the date the action occasioning the trial becomes final if the unavailability of witnesses or other factors resulting from the passage of time shall make trial within seventy days impractical. The periods

of delay enumerated in section 3161(h) are excluded in computing the time limitations specified in this section. The sanctions of section 3162 apply to this subsection.

(e) If the defendant is to be tried again following a declaration by the trial judge of a mistrial or following an order of such judge for a new trial, the trial shall commence within seventy days from the date the action occasioning the retrial becomes final. If the defendant is to be tried again following an appeal or a collateral attack, the trial shall commence within seventy days from the date the action occasioning the retrial becomes final, except that the court retrying the case may extend the period for retrial not to exceed one hundred and eighty days from the date the action occasioning the retrial becomes final if unavailability of witnesses or other factors resulting from passage of time shall make trial within seventy days impractical. The periods of delay enumerated in section 3161(h) are excluded in computing the time limitations specified in this section. The sanctions of section 3162 apply to this subsection.

* * *

(h) The following periods of delay shall be excluded in computing the time within which an information or an indictment must be filed, or in computing the time within which the trial of any such offense must commence:

(1) Any period of delay resulting from other proceedings concerning the defendant, including but not limited to—

(A) delay resulting from any proceeding, including any examinations, to determine the mental competency or physical capacity of the defendant;

(B) delay resulting from trial with respect to other charges against the defendant;

(C) delay resulting from any interlocutory appeal;

(D) delay resulting from any pretrial motion, from the filing of the motion through the conclusion of the hearing on, or other prompt disposition of, such motion;

(E) delay resulting from any proceeding relating to the transfer of a case or the removal of any defendant from another district under the Federal Rules of Criminal Procedure;

(F) delay resulting from transportation of any defendant from another district, or to and from places of examination or hospitalization, except that any time consumed in excess of ten days from the date an order of removal or an order directing such transportation, and the defendant's arrival at the destination shall be presumed to be unreasonable;

(G) delay resulting from consideration by the court of a proposed plea agreement to be entered into by the defendant and the attorney for the Government; and

(H) delay reasonably attributable to any period, not to exceed thirty days, during which any proceeding concerning the defendant is actually under advisement by the court.

(2) Any period of delay during which prosecution is deferred by the attorney for the Government pursuant to written agreement with the defendant, with the approval of the court, for the purpose of allowing the defendant to demonstrate his good conduct.

(3)(A) Any period of delay resulting from the absence or unavailability of the defendant or an essential witness.

(B) For purposes of subparagraph (A) of this paragraph, a defendant or an essential witness shall be considered absent when his whereabouts are unknown and, in addition, he is attempting to avoid apprehension or prosecution or his whereabouts cannot be determined by due diligence. For purposes of such subparagraph, a defendant or an essential witness shall be considered unavailable whenever his whereabouts are known but his presence for trial cannot be obtained by due diligence or he resists appearing at or being returned for trial.

(4) Any period of delay resulting from the fact that the defendant is mentally incompetent or physically unable to stand trial.

(5) If the information or indictment is dismissed upon motion of the attorney for the Government and thereafter a charge is filed against the defendant for the same offense, or any offense required to be joined with that offense, any period of delay from the date the charge was dismissed to the date the time limitation would commence to run as to the subsequent charge had there been no previous charge.

(6) A reasonable period of delay when the defendant is joined for trial with a codefendant as to whom the time for trial has not run and no motion for severance has been granted.

(7)(A) Any period of delay resulting from a continuance granted by any judge on his own motion or at the request of the defendant or his counsel or at the request of the attorney for the Government, if the judge granted such continuance on the basis of his findings that the ends of justice served by taking such action outweigh the best interest of the public and the defendant in a speedy trial. No such period of delay resulting from a continuance granted by the court in accordance with this paragraph shall be excludable under this subsection unless the court sets forth, in the record of the case, either orally or in writing, its reasons for finding that the ends of justice served by the granting of such continuance outweigh the best interests of the public and the defendant in a speedy trial.

(B) The factors, among others, which a judge shall consider in determining whether to grant a continuance under subparagraph (A) of this paragraph in any case are as follows:

(i) Whether the failure to grant such a continuance in the proceeding would be likely to make a continuation of such proceeding impossible, or result in a miscarriage of justice.

(ii) Whether the case is so unusual or so complex, due to the number of defendants, the nature of the prosecution, or the existence of novel questions of fact or law, that it is unreasonable to expect adequate preparation for pretrial proceedings or for the trial itself within the time limits established by this section.

(iii) Whether, in a case in which arrest precedes indictment, delay in the filing of the indictment is caused because the arrest occurs at a time such that it is unreasonable to expect return and filing of the indictment within the period specified in section 3161(b), or because the facts upon which the grand jury must base its determination are unusual or complex.

(iv) Whether the failure to grant such a continuance in a case which, taken as a whole, is not so unusual or so complex as to fall within clause (ii), would deny the defendant reasonable time to obtain counsel, would unreasonably deny the defendant or the Government continuity of counsel, or would deny counsel for the defendant or the attorney for the Government the reasonable time necessary for effective preparation, taking into account the exercise of due diligence.

(C) No continuance under subparagraph (A) of this paragraph shall be granted because of general congestion of the court's calendar, or lack of diligent preparation or failure to obtain available witnesses on the part of the attorney for the Government.

(8) Any period of delay, not to exceed one year, ordered by a district court upon an application of a party and a finding by a preponderance of the evidence that an official request, as defined in section 3292 of this title, has been made for evidence of any such offense and that it reasonably appears, or reasonably appeared at the time the request was made, that such evidence is, or was, in such foreign country.

(i)   If trial did not commence within the time limitation specified in section 3161 because the defendant had entered a plea of guilty or nolo contendere subsequently withdrawn to any or all charges in an indictment or information, the defendant shall be deemed indicted with respect to all charges therein contained within the meaning of section 3161, on the day the order permitting withdrawal of the plea becomes final.

(j)(1) If the attorney for the Government knows that a person charged with an offense is serving a term of imprisonment in any penal institution, he shall promptly—

(A) undertake to obtain the presence of the prisoner for trial; or

(B) cause a detainer to be filed with the person having custody of the prisoner and request him to so advise the prisoner and to advise the prisoner of his right to demand trial.

(2) If the person having custody of such prisoner receives a detainer, he shall promptly advise the prisoner of the charge and of the prisoner's right to demand trial. If at any time thereafter the prisoner informs the person having custody that he does demand trial, such person shall cause notice to that effect to be sent promptly to the attorney for the Government who caused the detainer to be filed.

(3) Upon receipt of such notice, the attorney for the Government shall promptly seek to obtain the presence of the prisoner for trial.

(4) When the person having custody of the prisoner receives from the attorney for the Government a properly

supported request for temporary custody of such prisoner for trial, the prisoner shall be made available to that attorney for the Government (subject, in cases of interjurisdictional transfer, to any right of the prisoner to contest the legality of his delivery).

(k)(1) If the defendant is absent (as defined by subsection (h)(3)) on the day set for trial, and the defendant's subsequent appearance before the court on a bench warrant or other process or surrender to the court occurs more than 21 days after the day set for trial, the defendant shall be deemed to have first appeared before a judicial officer of the court in which the information or indictment is pending within the meaning of subsection (c) on the date of the defendant's subsequent appearance before the court.

(2) If the defendant is absent (as defined by subsection (h)(3)) on the day set for trial, and the defendant's subsequent appearance before the court on a bench warrant or other process or surrender to the court occurs not more than 21 days after the day set for trial, the time limit required by subsection (c), as extended by subsection (h), shall be further extended by 21 days.

18 U.S.C. § 3162. Sanctions

(a)(1) If, in the case of any individual against whom a complaint is filed charging such individual with an offense, no indictment or information is filed within the time limit required by section 3161(b) as extended by section 3161(h) of this chapter, such charge against that individual contained in such complaint shall be dismissed or otherwise dropped. In determining whether to dismiss the case with or without prejudice, the court shall consider, among others, each of the following factors: the seriousness of the offense; the facts and circumstances of the case which led to the dismissal; and the impact of a reprosecution on the administration of this chapter and on the administration of justice.

(2) If a defendant is not brought to trial within the time limit required by section 3161(c) as extended by section 3161(h), the information or indictment shall be dismissed on motion of the defendant. The defendant shall have the burden of proof of supporting such motion but the Government shall have the burden of going forward with the evidence in connection with any exclusion of time under subparagraph 3161(h) (3). In determining whether to dismiss the case with or without prejudice, the court shall consider, among others, each of the following factors: the seriousness of the offense; the facts and circumstances of the case which led to the dismissal; and the impact of a reprosecution on the administration of this chapter and on

the administration of justice. Failure of the defendant to move for dismissal prior to trial or entry of a plea of guilty or nolo contendere shall constitute a waiver of the right to dismissal under this section.

(b) In any case in which counsel for the defendant or the attorney for the Government (1) knowingly allows the case to be set for trial without disclosing the fact that a necessary witness would be unavailable for trial; (2) files a motion solely for the purpose of delay which he knows is totally frivolous and without merit; (3) makes a statement for the purpose of obtaining a continuance which he knows to be false and which is material to the granting of a continuance; or (4) otherwise willfully fails to proceed to trial without justification consistent with section 3161 of this chapter, the court may punish any such counsel or attorney, as follows:

(A) in the case of an appointed defense counsel, by reducing the amount of compensation that otherwise would have been paid to such counsel pursuant to section 3006A of this title in an amount not to exceed 25 per centum thereof;

(B) in the case of a counsel retained in connection with the defense of a defendant, by imposing on such counsel a fine of not to exceed 25 per centum of the compensation to which he is entitled in connection with his defense of such defendant;

(C) by imposing on any attorney for the Government a fine of not to exceed $250;

(D) by denying any such counsel or attorney for the Government the right to practice before the court considering such case for a period of not to exceed ninety days; or

(E) by filing a report with an appropriate disciplinary committee.

The authority to punish provided for by this subsection shall be in addition to any other authority or power available to such court.

(c) The court shall follow procedures established in the Federal Rules of Criminal Procedure in punishing any counsel or attorney for the Government pursuant to this section.

* * *

18 U.S.C. § 3173. Sixth amendment rights

No provision of this chapter shall be interpreted as a bar to any claim of denial of speedy trial as required by amendment VI of the Constitution.

* * *

NOTES ON THE SPEEDY TRIAL ACT

The Speedy Trial Act is lengthy but worth studying closely. One of the provisions not included in the above excerpt is section 3165, which, along with section 3166, requires district courts to prepare "speedy trial plans" geared toward ensuring the prompt "disposition of criminal cases in the district consistent with the time standards of this chapter and the objectives of effective law enforcement, fairness to accused persons, efficient judicial administration, and increased knowledge concerning the proper functioning of the criminal law." 18 U.S.C. § 3166. There is also a provision of the statute under which a district court may apply for a suspension of various time limits in the act due to judicial emergency. *See* 18 U.S.C. § 3174. Finally, it should be noted that section 3162, which is addressed to sanctions, provides a court confronted with a violation of the statute the option of dismissing the case either with or without prejudice, unlike the sanction for a constitutional speedy trial violation, which can only be remedied by dismissal with prejudice. For a state perspective on the speedy trial issue, *see* Daniel Hamburg, *A Broken Clock: Fixing New York's Speedy Trial Statute*, 48 COLUM. J.L. & SOC. PROBS. 223 (2015).

* * *

Rule 48 of the Federal Rules of Criminal Procedure clarifies that the court may dismiss a charging document because of undue delay in prosecution of the case:

Rule 48. Dismissal

(a) By the Government. The government may, with leave of court, dismiss an indictment, information, or complaint. The government may not dismiss the prosecution during trial without the defendant's consent.

(b) By the Court. The court may dismiss an indictment, information, or complaint if unnecessary delay occurs in:

    (1) presenting a charge to a grand jury;

    (2) filing an information against a defendant; or

    (3) bringing a defendant to trial.

COUNSEL EXERCISE 11A: Motion to Dismiss the Indictment on Speedy Trial Grounds (Defense)

The defense should draft a motion to dismiss (with or without prejudice) the indictment with a memorandum in support setting out the strongest constitutional, statutory, or rule-based arguments for dismissal on speedy trial grounds. Assume, for purposes of this exercise, that the defendant's trial will begin 120 days following the arraignment on the indictment in the case. Included with the motion should be a supporting brief or memorandum of law, a proposed order, and a certificate of service.

COUNSEL EXERCISE 11B: Motion to Dismiss the Indictment on Speedy Trial Grounds (Prosecution)

The government should oppose the defense motion, setting out the best arguments for why no such relief should be granted on these grounds. Included with the motion should be a supporting brief or memorandum of law, a proposed order, and a certificate of service.

CHAPTER 12

TRIAL BY JURY

I. INTRODUCTION

"The Trial of all Crimes . . . shall be by Jury."

U.S. CONST., art. III, § 2.

"In all criminal prosecutions, the accused shall enjoy the right to a . . . trial, by an impartial jury."

U.S CONST., amend. VI.

As is discussed in Chapter Six, nearly all criminal convictions derive from guilty pleas and very few cases go to trial. However, many of the procedural rights examined in this textbook operate in the long shadow of the right to jury trial. This Chapter will examine the Sixth Amendment right to jury trial, and the many procedural issues it implicates.

II. THE SIXTH AMENDMENT RIGHT

Duncan v. Louisiana
Supreme Court of the United States, 1968
391 U.S. 145

■ MR. JUSTICE WHITE delivered the opinion of the Court.

Appellant, Gary Duncan, was convicted of simple battery in the Twenty-fifth Judicial District Court of Louisiana. Under Louisiana law simple battery is a misdemeanor, punishable by a maximum of two years' imprisonment and a $300 fine. Appellant sought trial by jury, but because the Louisiana Constitution grants jury trials only in cases in which capital punishment or imprisonment at hard labor may be imposed, the trial judge denied the request. Appellant was convicted and sentenced to serve 60 days in the parish prison and pay a fine of $150. Appellant sought review in the Supreme Court of Louisiana, asserting that the denial of jury trial violated rights guaranteed to him by the United States Constitution. The Supreme Court, finding '(n)o error of law in the ruling complained of,' denied appellant a writ of certiorari. Pursuant to 28 U.S.C. § 1257(2) appellant sought review in this Court, alleging that the Sixth and Fourteenth Amendments to the United States Constitution secure the right to jury trial in state criminal prosecutions where a sentence as long as two years may be imposed. We noted probable jurisdiction, and set the case for oral argument with No. 52, *Bloom v. State of Illinois*, 391 U.S. 194, 88 S.Ct. 1477, 20 L.Ed.2d 522.

Appellant was 19 years of age when tried. While driving on Highway 23 in Plaquemines Parish on October 18, 1966, he saw two younger cousins engaged in a conversation by the side of the road with four white boys. Knowing his cousins, Negroes who had recently transferred to a formerly all-white high school, had reported the occurrence of racial incidents at the school, Duncan stopped the car, got out, and approached the six boys. At trial the white boys and a white onlooker testified, as did appellant and his cousins. The testimony was in dispute on many points, but the witnesses agreed that appellant and the white boys spoke to each other, that appellant encouraged his cousins to break off the encounter and enter his car, and that appellant was about to enter the car himself for the purpose of driving away with his cousins. The whites testified that just before getting in the car appellant slapped Herman Landry, one of the white boys, on the elbow. The Negroes testified that appellant had not slapped Landry, but had merely touched him. The trial judge concluded that the State had proved beyond a reasonable doubt that Duncan had committed simple battery, and found him guilty.

I.

The Fourteenth Amendment denies the States the power to 'deprive any person of life, liberty, or property, without due process of law.' In resolving conflicting claims concerning the meaning of this spacious language, the Court has looked increasingly to the Bill of Rights for guidance; many of the rights guaranteed by the first eight Amendments to the Constitution have been held to be protected against state action by the Due Process Clause of the Fourteenth Amendment. That clause now protects the right to compensation for property taken by the State; the rights of speech, press, and religion covered by the First Amendment; the Fourth Amendment rights to be free from unreasonable searches and seizures and to have excluded from criminal trials any evidence illegally seized; the right guaranteed by the Fifth Amendment to be free of compelled self-incrimination; and the Sixth Amendment rights to counsel, to a speedy and public trial, to confrontation of opposing witnesses, and to compulsory process for obtaining witnesses.

The test for determining whether a right extended by the Fifth and Sixth Amendments with respect to federal criminal proceedings is also protected against state action by the Fourteenth Amendment has been phrased in a variety of ways in the opinions of this Court. The question has been asked whether a right is among those "fundamental principles of liberty and justice which lie at the base of all our civil and political institutions," *Powell v. State of Alabama*, 287 U.S. 45, 67, 53 S.Ct. 55,

63, 77 L.Ed. 158 (1932); whether it is 'basic in our system of jurisprudence,' *In re Oliver*, 333 U.S. 257, 273, 68 S.Ct. 499, 507, 92 L.Ed. 682 (1948); and whether it is 'a fundamental right, essential to a fair trial,' *Gideon v. Wainwright*, 372 U.S. 335, 343–344, 83 S.Ct. 792, 796, 9 L.Ed.2d 799 (1963); *Malloy v. Hogan*, 378 U.S. 1, 6, 84 S.Ct. 1489, 1492, 12 L.Ed.2d 653 (1964); *Pointer v. State of Texas*, 380 U.S. 400, 403, 85 S.Ct. 1065, 1067, 13 L.Ed.2d 923 (1965). The claim before us is that the right to trial by jury guaranteed by the Sixth Amendment meets these tests. The position of Louisiana, on the other hand, is that the Constitution imposes upon the States no duty to give a jury trial in any criminal case, regardless of the seriousness of the crime or the size of the punishment which may be imposed. Because we believe that trial by jury in criminal cases is fundamental to the American scheme of justice, we hold that the Fourteenth Amendment guarantees a right of jury trial in all criminal cases which—were they to be tried in a federal court—would come within the Sixth Amendment's guarantee. Since we consider the appeal before us to be such a case, we hold that the Constitution was violated when appellant's demand for jury trial was refused.

The history of trial by jury in criminal cases has been frequently told. It is sufficient for present purposes to say that by the time our Constitution was written, jury trial in criminal cases had been in existence in England for several centuries and carried impressive credentials traced by many to Magna Carta. Its preservation and proper operation as a protection against arbitrary rule were among the major objectives of the revolutionary settlement which was expressed in the Declaration and Bill of Rights of 1689. In the 18th century Blackstone could write:

'Our law has therefore wisely placed this strong and two-fold barrier, of a presentment and a trial by jury, between the liberties of the people and the prerogative of the crown. It was necessary, for preserving the admirable balance of our constitution, to vest the executive power of the laws in the prince: and yet this power might be dangerous and destructive to that very constitution, if exerted without check or control, by justices of oyer and terminer occasionally named by the crown; who might then, as in France or Turkey, imprison, dispatch, or exile any man that was obnoxious to the government, by an instant declaration that such is their will and pleasure. But the founders of the English law have, with excellent forecast, contrived that * * * the truth of every accusation, whether preferred in the shape of indictment, information, or appeal, should afterwards be confirmed by the unanimous suffrage of twelve of his equals and neighbours, indifferently chosen and superior to all suspicion.'

Jury trial came to America with English colonists, and received strong support from them. Royal interference with the jury trial was deeply resented. Among the resolutions adopted by the First Congress of the American Colonies (the Stamp Act Congress) on October 19, 1765—resolutions deemed by their authors to state 'the most essential rights and liberties of the colonists'—was the declaration:

> 'That trial by jury is the inherent and invaluable right of every British subject in these colonies.'

The First Continental Congress, in the resolve of October 14, 1774, objected to trials before judges dependent upon the Crown alone for their salaries and to trials in England for alleged crimes committed in the colonies; the Congress therefore declared:

> 'That the respective colonies are entitled to the common law of England, and more especially to the great and inestimable privilege of being tried by their peers of the vicinage, according to the course of that law.'

The Declaration of Independence stated solemn objections to the King's making 'judges dependent on his will alone, for the tenure of their offices, and the amount and payment of their salaries,' to his 'depriving us in many cases, of the benefits of Trial by Jury,' and to his 'transporting us beyond Seas to be tried for pretended offenses.' The Constitution itself, in Art. III, § 2, commanded:

> 'The Trial of all Crimes, except in Cases of Impeachment, shall be by Jury; and such Trial shall be held in the State where the said Crimes shall have been committed.'

Objections to the Constitution because of the absence of a bill of rights were met by the immediate submission and adoption of the Bill of Rights. Included was the Sixth Amendment which, among other things, provided:

> 'In all criminal prosecutions, the accused shall enjoy the right to a speedy and public trial, by an impartial jury of the State and district wherein the crime shall have been committed.'

The constitutions adopted by the original States guaranteed jury trial. Also, the constitution of every State entering the Union thereafter in one form or another protected the right to jury trial in criminal cases.

Even such skeletal history is impressive support for considering the right to jury trial in criminal cases to be fundamental to our system of justice, an importance frequently recognized in the opinions of this Court. For example, the Court has said:

'Those who emigrated to this country from England brought with them this great privilege 'as their birthright and inheritance, as a part of that admirable common law which had fenced around and interposed barriers on every side against the approaches of arbitrary power."

Jury trial continues to receive strong support. The laws of every State guarantee a right to jury trial in serious criminal cases; no State has dispensed with it; nor are there significant movements underway to do so. Indeed, the three most recent state constitutional revisions, in Maryland, Michigan, and New York, carefully preserved the right of the accused to have the judgment of a jury when tried for a serious crime.

We are aware of prior cases in this Court in which the prevailing opinion contains statements contrary to our holding today that the right to jury trial in serious criminal cases is a fundamental right and hence must be recognized by the States as part of their obligation to extend due process of law to all persons within their jurisdiction. Louisiana relies especially on *Maxwell v. Dow*, 176 U.S. 581, 20 S.Ct. 448, 44 L.Ed. 597 (1900); *Palko v. State of Connecticut*, 302 U.S. 319, 58 S.Ct. 149, 82 L.Ed. 288 (1937); and *Snyder v. Commonwealth of Massachusetts*, 291 U.S. 97, 54 S.Ct. 330, 78 L.Ed. 674 (1934). None of these cases, however, dealt with a State which had purported to dispense entirely with a jury trial in serious criminal cases. Maxwell held that no provision of the Bill of Rights applied to the States—a position long since repudiated—and that the Due Process Clause of the Fourteenth Amendment did not prevent a State from trying a defendant for a noncapital offense with fewer than 12 men on the jury. It did not deal with a case in which no jury at all had been provided. In neither Palko nor Snyder was jury trial actually at issue, although both cases contain important dicta asserting that the right to jury trial is not essential to ordered liberty and may be dispensed with by the States regardless of the Sixth and Fourteenth Amendments. These observations, though weighty and respectable, are nevertheless dicta, unsupported by holdings in this Court that a State may refuse a defendant's demand for a jury trial when he is charged with a serious crime. Perhaps because the right to jury trial was not directly at stake, the Court's remarks about the jury in Palko and Snyder took no note of past or current developments regarding jury trials, did not consider its purposes and functions, attempted no inquiry into how well it was performing its job, and did not discuss possible distinctions between civil and criminal cases. In *Malloy v. Hogan*, supra, the Court rejected Palko's discussion of the self-incrimination clause. Respectfully, we reject the prior dicta regarding jury trial in criminal cases.

The guarantees of jury trial in the Federal and State Constitutions reflect a profound judgment about the way in which law should be enforced and justice administered. A right to jury trial is granted to criminal defendants in order to prevent oppression by the Government. Those who wrote our constitutions knew from history and experience that it was necessary to protect against unfounded criminal charges brought to eliminate enemies and against judges too responsive to the voice of higher authority. The framers of the constitutions strove to create an independent judiciary but insisted upon further protection against arbitrary action. Providing an accused with the right to be tried by a jury of his peers gave him an inestimable safeguard against the corrupt or overzealous prosecutor and against the compliant, biased, or eccentric judge. If the defendant preferred the common-sense judgment of a jury to the more tutored but perhaps less sympathetic reaction of the single judge, he was to have it. Beyond this, the jury trial provisions in the Federal and State Constitutions reflect a fundamental decision about the exercise of official power—a reluctance to entrust plenary powers over the life and liberty of the citizen to one judge or to a group of judges. Fear of unchecked power, so typical of our State and Federal Governments in other respects, found expression in the criminal law in this insistence upon community participation in the determination of guilt or innocence. The deep commitment of the Nation to the right of jury trial in serious criminal cases as a defense against arbitrary law enforcement qualifies for protection under the Due Process Clause of the Fourteenth Amendment, and must therefore be respected by the States.

Of course jury trial has 'its weaknesses and the potential for misuse,' *Singer v. United States*, 380 U.S. 24, 35, 85 S.Ct. 783, 790, 13 L.Ed.2d 630 (1965). We are aware of the long debate, especially in this century, among those who write about the administration of justice, as to the wisdom of permitting untrained laymen to determine the facts in civil and criminal proceedings. Although the debate has been intense, with powerful voices on either side, most of the controversy has centered on the jury in civil cases. Indeed, some of the severest critics of civil juries acknowledge that the arguments for criminal juries are much stronger. In addition, at the heart of the dispute have been express or implicit assertions that juries are incapable of adequately understanding evidence or determining issues of fact, and that they are unpredictable, quixotic, and little better than a roll of dice. Yet, the most recent and exhaustive study of the jury in criminal cases concluded that juries do understand the evidence and come to sound conclusions in most of the cases presented to them and that when juries differ with the result at which the judge would have arrived, it is usually because they are serving some of the very purposes for which they were created and for which they are now employed.

The State of Louisiana urges that holding that the Fourteenth Amendment assures a right to jury trial will cast doubt on the integrity of every trial conducted without a jury. Plainly, this is not the import of our holding. Our conclusion is that in the American States, as in the federal judicial system, a general grant of jury trial for serious offenses is a fundamental right, essential for preventing miscarriages of justice and for assuring that fair trials are provided for all defendants. We would not assert, however, that every criminal trial—or any particular trial—held before a judge alone is unfair or that a defendant may never be as fairly treated by a judge as he would be by a jury. Thus we hold no constitutional doubts about the practices, common in both federal and state courts, of accepting waivers of jury trial and prosecuting petty crimes without extending a right to jury trial. However, the fact is that in most places more trials for serious crimes are to juries than to a court alone; a great many defendants prefer the judgment of a jury to that of a court. Even where defendants are satisfied with bench trials, the right to a jury trial very likely serves its intended purpose of making judicial or prosecutorial unfairness less likely.

II.

Louisiana's final contention is that even if it must grant jury trials in serious criminal cases, the conviction before us is valid and constitutional because here the petitioner was tried for simple battery and was sentenced to only 60 days in the parish prison. We are not persuaded. It is doubtless true that there is a category of petty crimes or offenses which is not subject to the Sixth Amendment jury trial provision and should not be subject to the Fourteenth Amendment jury trial requirement here applied to the States. Crimes carrying possible penalties up to six months do not require a jury trial if they otherwise qualify as petty offenses, *Cheff v. Schnackenberg*, 384 U.S. 373, 86 S.Ct. 1523, 16 L.Ed.2d 629 (1966). But the penalty authorized for a particular crime is of major relevance in determining whether it is serious or not and may in itself, if severe enough, subject the trial to the mandates of the Sixth Amendment. *District of Columbia v. Clawans*, 300 U.S. 617, 57 S.Ct. 660, 81 L.Ed. 843 (1937). The penalty authorized by the law of the locality may be taken 'as a gauge of its social and ethical judgments.' 300 U.S., at 628, 57 S.Ct., at 663, of the crime in question. In *Clawans* the defendant was jailed for 60 days, but it was the 90-day authorized punishment on which the Court focused in determining that the offense was not one for which the Constitution assured trial by jury. In the case before us the Legislature of Louisiana has made simple battery a criminal offense punishable by imprisonment for up to two years and a fine. The question, then, is whether a crime carrying such a penalty is an offense which Louisiana may insist on trying without a jury.

We think not. So-called petty offenses were tried without juries both in England and in the Colonies and have always been held to be exempt from the otherwise comprehensive language of the Sixth Amendment's jury trial provisions. There is no substantial evidence that the Framers intended to depart from this established common-law practice, and the possible consequences to defendants from convictions for petty offenses have been thought insufficient to outweigh the benefits to efficient law enforcement and simplified judicial administration resulting from the availability of speedy and inexpensive nonjury adjudications. These same considerations compel the same result under the Fourteenth Amendment. Of course the boundaries of the petty offense category have always been ill-defined, if not ambulatory. In the absence of an explicit constitutional provision, the definitional task necessarily falls on the courts, which must either pass upon the validity of legislative attempts to identify those petty offenses which are exempt from jury trial or, where the legislature has not addressed itself to the problem, themselves face the question in the first instance. In either case it is necessary to draw a line in the spectrum of crime, separating petty from serious infractions. This process, although essential, cannot be wholly satisfactory, for it requires attaching different consequences to events which, when they lie near the line, actually differ very little.

In determining whether the length of the authorized prison term or the seriousness of other punishment is enough in itself to require a jury trial, we are counseled by *District of Columbia v. Clawans*, supra, to refer to objective criteria, chiefly the existing laws and practices in the Nation. In the federal system, petty offenses are defined as those punishable by no more than six months in prison and a $500 fine. In 49 of the 50 States crimes subject to trial without a jury, which occasionally include simple battery, are punishable by no more than one year in jail. Moreover, in the late 18th century in America crimes triable without a jury were for the most part punishable by no more than a six-month prison term, although there appear to have been exceptions to this rule. We need not, however, settle in this case the exact location of the line between petty offenses and serious crimes. It is sufficient for our purposes to hold that a crime punishable by two years in prison is, based on past and contemporary standards in this country, a serious crime and not a petty offense. Consequently, appellant was entitled to a jury trial and it was error to deny it.

The judgment below is reversed and the case is remanded for proceedings not inconsistent with this opinion.

Reversed and remanded.

The Purpose of the Right to Jury Trial

Duncan v. Louisiana incorporated the right to jury trial to apply to the states. As such, the cases produced numerous concurring and dissenting opinions (not included in the excerpt) by justices who weighed in on the debate between the selective incorporation and total incorporation. However, the case is also important as an opportunity for the Court to take inventory of the central purposes of the right to be tried by a jury in a criminal case. What are some of these key purposes identified by the Court? Which of these purposes relate to community or systemic interests and which relate to the interests of the accused? Professor Fairfax, in his article, *Harmless Constitutional Error and the Institutional Significance of the Jury*, 76 FORDHAM L. REV. 2027 (2008), discusses these questions:

> The guarantee of "trial by jury . . . is fundamental to the American scheme of justice," so much so that is has been described as "the spinal column of American democracy." A review of Article III's mandate that "[t]he Trial of all Crimes . . . shall be by Jury'" immediately highlights the structural significance of the jury. The framers saw the jury as an indispensable organ of government. Although the Sixth Amendment guarantees to individuals the right to jury trial, the Article III Jury Clause cements the permanent role of the jury in the framework of government itself. As Professor Akhil Amar persuasively has argued, "[I]t is anachronistic to see jury trial as an issue of individual right rather than (also, and more fundamentally) a question of government structure." Likewise, under state constitutions, the jury has had a celebrated role; all the early state constitutions, many of which were drafted by those involved with the framing of the Federal Constitution, held the right to jury trial in high esteem. Indeed, on both the federal and state levels, the jury was thought to be a key protection of individual freedom against the excesses of the branches of tripartite government.

> Although the importance of the jury's role in the American criminal justice system requires no extended discussion, it bears emphasizing the community voice function the jury performs. As the Supreme Court in *Duncan* noted, in affirming the applicability of the Sixth Amendment to the States, "Fear of unchecked power, so typical of our State and Federal Governments in other respects, found expression in the criminal law in this insistence upon community participation in the determination of guilt or innocence." This structural role of the jury is meant to ensure the input of the citizenry in the operation of the courts and government more generally. Even

recently, the Supreme Court has noted that Sixth Amendment right to jury trial is "no mere procedural formality, but a fundamental reservation of power in our constitutional structure . . . meant to ensure [the people's] control in the judiciary." The moral values of the community are expressed through jury service, deliberation, and verdict, and that expression is a function and prerogative of the jury that is independent of the right of the criminal defendant to demand it.

The framers saw the jury as the means for the citizenry to hold ultimate sway over the judicial function of government, in the same way power was given, by means of the ballot, over the legislative and executive functions. Indeed, Thomas Jefferson even expressed a preference for citizen oversight of the affairs of the judiciary through jury service over analogous oversight of the legislative branch through the cherished model of representative government.

Another institutional prerogative of the jury derives from the Double Jeopardy Clause and its mandate that jury verdicts of acquittal remain inviolate. Juries can, of course, engage in nullification, introducing mercy into the criminal justice system or communicating their messages to the legislature regarding the wisdom of its laws, the judiciary regarding its sentencing and process oversight, and the executive regarding its enforcement and prosecution priorities. Regardless of the normative merits of whether juries should engage in nullification, this ancient power of the petit jury is plenary and unreviewable. Furthermore, although this "voice of the community role" includes the power of citizens to nullify, its function extends beyond that. Lay jurors bring a perspective to the criminal fact-finding process the framers thought valuable enough to enshrine in the body of the Constitution. Juries also serve the institutional function of training the citizen-jurors in the processes of democratic governance. Through jury service, citizens participate in the machinery of government, learning about it while influencing and shaping it at the same time. As Alexis de Tocqueville remarked when commenting upon the manner in which the American jury serves as a vehicle for the education of the citizenry, "[T]he jury, which is the most energetic form of popular rule, is also the most effective means of teaching people how to rule."

These constitutional and traditional institutional functions of the jury, many of which are separate and distinct from the role of securing the individual rights of criminal defendants, have begun to receive the greater recognition they deserve. The late twentieth-century renaissance of the jury trial right, marked by *Apprendi* and its progeny, may have been prompted more by respect for the institutional legitimacy of the jury and its constitutional role and prerogatives than for the jury rights of criminal defendants.

* * *

III. FEDERAL RULE OF CRIMINAL PROCEDURE 23

Rule 23 of the Federal Rules of Criminal Procedure provides the parameters of the federal criminal trial jury right. Whereas Rule 24 governs jury selection, Rule 30 governs jury instructions, and Rule 31 governs the jury verdict, Rule 23 governs the question whether jury trial may be waived and the size of the jury.

Rule 23. Jury or Nonjury Trial

(a) **Jury Trial.** If the defendant is entitled to a jury trial, the trial must be by trial unless:

(1)   the defendant waives a jury trial in writing;

(2)   the government consents; and

(3)   the court approves.

Entitlement to the Jury Trial Right for Non-Petty Offenses

Rule 23(a) provides that, absent waiver, the trial must be by jury *if the defendant is entitled to a jury trial*. But when is the defendant entitled to a jury trial? The Supreme Court has held that an offense that is punishable by more than six months incarceration triggers the right to jury trial. *See Baldwin v. New York*, 399 U.S. 66 (1970).

It is important to keep in mind that this jury trial right is triggered not by the sentence the defendant actually receives, but the sentence that is *authorized* under the statute. *See Frank v. United States,* 395 U.S. 147 (1969); *District of Columbia v. Clawans*, 300 U.S. 617 (1937). Thus, if a defendant is denied a jury trial and is convicted of an offense punishable by two years incarceration, but is sentenced to only three months incarceration, her Sixth Amendment right to jury trial still has been violated. *But see Lewis v. United States*, 518 U.S. 322 (1996) (possibility of consecutive petty offense sentences that, in the aggregate, would mean incarceration in excess of six months does not trigger jury right).*

---

*   The Court in *Lewis* distinguished *Codispoti v. Pennsylvania*, 418 U.S. 506 (1974) (in which the Court held that the jury trial right was triggered when multiple contempt sentences of less than six months were aggregated for a total term of incarceration of longer than six months), on the grounds that criminal contempt presents a unique situation and that there

Furthermore, it is only presumed that a petty offense (an offense punishable by no more than six months incarceration) does not carry the right to jury trial. An offense for which the authorized incarceration is six months or less, but which carries severe collateral penalties *could* also trigger the right to jury trial, but the threshold is high. *See Blanton v. City of North Las Vegas*, 489 U.S. 538 (1989) (statutory penalties of six months incarceration, maximum $1,000 fine, temporary loss of driver's license, forced community service in identifiable clothing, and required alcohol abuse course "viewed together . . . are not so severe that DUI must be considered a 'serious' offense for purposes of the Sixth Amendment").

Waiver of the Right to Jury Trial

Note that Rule 23(a) only permits the defendant to waive jury trial if the government consents and the court approves the waiver. Does the rule properly give the government and the court the ability to frustrate the defendant's desire to have a case tried before a judge, rather than before a jury? The Supreme Court, in *Singer v. United States*, 380 U.S. 24 (1965), answered this question in the affirmative:

> We can find no evidence that the common law recognized that defendants had the right to choose between court and jury trial. Although instances of waiver of jury trial can be found in certain of the colonies prior to the adoption of the Constitution, they were isolated instances occurring pursuant to colonial 'constitutions' or statutes and were clear departures from the common law. There is no indication that the colonists considered the ability to waive a jury trial to be of equal importance to the right to demand one. Having found that the Constitution neither confers nor recognizes a right of criminal defendants to have their cases tried before a judge alone, we also conclude that Rule 23(a) sets forth a reasonable procedure governing attempted waivers of jury trials. * * *

> The Constitution recognizes an adversary system as the proper method of determining guilt, and the Government, as a litigant, has a legitimate interest in seeing that cases in which it believes a conviction is warranted are tried before the tribunal which the Constitution regards as most likely to produce a fair result. * * *

> In upholding the validity of Rule 23(a), we reiterate the sentiment expressed in *Berger v. United States*, 295 U.S. 78, 88, 55 S.Ct. 629, 633, 79 L.Ed. 1314, that the government attorney in a criminal prosecution is not an ordinary party to a

---

was no maximum penalty for the contempt punishment in the case. *See Lewis*, 518 U.S. at 328–29.

controversy, but a 'servant of the law' with a 'twofold aim * * * that guilt shall not escape or innocence suffer.' It was in light of this concept of the role of prosecutor that Rule 23(a) was framed, and we are confident that it is in this light that it will continue to be invoked by government attorneys. Because of this confidence in the integrity of the federal prosecutor, Rule 23(a) does not require that the Government articulate its reasons for demanding a jury trial at the time it refuses to consent to a defendant's proffered waiver. Nor should we assume that federal prosecutors would demand a jury trial for an ignoble purpose.

Recall the two constitutional provisions relating to the jury trial. Article III, section 2 of the United States Constitution mandates that "[t]he Trial of all Crimes ... shall be by Jury." Furthermore, the Sixth Amendment requires that "[i]n all criminal prosecutions, the accused shall enjoy the right to a ... trial, by an impartial jury." Do either of these provisions support the argument that jury trial is something a criminal defendant can waive?

NOTE ON STATE PRACTICE

What are the rules governing a criminal defendant's ability to waive jury trial in the jurisdiction in which you intend to practice? *See, e.g.,* W. Va. R. Crim. P. 23.

* * *

Rule 23. Jury or Nonjury Trial

(b) Jury Size.

(1) In General. A jury consists of 12 persons unless this rule provides otherwise.

(2) Stipulation for a Smaller Jury. At any time before the verdict, the parties may, with the court's approval, stipulate in writing that:

(A) the jury may consist of fewer than 12 persons; or

(B) a jury of fewer than 12 persons may return a verdict if the court finds it necessary to excuse a juror for good cause after the trial begins.

(3) Court Order for a Jury of 11. After the jury has retired to deliberate, the court may permit a jury of 11 persons to return a verdict, even without a stipulation by the parties, if the court finds good cause to excuse a juror.

(c) Nonjury Trial. In a case tried without a jury, the court must find the defendant guilty or not guilty. If a party requests before the finding of guilty or not guilty, the court must state its specific findings of fact in open court or in written decision or opinion.

Jury Size

Williams v. Florida

Supreme Court of the United States, 1970
399 U.S. 78

■ MR. JUSTICE WHITE delivered the opinion of the Court.

Prior to his trial for robbery in the State of Florida, petitioner filed * * * a pretrial motion to impanel a 12-man jury instead of the six-man jury provided by Florida law in all but capital cases. That motion * * * was denied. Petitioner was convicted as charged and was sentenced to life imprisonment. The District Court of Appeal affirmed, rejecting petitioner's claims that his * * * Sixth Amendment right[ ] had been violated. We granted certiorari. 396 U.S. 955, 90 S.Ct. 439, 24 L.Ed.2d 420 (1969).

* * *

II

In *Duncan v. Louisiana*, 391 U.S. 145, 88 S.Ct. 1444, 20 L.Ed.2d 491 (1968), we held that the Fourteenth Amendment guarantees a right to trial by jury in all criminal cases that—were they to be tried in a federal court—would come within the Sixth Amendment's guarantee. Petitioner's trial for robbery on July 3, 1968, clearly falls within the scope of that holding. See *Baldwin v. New York*, 399 U.S. 66, 90 S.Ct. 1886, 26 N.E.2d 437; *DeStefano v. Woods,* 392 U.S. 631, 88 S.Ct. 2093, 20 L.Ed.2d 1308 (1968). The question in this case then is whether the constitutional guarantee of a trial by 'jury' necessarily requires trial by exactly 12 persons, rather than some lesser number—in this case six. We hold that the 12-man panel is not a necessary ingredient of 'trial by jury,' and that respondent's refusal to impanel more than the six members provided for by Florida law did not violate petitioner's Sixth Amendment rights as applied to the States through the Fourteenth.

We had occasion in *Duncan v. Louisiana*, supra, to review briefly the oft-told history of the development of trial by jury in criminal cases. That history revealed a long tradition attaching great importance to the concept of relying on a body of one's peers to determine guilt or innocence as a safeguard against arbitrary law enforcement. That same history, however, affords little insight into the considerations that gradually led the size of that body to be generally fixed at 12. Some have suggested that the number 12 was fixed upon simply because that was the number of the presentment jury from the hundred, from which the petit jury developed. Other, less circular but more fanciful reasons for the number 12 have been given, 'but they were all brought forward after the number was fixed,' and rest on little more than mystical or superstitious insights into the significance of '12.' Lord Coke's explanation that the 'number of twelve is much respected in holy writ, as 12 apostles, 12 stones, 12 tribes, etc.,' is typical. In short, while sometime in the 14th century the size of the jury at common law came to be fixed generally at 12, that particular feature of the jury system appears to have been a historical accident, unrelated to the great purposes which gave rise to the jury in the first place. The question before us is whether this accidental feature of the jury has been immutably codified into our Constitution.

This Court's earlier decisions have assumed an affirmative answer to this question. The leading case so construing the Sixth Amendment is *Thompson v. Utah*, 170 U.S. 343, 18 S.Ct. 620, 42 L.Ed. 1061 (1898). There the defendant had been tried and convicted by a 12-man jury for a crime committed in the Territory of Utah. A new trial was granted, but by that time Utah had been admitted as a State. The defendant's new trial proceeded under Utah's Constitution, providing for a jury of only eight members. This Court reversed the resulting conviction, holding that Utah's constitutional provision was an ex post facto law as applied to the defendant. In reaching its conclusion, the Court announced that the Sixth Amendment was applicable to the defendant's trial when Utah was a Territory, and that the jury referred to in the Amendment was a jury 'constituted, as it was at common law, of twelve persons, neither more nor less.' 170 U.S., at 349, 18 S.Ct., at 622. Arguably unnecessary for the result, this announcement was supported simply by referring to the Magna Carta, and by quoting passages from treatises which noted—what has already been seen—that at common law the jury did indeed consist of 12. Noticeably absent was any discussion of the essential step in the argument: namely, that every feature of the jury as it existed at common law—whether incidental or essential to that institution—was necessarily included in the Constitution wherever that document referred to a 'jury.' Subsequent decisions have reaffirmed the announcement in Thompson often in dictum and usually by relying—where there was any discussion of the issue at all—solely on the fact that the common-law jury consisted of 12. See *Patton v. United States*, 281 U.S. 276, 288, 50 S.Ct. 253, 254, 74 L.Ed. 854 (1930); *Rassmussen v. United States*, 197 U.S. 516, 519, 25 S.Ct. 514, 515, 49 L.Ed. 862 (1905); *Maxwell v. Dow*, 176 U.S. 581, 586, 20 S.Ct. 448, 450, 451, 44 L.Ed. 597 (1900).

While 'the intent of the Framers' is often an elusive quarry, the relevant constitutional history casts considerable doubt on the easy assumption in our past decisions that if a given feature existed in a jury at common law in 1789, then it was necessarily preserved in the Constitution. Provisions for jury trial were first placed in the Constitution in Article III's provision that '(t)he Trial of all Crimes * * * shall be by Jury; and such Trial shall be held in the State where the said Crimes shall have been committed.' The 'very scanty history (of this provision) in the records of the Constitutional Convention' sheds little light either way on the intended correlation between Article III's 'jury' and the features of the jury at common law. Indeed, pending and after the adoption of the Constitution, fears were expressed that Article III's provision failed to preserve the common-law right to be tried by a 'jury of the vicinage.' That concern, as well as the concern to preserve the right to jury in civil as well as criminal cases, furnished part of the impetus for introducing amendments to the Constitution that ultimately resulted in the jury trial provisions of the Sixth and Seventh Amendments. As introduced by James Madison in the House, the Amendment relating to jury trial in criminal cases would have provided that:

> 'The trial of all crimes * * * shall be by an impartial jury of freeholders of the vicinage, with the requisite of unanimity for conviction, of the right of challenge, and other accustomed requisites. * * *'

The Amendment passed the House in substantially this form, but after more than a week of debate in the Senate it returned to the House considerably altered. While records of the actual debates that occurred in the Senate are not available, a letter from Madison to Edmund Pendleton on September 14, 1789, indicates that one of the Senate's major objections was to the 'vicinage' requirement in the House version. A conference committee was appointed. As reported in a second letter by Madison on September 23, 1789, the Senate remained opposed to the vicinage requirement, partly because in its view the then-pending judiciary bill—which was debated at the same time as the Amendments—adequately preserved the common-law vicinage feature, making it unnecessary to freeze that requirement into the Constitution. 'The Senate,' wrote Madison:

> 'are * * * inflexible in opposing a definition of the locality of Juries. The vicinage they contend is either too vague or too strict a term; too vague if depending on limits to be fixed by the pleasure of the law, too strict if limited to the county. It was proposed to insert after the word Juries, 'with the accustomed requisites,' leaving the definition to be construed according to the judgment of professional men. Even this could not be obtained. * * * The Senate suppose, also, that the provision for vicinage in the Judiciary bill will sufficiently quiet the fears which called for an amendment on this point.'

The version that finally emerged from the Committee was the version that ultimately became the Sixth Amendment, ensuring an accused:

> 'the right to a speedy and public trial, by an impartial jury of the State and district wherein the crime shall have been committed, which district shall have been previously ascertained by law * * *.'

Gone were the provisions spelling out such common-law features of the jury as 'unanimity,' or 'the accustomed requisites.' And the 'vicinage' requirement itself had been replaced by wording that reflected a compromise between broad and narrow definitions of that term, and that left Congress the power to determine the actual size of the 'vicinage' by its creation of judicial districts.

Three significant features may be observed in this sketch of the background of the Constitution's jury trial provisions. First, even though the vicinage requirement was as much a feature of the common-law jury as was the 12-man requirement, the mere reference to 'trial by jury' in Article III was not interpreted to include that feature. Indeed, as the subsequent debates over the Amendments indicate, disagreement arose over whether the feature should be included at all in its common-law sense, resulting in the compromise described above. Second, provisions that would have explicitly tied the 'jury' concept to the 'accustomed requisites' of the time were eliminated. Such action is concededly open to the explanation that the 'accustomed requisites' were thought to be already included in the concept of a 'jury.' But that explanation is no more plausible than the contrary one: that the deletion had some substantive effect. Indeed, given the clear expectation that a substantive change would be effected by the inclusion or deletion of an explicit 'vicinage' requirement, the latter explanation is, if anything, the more plausible. Finally, contemporary legislative and constitutional provisions indicate that where Congress wanted to leave no doubt that it was incorporating existing common-law features of the jury system, it knew how to use express language to that effect. Thus, the Judiciary bill, signed by the President on the same day that the House and Senate finally agreed on the form of the Amendments to be submitted to the States, provided in certain cases for the narrower 'vicinage' requirements that the House had wanted to include in the Amendments. And the Seventh Amendment, providing for jury trial in civil cases, explicitly added that 'no fact tried by a jury, shall be otherwise re-examined in any Court of the United States, than according to the rules of the common law.'

We do not pretend to be able to divine precisely what the word 'jury' imported to the Framers, the First Congress, or the States in 1789. It may well be that the usual expectation was that the jury would consist of 12, and that hence, the most likely conclusion to be drawn is simply that little thought was actually given to the specific question we face today. But there is absolutely no indication in 'the intent of the Framers' of an explicit decision to equate the constitutional and common-law characteristics of the jury. Nothing in this history suggests, then, that we do violence to the letter of the Constitution by turning to other than purely historical considerations to determine which features of the jury system, as it existed at common law, were preserved in the Constitution. The relevant inquiry, as we see it, must be the function that the particular feature performs and its relation to the purposes of the jury trial. Measured by this standard, the 12-man requirement cannot be regarded as an indispensable component of the Sixth Amendment.

The purpose of the jury trial, as we noted in Duncan, is to prevent oppression by the Government. 'Providing an accused with the right to be tried by a jury of his peers gave him an inestimable safeguard against the corrupt or overzealous prosecutor and against the compliant, biased, or eccentric judge.' *Duncan v. Louisiana*, supra, 391 U.S., at 156, 88 S.Ct., at 1451. Given this purpose, the essential feature of a jury obviously lies in the interposition between the accused and his accuser of the commonsense judgment of a group of laymen, and in the community participation and shared responsibility that results from that group's determination of guilt or innocence. The performance of this role is not a function of the particular number of the body that makes up the jury. To be sure, the number should probably be large enough to promote group deliberation, free from outside attempts at intimidation, and to provide a fair possibility for obtaining a representatives cross-section of the community. But we find little reason to think that these goals are in any meaningful sense less likely to be achieved when the jury numbers six, than when it numbers 12— particularly if the requirement of unanimity is retained. And, certainly the reliability of the jury as a factfinder hardly seems likely to be a function of its size.

It might be suggested that the 12-man jury gives a defendant a greater advantage since he has more 'chances' of finding a juror who will insist on acquittal and thus prevent conviction. But the advantage might just as easily belong to the State, which also needs only one juror out of twelve insisting on guilt to prevent acquittal. What few experiments have occurred—usually in the civil area—indicate that there is no discernible difference between the results reached by the two different-sized juries. In short, neither currently available evidence nor theory suggests that the 12-man jury is necessarily more advantageous to the defendant than a jury composed of fewer members.

Similarly, while in theory the number of viewpoints represented on a randomly selected jury ought to increase as the size of the jury increases, in practice the difference between the 12-man and the six-man jury in terms of the cross-section of the community represented seems likely to be negligible. Even the 12-man jury cannot insure representation of every distinct voice in the community, particularly given the use of the peremptory challenge. As long as arbitrary exclusions of a particular class from the jury rolls are forbidden, see, e.g., *Carter v. Jury Commission*, 396 U.S. 320, 329–330, 90 S.Ct. 518, 523, 24 L.Ed.2d 549 (1970), the concern that the cross-section will be significantly diminished if the jury is decreased in size from 12 to six seems an unrealistic one.

We conclude, in short, as we began: the fact that the jury at common law was composed of precisely 12 is a historical accident, unnecessary to effect the purposes of the jury system and wholly without significance 'except to mystics.' *Duncan v. Louisiana*, supra, 391 U.S., at 182, 88 S.Ct. at 1466 (Harlan, J., dissenting). To read the Sixth Amendment as forever codifying a feature so incidental to the real purpose of the Amendment is to ascribe a blind formalism to the Framers which would require considerably more evidence than we have been able to discover in the history and language of the Constitution or in the reasoning of our past decisions. We do not mean to intimate that legislatures can never have good reasons for concluding that the 12-man jury is preferable to the smaller jury, or that such conclusions—reflected in the provisions of most States and in our federal system—are in any sense unwise. Legislatures may well have their own views about the relative value of the larger and smaller juries, and may conclude that, wholly apart from the jury's primary function, it is desirable to spread the collective responsibility for the determination of guilt among the larger group. In capital cases, for example, it appears that no State provides for less than 12 jurors—a fact that suggests implicit recognition of the value of the larger body as a means of legitimating society's decision to impose the death penalty. Our holding does no more than leave these considerations to Congress and the States, unrestrained by an interpretation of the Sixth Amendment that would forever dictate the precise number that can constitute a jury. Consistent with this holding, we conclude that petitioner's Sixth Amendment rights, as applied to the States through the Fourteenth Amendment, were not violated by Florida's decision to provide a six-man rather than a 12-man jury. The judgment of the Florida District Court of Appeal is

Affirmed.

Minimum Size of the Jury

As *Williams v. Florida* held, the Sixth Amendment right to jury trial does not require 12 jurors. Rule 23(b) sets the number of jurors at twelve, with limited exceptions. Although most states have 12-person juries, some utilize smaller juries. Does the Sixth Amendment require a minimum size for a criminal jury? The Supreme Court has held that six jurors is the minimum threshold in a trial for a non-petty offense. *See Ballew v. Georgia*, 435 U.S. 223 (1978). In reaching its decision, the Court took notice of academic studies suggesting that deliberations of smaller juries tend to reach less accurate outcomes, and that smaller jury sizes can diminish the representation of minority groups in the process. Thus, a criminal jury may have as few as six jurors consistent with the Sixth Amendment. However, if the jury is as small as six, the verdict must be unanimous. *See Burch v. Louisiana*, 441 U.S. 130 (1979). Is there an appreciable difference between five jurors and six jurors? What about between six jurors and twelve jurors?

* * *

Motions in Limine

Motions in limine are motions, often made on the eve of trial, requesting clarification on issues important to the presentation or admissibility of certain evidence. Although evidentiary issues can be argued during trial, often as the result of an objection, the motion in limine can help prevent the jury from hearing evidence the court will later declare to be inadmissible. In addition, a motion in limine can give the parties more certainty about whether certain evidence will be admitted so they can adapt their trial strategies accordingly.

ADVOCACY POINT

Written motions in limine, supported by memoranda of law or supporting briefs, can by particularly effective in persuading the court to adopt a particular position. Although it may not always be possible to fully brief an issue given the time constraints associated with trials, to the extent an attorney can anticipate issues that will need to be resolved just before trial, and can provide quality, written pleadings, the greater the likelihood of success. The same holds true when opposing a motion in limine.

COUNSEL EXERCISE 12: Motions in Limine
(Prosecution and Defense)

For purposes of this exercise, assume that if the defendant testifies at trial, the government will seek to enter into evidence a recent conviction for domestic violence in a neighboring state. Further assume that the defense intends to introduce evidence that the case agent was convicted for felony check fraud when in college twenty years ago. Each side should prepare a written motion in limine, setting out the best arguments for or against the admission of the relevant evidence. Included with the motion should be a supporting brief or memorandum of law, a proposed order, and a certificate of service.

CHAPTER 13

SELECTING THE PETIT JURY

I. CONSTITUTIONAL RESTRICTIONS

There are two primary constitutional restrictions relevant to how the jury is composed. The first is the fair cross-section requirement of the Sixth Amendment, and the second is the non-discrimination principle of the Fourteenth Amendment's Equal Protection Clause.

A. FAIR CROSS-SECTION REQUIREMENT

"In all criminal prosecutions, the accused shall enjoy the right to a . . . trial, by an impartial jury of the State and district wherein the crime shall have been committed."

U.S. CONST., amend. VI.

It is often said that the fair cross-section requirement is grounded in the notion that to ensure impartiality the members of the jury should be representative of the community from which they are drawn. This requirement, however, does not apply to the actual jury selected; instead, it is concerned with the venire (or "jury pool") from which the actual jury is drawn. *See Holland v. Illinois*, 493 U.S. 474 (1990). (Note: scrutiny of the membership of the selected petit jury is addressed later in this chapter in the context of peremptory challenges and jury selection.)

The Supreme Court, in the following case, explained the framework for proving a violation of the fair cross-section requirement.

Duren v. Missouri
Supreme Court of the United States, 1979
439 U.S. 357

■ MR. JUSTICE WHITE delivered the opinion of the Court.

In *Taylor v. Louisiana*, 419 U.S. 522, 95 S.Ct. 692, 42 L.Ed.2d 690 (1975), this Court held that systematic exclusion of women during the jury-selection process, resulting in jury pools not "reasonably representative" of the community, denies a criminal defendant his right, under the Sixth and Fourteenth Amendments, to a petit jury selected from a fair cross section of the community. Under the system invalidated in Taylor, a woman could not serve on a jury unless she filed a written declaration of her willingness to do so. As a result, although 53% of the persons eligible for jury service were women, less than 1% of the 1,800 persons whose names were drawn from the jury wheel during the year in which appellant Taylor's jury was chosen were female. Id., at 524.

At the time of our decision in Taylor no other State provided that women could not serve on a jury unless they volunteered to serve. However, five States, including Missouri, provided an automatic exemption from jury service for any women requesting not to serve. Subsequent to Taylor, three of these States eliminated this exemption. Only Missouri, respondent in this case, and Tennessee continue to exempt women from jury service upon request. Today we hold that such systematic exclusion of women that results in jury venires averaging less than 15% female violates the Constitution's fair-cross-section requirement.

I

Petitioner Duren was indicted in 1975 in the Circuit Court of Jackson County, Mo., for first-degree murder and first-degree robbery. In a pretrial motion to quash his petit jury panel and again in a post-conviction motion for a new trial, he contended that his right to trial by a jury chosen from a fair cross section of his community was denied by provisions of Missouri law granting women who so request an automatic exemption from jury service. Both motions were denied.

At hearings on these motions, petitioner established that the jury-selection process in Jackson County begins with the annual mailing of a questionnaire to persons randomly selected from the Jackson County voter registration list. Approximately 70,000 questionnaires were mailed in 1975. The questionnaire contains a list of occupations and other categories which are the basis under Missouri law for either disqualification or exemption from jury service. Included on the questionnaire is a paragraph prominently addressed "TO WOMEN" that states in part:

> "Any woman who elects not to serve will fill out this paragraph
> and mail this questionnaire to the jury commissioner at once."

A similar paragraph is addressed "TO MEN OVER 65 YEARS OF AGE," who are also statutorily exempt upon request.

The names of those sent questionnaires are placed in the master jury wheel for Jackson County, except for those returning the questionnaire who indicate disqualification or claim an applicable exemption. Summonses are mailed on a weekly basis to prospective jurors randomly drawn from the jury wheel. The summons, like the questionnaire, contains special directions to men over 65 and to women, this time advising them to return the summons by mail if they desire not to serve. The practice also is that even those women who do not return the summons are treated as having claimed exemption if they fail to appear for jury service on the appointed day. Other persons seeking to claim an exemption at this stage must make written or personal application to the court.

Petitioner established that according to the 1970 census, 54% of the adult inhabitants of Jackson County were women. He also showed that for the periods June-October 1975 and January-March 1976, 11,197 persons were summoned and that 2,992 of these or 26.7%, were women. Of those summoned, 741 women and 4,378 men appeared for service. Thus, 14.5% (741 of 5,119) of the persons on the postsummons weekly venires during the period in which petitioner's jury was chosen were female. In March 1976, when petitioner's trial began, 15.5% of those on the weekly venires were women (110 of 707). Petitioner's jury was selected from a 53-person panel on which there were 5 women; all 12 jurors chosen were men. None of the foregoing statistical evidence was disputed.

In affirming petitioner's conviction, the Missouri Supreme Court questioned two aspects of his statistical presentation. First, it considered the census figures inadequate because they were six years old and might not precisely mirror the percentage of women registered to vote. Second, petitioner had not unequivocally demonstrated the extent to which the low percentage of women appearing for jury service was due to the automatic exemption for women, rather than to sex-neutral exemptions such as that for persons over age 65.

The court went on to hold, however, that even accepting petitioner's statistical proof, "the number of female names in the wheel, those summoned and those appearing were well above acceptable constitutional standards." 556 S.W.2d 11, 15–17 (1977). We granted certiorari, 435 U.S. 1006, 98 S.Ct. 1875, 56 L.Ed.2d 387 (1978), because of concern that the decision below is not consistent with our decision in Taylor.

II

We think that in certain crucial respects the Missouri Supreme Court misconceived the nature of the fair-cross-section inquiry set forth in Taylor. In holding that "petit juries must be drawn from a source fairly representative of the community," 419 U.S., at 538, 95 S.Ct., at 702, we explained that

> "jury wheels, pools of names, panels, or venires from which juries are drawn must not systematically exclude distinctive groups in the community and thereby fail to be reasonably representative thereof." Ibid.

In order to establish a prima facie violation of the fair-cross-section requirement, the defendant must show (1) that the group alleged to be excluded is a "distinctive" group in the community; (2) that the representation of this group in venires from which juries are selected is not fair and reasonable in relation to the number of such persons in the community; and (3) that this underrepresentation is due to systematic exclusion of the group in the jury-selection process.

A

With respect to the first part of the prima facie test, Taylor without doubt established that women "are sufficiently numerous and distinct from men" so that "if they are systematically eliminated from jury panels, the Sixth Amendment's fair-cross-section requirement cannot be satisfied." Id., at 531, 95 S.Ct., at 698.

B

The second prong of the prima facie case was established by petitioner's statistical presentation. Initially, the defendant must demonstrate the percentage of the community made up of the group alleged to be underrepresented, for this is the conceptual benchmark for the Sixth Amendment fair-cross-section requirement. In Taylor, the State had stipulated that 53% of the population eligible for jury service was female, while petitioner Duren has relied upon a census measurement of the actual percentage of women in the community (54%). In the trial court, the State of Missouri never challenged these data. Although the Missouri Supreme Court speculated that changing population patterns between 1970 and 1976 and unequal voter registration by men and women rendered the census figures a questionable frame of reference, there is no evidence whatsoever in the record to suggest that the 1970 census data significantly distorted the percentage of women in Jackson County at the time of trial. Petitioner's presentation was clearly adequate prima facie evidence of population characteristics for the purpose of making a fair-cross-section violation.

Given petitioner's proof that in the relevant community slightly over half of the adults are women, we must disagree with the conclusion of the court below that jury venires containing approximately 15% women are "reasonably representative" of this community. If the percentage of women appearing on jury pools in Jackson County had precisely mirrored the percentage of women in the population, more than one of every two prospective jurors would have been female. In fact, less than one of every six prospective jurors was female; 85% of the average jury was male. Such a gross discrepancy between the percentage of women in jury venires and the percentage of women in the community requires the conclusion that women were not fairly represented in the source from which petit juries were drawn in Jackson County.

C

Finally, in order to establish a prima facie case, it was necessary for petitioner to show that the underrepresentation of women, generally and on his venire, was due to their systematic exclusion in the jury-selection process. Petitioner's proof met this requirement. His undisputed demonstration that a large discrepancy occurred not just occasionally but in every weekly venire for a period of nearly a year manifestly indicates that the cause of the underrepresentation was systematic—that is, inherent in the particular jury-selection process utilized.

Petitioner Duren's statistics and other evidence also established when in the selection process the systematic exclusion took place. There was no indication that underrepresentation of women occurred at the first stage of the selection process—the questionnaire canvass of persons randomly selected from the relevant voter registration list. The first sign of a systematic discrepancy is at the next stage—the construction of the jury wheel from which persons are randomly summoned for service. Less than 30% of those summoned were female, demonstrating that a substantially larger number of women answering the questionnaire claimed either ineligibility or exemption from jury service. Moreover, at the summons stage women were not only given another opportunity to claim exemption, but also were presumed to have claimed exemption when they did not respond to the summons. Thus, the percentage of women at the final, venire, stage (14.5%) was much lower than the percentage of women who were summoned for service (26.7%).

The resulting disproportionate and consistent exclusion of women from the jury wheel and at the venire stage was quite obviously due to the system by which juries were selected. Petitioner demonstrated that the underrepresentation of women in the final pool of prospective jurors was due to the operation of Missouri's exemption criteria—whether the automatic exemption for women or other statutory exemptions—as implemented in Jackson County. Women were therefore systematically underrepresented within the meaning of Taylor.

III

The demonstration of a prima facie fair-cross-section violation by the defendant is not the end of the inquiry into whether a constitutional violation has occurred. We have explained that "States remain free to prescribe relevant qualifications for their jurors and to provide reasonable exemptions so long as it may be fairly said that the jury lists or panels are representative of the community." Taylor, 419 U.S., at 538, 95 S.Ct., at 701. However, we cautioned that "[t]he right to a proper jury cannot be overcome on merely rational grounds," id., at 534, 95 S.Ct., at 699, 700. Rather, it requires that a significant state interest be manifestly and primarily advanced by those aspects of the jury-selection process, such as exemption criteria, that result in the disproportionate exclusion of a distinctive group.

The Supreme Court of Missouri suggested that the low percentage of women on jury venires in Jackson County may have been due to a greater number of women than of men qualifying for or claiming permissible exemptions, such as those for persons over 65, teachers, and government workers. 556 S.W.2d, at 16. Respondent further argues that petitioner has not proved that the exemption for woman had "any effect" on or was responsible for the underrepresentation of women on venires. Brief for Respondent 15.

However, once the defendant has made a prima facie showing of an infringement of his constitutional right to a jury drawn from a fair cross section of the community, it is the State that bears the burden of justifying this infringement by showing attainment of a fair cross section to be incompatible with a significant state interest. See Taylor, 419 U.S., at 533–535, 95 S.Ct., at 699–700. Assuming, arguendo, that the exemptions mentioned by the court below would justify failure to achieve a fair community cross section on jury venires, the State must demonstrate that these exemptions caused the underrepresentation complained of. The record contains no such proof, and mere suggestions or assertions to that effect are insufficient.

The other possible cause of the disproportionate exclusion of women on Jackson County jury venires is, of course, the automatic exemption for women. Neither the Missouri Supreme Court nor respondent in its brief has offered any substantial justification for this exemption. In response to questioning at oral argument, counsel for respondent ventured that the only state interest advanced by the exemption is safeguarding the important role played by women in home and family life. But exempting all women because of the preclusive domestic responsibilities of some women is insufficient justification for their disproportionate exclusion on jury venires. What we stated in Taylor with respect to the system there challenged under which women could "opt in" for jury service is equally applicable to Missouri's "opt out" exemption:

> "It is untenable to suggest these days that it would be a special hardship for each and every woman to perform jury service or that society cannot spare any women from their present duties. This may be the case with many, and it may be burdensome to sort out those who should be exempted from those who should serve. But that task is performed in the case of men and the administrative convenience in dealing with women as a class is insufficient justification for diluting the quality of community judgment represented by the jury in criminal trials.

> "If it was ever the case that women were unqualified to sit on juries or were so situated that none of them should be required to perform jury service, that time has long since passed." 419 U.S., at 534–535, 537, 95 S.Ct., at 700, 701 (footnote omitted).

We recognize that a State may have an important interest in assuring that those members of the family responsible for the care of children are available to do so. An exemption appropriately tailored to this interest would, we think, survive a fair-cross-section challenge. We stress, however, that the constitutional guarantee to a jury drawn from a fair cross section of the community requires that States exercise proper caution in exempting broad categories of persons from jury service. Although most occupational and other reasonable exemptions may inevitably involve some degree of overinclusiveness or underinclusiveness, any category expressly limited to a group in the community of sufficient magnitude and distinctiveness so as to be within the fair-cross-section requirement—such as women—runs the danger of resulting in underrepresentation sufficient to constitute a prima facie violation of that constitutional requirement. We also repeat the observation made in Taylor that it is unlikely that reasonable exemptions, such as those based on special hardship, incapacity, or community needs, "would pose substantial threats that the remaining pool of jurors would not be representative of the community." Id., at 534, 95 S.Ct., at 700.

The judgment of the Missouri Supreme Court is reversed, and the case is remanded for further proceedings not inconsistent with this opinion.

So ordered.

Excluded Groups and Standing to Bring Fair Cross-Section Claims

As *Duren v. Missouri* instructs, in addition to prohibiting the exclusion of women from jury service unless they affirmatively volunteer to serve, *see Taylor v. Louisiana*, 419 U.S. 522 (1975), the Sixth Amendment is violated by a system in which the automatic exemption of women from jury service leads to their underrepresentation in the pool from which jurors are selected. You may note that although the exclusion of *female* prospective jurors was at issue, the petitioner in *Duren* was male. The Court has made clear that the defendant does not need to be a member of the excluded group in order to have standing to raise a fair cross-section claim. *See Peters v. Kiff*, 407 U.S. 493 (1972) (holding that white defendant had standing to challenge the systematic exclusion of African Americans from the grand jury and petit jury that indicted and convicted him).

B. NON-DISCRIMINATION AND EQUAL PROTECTION

". . . nor shall any State . . . deny to any person within its jurisdiction the equal protection of the laws.

U.S. CONST., amend. XIV, § 1.

The Equal Protection Clause of the Fourteenth Amendment is violated when individuals are excluded from the jury pool on the basis of suspect classifications. In *Strauder v. West Virginia*, 100 U.S. 303 (1880), the Supreme Court was confronted with a state statute that plainly limited jury service to "[a]ll white male persons who are twenty-one years of age and who are citizens of this State." The African American defendant challenged his conviction based on the wholesale exclusion of members of his race from the grand jury and petit jury. In overturning the conviction, the Supreme Court explained that the discriminatory West Virginia statute violated the Equal Protection Clause:

> That the West Virginia statute respecting juries—the statute that controlled the selection of the grand and petit jury in the case of the plaintiff in error—is such a discrimination ought not to be doubted. Nor would it be if the persons excluded by it were white men. If in those States where the colored people constitute a majority of the entire population a law should be enacted excluding all white men from jury service, thus denying to them the privilege of participating equally with the blacks in the administration of justice, we apprehend no one would be heard to claim that it would not be a denial to white men of the equal protection of the laws. Nor if a law should be passed excluding all naturalized Celtic Irishmen, would there by any doubt of its inconsistency with the spirit of the amendment. The very fact that colored people are singled out and expressly denied by a statute all right to participate in the administration of the law, as jurors, because of their color, though they are citizens, and may be in other respects fully qualified, is practically a brand upon them, affixed by the law, an assertion of their inferiority, and a stimulant to that race prejudice which is an impediment to securing to individuals of the race that equal justice which the law aims to secure to all others.

The Court would extend *Strauder*'s reasoning to less straightforward discriminatory schemes, such as when a facially-neutral jury qualification statute was applied in a way to exclude African Americans from jury service. *See Neal v. Delaware,* 103 U.S. 370 (1880).

Although much of the jurisprudence surrounding discriminatory exclusion from jury service involved African American defendants challenging discriminatory state efforts to exclude African Americans from grand jury or petit jury service, *see* Roger A. Fairfax, Jr., Batson's *Grand Jury DNA*, 97 IOWA L. REV. 1511 (2012), a defendant need not be a member of the excluded class. As the Supreme Court held in *Powers v. Ohio*, 499 U.S. 400 (1991), any criminal defendant possesses standing to challenge the violation of the equal protection rights of excluded jurors, even if the defendant is not of the same race as those jurors.

Gender and Non-Discrimination

Both the *Powers* standing rule and the general Equal Protection Clause prohibition against discriminatory exclusion of suspect classes from jury service apply in the context of gender. However, these protections did not always apply to gender, as the following passage from the *Strauder* opinion makes clear:

> We do not say that within the limits from which it is not excluded by the amendment a State may not prescribe the qualifications of its jurors, and in so doing make discriminations. It may confine the selection to males, to freeholders, to citizens, to persons within certain ages, or to persons having educational qualifications. We do not believe the Fourteenth Amendment was ever intended to prohibit this. Looking at its history, it is clear it had no such purpose. Its aim was against discrimination because of race or color. As we have said more than once, its design was to protect an emancipated race, and to strike down all possible legal discriminations against those who belong to it.

However, the Court held definitively in *J.E.B. v. Alabama ex rel. T.B.*, 511 U.S. 127 (1994), that the Equal Protection Clause prohibited the exclusion of individuals from jury service on the basis of gender. Although the *J.E.B.* case involved gender-based peremptory challenges, the Court addressed gender-based jury discrimination more broadly, noting "[w]ith respect to jury service, African Americans and women share a history of total exclusion, a history which came to an end for women many years after the embarrassing chapter in our history came to an end for African Americans."

The Court spoke with a clear voice in extending the protections against racial discrimination in jury selection to the context of gender: "Today we reaffirm what, by now, should be axiomatic: Intentional discrimination on the basis of gender by state actors violates the Equal Protection Clause, particularly where, as here, the discrimination serves to ratify and perpetuate invidious, archaic, and overbroad stereotypes about the relative abilities of men and women."

II. JURY SELECTION AND SERVICE ACT OF 1968

Title 28, Section 1861 et seq. of the United States Code codifies the Juror Selection and Service Act of 1968, which governs the process of summoning and selecting jurors and the juror qualifications that will apply in federal courts. Section 1861 sets out the "Declaration of Policy" of the Act:

> It is the policy of the United States that all litigants in Federal courts entitled to trial by jury shall have the right to grand and petit juries selected at random from a fair cross section of the community in the district or division wherein the court convenes. It is further the policy of the United States that all citizens shall have the opportunity to be considered for service on grand and petit juries in the district courts of the United States, and shall have an obligation to serve as jurors when summoned for that purpose.

Section 1862 contains the non-discrimination provision: "No citizen shall be excluded from service as a grand or petit juror in the district courts of the United States or in the Court of International Trade on account of race, color, religion, sex, national origin, or economic status."

Section 1863 imposes a requirement that each federal judicial district devise a jury selection plan that is designed to implement Sections 1861 and 1862. Included in the plan must be an indication of the source of names of prospective jurors, the groups of persons or occupational classes which are eligible for hardship excusals, and the declaration of exemptions or exclusions for certain military, public safety, and government officials.

Other provisions address the requirement of the maintenance of a master jury wheel and qualified jury wheel, qualifications for jury service, methods for challenging selection procedures, and fee payments and protections for individuals selected as jurors. *See* 28 U.S.C. §§ 1863–1878.

III. VOIR DIRE—FEDERAL RULE OF CRIMINAL PROCEDURE 24

Rule 24(a) of the Federal Rules of Criminal Procedure addresses the voir dire procedure in federal court.

Rule 24. Trial Jurors

(a) Examination.

> (1) *In General.* The court may examine prospective jurors or may permit the attorneys for the parties to do so.

> (2) *Court Examination.* If the court examines the jurors, it must permit the attorneys for the parties to:

>> (A) ask further questions that the court considers proper; or

(B) submit further questions that the court may ask if it considers them proper.

As the language of the rule reveals, the trial judge has broad discretion to conduct voir dire as he or she may see fit. Even where the court must permit counsel involvement in voir dire, it still retains discretion to determine the extent of that involvement.

As such, voir dire practices vary widely. The court may allow counsel to ask questions of the potential jurors directly, or the judge may pose all questions to the jury. Questions might be posed to potential jurors individually, or they may be posed to the entire panel at once, perhaps with follow-up questions to individual jurors. Also, judges may give attorneys wide latitude in the scope of questioning, or the court may permit only very narrow questioning with limited input from counsel.

There are, however, certain contexts in which the court must permit limited voir dire in order to protect the constitutional rights of the defendant. *See, e.g., Ham v. South Carolina*, 409 U.S. 534 (1973) (reversing a conviction of an African American defendant when the trial court denied defendant's request to voir dire the jurors on the question of racial prejudice against him); Cynthia Lee, *A New Approach to Voir Dire on Racial Bias*, 5 U.C. IRVINE L. REV. 843 (2015).

ADVOCACY NOTE

Given the wide variation in voir dire practice, it is incumbent upon the attorneys unfamiliar with a particular judge's practices to either observe the judge's voir dire procedures in another trial, or request that the court disclose its intentions in advance of jury selection.

IV. JURY SELECTION

A. CHALLENGES FOR CAUSE

One purpose of voir dire is to provide counsel on both sides of the case insight into whether potential jurors are unsuitable for service because they are unable to be impartial, either because they have some sort of bias or prejudice, they would be unable to follow the law or court instructions, their views have been tainted by publicity about the case, or because they otherwise have made up their minds about guilt or innocence before hearing the evidence in the case. When counsel has reason to believe he or she can make a showing that a juror is impaired on one of these bases, it is appropriate to challenge the juror for cause. If the court finds merit in the claim that the juror cannot be impartial, it must excuse the juror.

Below are excerpts from a set of model voir dire questions used by many United States District Court judges. As you will read, these questions are designed, in part, to highlight bases for challenges for cause.

Have you ever served as a juror in a criminal or civil case or as a member of a grand jury in either a federal or state court?

Have you, any member of your family, or any close friend ever been employed by a law enforcement agency?

Have you ever been involved, in any court, in a criminal matter that concerned yourself, any member of your family, or a close friend either as a defendant, a witness, or a victim?

[Only if the charged crime relates to illegal drugs or narcotics, ask:] Have you yourself, any member of your family, or any close friend had any experience involving the use or possession of illegal drugs or narcotics?

If you are selected to sit on this case, will you be able to render a verdict solely on the evidence presented at the trial and in the context of the law as I will give it to you in my instructions, disregarding any other ideas, notions, or beliefs about the law that you may have encountered in reaching your verdict?

Is there any member of the panel who has any special disability or problem that would make serving as a member of this jury difficult or impossible?

Having heard the questions put to you by the court, does any other reason suggest itself to you as to why you could not sit on this jury and render a fair verdict based on the evidence presented to you and in the context of the court's instructions to you on the law?

If appropriate, permit counsel to conduct additional direct voir dire examination, subject to such time and subject matter limitations as the court deems proper, or state to counsel that if there are additional questions that should have been asked or were overlooked, counsel may approach the bench and discuss them with the court.

FEDERAL JUDICIAL CENTER, BENCHBOOK FOR U.S. DISTRICT COURT JUDGES, § 2.06 (March 2013).

B. PEREMPTORY CHALLENGES

Another reason for voir dire is to provide counsel the opportunity to develop an impression about a juror and to make an educated guess whether a particular juror's participation would be helpful or harmful to his or her case. Although sometimes these assessments can be related to the types of concerns that underpin challenges for cause, often they are simply "gut reactions" about a juror based on mannerisms, tone, body language, or perceived attitude. An attorney with a strong feeling about a potential juror, if unsuccessful in challenging the juror for cause, may choose to exercise an available peremptory challenge against the juror.

However, peremptory challenges are not a requisite of due process under the federal constitution. *See Rivera v. Illinois*, 556 U.S. 148, 152 (2009) (citing *United States v. Martinez-Salazar*, 528 U.S. 304, 311 (2000)). A state may choose not to make peremptory challenges available. *See Rivera*, 556 U.S. at 152 (citing *Georgia v. McCollum*, 505 U.S. 42, 57 (1992)). In other words, it is up to state legislatures—and Congress on the federal level—whether peremptory challenges are made available to parties and in what quantity and manner. Nevertheless, the peremptory challenge is used in virtually every jurisdiction and is firmly established as a feature of the American criminal trial.

In the federal system, Rule 24(b) governs the provision and exercise of peremptory challenges:

Rule 24. Trial Jurors

(b) Peremptory Challenges. Each side is entitled to the number of peremptory challenges to prospective jurors specified below. The court may allow additional peremptory challenges to multiple defendants, and may allow the defendants to exercise those challenges separately or jointly.

(1) *Capital Case.* Each side has 20 peremptory challenges when the government seeks the death penalty.

(2) *Other Felony Case.* The government has 6 peremptory challenges and the defendant or defendants jointly have 10 peremptory challenges when the defendant is charged with a crime punishable by imprisonment of more than one year.

(3) *Misdemeanor Case.* Each side has 3 peremptory challenges when the defendant is charged with a crime punishable by fine, imprisonment of one year or less, or both.

Peremptory challenges are not required by any federal constitutional provision; they are made available by statute or rule. *See Ross v. Oklahoma*, 487 U.S. 81 (1988). The basic idea behind peremptory challenges is that they may be exercised by an attorney for any reason or for no reason at all. Can you think of reasons why an attorney might choose to use a peremptory challenge against a juror if they juror is not challengeable for cause?

Peremptory Challenges and the Equal Protection Clause

Even though an attorney theoretically can use a peremptory challenge to exclude a juror for any reason at all, would striking a juror on the basis of race violate the Equal Protection Clause? The Court provided an incomplete answer to this question in *Swain v. Alabama*, 380 U.S. 202 (1965). Professor Fairfax explains the *Swain* case in Batson's *Grand Jury DNA*, 97 IOWA L. REV. 1511 (2012):

> In *Swain*, the Court rejected a jury-discrimination challenge in a capital rape case. Despite the underrepresentation of black males on jury panels and the lack of any black petit jurors in Talladega County for over a decade, the Court concluded that it was "wholly obvious that Alabama has not totally excluded a racial group from either grand or petit jury panels," as the Court had determined in certain other cases. Also, recounting the "very old credentials" of the peremptory challenge, the Court rejected the notion that there should be scrutiny of a prosecutor's reasons for exercising any particular peremptory challenge in a given criminal case.
>
> The Court, however, did entertain the argument that exclusion of blacks from petit juries through the prosecutor's *systematic* use of peremptory challenges violated equal protection. Nevertheless, the Court determined that Swain had not made out a prima facie case because he presented only evidence of the peremptory challenges exercised in the instant case; proof of discrimination would require evidence of a pattern of discriminatory strikes across other cases. Furthermore, even though the record was clear that no blacks had served on a petit jury in over a decade, the Court noted that there was no proof that exclusion of blacks was not the result of defendants' peremptory strikes against black members of the venire. The dissent accused the majority of undermining *Strauder* and its progeny and "creat[ing] additional barriers to the elimination of jury discrimination practices which have operated in many communities to nullify the command of the Equal Protection Clause."

Swain launched a sustained run of Supreme Court cases examining how statistical evidence of jury discrimination should be weighed and considered in equal protection challenges.

So, after *Swain*, how does one prove that a peremptory challenge was used in such a discriminatory way? Is it reasonable to assume that a defendant would ever be able to prove a systematic pattern or practice of discriminatory peremptory challenges on the part of the prosecutor? The Court tackled these questions in the following landmark case.

Batson v. Kentucky

Supreme Court of the United States, 1986
476 U.S. 79

■ JUSTICE POWELL delivered the opinion of the Court.

This case requires us to reexamine that portion of *Swain v. Alabama*, 380 U.S. 202, 85 S.Ct. 824, 13 L.Ed.2d 759 (1965), concerning the evidentiary burden placed on a criminal defendant who claims that he has been denied equal protection through the State's use of peremptory challenges to exclude members of his race from the petit jury.

I

Petitioner, a black man, was indicted in Kentucky on charges of second-degree burglary and receipt of stolen goods. On the first day of trial in Jefferson Circuit Court, the judge conducted *voir dire* examination of the venire, excused certain jurors for cause, and permitted the parties to exercise peremptory challenges. The prosecutor used his peremptory challenges to strike all four black persons on the venire, and a jury composed only of white persons was selected. Defense counsel moved to discharge the jury before it was sworn on the ground that the prosecutor's removal of the black veniremen violated petitioner's rights under the Sixth and Fourteenth Amendments to a jury drawn from a cross section of the community, and under the Fourteenth Amendment to equal protection of the laws. Counsel requested a hearing on his motion. Without expressly ruling on the request for a hearing, the trial judge observed that the parties were entitled to use their peremptory challenges to "strike anybody they want to." The judge then denied petitioner's motion, reasoning that the cross-section requirement applies only to selection of the venire and not to selection of the petit jury itself.

The jury convicted petitioner on both counts. On appeal to the Supreme Court of Kentucky, petitioner pressed, among other claims, the argument concerning the prosecutor's use of peremptory challenges. Conceding that *Swain v. Alabama, supra,* apparently foreclosed an equal protection claim based solely on the prosecutor's conduct in this case, petitioner urged the court to follow decisions of other States, *People v. Wheeler*, 22 Cal.3d 258, 148 Cal.Rptr. 890, 583 P.2d 748 (1978); *Commonwealth v. Soares*, 377 Mass. 461, 387 N.E.2d 499, cert. denied, 444 U.S. 881, 100 S.Ct. 170, 62 L.Ed.2d 110 (1979), and to hold that such conduct violated his rights under the Sixth Amendment and § 11 of the Kentucky Constitution to a jury drawn from a cross section of the community. Petitioner also contended that the facts showed that the prosecutor had engaged in a "pattern" of discriminatory challenges in this case and established an equal protection violation under *Swain*.

The Supreme Court of Kentucky affirmed. In a single paragraph, the court declined petitioner's invitation to adopt the reasoning of *People v. Wheeler, supra,* and *Commonwealth v. Soares, supra.* The court observed that it recently had reaffirmed its reliance on *Swain*, and had held that a defendant alleging lack of a fair cross section must demonstrate systematic exclusion of a group of jurors from the venire. See *Commonwealth v. McFerron*, 680 S.W.2d 924 (1984). We granted certiorari, 471 U.S. 1052, 105 S.Ct. 2111, 85 L.Ed.2d 476 (1985), and now reverse.

II

In *Swain v. Alabama*, this Court recognized that a "State's purposeful or deliberate denial to Negroes on account of race of participation as jurors in the administration of justice violates the Equal Protection Clause." 380 U.S., at 203–204, 85 S.Ct., at 826–27. This principle has been "consistently and repeatedly" reaffirmed, *id.*, at 204, 85 S.Ct., at 827, in numerous decisions of this Court both preceding and following *Swain*. We reaffirm the principle today.

A

More than a century ago, the Court decided that the State denies a black defendant equal protection of the laws when it puts him on trial before a jury from which members of his race have been purposefully excluded. *Strauder v. West Virginia*, 10 Otto 303, 100 U.S. 303, 25 L.Ed. 664 (1880). That decision laid the foundation for the Court's unceasing efforts to eradicate racial discrimination in the procedures used to select the venire from which individual jurors are drawn. In *Strauder*, the Court explained that the central concern of the recently ratified Fourteenth Amendment was to put an end to governmental discrimination on account of race. *Id.*, at 306–307. Exclusion of black citizens from service as jurors constitutes a primary example of the evil the Fourteenth Amendment was designed to cure.

In holding that racial discrimination in jury selection offends the Equal Protection Clause, the Court in *Strauder* recognized, however, that a defendant has no right to a "petit jury composed in whole or in part of persons of his own race." *Id.*, at 305. "The number of our races and nationalities stands in the way of evolution of such a conception" of the demand of equal protection. *Akins v. Texas*, 325 U.S. 398, 403, 65 S.Ct. 1276, 1279, 89 L.Ed. 1692 (1945). But the defendant does have the right to be tried by a jury whose members are selected pursuant to nondiscriminatory criteria. *Martin v. Texas*, 200 U.S. 316, 321, 26 S.Ct. 338, 339, 50 L.Ed. 497 (1906); *Ex parte Virginia*, 10 Otto 339, 100 U.S. 339, 345, 25 L.Ed. 676 345 (1880). The Equal Protection Clause guarantees the defendant that the State will not exclude members of his race from the jury venire on account of race, *Strauder, supra*, 100 U.S., at 305, or on the false assumption that members of his race as a group are not qualified to serve as jurors, see *Norris v. Alabama*, 294 U.S. 587, 599, 55 S.Ct. 579, 584, 79 L.Ed. 1074 (1935); *Neal v. Delaware*, 13 Otto 370, 397, 103 U.S. 370, 397, 26 L.Ed. 567 (1881).

Purposeful racial discrimination in selection of the venire violates a defendant's right to equal protection because it denies him the protection that a trial by jury is intended to secure. "The very idea of a jury is a body . . . composed of the peers or equals of the person whose rights it is selected or summoned to determine; that is, of his neighbors, fellows, associates, persons having the same legal status in society as that which he holds." *Strauder, supra*, 100 U.S., at 308; see *Carter v. Jury Comm'n of Greene County*, 396 U.S. 320, 330, 90 S.Ct. 518, 524, 24 L.Ed.2d 549 (1970). The petit jury has occupied a central position in our system of justice by safeguarding a person accused of crime against the arbitrary exercise of power by prosecutor or judge. *Duncan v. Louisiana*, 391 U.S. 145, 156, 88 S.Ct. 1444, 1451, 20 L.Ed.2d 491 (1968). Those on the venire must be "indifferently chosen," to secure the defendant's right under the Fourteenth Amendment to "protection of life and liberty against race or color prejudice." *Strauder, supra*, 100 U.S., at 309.

Racial discrimination in selection of jurors harms not only the accused whose life or liberty they are summoned to try. Competence to serve as a juror ultimately depends on an assessment of individual qualifications and ability impartially to consider evidence presented at a trial. See *Thiel v. Southern Pacific Co.*, 328 U.S. 217, 223–224, 66 S.Ct. 984, 987–88, 90 L.Ed. 1181 (1946). A person's race simply "is unrelated to his fitness as a juror." *Id.*, at 227, 66 S.Ct., at 989 (Frankfurter, J., dissenting). As long ago as *Strauder*, therefore, the Court recognized that by denying a person participation in jury service on account of his race, the State unconstitutionally discriminated against the excluded juror. 100 U.S., at 308; see *Carter v. Jury Comm'n of Greene County, supra*, 396 U.S., at 329–330, 90 S.Ct., at 523–524; *Neal v. Delaware, supra*, 103 U.S., at 386.

The harm from discriminatory jury selection extends beyond that inflicted on the defendant and the excluded juror to touch the entire community. Selection procedures that purposefully exclude black persons from juries undermine public confidence in the fairness of our system of justice. See *Ballard v. United States*, 329 U.S. 187, 195, 67 S.Ct. 261, 265, 91 L.Ed. 181 (1946); *McCray v. New York*, 461 U.S. 961, 968, 103 S.Ct. 2438, 2443, 77 L.Ed.2d 1322 (1983) (MARSHALL, J., dissenting from denial of certiorari). Discrimination within the judicial system is most pernicious because it is "a stimulant to that race prejudice which is an impediment to securing to [black citizens] that equal justice which the law aims to secure to all others." *Strauder*, 100 U.S., at 308.

B

In *Strauder*, the Court invalidated a state statute that provided that only white men could serve as jurors. *Id.*, at 305. We can be confident that no State now has such a law. The Constitution requires, however, that we look beyond the face of the statute defining juror qualifications and also consider challenged selection practices to afford "protection against action of the State through its administrative officers in effecting the prohibited discrimination." *Norris v. Alabama, supra*, 294 U.S., at 589, 55 S.Ct. 579, 580, 79 L.Ed. 1074; see *Hernandez v. Texas*, 347 U.S. 475, 478–479, 74 S.Ct. 667, 670–71, 98 L.Ed. 866 (1954); *Ex parte Virginia, supra*, 100 U.S., at 346–347. Thus, the Court has found a denial of equal protection where the procedures implementing a neutral statute operated to exclude persons from the venire on racial grounds, and has made clear that the Constitution prohibits all forms of purposeful racial discrimination in selection of jurors. While decisions of this Court have been concerned largely with discrimination during selection of the venire, the principles announced there also forbid discrimination on account of race in selection of the petit jury. Since the Fourteenth Amendment protects an accused throughout the proceedings bringing him to justice, *Hill v. Texas*, 316 U.S. 400, 406, 62 S.Ct. 1159, 1162, 86 L.Ed. 1559 (1942), the State may not draw up its jury lists pursuant to neutral procedures but then resort to discrimination at "other stages in the selection process," *Avery v. Georgia*, 345 U.S. 559, 562, 73 S.Ct. 891, 893, 97 L.Ed. 1244 (1953); see *McCray v. New York, supra*, 461 U.S., at 965, 968, 103 S.Ct., at 2440, 2443 (MARSHALL, J., dissenting from denial of certiorari); see also *Alexander v. Louisiana*, 405 U.S. 625, 632, 92 S.Ct. 1221, 1226, 31 L.Ed.2d 536 (1972).

Accordingly, the component of the jury selection process at issue here, the State's privilege to strike individual jurors through peremptory challenges, is subject to the commands of the Equal Protection Clause. Although a prosecutor ordinarily is entitled to exercise permitted peremptory challenges "for any reason at all, as long as that reason is related to his view concerning the outcome" of the case to be tried,

United States v. Robinson, 421 F.Supp. 467, 473 (Conn.1976), mandamus granted *sub nom. United States v. Newman*, 549 F.2d 240 (CA2 1977), the Equal Protection Clause forbids the prosecutor to challenge potential jurors solely on account of their race or on the assumption that black jurors as a group will be unable impartially to consider the State's case against a black defendant.

III

The principles announced in *Strauder* never have been questioned in any subsequent decision of this Court. Rather, the Court has been called upon repeatedly to review the application of those principles to particular facts. A recurring question in these cases, as in any case alleging a violation of the Equal Protection Clause, was whether the defendant had met his burden of proving purposeful discrimination on the part of the State. *Whitus v. Georgia*, 385 U.S. 545, 550, 87 S.Ct. 643, 646–647, 17 L.Ed.2d 599 (1967); *Hernandez v. Texas, supra*, 347 U.S., at 478–481, 74 S.Ct., at 670–672; *Akins v. Texas*, 325 U.S., at 403–404, 65 S.Ct., at 1279; *Martin v. Texas*, 200 U.S. 316, 26 S.Ct. 338, 50 L.Ed. 497 (1906). That question also was at the heart of the portion of *Swain v. Alabama* we reexamine today.

A

Swain required the Court to decide, among other issues, whether a black defendant was denied equal protection by the State's exercise of peremptory challenges to exclude members of his race from the petit jury. 380 U.S., at 209–210, 85 S.Ct., at 830. The record in *Swain* showed that the prosecutor had used the State's peremptory challenges to strike the six black persons included on the petit jury venire. *Id.*, at 210, 85 S.Ct., at 830. While rejecting the defendant's claim for failure to prove purposeful discrimination, the Court nonetheless indicated that the Equal Protection Clause placed some limits on the State's exercise of peremptory challenges. *Id.*, at 222–224, 85 S.Ct., at 837–838.

The Court sought to accommodate the prosecutor's historical privilege of peremptory challenge free of judicial control, *id.*, at 214–220, 85 S.Ct., at 832–836, and the constitutional prohibition on exclusion of persons from jury service on account of race, *id.*, at 222–224, 85 S.Ct., at 837–838. While the Constitution does not confer a right to peremptory challenges, *id.*, at 219, 85 S.Ct., at 835 (citing *Stilson v. United States*, 250 U.S. 583, 586, 40 S.Ct. 28, 29–30, 63 L.Ed. 1154 (1919)), those challenges traditionally have been viewed as one means of assuring the selection of a qualified and unbiased jury, 380 U.S., at 219, 85 S.Ct., at 835.15 To preserve the peremptory nature of the prosecutor's challenge, the Court in *Swain* declined to scrutinize his actions in a particular case by relying on a presumption that he properly exercised the State's challenges. *Id.*, at 221–222, 85 S.Ct., at 836–837.

The Court went on to observe, however, that a State may not exercise its challenges in contravention of the Equal Protection Clause. It was impermissible for a prosecutor to use his challenges to exclude blacks from the jury "for reasons wholly unrelated to the outcome of the particular case on trial" or to deny to blacks "the same right and opportunity to participate in the administration of justice enjoyed by the white population." *Id.*, at 224, 85 S.Ct., at 838. Accordingly, a black defendant could make out a prima facie case of purposeful discrimination on proof that the peremptory challenge system was "being perverted" in that manner. *Ibid.* For example, an inference of purposeful discrimination would be raised on evidence that a prosecutor, "in case after case, whatever the circumstances, whatever the crime and whoever the defendant or the victim may be, is responsible for the removal of Negroes who have been selected as qualified jurors by the jury commissioners and who have survived challenges for cause, with the result that no Negroes ever serve on petit juries." *Id.*, at 223, 85 S.Ct., at 837. Evidence offered by the defendant in *Swain* did not meet that standard. While the defendant showed that prosecutors in the jurisdiction had exercised their strikes to exclude blacks from the jury, he offered no proof of the circumstances under which prosecutors were responsible for striking black jurors beyond the facts of his own case. *Id.*, at 224–228, 85 S.Ct., at 838–840.

A number of lower courts following the teaching of *Swain* reasoned that proof of repeated striking of blacks over a number of cases was necessary to establish a violation of the Equal Protection Clause. Since this interpretation of *Swain* has placed on defendants a crippling burden of proof, prosecutors' peremptory challenges are now largely immune from constitutional scrutiny. For reasons that follow, we reject this evidentiary formulation as inconsistent with standards that have been developed since *Swain* for assessing a prima facie case under the Equal Protection Clause.

B

Since the decision in *Swain*, we have explained that our cases concerning selection of the venire reflect the general equal protection principle that the "invidious quality" of governmental action claimed to be racially discriminatory "must ultimately be traced to a racially discriminatory purpose." *Washington v. Davis*, 426 U.S. 229, 240, 96 S.Ct. 2040, 2048, 48 L.Ed.2d 597 (1976). As in any equal protection case, the "burden is, of course," on the defendant who alleges discriminatory selection of the venire "to prove the existence of purposeful discrimination." *Whitus v. Georgia*, 385 U.S., at 550, 87 S.Ct., at 646–47 (citing *Tarrance v. Florida*, 188 U.S. 519, 23 S.Ct. 402, 47 L.Ed. 572 (1903)). In deciding if the defendant has carried his burden of persuasion, a court must undertake "a sensitive inquiry into such circumstantial and direct evidence of intent as may be available." *Arlington Heights v. Metropolitan Housing Development Corp.*, 429 U.S. 252, 266, 97 S.Ct. 555, 564, 50 L.Ed.2d 450 (1977). Circumstantial evidence of invidious intent may include proof of disproportionate impact. *Washington v. Davis*, 426 U.S., at 242, 96 S.Ct., at 2049. We have observed that under some circumstances proof of discriminatory impact "may for all practical purposes demonstrate unconstitutionality because in various circumstances the discrimination is very difficult to explain on nonracial grounds." *Ibid.* For example, "total or seriously disproportionate exclusion of Negroes from jury venires," *ibid.*, "is itself such an 'unequal application of the law ... as to show intentional discrimination,'" *id.*, at 241, 96 S.Ct., at 2048 (quoting *Akins v. Texas*, 325 U.S., at 404, 65 S.Ct., at 1279).

Moreover, since *Swain*, we have recognized that a black defendant alleging that members of his race have been impermissibly excluded from the venire may make out a prima facie case of purposeful discrimination by showing that the totality of the relevant facts gives rise to an inference of discriminatory purpose. *Washington v. Davis, supra*, 426 U.S., at 239–242, 96 S.Ct., at 2047–49. Once the defendant makes the requisite showing, the burden shifts to the State to explain adequately the racial exclusion. *Alexander v. Louisiana*, 405 U.S., at 632, 92 S.Ct., at 1226. The State cannot meet this burden on mere general assertions that its officials did not discriminate or that they properly performed their official duties. See *Alexander v. Louisiana, supra*, 405 U.S., at 632, 92 S.Ct., at 1226; *Jones v. Georgia*, 389 U.S. 24, 25, 88 S.Ct. 4, 5, 19 L.Ed.2d 25 (1967). Rather, the State must demonstrate that "permissible racially neutral selection criteria and procedures have produced the monochromatic result." *Alexander v. Louisiana, supra*, at 632, 92 S.Ct., at 1226; see *Washington v. Davis, supra*, 426 U.S., at 241, 96 S.Ct., at 2048.

The showing necessary to establish a prima facie case of purposeful discrimination in selection of the venire may be discerned in this Court's decisions. *E.g., Castaneda v. Partida*, 430 U.S. 482, 494–495, 97 S.Ct. 1272, 1280, 51 L.Ed.2d 498 (1977); *Alexander v. Louisiana, supra*, 405 U.S., at 631–632, 92 S.Ct., at 1225–1226. The defendant initially must show that he is a member of a racial group capable of being singled out for differential treatment. *Castaneda v. Partida, supra*, 430 U.S., at 494, 97 S.Ct., at 1280. In combination with that evidence, a defendant may then make a prima facie case by proving that in the particular jurisdiction members of his race have not been summoned for jury service over an extended period of time. *Id.*, at 494, 97 S.Ct., at 1280. Proof of systematic exclusion from the venire raises an inference of purposeful discrimination because the "result bespeaks discrimination." *Hernandez v. Texas*, 347 U.S., at 482, 74 S.Ct., at 672–

73; see *Arlington Heights v. Metropolitan Housing Development Corp.,
supra*, 429 U.S., at 266, 97 S.Ct., at 564.

Since the ultimate issue is whether the State has discriminated in
selecting the defendant's venire, however, the defendant may establish
a prima facie case "in other ways than by evidence of long-continued
unexplained absence" of members of his race "from many panels."
Cassell v. Texas, 339 U.S. 282, 290, 70 S.Ct. 629, 633, 94 L.Ed. 839
(1950) (plurality opinion). In cases involving the venire, this Court has
found a prima facie case on proof that members of the defendant's race
were substantially underrepresented on the venire from which his jury
was drawn, and that the venire was selected under a practice providing
"the opportunity for discrimination." *Whitus v. Georgia, supra*, 385 U.S.,
at 552, 87 S.Ct., at 647; see *Castaneda v. Partida, supra*, 430 U.S., at
494, 97 S.Ct., at 1280; *Washington v. Davis, supra*, 426 U.S., at 241, 96
S.Ct., at 2048; *Alexander v. Louisiana, supra*, 405 U.S., at 629–631, 92
S.Ct., at 1224–26. This combination of factors raises the necessary
inference of purposeful discrimination because the Court has declined
to attribute to chance the absence of black citizens on a particular jury
array where the selection mechanism is subject to abuse. When
circumstances suggest the need, the trial court must undertake a
"factual inquiry" that "takes into account all possible explanatory
factors" in the particular case. *Alexander v. Louisiana, supra*, at 630, 92
S.Ct., at 1225.

Thus, since the decision in *Swain*, this Court has recognized that a
defendant may make a prima facie showing of purposeful racial
discrimination in selection of the venire by relying solely on the facts
concerning its selection *in his case*. These decisions are in accordance
with the proposition, articulated in *Arlington Heights v. Metropolitan
Housing Department Corp.*, that "a consistent pattern of official racial
discrimination" is not "a necessary predicate to a violation of the Equal
Protection Clause. A single invidiously discriminatory governmental
act" is not "immunized by the absence of such discrimination in the
making of other comparable decisions." 429 U.S., at 266, n. 14, 97 S.Ct.,
at 564, n. 14. For evidentiary requirements to dictate that "several
must suffer discrimination" before one could object, *McCray v. New
York*, 461 U.S., at 965, 103 S.Ct., at 2440 (MARSHALL, J., dissenting
from denial of certiorari), would be inconsistent with the promise of
equal protection to all.

C

The standards for assessing a prima facie case in the context of
discriminatory selection of the venire have been fully articulated since
Swain. See *Castaneda v. Partida, supra*, 430 U.S., at 494–495, 97 S.Ct.,
at 1280; *Washington v. Davis*, 426 U.S., at 241–242, 96 S.Ct., at 2048–
2049; *Alexander v. Louisiana, supra*, 405 U.S., at 629–631, 92 S.Ct., at

1224–1226. These principles support our conclusion that a defendant may establish a prima facie case of purposeful discrimination in selection of the petit jury solely on evidence concerning the prosecutor's exercise of peremptory challenges at the defendant's trial. To establish such a case, the defendant first must show that he is a member of a cognizable racial group, *Castaneda v. Partida, supra*, 430 U.S., at 494, 97 S.Ct., at 1280, and that the prosecutor has exercised peremptory challenges to remove from the venire members of the defendant's race. Second, the defendant is entitled to rely on the fact, as to which there can be no dispute, that peremptory challenges constitute a jury selection practice that permits "those to discriminate who are of a mind to discriminate." *Avery v. Georgia*, 345 U.S., at 562, 73 S.Ct., at 892. Finally, the defendant must show that these facts and any other relevant circumstances raise an inference that the prosecutor used that practice to exclude the veniremen from the petit jury on account of their race. This combination of factors in the empaneling of the petit jury, as in the selection of the venire, raises the necessary inference of purposeful discrimination.

In deciding whether the defendant has made the requisite showing, the trial court should consider all relevant circumstances. For example, a "pattern" of strikes against black jurors included in the particular venire might give rise to an inference of discrimination. Similarly, the prosecutor's questions and statements during *voir dire* examination and in exercising his challenges may support or refute an inference of discriminatory purpose. These examples are merely illustrative. We have confidence that trial judges, experienced in supervising *voir dire*, will be able to decide if the circumstances concerning the prosecutor's use of peremptory challenges creates a prima facie case of discrimination against black jurors.

Once the defendant makes a prima facie showing, the burden shifts to the State to come forward with a neutral explanation for challenging black jurors. Though this requirement imposes a limitation in some cases on the full peremptory character of the historic challenge, we emphasize that the prosecutor's explanation need not rise to the level justifying exercise of a challenge for cause. See *McCray v. Abrams*, 750 F.2d, at 1132; *Booker v. Jabe*, 775 F.2d 762, 773 (CA6 1985), cert. pending, No. 85–1028. But the prosecutor may not rebut the defendant's prima facie case of discrimination by stating merely that he challenged jurors of the defendant's race on the assumption-or his intuitive judgment-that they would be partial to the defendant because of their shared race. Cf. *Norris v. Alabama*, 294 U.S., at 598–599, 55 S.Ct., at 583–84; see *Thompson v. United States*, 469 U.S. 1024, 1026, 105 S.Ct. 443, 445, 83 L.Ed.2d 369 (1984) (BRENNAN, J., dissenting from denial of certiorari). Just as the Equal Protection Clause forbids the States to exclude black persons from the venire on the assumption that blacks as a group are unqualified to serve as jurors, *supra*, at 1716, so it forbids the States to strike black veniremen on the assumption that they will be biased in a particular case simply because the defendant is black. The core guarantee of equal protection, ensuring citizens that their State will not discriminate on account of race, would be meaningless were we to approve the exclusion of jurors on the basis of such assumptions, which arise solely from the jurors' race. Nor may the prosecutor rebut the defendant's case merely by denying that he had a discriminatory motive or "affirm[ing] [his] good faith in making individual selections." *Alexander v. Louisiana*, 405 U.S., at 632, 92 S.Ct., at 1226. If these general assertions were accepted as rebutting a defendant's prima facie case, the Equal Protection Clause "would be but a vain and illusory requirement." *Norris v. Alabama, supra*, 294 U.S. at 598, 55 S.Ct., at 583–84. The prosecutor therefore must articulate a neutral explanation related to the particular case to be tried. The trial court then will have the duty to determine if the defendant has established purposeful discrimination.

IV

The State contends that our holding will eviscerate the fair trial values served by the peremptory challenge. Conceding that the Constitution does not guarantee a right to peremptory challenges and that *Swain* did state that their use ultimately is subject to the strictures of equal protection, the State argues that the privilege of unfettered exercise of the challenge is of vital importance to the criminal justice system.

While we recognize, of course, that the peremptory challenge occupies an important position in our trial procedures, we do not agree that our decision today will undermine the contribution the challenge generally makes to the administration of justice. The reality of practice, amply reflected in many state- and federal-court opinions, shows that the challenge may be, and unfortunately at times has been, used to discriminate against black jurors. By requiring trial courts to be sensitive to the racially discriminatory use of peremptory challenges, our decision enforces the mandate of equal protection and furthers the ends of justice. In view of the heterogeneous population of our Nation, public respect for our criminal justice system and the rule of law will be strengthened if we ensure that no citizen is disqualified from jury service because of his race.

Nor are we persuaded by the State's suggestion that our holding will create serious administrative difficulties. In those States applying a version of the evidentiary standard we recognize today, courts have not experienced serious administrative burdens, and the peremptory challenge system has survived. We decline, however, to formulate particular procedures to be followed upon a defendant's timely objection to a prosecutor's challenges.

V

In this case, petitioner made a timely objection to the prosecutor's removal of all black persons on the venire. Because the trial court flatly rejected the objection without requiring the prosecutor to give an explanation for his action, we remand this case for further proceedings. If the trial court decides that the facts establish, prima facie, purposeful discrimination and the prosecutor does not come forward with a neutral explanation for his action, our precedents require that petitioner's conviction be reversed. *E.g., Whitus v. Georgia*, 385 U.S., at 549–550, 87 S.Ct., at 646–47; *Hernandez v. Texas*, 347 U.S., at 482, 74 S.Ct., at 672–673; *Patton v. Mississippi*, 332 U.S., at 469, 68 S.Ct., at 187.

It is so ordered.

Should Peremptory Challenges Be Abolished?

Justice Marshall's concurrence in *Batson* is noteworthy for its call to end the practice of peremptory challenges altogether—for both prosecutors and defense attorneys. Marshall argued that it is far too difficult to detect discriminatory peremptory strikes and too easy to articulate a race-neutral reason for a discriminatory challenge. Justice Marshall also worried that conscious or subconscious racism may lead attorneys to draw adverse conclusions about potential jurors of certain races based on innocuous features of their appearance or mannerisms. Do you think peremptory challenges should be abolished?

The U.S. Supreme Court has decided a number of Batson-related cases in recent years, finding that peremptory challenges had been exercised in an unconstitutional manner. *See, e.g., Foster v. Chatman*, 136 S.Ct. 1737 (2016); *Snyder v. Louisiana*, 552 U.S. 472 (2008); *Miller-El v. Dretke*, 545 U.S. 231 (2005).

Extensions of Batson

The Supreme Court extended *Batson* to the civil litigation context in *Edmonson v. Leesville Concrete Co.*, 500 U.S. 614 (1991). Also, *Batson* has been applied to defense counsel's exercise of race-based peremptory challenges. Furthermore, as discussed earlier in the chapter, gender-based peremptory challenges violate the Equal Protection Clause, *see J.E.B. v. Alabama ex rel. T.B.*, 511 U.S. 127 (1994), and a defendant has standing to bring a *Batson* challenge even if not a member of the group against which the allegedly discriminatory strike was made. See *Powers v. Ohio,* 499 U.S. 400 (1991). A recent Ninth Circuit case also found that peremptory strikes on the basis of sexual orientation violate the Equal

Protection Clause. *See SmithKline Beecham Corp. v. Abbott Laboratories*, 740 F.3d 471 (9th Cir. 2014).

* * *

Selection of Alternate Jurors

For any number of reasons, one or more jurors may need to be excused during the course of a trial. Given possible requirements that there be a minimum number of jurors participating in the trial and deliberating regarding the verdict, it is sometimes necessary to replace a juror who is dismissed or excused during the trial. Rather than start the entire voir dire process anew, courts will sometimes select an alternate juror during the initial jury selection process.

Rule 24(c) governs the selection of alternate jurors in the federal system. Note that a certain number of additional peremptory challenges are made available for the selection of alternate jurors.

Rule 24. Trial Jurors

(c)   Alternate Jurors.

(1) *In General*. The court may impanel up to 6 alternate jurors to replace any jurors who are unable to perform or who are disqualified from performing their duties.

(2) *Procedure*.

(A) Alternate jurors must have the same qualifications and be selected and sworn in the same manner as any other juror.

(B) Alternate jurors replace jurors in the same sequence in which the alternates were selected. An alternate juror who replaces a juror has the same authority as the other jurors.

(3) *Retaining Alternate Jurors*. The court may retain alternate jurors after the jury retires to deliberate. The court must ensure that a retained alternate does not discuss the case with anyone until that alternate replaces a juror or is discharged. If an alternate replaces a juror after deliberations have begun, the court must instruct the jury to begin its deliberations anew.

(4) *Peremptory Challenges*. Each side is entitled to the number of additional peremptory challenges to prospective alternate jurors specified below. These additional challenges may be used only to remove alternate jurors.

(A) *One or Two Alternates.* One additional peremptory challenge is permitted when one or two alternates are impaneled.

(B) *Three or Four Alternates.* Two additional peremptory challenges are permitted when three or four alternates are impaneled.

(C) *Five or Six Alternates.* Three additional peremptory challenges are permitted when five or six alternates are impaneled.

NOTE ON STATE PRACTICE

Does the jurisdiction in which you plan to practice provide peremptory challenges in criminal cases? How many are provided to each side? *See, e.g.,* Ariz. R. Crim. P. 18.4(c).

ADVOCACY POINT

There are a number of methods courts utilize to manage the use of peremptory challenges. Some involve filling all of the seats in the jury box with qualified jurors (those not challenged for cause) and allowing counsel to exercise peremptory challenges on any jurors they choose. Other methods require counsel to exercise a peremptory challenge on a juror before the juror is seated in the jury box. Given the variation in practice, it is important for counsel to research a particular judge's practice and prepare to use peremptory challenges effectively during the often fast-paced jury selection phase of the trial.

COUNSEL EXERCISE 13: Jury Selection
(Prosecution and Defense)

Each side should draft a pleading presenting to the court a set of voir dire questions you would like posed to the prospective jurors. Your proposed voir dire questions should address any concerns you have about potential biases jurors might have as relates to your case. In crafting your proposed questions, you should think about the jury you would like to have, and how your questions might provide the information you need to effectively: (1) challenge potential jurors for cause; and (2) exercise your peremptory challenges against undesirable potential jurors.

In addition to the written assignment, you may participate in an in-class simulation of jury selection.

CHAPTER 14

JURY INSTRUCTIONS AND PROOF REQUIREMENTS

I. TRIAL CONTEXT

Although the basic Adjudicatory Criminal Procedure course is not typically designed to cover trial practice, it is worth addressing a few key features of the context in which the jury trial takes place.

A. OPENING STATEMENT

The opening statement is an opportunity for counsel to set the stage for the anticipated evidentiary presentation to take place during trial. Note that it traditionally is referred to as the opening *statement*, not the opening *argument*. Counsel should endeavor to ensure that the opening statement is not argumentative, and prosecutors in particular should limit the opening statement to a preview of facts he or she expects, in good faith, to be able to establish with available evidence. If an attorney makes an improper remark in the opening statement, the court may give the jury a limiting instruction designed to cure the error and prevent the need for a mistrial or the reversal of a conviction.

Although criminal defendants have no burden of proof and therefore may stand silent at any point of the trial, defense attorneys often will choose to make an opening statement. On occasion, a defense attorney will wish to reserve making an opening statement until after the government has rested in its case-in-chief. However, the court generally has discretion as to when opening statements are made, and whether they may be made at all.

> **COUNSEL EXERCISE 14A: Opening Statement**
> **(Prosecution)**
>
> Prepare to deliver an opening statement in the case. Make sure that the key elements of the government's theory of the case are highlighted, and that the statement communicates to the jury what the evidence will show in the trial.

COUNSEL EXERCISE 14B: Opening Statement (Defense)

Prepare to deliver an opening statement in the case. Endeavor to set the stage for the ways you will cast doubt in the minds of the jurors regarding the government's theory of the case.

B. TESTIMONY

As Federal Rule of Criminal Procedure 26 states, "[i]n every trial the testimony of witnesses must be taken in open court, unless otherwise provided by a statute or by rules adopted under [statutes regarding the federal courts' rulemaking authority]."

Counsel should not ask a question without having a good faith basis for doing so. For example, asking a witness whether he or she still sells drugs is improper if there is no good faith basis to believe that the witness was ever engaged in such activity. Also, it is improper to put a witness on the stand simply to have them invoke the Fifth Amendment in front of the jury.

Under Federal Rule of Evidence 609(a), the government may be given the opportunity to impeach a testifying defendant with a prior conviction involving a false statement or other act of dishonesty. A defendant typically will seek a ruling from the court, through a motion in limine, to exclude such evidence in the event the defendant decides to take the stand. If the court allows the impeachment evidence, the defendant may appeal the court's decision, but only if he or she actually testifies. *See Luce v. United States*, 469 U.S. 38 (1984).

Also, the government may not threaten to prosecute a witness for the defense with perjury in order to dissuade the witness from testifying at trial. *See Webb v. Texas*, 409 U.S. 95 (1972).

C. CLOSING ARGUMENT

Under Federal Rule of Criminal Procedure 29.1, the government delivers its closing argument first, the defense goes second, and the government then may have a rebuttal argument. Although courts have discretion with regard to the length and other attributes of closing arguments, they do not have discretion to deny them altogether. Unlike with opening statement, the closing argument is viewed as an essential element of the Sixth Amendment right to assistance of counsel in a criminal trial. *See Herring v. New York*, 422 U.S. 853 (1975). Even in a bench trial, the defendant must be afforded the opportunity to present a summation at the end of trial. *See id.*

Although attorneys are generally given wide latitude in closing arguments, they may not vouch or make personal assessments regarding facts or credibility. Of course, counsel may not misrepresent the evidence that was presented at trial. Also, the prosecutor may not comment on the defendant's failure to testify, as this violates the Fifth Amendment's privilege against self-incrimination. *See Griffin v. California*, 380 U.S. 609 (1965); *but see Salinas v. Texas*, 133 S.Ct. 2174 (2013).

COUNSEL EXERCISE 14C: Closing Argument (Prosecution)

Prepare to deliver the closing argument in the case. Summarize the evidence presented in the case, making sure to communicate to the jury that there is evidence to satisfy each and every element of the charged offenses. Try to contextualize the proof beyond a reasonable doubt standard with the evidence in the case, and leave the jury with a plausible theory of the case supported by the evidence.

COUNSEL EXERCISE 14D: Closing Argument (Defense)

Prepare to deliver the closing argument in the case. Be sure to emphasize that your client enjoys the presumption of innocence and that the government has the burden of proving each element of the charged offenses beyond a reasonable doubt. Try to highlight any weaknesses in the government's theory of the case or evidence presented, including any credibility or other testimonial capacity issues with government witnesses.

II. FEDERAL RULE OF CRIMINAL PROCEDURE 30

Federal Rule of Criminal Procedure 30 governs jury instructions, which guide the jurors on the law they are to follow in the case.

Rule 30. Jury Instructions

(a) **In General.** Any party may request in writing that the court instruct the jury on the law as specified in the request. The request must be made at the close of the evidence or at any earlier time that the court reasonably sets. When the request is made, the requesting party must furnish a copy to every other party.

(b) Ruling on a Request. The court must inform the parties before closing arguments how it intends to rule on the requested instructions.

(c) Time for Giving Instructions. The court may instruct the jury before or after the arguments are completed, or at both times.

(d) Objections to Instructions. A party who objects to any portion of the instructions or to a failure to give a requested instruction must inform the court of the specific objection and the grounds for the objection before the jury retires to deliberate. An opportunity must be given to object out of the jury's hearing and, on request, out of the jury's presence. Failure to object in accordance with this rule precludes appellate review, except as permitted under Rule 52(b).

The court may deliver the instructions to the jury before closing arguments, after closing arguments, or both before and after closing arguments. *See* Fed. R. Crim. P. 30(c). Note that, under Rule 30(b), "[t]he court must inform the parties before closing arguments how it intends to rule on the requested instructions." This is so counsel might tailor their closing arguments to the law as the jury is instructed on it.

Although judges typically have a set of standard or pattern jury instructions (or instructions drafted by a law clerk) from which they will work, parties may request specific jury instructions under Rule 30(a). Typically, there will be a conference, either in open court or in chambers, to work out which instructions the court will deliver to the jury. Regardless of when or how the decision is made by the court regarding the instructions it will give the jury, counsel must make any objections related to the instructions before the jury retires to deliberate. *See* Fed. R. Crim. P. 30(d). This objection will trigger a hearing, but failure to object waives the issue for purposes of appeal. *See id.*

ADVOCACY POINT

When drafting proposed jury instructions, often pattern jury instructions (available on Westlaw or in law libraries) are a helpful guide. Even if there are no pattern jury instructions in your circuit or jurisdiction, you may be able to borrow approaches from the pattern jury instructions of other circuits. In addition, you should review the case law of your circuit or jurisdiction in relation to any issues of law that might affect the jury instructions.

COUNSEL EXERCISE 14E: Jury Instructions (Prosecution and Defense)

Assume for purposes of this exercise that all counts of the indictment are being considered by the jury. The District Court has ordered both sides to submit proposed jury instructions, which should cover the counts of the indictment, the burden of proof, particular evidentiary issues, and any other proposed instructions you deem appropriate and advantageous to your case.

III. PROOF REQUIREMENTS

A. REASONABLE DOUBT

In the case of *In re Winship*, 397 U.S. 358 (1970), the Supreme Court was confronted with the question whether its earlier ruling in *In re Gault*, 387, U.S. 1 (1967), requiring "the essentials of due process and fair hearing" in juvenile delinquency proceedings, included the requirement that such proceedings utilize a proof beyond a reasonable doubt standard when criminal conduct is alleged. The *Winship* Court stated clearly that "[l]est there remain any doubt about the constitutional stature of the reasonable-doubt standard, we explicitly hold that the Due Process Clause protects the accused against conviction except upon proof beyond a reasonable doubt of every fact necessary to constitute the crime with which he is charged." *Winship*, 397 U.S. at 364.

Although the presumption of innocence remains an important feature of due process in criminal cases, *see, e.g., Nelson v. Colorado*, 581 U.S. ___, 137 S.Ct. 1249 (2017), a presumption of innocence instruction is not necessarily mandated by the Constitution, *see Kentucky v. Whorton*, 441 U.S. 786 (1979). In contrast, a reasonable doubt instruction is absolutely required. Indeed, a court's failure—actual or constructive—to provide a reasonable doubt instruction to the jury results in the automatic reversal of the conviction. *See Sullivan v. Louisiana*, 508 U.S. 275 (1993).

Why is there such an emphasis on the reasonable doubt instruction in criminal cases? The following excerpt from *In re Winship* provides some insight on the centrality of the reasonable doubt standard in our system:

> The requirement that guilt of a criminal charge be established by proof beyond a reasonable doubt dates at least from our early years as a Nation. The 'demand for a higher degree of persuasion in criminal cases was recurrently expressed from ancient times, (though) its crystallization into the formula 'beyond a reasonable doubt' seems to have occurred as late as 1798. It is now accepted in common law jurisdictions as the measure of persuasion by which the prosecution must convince the trier of all the essential elements of guilt.' C. McCormick, Evidence § 321, pp. 681–682 (1954); see also 9 J. Wigmore, Evidence, § 2497 (3d ed. 1940). Although virtually unanimous adherence to the reasonable-doubt standard in common-law jurisdictions may not conclusively establish it as a requirement of due process, such adherence does 'reflect a profound judgment about the way in which law should be enforced and justice administered.' *Duncan v. Louisiana*, 391 U.S. 145, 155, 88 S.Ct. 1444, 1451, 20 L.Ed.2d 491 (1968).
>
> Expressions in many opinions of this Court indicate that it has long been assumed that proof of a criminal charge beyond a reasonable doubt is constitutionally required. * * * Mr. Justice Frankfurter stated that '(i)t the duty of the Government to establish * * * guilt beyond a reasonable doubt. This notion— basic in our law and rightly one of the boasts of a free society— is a requirement and a safeguard of due process of law in the historic, procedural content of 'due process.'' *Leland v. Oregon*, supra, 343 U.S., at 802–803, 72 S.Ct., at 1009 (dissenting opinion). In a similar vein, the Court said in *Brinegar v. United States*, supra, 338 U.S., at 174, 69 S.Ct., at 1310, that '(g)uilt in a criminal case must be proved beyond a reasonable doubt and by evidence confined to that which long experience in the common-law tradition, to some extent embodied in the Constitution, has crystallized into rules of evidence consistent with that standard. These rules are historically grounded rights of our system, developed to safeguard men from dubious and unjust convictions, with resulting forfeitures of life, liberty and property.' *Davis v. United States*, supra, 160 U.S., at 488, 16 S.Ct., at 358 stated that the requirement is implicit in 'constitutions * * * (which) recognize the fundamental

principles that are deemed essential for the protection of life and liberty.' In Davis a murder conviction was reversed because the trial judge instructed the jury that it was their duty to convict when the evidence was equally balanced regarding the sanity of the accused. This Court said: 'On the contrary, he is entitled to an acquittal of the specific crime charged, if upon all the evidence, there is reasonable doubt whether he was capable in law of committing crime. * * * No man should be deprived of his life under the forms of law unless the jurors who try him are able, upon their consciences, to say that the evidence before them * * * is sufficient to show beyond a reasonable doubt the existence of every fact necessary to constitute the crime charged.' Id., at 484, 493, 16 S.Ct., at 357, 360.

The reasonable-doubt standard plays a vital role in the American scheme of criminal procedure. It is a prime instrument for reducing the risk of convictions resting on factual error. The standard provides concrete substance for the presumption of innocence—that bedrock 'axiomatic and elementary' principle whose 'enforcement lies at the foundation of the administration of our criminal law.' *Coffin v. United States*, supra, 156 U.S., at 453, 15 S.Ct., at 403. As the dissenters in the New York Court of Appeals observed, and we agree, 'a person accused of a crime * * * would be at a severe disadvantage, a disadvantage amounting to a lack of fundamental fairness, if he could be adjudged guilty and imprisoned for years on the strength of the same evidence as would suffice in a civil case.' 24 N.Y.2d, at 205, 299 N.Y.S.2d, at 422, 247 N.E.2d, at 259.

The requirement of proof beyond a reasonable doubt has this vital role in our criminal procedure for cogent reasons. The accused during a criminal prosecution has at stake interest of immense importance, both because of the possibility that he may lose his liberty upon conviction and because of the certainty that he would be stigmatized by the conviction. Accordingly, a society that values the good name and freedom of every individual should not condemn a man for commission of a crime when there is reasonable doubt about his guilt. As we said in *Speiser v. Randall*, supra, 357 U.S., at 525–526, 78 S.Ct., at 1342: 'There is always in litigation a margin of error, representing error in factfinding, which both parties must take into account. Where one party has at stake an interest of transcending value—as a criminal defendant his liberty—this margin of error is reduced as to him by the process of placing on the other party the burden of * * * persuading the factfinder at the conclusion of the trial of his guilt beyond a reasonable doubt. Due process commands that no man shall lose his liberty unless the Government has borne the burden of * * * convincing the factfinder of his guilt.' To this end, the reasonable-doubt standard is indispensable, for it 'impresses on the trier of fact the necessity of reaching a subjective state of certitude of the facts in issue.' Dorsen & Rezneck, In Re Gault and the Future of Juvenile Law, 1 Family Law Quarterly, No. 4, pp. 1, 26 (1967).

Moreover, use of the reasonable-doubt standard is indispensable to command the respect and confidence of the community in applications of the criminal law. It is critical that the moral force of the criminal law not be diluted by a standard of proof that leaves people in doubt whether innocent men are being condemned. It is also important in our free society that every individual going about his ordinary affairs have confidence that his government cannot adjudge him guilty of a criminal offense without convincing a proper factfinder of his guilt with utmost certainty.

Because the wording of the instruction can lead to reversible error, courts do not often "stray from the script" so to speak when instructing the jury on proof beyond a reasonable doubt. The following excerpt from *Cage v. Louisiana*, 498 U.S. 39 (1990) demonstrates how the language used in the jury instructions can be parsed on appeal:

In state criminal trials, the Due Process Clause of the Fourteenth Amendment "protects the accused against conviction except upon proof beyond a reasonable doubt of every fact necessary to constitute the crime with which he is charged." *In re Winship*, 397 U.S. 358, 364, 90 S.Ct. 1068, 1073, 25 L.Ed.2d 368 (1970); see also *Jackson v. Virginia*, 443 U.S. 307, 315–316, 99 S.Ct. 2781, 2787, 61 L.Ed.2d 560 (1979). This reasonable doubt standard "plays a vital role in the American scheme of criminal procedure." Winship, 397 U.S., at 363, 90 S.Ct., at 1072. Among other things, "it is a prime instrument for reducing the risk of convictions resting on factual error." Ibid. The issue before us is whether the reasonable doubt instruction in this case complied with Winship.

Petitioner was convicted in a Louisiana trial court of first-degree murder and was sentenced to death. He appealed to the Supreme Court of Louisiana, arguing, inter alia, that the reasonable doubt instruction used in the guilt phase of his trial was constitutionally defective. The instruction provided in relevant part:

> "If you entertain a reasonable doubt as to any fact or element necessary to constitute the defendant's guilt, it is your duty to give him the benefit of that doubt and return a verdict of not guilty. Even where the evidence demonstrates a probability of guilt, if it does not establish such guilt beyond a reasonable doubt, you must acquit the accused. This doubt, however, must be a reasonable one; that is one that is founded upon a real tangible substantial basis and not upon mere caprice and conjecture. It must be such doubt as would give rise to a grave uncertainty, raised in your mind by reasons of the unsatisfactory character of the evidence or lack thereof. A reasonable doubt is not a mere possible doubt. It is an actual substantial doubt. It is a doubt that a reasonable man can seriously entertain. What is required is not an absolute or mathematical certainty, but a moral certainty." 554 So.2d 39, 41 (La.1989) (emphasis added).

The Supreme Court of Louisiana rejected petitioner's argument. The court first observed that the use of the phrases "grave uncertainty" and "moral certainty" in the instruction, "if taken out of context, might overstate the requisite degree of uncertainty and confuse the jury." Ibid. But "taking the charge as a whole," the court concluded that "reasonable persons of ordinary intelligence would understand the definition of 'reasonable doubt.'" Ibid. It is our view, however, that the instruction at issue was contrary to the "beyond a reasonable doubt" requirement articulated in Winship.

In construing the instruction, we consider how reasonable jurors could have understood the charge as a whole.* *Francis v. Franklin*, 471 U.S. 307, 316, 105 S.Ct. 1965, 1972, 85 L.Ed.2d 344 (1985). The charge did at one point instruct that to convict, guilt must be found beyond a reasonable doubt; but it then equated a reasonable doubt with a "grave uncertainty" and an "actual substantial doubt," and stated that what was required was a "moral certainty" that the defendant was guilty. It is plain to us that the words "substantial" and "grave," as they are commonly understood, suggest a higher degree of doubt than is required for acquittal under the reasonable doubt

---

* Ed. Note: The Court has since made clear that the inquiry when reviewing the reasonable doubt instruction is "not whether the instruction 'could have' been applied in unconstitutional manner, but whether there is a reasonable likelihood that the jury *did* so apply it." *Victor v. Nebraska*, 511 U.S. 1 (1994) (citing *Estelle v. McGuire*, 502 U.S. 62 (1991)).

standard. When those statements are then considered with the reference to "moral certainty," rather than evidentiary certainty, it becomes clear that a reasonable juror could have interpreted the instruction to allow a finding of guilt based on a degree of proof below that required by the Due Process Clause.

Later, in a pair of cases, *Victor v. Nebraska, Sandoval v. California*, 511 U.S. 1 (1994), the Court upheld two reasonable doubt instructions—both of which utilized the moral certainty language used in *Cage*. The difference, the Court pointed out, was that there was enough accompanying explanatory language to adequately convey to the jury the meaning of reasonable doubt. Although the Court seemed to discourage the state courts' use of some of the language in the two instructions, it did not find the instructions constitutionally deficient. In her concurring opinion, Justice Ginsburg described the federal pattern jury instructions' articulation of the reasonable doubt standard (quoted below) as "clear, straightforward, and accurate":

> Proof beyond a reasonable doubt is proof that leaves you firmly convinced of the defendant's guilt. There are very few things in this world that we know with absolute certainty, and in criminal cases the law does not require proof that overcomes every possible doubt. If, based on your consideration of the evidence, you are firmly convinced that the defendant is guilty of the crime charged, you must find him guilty. If on the other hand, you think there is a real possibility that he is not guilty, you must give him the benefit of the doubt and find him not guilty.

> Federal Judicial Center, Pattern Criminal Jury Instructions 17–18 (1987) (instruction 21).

Do you find the proof beyond a reasonable doubt instruction helpful? What is the likelihood a jury of laypeople will be able to comprehend it and apply it appropriately?

B. AFFIRMATIVE DEFENSES

A jurisdiction might make available a defense that can mitigate or eliminate entirely a defendant's culpability for a crime, even though the government can prove each element of the crime beyond a reasonable doubt. This is typically described as an affirmative defense. Self-defense is a classic example. Even where the prosecutor can prove beyond a reasonable doubt the mens rea and actus reus of a criminal homicide offense, the defendant still may be acquitted if it is shown that the killing occurred in response to a threat of death or serious bodily injury and that the use of deadly force was both necessary and proportional to the threat.

As discussed above, *In re Winship* makes clear that the government must prove every element of the crime beyond a reasonable doubt. The burden of proof is always on the government and never on the defendant. Thus, a defendant never bears responsibility for *disproving* an element of the crime. However, what happens when the jurisdiction creates an affirmative defense, such as self-defense?

Some jurisdictions may require the defendant to prove the elements of self-defense by a preponderance of the evidence. This is perfectly valid from a constitutional standpoint. *See Smith v. United States*, 568 U.S. 106 (2013) (withdrawal from a conspiracy); *Martin v. Ohio*, 480 U.S. 228 (1987) (self-defense); *Patterson v. New York*, 432 U.S. 197 (1977) (insanity). Recall that even when an affirmative defense is made available to the defendant by law, the government still retains the burden of proving every element of the charged crime beyond a reasonable doubt.

However, although the Due Process Clause does not require the government to disprove affirmative defenses beyond a reasonable doubt (though some jurisdictions may), it is not always easy to distinguish such affirmative defenses from elements of the crime. As the Court explained in *Smith v. United States*:

> While the Government must prove beyond a reasonable doubt "every fact necessary to constitute the crime with which [the defendant] is charged," *In re Winship*, 397 U.S. 358, 364 (1970), "[p]roof of the nonexistence of all affirmative defenses has never been constitutionally required," *Patterson v. New York*, 432 U.S. 197, 210 (1977). The State is foreclosed from shifting the burden of proof to the defendant only "when an affirmative defense *does* negate an element of the crime." *Martin v. Ohio, 480 U.S. 228, 237 (1987)* (Powell, J., dissenting). Where instead it "excuse[s] conduct that would otherwise be punishable," but "does not controvert any of the elements of the offense itself," the Government has no constitutional duty to overcome the defense beyond a reasonable doubt. *Dixon v. United States*, 548 U.S. 1, 6 (2006).

For instance, you may recall from your Criminal Law course that the presence or absence of provocation can determine the difference between voluntary manslaughter and murder. Thus, if a jurisdiction's definition of murder requires the absence of provocation, is this a fact the defendant can be made to prove by a preponderance of the evidence, or, instead, is it something the government must prove beyond a reasonable doubt? The Court, in *Mullaney v. Wilbur*, 421 U.S. 684

(1975), held that the Due Process Clause mandates that the government be required to disprove provocation beyond a reasonable doubt. *See id.* at 703. The Maine statute in question, the Court reasoned, made the absence of provocation essentially an element of the crime of murder, and, therefore, it would violate the Due Process Clause to relieve the prosecutor of the responsibility of proving it beyond a reasonable doubt. *See id.*

C. PRESUMPTIONS

The following excerpt from *County Court of Ulster County, NY v. Allen*, 442 U.S. 140 (1979), provides a useful summary of how presumptions are used in criminal cases:

> Inferences and presumptions are a staple of our adversary system of factfinding. It is often necessary for the trier of fact to determine the existence of an element of the crime—that is, an "ultimate" or "elemental" fact—from the existence of one or more "evidentiary" or "basic" facts. * * * The value of these evidentiary devices, and their validity under the Due Process Clause, vary from case to case, however, depending on the strength of the connection between the particular basic and elemental facts involved and on the degree to which the device curtails the factfinder's freedom to assess the evidence independently. Nonetheless, in criminal cases, the ultimate test of any device's constitutional validity in a given case remains constant: the device must not undermine the factfinder's responsibility at trial, based on evidence adduced by the State, to find the ultimate facts beyond a reasonable doubt. See *In re Winship*, 397 U.S. 358, 364; *Mullaney v. Wilbur*, 421 U.S., at 702–703, n. 31.

> The most common evidentiary device is the entirely permissive inference or presumption, which allows—but does not require—the trier of fact to infer the elemental fact from proof by the prosecutor of the basic one and which places no burden of any kind on the defendant. * * * In that situation the basic fact may constitute prima facie evidence of the elemental fact. * * * When reviewing this type of device, the Court has required the party challenging it to demonstrate its invalidity as applied to him. * * * Because this permissive presumption leaves the trier of fact free to credit or reject the inference and does not shift the burden of proof, it affects the application of the "beyond a reasonable doubt" standard only if, under the facts of the case, there is no rational way the trier could make the connection permitted by the inference. For only in that situation is there any risk that an explanation of the

permissible inference to a jury, or its use by a jury, has caused the presumptively rational factfinder to make an erroneous factual determination.

A mandatory presumption is a far more troublesome evidentiary device. For it may affect not only the strength of the "no reasonable doubt" burden but also the placement of that burden; it tells the trier that he or they *must* find the elemental fact upon proof of the basic fact, at least unless the defendant has come forward with some evidence to rebut the presumed connection between the two facts. * * *

The passage above describes two basic types of presumptions—permissive and mandatory. A permissive presumption permits but does not require the factfinder to infer an elemental fact if the government proves a basic fact. A mandatory presumption may be either conclusive or rebuttable; the former requires the factfinder to find the elemental fact if the government proves the basic fact, whereas the latter allows for the possibility that the defendant will produce evidence to rebut the connection between the basic and elemental facts. Mandatory presumptions "violate the Due Process Clause if they relieve the State of the burden of persuasion on an element of an offense." *Francis v. Franklin*, 471 U.S. 307 (1985); *see also United States v. United States Gypsum Co.*, 438 U.S. 422 (1978); *Morrisette v. United States*, 342 U.S. 246 (1952).

As difficult as presumptions may be to comprehend, they are, in fact, designed to make the factfinder's job easier. However, as the Court reminds in *County Court v. Allen*, such presumptions "must not undermine the factfinder's responsibility at trial, based on evidence adduced by the State, to find the ultimate facts beyond a reasonable doubt." For, if a presumption is deemed to have usurped the prosecution's burden of proving beyond a reasonable doubt any element of the charged offense, it is error. *See, e.g., Sandstrom v. Montana*, 442 U.S. 510 (1979); *see also Rose v. Clark*, 478 U.S. 570 (1986) (holding that such error can be treated as harmless error).

D. ELEMENTS AND SENTENCING FACTORS

As discussed throughout this Section, the Due Process Clause requires that the government prove beyond a reasonable doubt each and every element of the charged crime before a conviction may properly be obtained. *See In re Winship, supra.* However, there are certain facts that go not to an element of the crime, but to the question of what sentence might be appropriate, or whether a sentencing enhancement might apply. For example, the quantity of narcotics sold could drive the length of a sentence, or whether racial animus motivated an assault could determine whether a hate crime enhancement to a sentence for assault is properly applied. If a fact is a sentencing factor rather than an element of the crime, it may proved to a judge by a preponderance of the evidence, rather than to a jury beyond a reasonable doubt.

In *McMillan v. Pennsylvania*, 477 U.S. 79 (1986), the Court considered a Pennsylvania statute which imposed a mandatory minimum sentence in certain cases where the judge found by a preponderance of the evidence that the defendant visibly possessed a firearm when he committed the offense. In holding that the firearm possession was a sentencing factor rather than an element of the crime and, thus, the statute did not violate the Due Process Clause, the Court noted that the law did not create a new offense, change the maximum punishment that could be imposed for the underlying offense, create a presumption of guilt, or diminish the government's burden of proving the underlying offense.

However, in the landmark case that follows, the Court was confronted with a statute that increased the *maximum* sentence based upon a judge's finding of fact by a preponderance of the evidence.

Apprendi v. New Jersey
Supreme Court of the United States, 2000
530 U.S. 466

■ JUSTICE STEVENS delivered the opinion of the Court.

A New Jersey statute classifies the possession of a firearm for an unlawful purpose as a "second-degree" offense. N. J. Stat. Ann. § 2C:39–4(a) (West 1995). Such an offense is punishable by imprisonment for "between five years and 10 years." § 2C:43–6(a)(2). A separate statute, described by that State's Supreme Court as a "hate crime" law, provides for an "extended term" of imprisonment if the trial judge finds, by a preponderance of the evidence, that "the defendant in committing the crime acted with a purpose to intimidate an individual or group of individuals because of race, color, gender, handicap, religion, sexual orientation or ethnicity." N. J. Stat. Ann. § 2C:44–3(e) (West Supp. 2000). The extended term authorized by the hate crime law for second-degree offenses is imprisonment for "between 10 and 20 years." § 2C:43–7(a)(3).

The question presented is whether the Due Process Clause of the Fourteenth Amendment requires that a factual determination authorizing an increase in the maximum prison sentence for an offense from 10 to 20 years be made by a jury on the basis of proof beyond a reasonable doubt.

I

At 2:04 a.m. on December 22, 1994, petitioner Charles C. Apprendi, Jr., fired several .22-caliber bullets into the home of an African-American family that had recently moved into a previously all-white neighborhood in Vineland, New Jersey. Apprendi was promptly arrested and, at 3:05 a.m., admitted that he was the shooter. After further questioning, at 6:04 a.m., he made a statement—which he later retracted—that even though he did not know the occupants of the house personally, "because they are black in color he does not want them in the neighborhood." * * *

A New Jersey grand jury returned a 23-count indictment charging Apprendi with four first-degree, eight second-degree, six third-degree, and five fourth-degree offenses. The charges alleged shootings on four different dates, as well as the unlawful possession of various weapons. None of the counts referred to the hate crime statute, and none alleged that Apprendi acted with a racially biased purpose.

The parties entered into a plea agreement, pursuant to which Apprendi pleaded guilty to two counts (3 and 18) of second-degree possession of a firearm for an unlawful purpose, N. J. Stat. Ann. § 2C:39–4a (West 1995), and one count (22) of the third-degree offense of unlawful possession of an antipersonnel bomb, § 2C:39–3a; the prosecutor dismissed the other 20 counts. Under state law, a second-degree offense carries a penalty range of 5 to 10 years, § 2C:43–6(a)(2); a third-degree offense carries a penalty range of between 3 and 5 years, § 2C:43–6(a)(3). As part of the plea agreement, however, the State reserved the right to request the court to impose a higher "enhanced" sentence on count 18 (which was based on the December 22 shooting) on the ground that that offense was committed with a biased purpose, as described in § 2C:44–3(e). Apprendi, correspondingly, reserved the right to challenge the hate crime sentence enhancement on the ground that it violates the United States Constitution.

At the plea hearing, the trial judge heard sufficient evidence to establish Apprendi's guilt on counts 3, 18, and 22; the judge then confirmed that Apprendi understood the maximum sentences that could be imposed on those counts. Because the plea agreement provided that the sentence on the sole third-degree offense (count 22) would run concurrently with the other sentences, the potential sentences on the two second-degree counts were critical. If the judge found no basis for the biased purpose enhancement, the maximum consecutive sentences on those counts would amount to 20 years in aggregate; if, however, the judge enhanced the sentence on count 18, the maximum on that count alone would be 20 years and the maximum for the two counts in aggregate would be 30 years, with a 15-year period of parole ineligibility.

After the trial judge accepted the three guilty pleas, the prosecutor filed a formal motion for an extended term. The trial judge thereafter held an evidentiary hearing on the issue of Apprendi's "purpose" for the shooting on December 22. Apprendi adduced evidence from a psychologist and from seven character witnesses who testified that he did not have a reputation for racial bias. He also took the stand himself, explaining that the incident was an unintended consequence of overindulgence in alcohol, denying that he was in any way biased against African-Americans, and denying that his statement to the police had been accurately described. The judge, however, found the police officer's testimony credible, and concluded that the evidence supported a finding "that the crime was motivated by racial bias." App. to Pet. for Cert. 143a. Having found "by a preponderance of the evidence" that Apprendi's actions were taken "with a purpose to intimidate" as provided by the statute, *id.* at 138a, 139a, 144a, the trial judge held that the hate crime enhancement applied. Rejecting Apprendi's constitutional challenge to the statute, the judge sentenced him to a 12-year term of imprisonment on count 18, and to shorter concurrent sentences on the other two counts.

Apprendi appealed, arguing, *inter alia*, that the Due Process Clause of the United States Constitution requires that the finding of bias upon which his hate crime sentence was based must be proved to a jury beyond a reasonable doubt, *In re Winship*, 397 U.S. 358, 25 L. Ed. 2d 368, 90 S.Ct. 1068 (1970). Over dissent, the Appellate Division of the Superior Court of New Jersey upheld the enhanced sentence. * * * Relying on our decision in *McMillan v. Pennsylvania*, 477 U.S. 79, 91 L. Ed. 2d 67, 106 S.Ct. 2411 (1986), the appeals court found that the state legislature decided to make the hate crime enhancement a "sentencing factor," rather than an element of an underlying offense—and that decision was within the State's established power to define the elements of its crimes. The hate crime statute did not create a presumption of guilt, the court determined, and did not appear "tailored to permit the . . . finding to be a tail which wags the dog of the substantive offense." * * * Characterizing the required finding as one of "motive," the court described it as a traditional "sentencing factor," one not considered an "essential element" of any crime unless the legislature so provides. * * * While recognizing that the hate crime law did expose defendants to "greater and additional punishment," * * * (quoting *McMillan*, 477 U.S. at 88), the court held that that "one factor standing alone" was not sufficient to render the statute unconstitutional, *Ibid.*

A divided New Jersey Supreme Court affirmed.

* * *

We granted certiorari, * * * and now reverse.

II

* * *

* * * [B]ecause there is no ambiguity in New Jersey's statutory scheme, this case does not raise any question concerning the State's power to manipulate the prosecutor's burden of proof by, for example, relying on a presumption rather than evidence to establish an element of an offense, cf. *Mullaney v. Wilbur*, 421 U.S. 684, 44 L. Ed. 2d 508, 95 S.Ct. 1881 (1975); *Sandstrom v. Montana*, 442 U.S. 510, 61 L. Ed. 2d 39, 99 S.Ct. 2450 (1979), or by placing the affirmative defense label on "at least some elements" of traditional crimes, *Patterson v. New York*, 432 U.S. 197, 210, 53 L. Ed. 2d 281, 97 S.Ct. 2319 (1977). The prosecutor did not invoke any presumption to buttress the evidence of racial bias and did not claim that Apprendi had the burden of disproving an improper motive. The question whether Apprendi had a constitutional right to have a jury find such bias on the basis of proof beyond a reasonable doubt is starkly presented.

Our answer to that question was foreshadowed by our opinion in *Jones v. United States*, 526 U.S. 227, 143 L. Ed. 2d 311, 119 S.Ct. 1215 (1999), construing a federal statute. We there noted that "under the Due Process Clause of the Fifth Amendment and the notice and jury trial guarantees of the Sixth Amendment, any fact (other than prior conviction) that increases the maximum penalty for a crime must be charged in an indictment, submitted to a jury, and proven beyond a reasonable doubt." 526 U.S. at 243, n. 6. The Fourteenth Amendment commands the same answer in this case involving a state statute.

III

In his 1881 lecture on the criminal law, Oliver Wendell Holmes, Jr., observed: "The law threatens certain pains if you do certain things, intending thereby to give you a new motive for not doing them. If you persist in doing them, it has to inflict the pains in order that its threats may continue to be believed." New Jersey threatened Apprendi with certain pains if he unlawfully possessed a weapon and with additional pains if he selected his victims with a purpose to intimidate them because of their race. As a matter of simple justice, it seems obvious that the procedural safeguards designed to protect Apprendi from unwarranted pains should apply equally to the two acts that New Jersey has singled out for punishment. Merely using the label "sentence enhancement" to describe the latter surely does not provide a principled basis for treating them differently.

At stake in this case are constitutional protections of surpassing importance: the proscription of any deprivation of liberty without "due process of law," Amdt. 14, and the guarantee that "in all criminal prosecutions, the accused shall enjoy the right to a speedy and public trial, by an impartial jury," Amdt. 6. Taken together, these rights indisputably entitle a criminal defendant to "a jury determination that [he] is guilty of every element of the crime with which he is charged, beyond a reasonable doubt." *United States v. Gaudin*, 515 U.S. 506, 510, 132 L. Ed. 2d 444, 115 S.Ct. 2310 (1995); see also *Sullivan v. Louisiana*, 508 U.S. 275, 278, 124 L. Ed. 2d 182, 113 S.Ct. 2078 (1993); *Winship*, 397 U.S. at 364 (The Due Process Clause protects the accused against conviction except upon proof beyond a reasonable doubt of every fact necessary to constitute the crime with which he is charged").

As we have, unanimously, explained, *Gaudin*, 515 U.S. at 510–511, the historical foundation for our recognition of these principles extends down centuries into the common law.

* * *

Equally well founded is the companion right to have the jury verdict based on proof beyond a reasonable doubt.

* * *

Any possible distinction between an "element" of a felony offense and a "sentencing factor" was unknown to the practice of criminal indictment, trial by jury, and judgment by court as it existed during the years surrounding our Nation's founding.

* * *

We should be clear that nothing in this history suggests that it is impermissible for judges to exercise discretion—taking into consideration various factors relating both to offense and offender—in imposing a judgment *within the range* prescribed by statute. We have often noted that judges in this country have long exercised discretion of this nature in imposing sentence *within statutory limits* in the individual case. * * *

* * *

The historic link between verdict and judgment and the consistent limitation on judges' discretion to operate within the limits of the legal penalties provided highlight the novelty of a legislative scheme that removes the jury from the determination of a fact that, if found, exposes the criminal defendant to a penalty *exceeding* the maximum he would receive if punished according to the facts reflected in the jury verdict alone.

We do not suggest that trial practices cannot change in the course of centuries and still remain true to the principles that emerged from the Framers' fears "that the jury right could be lost not only by gross denial, but by erosion." *Jones*, 526 U.S. at 247–248. But practice must at least adhere to the basic principles undergirding the requirements of trying to a jury all facts necessary to constitute a statutory offense, and proving those facts beyond reasonable doubt. * * *

* * *

IV

It was in *McMillan v. Pennsylvania*, that this Court, for the first time, coined the term "sentencing factor" to refer to a fact that was not found by a jury but that could affect the sentence imposed by the judge. * * *

* * *

Finally, as we made plain in *Jones* last Term, *Almendarez-Torres v. United States*, 523 U.S. 224, 140 L. Ed. 2d 350, 118 S.Ct. 1219 (1998), represents at best an exceptional departure from the historic practice that we have described. In that case, we considered a federal grand jury indictment, which charged the petitioner with "having been 'found in the United States . . . after being deported,'" in violation of 8 U.S.C. § 1326(a)—an offense carrying a maximum sentence of two years. 523 U.S. at 227. Almendarez-Torres pleaded guilty to the indictment, admitting at the plea hearing that he had been deported, that he had unlawfully reentered this country, and that "the earlier deportation had taken place 'pursuant to' three earlier 'convictions' for aggravated felonies." *Ibid*. The Government then filed a presentence report indicating that Almendarez-Torres' offense fell within the bounds of § 1326(b) because, as specified in that provision, his original deportation had been subsequent to an aggravated felony conviction; accordingly, Almendarez-Torres could be subject to a sentence of up to 20 years. Almendarez-Torres objected, contending that because the indictment "had not mentioned his earlier aggravated felony convictions," he could be sentenced to no more than two years in prison. *Ibid*.

Rejecting Almendarez-Torres' objection, we concluded that sentencing him to a term higher than that attached to the offense alleged in the indictment did not violate the strictures of *Winship* in that case. Because Almendarez-Torres had *admitted* the three earlier convictions for aggravated felonies—all of which had been entered pursuant to proceedings with substantial procedural safeguards of their own—no question concerning the right to a jury trial or the standard of proof that would apply to a contested issue of fact was before the Court. Although our conclusion in that case was based in part on our application of the criteria we had invoked in *McMillan*, the specific question decided concerned the sufficiency of the indictment. More important, as *Jones* made crystal clear, 526 U.S. at 248–249, our conclusion in *Almendarez-Torres* turned heavily upon the fact that the additional sentence to which the defendant was subject was "the prior commission of a serious crime." 523 U.S. at 230; see also 526 U.S. at 243 (explaining that "recidivism . . . is a traditional, if not the most traditional, basis for a sentencing court's increasing an offender's sentence"); 526 U.S. at 244(emphasizing "the fact that recidivism 'does not relate to the commission of the offense . . .'"); *Jones*, 526 U.S. at 249–250, n. 10 ("The majority and the dissenters in *Almendarez-Torres* disagreed over the legitimacy of the Court's decision to restrict its holding to recidivism, but both sides agreed that the Court had done just that"). Both the certainty that procedural safeguards attached to any "fact" of prior conviction, and the reality that Almendarez-Torres did not challenge the accuracy of that "fact" in his case, mitigated the due process and Sixth Amendment concerns otherwise implicated in allowing a judge to determine a "fact" increasing punishment beyond the maximum of the statutory range.

Even though it is arguable that *Almendarez-Torres* was incorrectly decided, and that a logical application of our reasoning today should apply if the recidivist issue were contested, Apprendi does not contest the decision's validity and we need not revisit it for purposes of our decision today to treat the case as a narrow exception to the general rule we recalled at the outset. Given its unique facts, it surely does not warrant rejection of the otherwise uniform course of decision during the entire history of our jurisprudence.

In sum, our reexamination of our cases in this area, and of the history upon which they rely, confirms the opinion that we expressed in *Jones*. Other than the fact of a prior conviction, any fact that increases the penalty for a crime beyond the prescribed statutory maximum must be submitted to a jury, and proved beyond a reasonable doubt. With that exception, we endorse the statement of the rule set forth in the concurring opinions in that case: "It is unconstitutional for a legislature to remove from the jury the assessment of facts that increase the prescribed range of penalties to which a criminal defendant is exposed. It is equally clear that such facts must be established by proof beyond a reasonable doubt." 526 U.S. at 252–253 (opinion of STEVENS, J.); see also 526 U.S. at 253(opinion of SCALIA, J.).

V

The New Jersey statutory scheme that Apprendi asks us to invalidate allows a jury to convict a defendant of a second-degree offense based on its finding beyond a reasonable doubt that he unlawfully possessed a prohibited weapon; after a subsequent and separate proceeding, it then allows a judge to impose punishment identical to that New Jersey provides for crimes of the first degree, N. J. Stat. Ann. § 2C:43–6(a)(1) (West 1999), based upon the judge's finding, by a preponderance of the evidence, that the defendant's "purpose" for unlawfully possessing the weapon was "to intimidate" his victim on the basis of a particular characteristic the victim possessed. In light of the constitutional rule explained above, and all of the cases supporting it, this practice cannot stand.

New Jersey's defense of its hate crime enhancement statute has three primary components: (1) the required finding of biased purpose is not an "element" of a distinct hate crime offense, but rather the traditional "sentencing factor" of motive; (2) *McMillan* holds that the legislature can authorize a judge to find a traditional sentencing factor on the basis of a preponderance of the evidence; and (3) *Almendarez-Torres* extended *McMillan's* holding to encompass factors that authorize a judge to impose a sentence beyond the maximum provided by the substantive statute under which a defendant is charged. None of these persuades us that the constitutional rule that emerges from our history and case law should incorporate an exception for this New Jersey statute.

* * *

The New Jersey procedure challenged in this case is an unacceptable departure from the jury tradition that is an indispensable part of our criminal justice system. Accordingly, the judgment of the Supreme Court of New Jersey is reversed, and the case is remanded for further proceedings not inconsistent with this opinion.

It is so ordered.

Apprendi's *Impact*

The holding of *Apprendi*—"other than the fact of a prior conviction, any fact that increases the penalty of a crime beyond the prescribed statutory maximum must be submitted to a jury, and proved beyond a reasonable doubt"—had profound implications for the administration of American criminal justice. First and foremost, it required courts to reconsider which facts were to be presented to juries and how this was to be accomplished. This would entail juries hearing evidence on issue they previously had not, and prosecutors having to provide, at the earliest stages of a case, evidence on issues traditionally reserved for the post-trial sentencing hearing.

Further, the logic of the ruling had the potential to impact situations beyond the context of facts that increased the length of a sentence above a statutory maximum. Although the Court initially declined to apply the reasoning of *Apprendi* to judicial factfinding that would trigger a mandatory minimum sentence, *see Harris v. United States*, 536 U.S. 545 (2002), it changed course in *Alleyne v. United States*, 133 S.Ct. 2151 (2013), overruling *Harris*, and holding that the Sixth Amendment required a jury finding of any fact that determined the statutory sentencing range, both the minimum and maximum. *See id.*; *see also Cunningham v. California*, 549 U.S. 270 (2007) (holding that California's Determinate Sentencing Law violates *Apprendi*).

Likewise, in *Ring v. Arizona*, 536 U.S. 584 (2002), the Court held that a sentencing scheme which permitted judicial factfinding of enumerated aggravating factors sufficient to impose the death penalty violated the Sixth Amendment. *See also Hurst v. Florida*, 136 S.Ct. 616 (2016). The Court also applied *Apprendi* to the other end of the spectrum of punishment severity, holding in *Southern Union v. United States*, 567 U.S. 343 (2012), that the Sixth Amendment requires jury factfinding in the context of the imposition of criminal fines. However, the Court declined to apply *Apprendi* to the decision whether multiple sentences would run consecutively or concurrently, deferring to states' prerogative in administering their criminal justice systems, and reasoning that the jury historically had no role in this sentencing determination. *See Oregon v. Ice*, 555 U.S. 160 (2009).

Perhaps the most significant extension of *Apprendi* was its application to the federal sentencing guidelines scheme, a topic addressed later in Chapter 18. In her dissent in *Apprendi*, Justice O'Connor predicted that the decision would have implications for the federal sentencing guidelines, which were built around a model dependent on extensive judicial factfinding in fashioning sentences in accordance with those guidelines.

Justice O'Connor's prediction was bolstered by the Court's decision in *Blakely v. Washington*, 542 U.S. 296 (2004), which applied *Apprendi* to the Washington state sentencing guidelines scheme and held that any fact that would increase a sentence above the *guidelines* maximum (even if it remains under the statutory maximum) must be proven to a jury beyond a reasonable doubt. Only one year after *Blakeley*, the Court declared the federal sentencing guidelines unconstitutional in *United States v. Booker*, 543 U.S. 220 (2005).

The *Booker* Court held that there was no significant distinction between the federal guidelines and the Washington state guidelines invalidated in *Blakeley*. Because the district judge, rather than the jury, finds facts that form the basis of sentencing enhancements under the federal guidelines, those guidelines violate the Sixth Amendment. However, as is discussed later in Chapter 18 *infra*, the Court severed the mandatory provisions of the governing statute in order to save the Guidelines, which are now advisory.

CHAPTER 15

JURY DELIBERATIONS AND VERDICT

I. JURY DELIBERATIONS

The classic 1957 film "12 Angry Men" provides a dramatic depiction of the jury's deliberation process in a murder trial. Much has changed since this film was nominated for the Best Picture Academy Award in 1958. The fair cross-section and non-discrimination principles discussed earlier in Chapter 13, today, likely would produce a more racially diverse jury and one better characterized as "12 Angry *People*." However, the film's core element—the jurors' struggle with the solemn and difficult task of sitting in judgment of another—has stood the test of time.

Two passages from Juror #8, played by Henry Fonda, highlight some of the tensions inherent in the jurors' role:

> According to the testimony, the boy looks guilty. . . maybe he is. I sat there in court for six days listening while the evidence built up. Everybody sounded so positive, you know, I . . . I began to get a peculiar feeling about this trial. I mean, nothing is that positive. There're a lot of questions I'd have liked to ask. I don't know, maybe they wouldn't have meant anything, but . . . I began to get the feeling that the defense counsel wasn't conducting a thorough enough cross-examination. I mean, he . . . he let too many things go by . . . little things that. . .

> It's always difficult to keep personal prejudice out of a thing like this. And wherever you run into it, prejudice always obscures the truth. I don't really know what the truth is. I don't suppose anybody will ever really know. Nine of us now seem to feel that the defendant is innocent, but we're just gambling on probabilities—we may be wrong. We may be trying to let a guilty man go free, I don't know. Nobody really can. But we have a reasonable doubt, and that's something that's very valuable in our system. No jury can declare a man guilty unless it's sure.

> "12 Angry Men," MGM Studios (1957).

A. BREAKING DEADLOCKS

Of course, the Sixth Amendment assigns to jurors the fact-finding function in criminal trials. As the dialogue excerpts above reveal, jury deliberations are anything but scientific, and commentators often debate how lay jurors fare in reaching accurate results. Also, as discussed in the earlier materials on jury composition, there has been a great deal of academic commentary on the ideal size of a jury and what factors are relevant to the quality of deliberation in which jurors engage.

However, when all is said and done, there will be (typically) twelve humans in a room, bringing their common sense, lived experiences, and intuitions to the task of trying to reach a verdict. What happens when, despite best efforts, the jurors' deliberations are not able to produce an agreed-upon verdict? Is there anything the court can do, short of declaring a mistrial? The next case provides a framework for a court confronted with this problem.

Allen v. United States

Supreme Court of the United States, 1896
164 U.S. 492

■ MR. JUSTICE BROWN delivered the opinion of the court.

This was a writ of error to a judgment of the Circuit Court of the United States for the Western District of Arkansas sentencing the plaintiff in error to death for the murder of Philip Henson, a white man, in the Cherokee Nation of the Indian Territory. The defendant was tried and convicted in 1893, and upon such conviction being set aside by this court, 150 U.S. 551, was again tried and convicted in 1894. The case was again reversed, 157 U.S. 675, when Allen was tried for the third time and convicted, and this writ of error was sued out.

The facts are so fully set forth in the previous reports of the case that it is unnecessary to repeat them here.

We are somewhat embarrassed in the consideration of this case by the voluminousness of the charge, and of the exceptions taken thereto, as well as by the absence of a brief on the part of the plaintiff in error; but the principal assignments of error, set forth in the record, will be noticed in this opinion.

* * *

9. The seventeenth and eighteenth assignments were taken to instructions given to the jury after the main charge was delivered, and when the jury had returned to the court, apparently for further instructions. These instructions were quite lengthy and were, in substance, that in a large proportion of cases absolute certainty could not be expected; that although the verdict must be the verdict of each individual juror, and not a mere acquiescence in the conclusion of his fellows, yet they should examine the question submitted with candor

and with a proper regard and deference to the opinions of each other; that it was their duty to decide the case if they could conscientiously do so; that they should listen, with a disposition to be convinced, to each other's arguments; that, if much the larger number were for conviction, a dissenting juror should consider whether his doubt was a reasonable one which made no impression upon the minds of so many men, equally honest, equally intelligent with himself. If, upon the other hand, the majority was for acquittal, the minority ought to ask themselves whether they might not reasonably doubt the correctness of a judgement which was not concurred in by the majority. These instructions were taken literally from a charge in a criminal case which was approved of by the Supreme Court of Massachusetts in *Commonwealth v. Tuey*, 8 Cush. 1, and by the Supreme Court of Connecticut in *State v. Smith*, 49 Connecticut, 376, 386.

While, undoubtedly, the verdict of the jury should represent the opinion of each individual juror, it by no means follows that opinions may not be changed by conference in the juryroom. The very object of the jury system is to secure unanimity by a comparison of views, and by arguments among the jurors themselves. It certainly cannot be the law that each juror should not listen with deference to the arguments and with a distrust of his own judgment, if he finds a large majority of the jury taking a different view of the case from what he does himself. It cannot be that each juror should go to the jury-room with a blind determination that the verdict shall represent his opinion of the case at that moment; or, that he should close his ears to the arguments of men who are equally honest and intelligent as himself. There was no error in these instructions.

Several other assignments were made, to which it is unnecessary to call attention.

For the reasons above stated the judgment of the court below will be affirmed.

The Allen *"Dynamite" Charge*

As Judge John Minor Wisdom once explained, "[t]he *Allen* or 'dynamite' charge is designed to blast loose a deadlocked jury." *Green v. United States*, 309 F.2d 852, 854 (5th Cir. 1962). The *Allen* case is often relied upon by courts attempting to encourage a seemingly deadlocked jury to give further deliberations another try. *See* Fed. R. Crim. P. 31(d). However, despite its ubiquity, the *Allen* "dynamite" charge has long been the subject of criticism. *See, e.g.*, Paul Marcus, *The* Allen *Instruction in Criminal Cases: Is the Dynamite Charge About to be Permanently Diffused?*, 43 MISSOURI L. REV. 613 (1978); *Deadlocked*

Juries and Dynamite: A Critical Look at the "Allen Charge," 31 CHICAGO L. REV. 386 (1964).

Chief among the concerns about the *Allen* charge is the possibility that a juror with a minority view will be pressured by the court into abandoning his or her conscientiously-held position for reasons other than the natural shifting of views during the deliberation process. Indeed, many believe that juries tend to convict defendants following an *Allen* charge. *See, e.g.*, Joe Saint-Veltri, *Judicial Tyranny and the* Allen *Charge*, 40 LITIGATION (American Bar Association) (Summer 2014). Also, criminal defendants may benefit from a hung trial, either because the government may decide to drop the prosecution or bargain for a lesser offense. In addition, in the capital context, a hung jury at the penalty phase may mandate a life sentence.

Although *Allen* charges are permitted, courts may not explicitly demand that jurors arrive at a verdict. *See Jenkins v. United States*, 380 U.S. 445 (1965) (holding judge's statement to jury that "[y]ou have got to reach a decision in this case" was coercive).* In addition, courts have fashioned safeguards to ensure that *Allen* charges are not coercive. *See Lowenfield v. Phelps*, 484 U.S. 231 (1988) (differentiating between judicial "inquir[ies] as to the numerical division" of the jury on the merits and judicial inquiries as to "how they stood on the question of whether further deliberations might assist them in returning a verdict"). These modified *Allen* charges will avoid conveying a sense of urgency to the jurors or dilute the jurors' understanding that the government retains the burden of proof beyond a reasonable doubt. They also will call upon jurors in both the majority camp and the minority camp to reassess their views, but will discourage jurors from straying from their conscientiously held views.

Below is a model modified *Allen* charge taken from a popular compendium of pattern jury instructions that surveys the case law of a number of federal circuits:

> The Court wishes to suggest a few thoughts to you which you may consider in your deliberations. You should think about these concepts along with the evidence received during the trial and all the instructions previously given to you.
>
> This is an important case. The trial has required time, effort, and money from both the defense and the prosecution. If you should fail to agree on a verdict, the case is left open and undecided. Like all cases, it must be resolved at some time. A

---

* Note, however, that the court has the ability to remove a juror who simply refuses to engage in deliberations. *See, e.g., United States v. Kemp*, 500 F.3d 257, 303 (3d Cir. 2007); *United States v. Thomas*, 116 F.3d 606 (2d Cir. 1997); *see also* Jeffrey Bellin, *An Inestimable Safeguard Gives Way to Practicality: Eliminating the Juror Who "Refuses to Deliberate" Under Federal Rule of Criminal Procedure 23(b)(3)*, 36 U. MEM. L. REV. 631 (2006).

second trial will also be costly to both sides. There is no reason to believe that the case can be tried again, by either side, better or more exhaustively than it has been tried before you. There is no reason to believe that more evidence or better evidence would be produced at a second trial. Any future jury would be selected in the same manner and from the same source as you were chosen. So, there appears no reason to believe that the case could ever be submitted to twelve people more conscientious, more impartial, or more competent to decide it.

These concepts are, of course, clear to all of us who have participated in this trial. The only reason that I mention these facts now is because some of them may have escaped your attention while you have been fully occupied in reviewing the evidence in the case in the light of the instructions with your fellow jurors. These are all matters which remind us how desirable it is that you unanimously agree upon a verdict.

As stated in the instructions given at the time the case was first submitted to you for decision, you should not surrender your honest beliefs as to the weight or effect of evidence solely because of the opinion of other jurors or for the mere purpose of returning a unanimous verdict.

It is your duty as jurors, however, to consult with one another and to deliberate with a view to reaching an agreement if you can do so without violence to individual judgment. Each of you must decide the case for yourself, but you should do so only after a consideration of the evidence in the case with your fellow jurors. In the course of your deliberations you should not hesitate to reexamine your own views and change your opinion if convinced it is erroneous.

In order to bring twelve minds to a unanimous result you must examine the questions submitted to you with candor and frankness and with proper deference to and regard for the opinions of each other. That is to say, in conferring together, each of you should pay due attention and respect to the views of the others and listen to each other's arguments with a disposition to reexamine your own views.

If the greater majority of you are for a conviction, each dissenting juror ought to consider whether a doubt in his or her own mind is a reasonable one since it makes no effective impression upon the minds of so many equally honest and equally conscientious fellow jurors who bear the same responsibility, serve under the same oath, and have heard the same evidence with, we may assume, the same attention and an equal desire to arrive at the truth.

If on the other hand, a majority or even a lesser number of you are for acquittal, other jurors ought to seriously ask themselves again, and most thoughtfully, whether they do not have reason to doubt the correctness of a judgment which is not concurred in by many of their fellow jurors and whether they should not distrust the weight and sufficiency of evidence which fails to convince the minds of several of their fellow jurors beyond a reasonable doubt.

You are not partisans. You are judges—judges of the facts. Your sole responsibility here is to determine whether the government has proven each essential element of *[the] [each]* charge concerning *[the] [each]* defendant beyond a reasonable doubt. You are the exclusive judges of the credibility of all the witnesses and of the weight and effect of all the evidence.

Remember, at all times, that no juror is expected to yield a conscientious belief he or she may have as to the weight or effect of evidence. But remember also that after full deliberation and consideration of all the evidence in the case, it is your duty to agree upon a verdict if you can do so without violating your individual judgment and your conscience. Remember too, if the evidence in the case fails to establish guilt beyond a reasonable doubt, *[the] [each]* defendant should have your unanimous verdict of "not guilty."

In order to make a decision more practicable, the law imposes the burden of proof on one party or the other in all cases. In a criminal case, the burden of proof is on the government.

Above all, keep constantly in mind that, unless your final conscientious appraisal of the evidence in the case clearly requires it, the defendant should never be exposed to the risk of having to twice run the gauntlet of a criminal prosecution and to endure a second time the mental, emotional, and financial strain of a criminal trial.

You may conduct your deliberations as you choose, but I suggest that you now carefully reexamine and reconsider all the evidence in the case bearing upon the questions before you in the light of the Court's instructions on the law.

You may be as leisurely in your deliberations as the occasion may require and you may take all the time which you may feel is necessary. * * *

You may now retire and continue your deliberations in such manner as shall be determined by your good and conscientious judgment as reasonable men and women.

1A Fed. Jury Practice & Instructions, § 20:08 (6th ed.).

What do you think about the potential effectiveness of these instructions to a deadlocked jury? Is it too coercive? Might it be not coercive enough?

B. Protecting the Integrity of Jury Deliberations

As the Court stated in *Remmer v. United States*, 347 U.S. 227 (1954):

> In a criminal case, any private communication, contact, or tampering, directly or indirectly, with a juror during a trial about the matter pending before the jury is, for obvious reasons, deemed presumptively prejudicial, if not made in pursuance of known rules of the court and the instructions and directions of the court made during the trial, with full knowledge of the parties. The presumption is not conclusive, but the burden rests heavily upon the Government to establish, after notice to and hearing of the defendant, that such contact with the juror was harmless to the defendant.

There are a number of measures taken to ensure that juries are able to deliberate without the taint of tampering or improper influence. Prosecutors and judges must avoid having ex parte contact with jury, either inside or outside of the courthouse. The above excerpt from *Remmer* conveys the harm associated with such ex parte contact, and the burden on the rights of the defendant in a criminal case.

Of course, defendants also have a duty to refrain from interfering with the jury. As a general matter, the names of the jurors are disclosed to defense counsel at the jury selection stage. However, courts retain the authority to withhold information or set in place protective measures if there is a showing that a defendant has attempted or may attempt to intimidate a juror or obstruct justice. One of the protective measures a court may undertake is the sequestration of the jury for the jury's protection. What problems might be associated with a court's decision to sequester a jury for their protection during a criminal case?

More commonly, a jury may be sequestered to ensure that the jurors are not tainted by trial publicity. However, while it once may have been feasible to put jurors up in a hotel room and deny them a television and the morning newspaper, is it possible to cut off jurors from the vast and rapid access to information made possible through the Internet and social media? For an analysis of the problems social media poses to the quest for juror impartiality, *see* Nicole Waters &

Paula Hannaford-Agor, *Jurors 24/7: The Impact of New Media on Jurors, Public Perceptions of the Jury System, and the American Criminal Justice System* (2013); Ralph Artigliere, *Sequestration for the Twenty-First Century: Disconnecting Jurors from the Internet*, 59 DRAKE L. REV. 621 (2011).

What happens if, after the jury has rendered a verdict, there arises a concern that there has been some sort of influence on the jury? Although the law is clear that courts cannot probe the internal deliberations of the jurors, it may be permissible to investigate whether there had been external influence on the jury's deliberations. The challenge, however, is in determining whether a matter is of an external nature or related to the internal deliberations of the jury.

Tanner v. United States

Supreme Court of the United States, 1987
483 U.S. 107

■ JUSTICE O'CONNOR delivered the opinion of the Court.

Petitioners William Conover and Anthony Tanner were convicted of conspiring to defraud the United States in violation of 18 U.S. C. § 371, and of committing mail fraud in violation of 18 U.S. C. § 1341. The United States Court of Appeals for the Eleventh Circuit affirmed the convictions. 772 F.2d 765 (1985). Petitioners argue that the District Court erred in refusing to admit juror testimony at a post-verdict hearing on juror intoxication during the trial; and that the conspiracy count of the indictment failed to charge a crime against the United States. We affirm in part and remand.

* * *

The day before petitioners were scheduled to be sentenced, Tanner filed a motion, in which Conover subsequently joined, seeking continuance of the sentencing date, permission to interview jurors, an evidentiary hearing, and a new trial. According to an affidavit accompanying the motion, Tanner's attorney had received an unsolicited telephone call from one of the trial jurors, Vera Asbul. App. 246. Juror Asbul informed Tanner's attorney that several of the jurors consumed alcohol during the lunch breaks at various times throughout the trial, causing them to sleep through the afternoons. *Id.*, at 247. The District Court continued the sentencing date, ordered the parties to file memoranda, and heard argument on the motion to interview jurors. The District Court concluded that juror testimony on intoxication was inadmissible under Federal Rule of Evidence 606(b) to impeach the jury's verdict. The District Court invited petitioners to call any nonjuror witnesses, such as courtroom personnel, in support of the motion for new trial. Tanner's counsel took the stand and testified that he had observed one of the jurors "in a sort of giggly mood" at one point during the trial but did not bring this to anyone's attention at the time. *Id.*, at 170.

Earlier in the hearing the judge referred to a conversation between defense counsel and the judge during the trial on the possibility that jurors were sometimes falling asleep. During that extended exchange the judge twice advised counsel to immediately inform the court if they observed jurors being inattentive, and suggested measures the judge would take if he were so informed:

"MR. MILBRATH [defense counsel]: But, in any event, I've noticed over a period of several days that a couple of jurors in particular have been taking long naps during the trial.

"THE COURT: Is that right. Maybe I didn't notice because I was—

"MR. MILBRATH: I imagine the Prosecutors have noticed that a time or two.

"THE COURT: What's your solution?

"MR. MILBRATH: Well, I just think a respectful comment from the Court that if any of them are getting drowsy, they just ask for a break or something might be helpful.

"THE COURT: Well, here's what I have done in the past—and, you have to do it very diplomatically, of course: I once said, I remember, 'I think we'll just let everybody stand up and stretch, it's getting a little sleepy in here,' I said, but that doesn't sound good in the record.

"I'm going to—not going to take on that responsibility. If any of you think you see that happening, ask for a bench conference and come up and tell me about it and I'll figure out what to do about it, and I won't mention who suggested it.

"MR. MILBRATH: All right.

"THE COURT: But, I'm not going to sit here and watch. I'm— among other things, I'm not going to see—this is off the record.

"(Discussion had off the record.)

". . . This is a new thing to this jury, and I don't know how interesting it is to them or not; some of them look like they're pretty interested.

. . . .

"And, as I say, if you don't think they are, come up and let me know and I'll figure how—either have a recess or—which is more than likely what I would do."

Tr. 12–10–12–101.

As the judge observed during the hearing, despite the above admonitions counsel did not bring the matter to the court again. App. 147.

The judge also observed that in the past courtroom employees had alerted him to problems with the jury. "Nothing was brought to my attention in this case about anyone appearing to be intoxicated," the judge stated, adding, "I saw nothing that suggested they were." *Id.*, at 172.

Following the hearing the District Court filed an order stating that "on the basis of the admissible evidence offered I specifically find that the motions for leave to interview jurors or for an evidentiary hearing at which jurors would be witnesses is not required or appropriate." The District Court also denied the motion for new trial. *Id.*, at 181–182.

While the appeal of this case was pending before the Eleventh Circuit, petitioners filed another new trial motion based on additional evidence of jury misconduct. In another affidavit, Tanner's attorney stated that he received an unsolicited visit at his residence from a second juror, Daniel Hardy. *Id.*, at 241. Despite the fact that the District Court had denied petitioners' motion for leave to interview jurors, two days after Hardy's visit Tanner's attorney arranged for Hardy to be interviewed by two private investigators. *Id.*, at 242. The interview was transcribed, sworn to by the juror, and attached to the new trial motion. In the interview Hardy stated that he "felt like . . . the jury was on one big party." *Id.*, at 209. Hardy indicated that seven of the jurors drank alcohol during the noon recess. Four jurors, including Hardy, consumed between them "a pitcher to three pitchers" of beer during various recesses. *Id.*, at 212. Of the three other jurors who were alleged to have consumed alcohol, Hardy stated that on several occasions he observed two jurors having one or two mixed drinks during the lunch recess, and one other juror, who was also the foreperson, having a liter of wine on each of three occasions. *Id.*, at 213–215. Juror Hardy also stated that he and three other jurors smoked marijuana quite regularly during the trial. *Id.*, at 216–223. Moreover, Hardy stated that during the trial he observed one juror ingest cocaine five times and another juror ingest cocaine two or three times. *Id.*, at 227. One juror sold a quarter pound of marijuana to another juror during the trial, and took marijuana, cocaine, and drug paraphernalia into the courthouse. *Id.*, at 234–235. Hardy noted that some of the jurors were falling asleep during the trial, and that one of the jurors described himself to Hardy as "flying." *Id.*, at 229. Hardy stated that before he visited Tanner's attorney at his residence, no one had contacted him concerning the jury's conduct, and Hardy had not been offered anything in return for his statement. *Id.*, at 232. Hardy said that he came forward "to clear my conscience" and "because I felt . . . that the people on the jury didn't have no business being on the jury. I felt . . . that Mr. Tanner should have a better opportunity to get somebody that would review the facts right." *Id.*, at 231–232.

The District Court, stating that the motions "contain supplemental allegations which differ quantitatively but not qualitatively from those in the April motions," *id.*, at 256, denied petitioners' motion for a new trial.

The Court of Appeals for the Eleventh Circuit affirmed. 772 F.2d 765 (1985). We granted certiorari, 479 U.S. 929 (1986), to consider whether the District Court was required to hold an evidentiary hearing, including juror testimony, on juror alcohol and drug use during the trial, and to consider whether petitioners' actions constituted a conspiracy to defraud the United States within the meaning of 18 U.S. C. § 371.

II

Petitioners argue that the District Court erred in not ordering an additional evidentiary hearing at which jurors would testify concerning drug and alcohol use during the trial. Petitioners assert that, contrary to the holdings of the District Court and the Court of Appeals, juror testimony on ingestion of drugs or alcohol during the trial is not barred by Federal Rule of Evidence 606(b). Moreover, petitioners argue that whether or not authorized by Rule 606(b), an evidentiary hearing including juror testimony on drug and alcohol use is compelled by their Sixth Amendment right to trial by a competent jury.

By the beginning of this century, if not earlier, the near-universal and firmly established common-law rule in the United States flatly prohibited the admission of juror testimony to impeach a jury verdict. See 8 J. Wigmore, Evidence § 2352, pp. 696–697 (J. McNaughton rev. ed. 1961) (common-law rule, originating from 1785 opinion of Lord Mansfield, "came to receive in the United States an adherence almost unquestioned").

Exceptions to the common-law rule were recognized only in situations in which an "extraneous influence," *Mattox v. United States*, 146 U.S. 140, 149 (1892), was alleged to have affected the jury. In *Mattox*, this Court held admissible the testimony of jurors describing how they heard and read prejudicial information not admitted into evidence. The Court allowed juror testimony on influence by outsiders in *Parker v. Gladden*, 385 U.S. 363, 365 (1966) (bailiff's comments on defendant), and *Remmer v. United States*, 347 U.S. 227, 228–230 (1954) (bribe offered to juror). See also *Smith v. Phillips*, 455 U.S. 209 (1982) (juror in criminal trial had submitted an application for employment at the District Attorney's office). In situations that did not fall into this exception for external influence, however, the Court adhered to the common-law rule against admitting juror testimony to impeach a verdict. *McDonald v. Pless*, 238 U.S. 264 (1915); *Hyde v. United States*, 225 U.S. 347, 384 (1912).

Lower courts used this external/internal distinction to identify those instances in which juror testimony impeaching a verdict would be admissible. The distinction was not based on whether the juror was literally inside or outside the jury room when the alleged irregularity took place; rather, the distinction was based on the nature of the allegation. Clearly a rigid distinction based only on whether the event took place inside or outside the jury room would have been quite unhelpful. For example, under a distinction based on location a juror could not testify concerning a newspaper read inside the jury room. Instead, of course, this has been considered an external influence about which juror testimony is admissible. See *United States v. Thomas*, 463 F.2d 1061 (CA7 1972). Similarly, under a rigid locational distinction jurors could be regularly required to testify after the verdict as to whether they heard and comprehended the judge's instructions, since the charge to the jury takes place outside the jury room. Courts wisely have treated allegations of a juror's inability to hear or comprehend at trial as an internal matter. See *Government of the Virgin Islands v. Nicholas*, 759 F.2d 1073 (CA3 1985); *Davis v. United States*, 47 F.2d 1071 (CA5 1931) (rejecting juror testimony impeaching verdict, including testimony that jurors had not heard a particular instruction of the court).

Most significant for the present case, however, is the fact that lower federal courts treated allegations of the physical or mental incompetence of a juror as "internal" rather than "external" matters. In *United States v. Dioguardi*, 492 F.2d 70 (CA2 1974), the defendant Dioguardi received a letter from one of the jurors soon after the trial in which the juror explained that she had "eyes and ears that . . . see things before [they] happen," but that her eyes "are only partly open" because "a curse was put upon them some years ago." *Id.*, at 75. Armed with this letter and the opinions of seven psychiatrists that the letter suggested that the juror was suffering from a psychological disorder, Dioguardi sought a new trial or in the alternative an evidentiary hearing on the juror's competence. The District Court denied the motion and the Court of Appeals affirmed. The Court of Appeals noted "the strong policy against any post-verdict inquiry into a juror's state of mind," *id.*, at 79, and observed:

> "The quickness with which jury findings will be set aside when there is proof of tampering or *external* influence, . . . parallel the reluctance of courts to inquire into jury deliberations when a verdict is valid on its face. . . . Such exceptions support

rather than undermine the rationale of the rule that possible *internal* abnormalities in a jury will not be inquired into except 'in the gravest and most important cases.' " *Id.*, at 79, n. 12, quoting *McDonald v. Pless, supra,* at 269 (emphasis in original).

The Court of Appeals concluded that when faced with allegations that a juror was mentally incompetent, "courts have refused to set aside a verdict, or even to make further inquiry, unless there be proof of an adjudication of insanity or mental incompetence closely in advance . . . of jury service," or proof of "a closely contemporaneous and independent post-trial adjudication of incompetency." 492 F.2d, at 80. See also *Sullivan v. Fogg*, 613 F.2d 465, 467 (CA2 1980) (allegation of juror insanity is internal consideration); *United States v. Allen*, 588 F.2d 1100, 1106, n. 12 (CA5 1979) (noting "specific reluctance to probe the minds of jurors once they have deliberated their verdict"); *United States v. Pellegrini*, 441 F.Supp. 1367 (ED Pa. 1977), aff'd, 586 F.2d 836 (CA3), cert. denied, 439 U.S. 1050 (1978) (whether juror sufficiently understood English language was not a question of "extraneous influence"). This line of federal decisions was reviewed in *Government of the Virgin Islands v. Nicholas, supra,* in which the Court of Appeals concluded that a juror's allegation that a hearing impairment interfered with his understanding of the evidence at trial was not a matter of "external influence." *Id.*, at 1079.

Substantial policy considerations support the common-law rule against the admission of jury testimony to impeach a verdict. As early as 1915 this Court explained the necessity of shielding jury deliberations from public scrutiny:

> "Let it once be established that verdicts solemnly made and publicly returned into court can be attacked and set aside on the testimony of those who took part in their publication and all verdicts could be, and many would be, followed by an inquiry in the hope of discovering something which might invalidate the finding. Jurors would be harassed and beset by the defeated party in an effort to secure from them evidence of facts which might establish misconduct sufficient to set aside a verdict. If evidence thus secured could be thus used, the result would be to make what was intended to be a private deliberation, the constant subject of public investigation—to the destruction of all frankness and freedom of discussion and conference." *McDonald v. Pless*, 238 U.S., at 267–268.

See also *Mattox v. United States*, 146 U.S. 140 (1892). The Court's holdings requiring an evidentiary hearing where extrinsic influence or relationships have tainted the deliberations do not detract from, but rather harmonize with, the weighty government interest in insulating the jury's deliberative process. See *Smith v. Phillips*, 455 U.S. 209 (1982) (juror in criminal trial had submitted an application for employment at the District Attorney's office); *Remmer v. United States*, 347 U.S. 227 (1954) (juror reported attempted bribe during trial and was subjected to investigation). The Court's statement in *Remmer* that "the integrity of jury proceedings must not be jeopardized by unauthorized invasions," *id.*, at 229, could also be applied to the inquiry petitioners seek to make into the internal processes of the jury.

There is little doubt that postverdict investigation into juror misconduct would in some instances lead to the invalidation of verdicts reached after irresponsible or improper juror behavior. It is not at all clear, however, that the jury system could survive such efforts to perfect it. Allegations of juror misconduct, incompetency, or inattentiveness, raised for the first time days, weeks, or months after the verdict, seriously disrupt the finality of the process. See, *e. g., Government of the Virgin Islands v. Nicholas, supra, at 1081* (one year and eight months after verdict rendered, juror alleged that hearing difficulties affected his understanding of the evidence). Moreover, full and frank discussion in the jury room, jurors' willingness to return an unpopular verdict, and the community's trust in a system that relies on the decisions of laypeople would all be undermined by a barrage of postverdict scrutiny of juror conduct. See Note, Public Disclosures of Jury Deliberations, 96 HARV. L. REV. 886, 888–892 (1983).

Federal Rule of Evidence 606(b) is grounded in the common-law rule against admission of jury testimony to impeach a verdict and the exception for juror testimony relating to extraneous influences. See *Government of the Virgin Islands v. Gereau*, 523 F.2d 140, 149, n. 22 (CA3 1975); S. Rep. No. 93–1277, p. 13 (1974) (observing that Rule 606(b) "embodied long-accepted Federal law"). Rule 606(b) states:

> "Upon an inquiry into the validity of a verdict or indictment, a juror may not testify as to any matter or statement occurring during the course of the jury's deliberations or to the effect of anything upon his or any other juror's mind or emotions as influencing him to assent to or dissent from the verdict or indictment or concerning his mental processes in connection therewith, except that a juror may testify on the question whether extraneous prejudicial information was improperly brought to the jury's attention or whether any outside influence was improperly brought to bear upon any juror. Nor may his affidavit or evidence of any statement by him concerning a matter about which he would be precluded from testifying be received for these purposes."

Petitioners have presented no argument that Rule 606(b) is inapplicable to the juror affidavits and the further inquiry they sought in this case, and, in fact, there appears to be virtually no support for such a proposition. See 3 D. Louisell & C. Mueller, Federal Evidence § 287, pp. 121–125 (1979) (under Rule 606(b), "proof to the following effects is excludable . . . : . . . that one or more jurors was inattentive during trial or deliberations, sleeping or thinking about other matters"); cf. Note, Impeachment of Verdicts by Jurors—Rule of Evidence 606(b), 4 Wm. Mitchell L. Rev. 417, 430–431, and n. 88 (1978) (observing that under Rule 606(b), "juror testimony as to . . . juror intoxication probably will be inadmissible"; note author suggests that "one possibility is for the courts to determine that certain acts, such as a juror becoming intoxicated outside the jury room, simply are not within the rule," but cites no authority in support of the suggestion). Rather, petitioners argue that substance abuse constitutes an improper "outside influence" about which jurors may testify under Rule 606(b). In our view the language of the Rule cannot easily be stretched to cover this circumstance. However severe their effect and improper their use, drugs or alcohol voluntarily ingested by a juror seems no more an "outside influence" than a virus, poorly prepared food, or a lack of sleep.

In any case, whatever ambiguity might linger in the language of Rule 606(b) as applied to juror intoxication is resolved by the legislative history of the Rule.

* * *

[Ed. Note: The Court reviews the legislative history of Federal Rule of Evidence 606(b)]

* * *

Thus, the legislative history demonstrates with uncommon clarity that Congress specifically understood, considered, and rejected a version of Rule 606(b) that would have allowed jurors to testify on juror conduct during deliberations, including juror intoxication. This legislative history provides strong support for the most reasonable reading of the language of Rule 606(b)—that juror intoxication is not an "outside influence" about which jurors may testify to impeach their verdict.

Finally, even if Rule 606(b) is interpreted to retain the common-law exception allowing postverdict inquiry of juror incompetence in cases of "substantial if not wholly conclusive evidence of incompetency," *Dioguardi*, 492 F.2d, at 80, the showing made by petitioners falls far short of this standard. The affidavits and testimony presented in support of the first new trial motion suggested, at worst, that several of the jurors fell asleep at times during the afternoons. The District Court Judge appropriately considered the fact that he had "an unobstructed view" of the jury, and did not see any juror sleeping. App. 147–149, 167–168; see *Government of the Virgin Islands v. Nicholas*, 759 F.2d, at 1077 ("It was appropriate for the trial judge to draw upon his personal knowledge and recollection in considering the factual allegations . . . that related to events that occurred in his presence"). The juror affidavit submitted in support of the second new trial motion was obtained in clear violation of the District Court's order and the court's local rule against juror interviews, MD Fla. Rule 2.04(c); on this basis alone the District Court would have been acting within its discretion in disregarding the affidavit. In any case, although the affidavit of juror Hardy describes more dramatic instances of misconduct, Hardy's allegations of *incompetence* are meager. Hardy stated that the alcohol consumption he engaged in with three other jurors did not leave any of them intoxicated. App. to Pet. for Cert. 47 ("I told [the prosecutor] that we would just go out and get us a pitcher of beer and drink it, but as far as us being drunk, no we wasn't"). The only allegations concerning the jurors' ability to properly consider the evidence were Hardy's observations that some jurors were "falling asleep all the time during the trial," and that his own reasoning ability was affected on one day of the trial. App. to Pet. for Cert. 46, 55. These allegations would not suffice to bring this case under the common-law exception allowing postverdict inquiry when an extremely strong showing of incompetency has been made.

Petitioners also argue that the refusal to hold an additional evidentiary hearing at which jurors would testify as to their conduct "violates the sixth amendment's guarantee to a fair trial before an impartial and *competent* jury." Brief for Petitioners 34 (emphasis in original).

This Court has recognized that a defendant has a right to "a tribunal both impartial and mentally competent to afford a hearing." *Jordan v. Massachusetts*, 225 U.S. 167, 176 (1912). In this case the District Court held an evidentiary hearing in response to petitioners' first new trial motion at which the judge invited petitioners to introduce any admissible evidence in support of their allegations. At issue in this case is whether the Constitution compelled the District Court to hold an additional evidentiary hearing including one particular kind of evidence inadmissible under the Federal Rules.

As described above, long-recognized and very substantial concerns support the protection of jury deliberations from intrusive inquiry. Petitioners' Sixth Amendment interests in an unimpaired jury, on the other hand, are protected by several aspects of the trial process. The suitability of an individual for the responsibility of jury service, of course, is examined during *voir dire*. Moreover, during the trial the jury is observable by the court, by counsel, and by court personnel. See *United States v. Provenzano*, 620 F.2d 985, 996–997 (CA3 1980) (marshal discovered sequestered juror smoking marijuana during early morning hours). Moreover, jurors are observable by each other, and may report inappropriate juror behavior to the court *before* they render a verdict. See *Lee v. United States*, 454 A. 2d 770 (DC App. 1982), cert. denied *sub nom. McIlwain v. United States, 464 U.S. 972 (1983)* (on second day of deliberations, jurors sent judge a note suggesting that foreperson was incapacitated).Finally, after the trial a party may seek to impeach the verdict by nonjuror evidence of misconduct. See *United States v. Taliaferro*, 558 F.2d 724, 725–726 (CA4 1977) (court considered records of club where jurors dined, and testimony of marshal who accompanied jurors, to determine whether jurors were intoxicated during deliberations). Indeed, in this case the District Court held an evidentiary hearing giving petitioners ample opportunity to produce nonjuror evidence supporting their allegations.

In light of these other sources of protection of petitioners' right to a competent jury, we conclude that the District Court did not err in deciding, based on the inadmissibility of juror testimony and the clear insufficiency of the nonjuror evidence offered by petitioners, that an additional postverdict evidentiary hearing was unnecessary.

* * *

The judgment of the Court of Appeals is affirmed in part and remanded for further proceedings consistent with this opinion.

It is so ordered.

_____

Do you agree with the *Tanner* Court's conclusion that the circumstances in the case did not warrant an evidentiary hearing? If so, what sort of allegation would compel such a hearing?

Racial Bias in Jury Deliberations as Basis for Evidentiary Hearing into Jury Deliberations

In *Pena-Rodriguez v. Colorado*, 137 S.Ct. 855 (2017), the United States Supreme Court announced an exception to the rule set forth in *Tanner. Pena-Rodriguez* involved a juror who had expressed racial bias against the defendant and a defense witness. The Colorado Supreme Court upheld the trial court's refusal to conduct an evidentiary hearing into the allegations of juror bias. Reversing the Colorado Supreme Court, the United States Supreme Court held that the Sixth Amendment defeats the no-impeachment rule to permit the trial court to conduct an evidentiary hearing in cases in which there is clear indication that a juror relied on racial animus during deliberations leading to a conviction. Does *Pena-Rodriguez* portend the end of *Tanner*? After *Pena-Rodriguez*, which dealt with racial animus, will courts consider evidentiary hearings in cases involving allegations of juror bias against other protected classes? If so, what about stereotypes unrelated to protected class status?

II. VERDICT

A. FEDERAL RULE OF CRIMINAL PROCEDURE 31

Federal Rule of Criminal Procedure 31 governs the jury verdict.

Rule 31. Jury Verdict

(a) Return. The jury must return its verdict to a judge in open court. The verdict must be unanimous.

* * *

By its plain terms, Rule 31(a) requires a unanimous verdict in federal criminal trials. However, does the Constitution require unanimity in *state* criminal jury trials? The Court considered this question in the following case.

Apodaca v. Oregon

Supreme Court of the United States, 1972
406 U.S. 404

■ MR. JUSTICE WHITE announced the judgment of the Court in an opinion in which THE CHIEF JUSTICE, MR. JUSTICE BLACKMUN, and MR. JUSTICE REHNQUIST joined.

Robert Apodaca, Henry Morgan Cooper, Jr., and James Arnold Madden were convicted respectively of assault with a deadly weapon, burglary in a dwelling, and grand larceny before separate Oregon juries, all of which returned less-than-unanimous verdicts. The vote in the cases of Apodaca and Madden was 11–1, while the vote in the case of Cooper was 10–2, the minimum requisite vote under Oregon law for sustaining a conviction.1 After their convictions had been affirmed by the Oregon Court of Appeals, 1 Or.App. 483, 462 P.2d 691 (1969), and review had been denied by the Supreme Court of Oregon, all three sought review in this Court upon a claim that conviction of crime by a less-than-unanimous jury violates the right to trial by jury in criminal cases specified by the Sixth Amendment and made applicable to the States by the Fourteenth. See *Duncan v. Louisiana*, 391 U.S. 145, 88 S.Ct. 1444, 20 L.Ed.2d 491 (1968). We granted certiorari to consider this claim, 400 U.S. 901, 91 S.Ct. 145, 27 L.Ed.2d 138 (1970), which we now find to be without merit.

In *Williams v. Florida*, 399 U.S. 78, 90 S.Ct. 1893, 26 L.Ed.2d 446 (1970), we had occasion to consider a related issue: whether the Sixth Amendment's right to trial by jury requires that all juries consist of 12 men. After considering the history of the 12-man requirement and the functions it performs in contemporary society, we concluded that it was not of constitutional stature. We reach the same conclusion today with regard to the requirement of unanimity.

I

Like the requirement that juries consist of 12 men, the requirement of unanimity arose during the Middle Ages and had become an accepted feature of the common-law jury by the 18th century. But, as we observed in Williams, 'the relevant constitutional history casts considerable doubt on the easy assumption . . . that if a given feature existed in a jury at common law in 1789, then it was necessarily preserved in the Constitution.' Id., at 92–93, 90 S.Ct., at 1902. The most salient fact in the scanty history of the Sixth Amendment, which we reviewed in full in Williams, is that, as it was introduced by James Madison in the House of Representatives, the proposed Amendment provided for trial

> 'by an impartial jury of freeholders of the vicinage, with the requisite of unanimity for conviction, of the right of challenge, and other accustomed requisites . . .' 1 Annals of Cong. 435 (1789).

Although it passed the House with little alteration, this proposal ran into considerable opposition in the Senate, particularly with regard to the vicinage requirement of the House version. The draft of the proposed Amendment was returned to the House in considerably altered form, and a conference committee was appointed. That committee refused to accept not only the original House language but also an alternate suggestion by the House conferees that juries be defined as possessing 'the accustomed requisites.' Letter from James Madison to Edmund Pendleton, Sept. 23, 1789, in 5 Writings of James Madison 424 (G. Hunt ed. 1904). Instead, the Amendment that ultimately emerged from the committee and then from Congress and the States provided only for trial

> 'by an impartial jury of the State and district wherein the crime shall have been committed, which district shall have been previously ascertained by law . . .'

As we observed in Williams, one can draw conflicting inferences from this legislative history. One possible inference is that Congress eliminated references to unanimity and to the other 'accustomed requisites' of the jury because those requisites were thought already to be implicit in the very concept of jury. A contrary explanation, which we found in Williams to be the more plausible, is that the deletion was intended to have some substantive effect. See 399 U.S., at 96–97, 90 S.Ct., at 1903–1904. Surely one fact that is absolutely clear from this history is that, after a proposal had been made to specify precisely which of the common-law requisites of the jury were to be preserved by the Constitution, the Framers explicitly rejected the proposal and instead left such specification to the future. As in Williams, we must accordingly consider what is meant by the concept 'jury' and determine whether a feature commonly associated with it is constitutionally required. And, as in Williams, our inability to divine 'the intent of the Framers' when they eliminated references to the 'accustomed requisites' requires that in determining what is meant by a jury we must turn to other than purely historical considerations.

II

Our inquiry must focus upon the function served by the jury in contemporary society. Cf. *Williams v. Florida*, supra, at 99–100, 90 S.Ct., at 1905. As we said in Duncan, the purpose of trial by jury is to prevent oppression by the Government by providing a 'safeguard against the corrupt or overzealous prosecutor and against the complaint, biased, or eccentric judge.' *Duncan v. Louisiana*, 391 U.S., at 156, 88 S.Ct., at 1451. 'Given this purpose, the essential feature of a jury obviously lies in the interposition between the accused and his accuser of the commonsense judgment of a group of laymen . . .' *Williams v. Florida*, supra, 399 U.S., at 100, 90 S.Ct., at 1906. A requirement of unanimity, however, does not materially contribute to the exercise of this commonsense judgment. As we said in Williams, a jury will come to such a judgment as long as it consists of a group of laymen representative of a cross section of the community who have the duty and the opportunity to deliberate, free from outside attempts at intimidation, on the question of a defendant's guilt. In terms of this function we perceive no difference between juries required to act unanimously and those permitted to convict or acquit by votes of 10 to two or 11 to one. Requiring unanimity would obviously produce hung juries in some situations where nonunanimous juries will convict or acquit. But in either case, the interest of the defendant in having the judgment of his peers interposed between himself and the officers of the State who prosecute and judge him is equally well served.

III

Petitioners nevertheless argue that unanimity serves other purposes constitutionally essential to the continued operation of the jury system. Their principal contention is that a Sixth Amendment 'jury trial' made mandatory on the States by virtue of the Due Process Clause of the Fourteenth Amendment, *Duncan v. Louisiana*, supra, should be held to require a unanimous jury verdict in order to give substance to the reasonable-doubt standard otherwise mandated by the Due Process Clause. See *In re Winship*, 397 U.S. 358, 363–364, 90 S.Ct. 1068, 1072, 25 L.Ed.2d 368 (1970).

We are quite sure, however, that the Sixth Amendment itself has never been held to require proof beyond a reasonable doubt in criminal cases. The reasonable-doubt standard developed separately from both the jury trial and the unanimous verdict. As the Court noted in the Winship case, the rule requiring proof of crime beyond a reasonable doubt did not crystallize in this country until after the Constitution was adopted. See id., at 361, 90 S.Ct., at 1070. And in that case, which held such a burden of proof to be constitutionally required, the Court purported to draw no support from the Sixth Amendment.

Petitioners' argument that the Sixth Amendment requires jury unanimity in order to give effect to the reasonable-doubt standard thus founders on the fact that the Sixth Amendment does not require proof beyond a reasonable doubt at all. The reasonable-doubt argument is rooted, in effect, in due process and has been rejected in *Johnson v. Louisiana*, 406 U.S. 356, 92 S.Ct. 1620, 32 L.Ed.2d 152.

IV

Petitioners also cite quite accurately a long line of decisions of this Court upholding the principle that the Fourteenth Amendment requires jury panels to reflect a cross section of the community. See, e.g., *Whitus v. Georgia*, 385 U.S. 545, 87 S.Ct. 643, 17 L.Ed.2d 599 (1967); *Smith v. Texas*, 311 U.S. 128, 61 S.Ct. 164, 85 L.Ed. 84 (1940); *Norris v. Alabama*, 294 U.S. 587, 55 S.Ct. 579, 79 L.Ed. 1074 (1935); *Strauder v. West Virginia*, 100 U.S. 303, 25 L.Ed. 664 (1880). They then contend that unanimity is a necessary precondition for effective application of the cross-section requirement, because a rule permitting less than unanimous verdicts will make it possible for convictions to occur without the acquiescence of minority elements within the community.

There are two flaws in this argument. One is petitioners' assumption that every distinct voice in the community has a right to be represented on every jury and a right to prevent conviction of a defendant in any case. All that the Constitution forbids, however, is systematic exclusion of identifiable segments of the community from jury panels and from the juries ultimately drawn from those panels; a defendant may not, for example, challenge the makeup of a jury merely because no members of his race are on the jury, but must prove that his race has been systematically excluded. See *Swain v. Alabama*, 380 U.S. 202, 208–209, 85 S.Ct. 824, 829, 13 L.Ed.2d 759 (1965); *Cassell v. Texas*, 339 U.S. 282, 286–287, 70 S.Ct. 629, 631, 94 L.Ed. 839 (1950); *Akins v. Texas*, 325 U.S. 398, 403–404, 65 S.Ct. 1276, 1279, 89 L.Ed. 1692 (1945); *Ruthenberg v. United States*, 245 U.S. 480, 38 S.Ct. 168, 62 L.Ed. 414 (1918). No group, in short, has the right to block convictions; it has only the right to participate in the overall legal processes by which criminal guilt and innocence are determined.

We also cannot accept petitioners' second assumption—that minority groups, even when they are represented on a jury, will not adequately represent the viewpoint of those groups simply because they may be outvoted in the final result. They will be present during all deliberations, and their views will be heard. We cannot assume that the majority of the jury will refuse to weigh the evidence and reach a decision upon rational grounds, just as it must now do in order to obtain unanimous verdicts, or that a majority will deprive a man of his liberty on the basis of prejudice when a minority is presenting a reasonable argument in favor of acquittal. We simply find no proof for the notion that a majority will disregard its instructions and cast its votes for guilt or innocence based on prejudice rather than the evidence.

We accordingly affirm the judgment of the Court of Appeals of Oregon.

It is so ordered.

Judgment affirmed.

When Is Unanimity Required?

As the Court stated in *Apodaca*, unanimity is not required in state trials, and 11–1 and 10–2 verdicts in favor of conviction were sufficient to support a conviction in accordance with the Constitution. The Court would later approve a 9–3 verdict in *Johnson v. Louisiana*, 406 U.S. 356 (1972). As discussed earlier in this Chapter, juries are not required to be made up of twelve members, and can be as small as six members. *See Ballew, supra*. However, six-member juries must be unanimous. *See Burch v. Louisiana*, 441 U.S. 130 (1979).

* * *

Rule 31. Jury Verdict

(b) Partial Verdicts, Mistrial, and Retrial.

(1) Multiple Defendants. If there are multiple defendants, the jury may return a verdict at any time during its deliberations as to any defendant about whom it has agreed.

(2) Multiple Counts. If the jury cannot agree on all counts as to any defendant, the jury may return a verdict on those counts on which it has agreed.

(3) Mistrial and Retrial. If the jury cannot agree on a verdict on one or more counts, the court may declare a mistrial on those counts. The government may retry any defendant on any count on which the jury could not agree.

(c) Lesser Offense or Attempt. A defendant may be found guilty of any of the following:

(1) an offense necessarily included in the offense charged;

(2) an attempt to commit the offense charged; or

(3) an attempt to commit an offense necessarily included in the offense charged, if the attempt is an offense in its own right.

* * *

Lesser Included Offenses

In *Schmuck v. United States*, 489 U.S. 705 (1989), the Supreme Court decided when a lesser included offense instruction is warranted under Rule 31(c):

Federal Rule of Criminal Procedure 31(c) provides in relevant part: "The defendant may be found guilty of an offense necessarily included in the offense charged." As noted above, the Courts of Appeals have adopted different tests to determine when, under this Rule, a defendant is entitled to a lesser included offense instruction. The Seventh Circuit's original panel opinion applied the "inherent relationship" approach formulated in *United States v. Whitaker*, 144 U.S. App. D. C. 344, 447 F. 2d 314 (1971):

"[D]efendant is entitled to invoke Rule 31(c) when a lesser offense is established by the evidence adduced at trial in proof of the greater offense, with the caveat that there must also be an 'inherent' relationship between the greater and lesser offenses, *i.e.*, they must relate to the protection of the same interests, and must be so related that in the general nature of these crimes, though not necessarily invariably, proof of the lesser offense is necessarily presented as part of the showing of the commission of the greater offense." *Id.*, at 349, 447 F. 2d, at 319.

The en banc Seventh Circuit rejected this approach in favor of the "traditional," or "elements" test. Under this test, one offense is not "necessarily included" in another unless the elements of the lesser offense are a subset of the elements of the charged offense. Where the lesser offense requires an element not required for the greater offense, no instruction is to be given under Rule 31(c).

We now adopt the elements approach to Rule 31(c). As the Court of Appeals noted, this approach is grounded in the language and history of the Rule and provides for greater certainty in its application. It, moreover, is consistent with past decisions of this Court which, though not specifically endorsing a particular test, employed the elements approach in cases involving lesser included offense instructions.

First, the wording of Rule 31(c), although not conclusive, supports the application of the elements approach. The Rule speaks in terms of an offense that is "necessarily included in the offense charged." This language suggests that the comparison to be drawn is between *offenses*. Since offenses are statutorily defined, that comparison is appropriately conducted by reference to the statutory elements of the offenses in question, and not, as the inherent relationship approach would mandate, by reference to conduct proved at trial regardless of the statutory definitions. Furthermore, the language of Rule 31(c) speaks of the necessary *inclusion* of the lesser offense in the greater. While the elements test is true to this requirement, the inherent relationship approach dispenses with the required relationship of necessary inclusion: the inherent relationship approach permits a lesser included offense instruction even if the proof of one offense does not invariably require proof of the other as long as the two offenses serve the same legislative goals.

In addition, the inherent relationship approach, in practice, would require that Rule 31(c) be applied in a manner inconsistent with its language. The Rule provides that a defendant "may be found guilty" of a lesser included offense, without distinguishing between a request for jury instructions made by the Government and one made by the defendant. In other words, the language of the Rule suggests that a lesser included offense instruction is available in equal measure to the defense and to the prosecution. Yet, under the inherent relationship approach, such mutuality is impossible.

It is ancient doctrine of both the common law and of our Constitution that a defendant cannot be held to answer a charge not contained in the indictment brought against him. See *Ex parte Bain*, 121 U.S. 1, 10 (1887); *Stirone v. United States*, 361 U.S. 212, 215–217 (1960); *United States v. Miller*, 471 U.S. 130, 140, 142–143 (1985). This stricture is based at least in part on the right of the defendant to notice of the charge brought against him. *United States v. Whitaker*, 144 U.S. App. D. C., at 350–351, 447 F. 2d, at 320–321. Were the prosecutor able to request an instruction on an offense whose elements were not charged in the indictment, this right to notice would be placed in jeopardy. Specifically, if, as mandated under the inherent relationship approach, the determination whether the offenses are sufficiently related to permit an instruction is delayed until all the evidence is developed at trial, the defendant may not have constitutionally sufficient notice to support a lesser included offense instruction requested by the prosecutor if the elements of that lesser offense are not part of the indictment. Accordingly, under the inherent relationship approach, the defendant, by in effect waiving his right to notice, may obtain a lesser offense instruction in circumstances where the constitutional restraint of notice to the defendant would prevent the prosecutor from seeking an identical instruction. The elements test, in contrast, permits lesser offense instructions only in those cases where the indictment contains the elements of both offenses and thereby gives notice to the defendant that he may be convicted on either charge. This approach preserves the mutuality implicit in the language of Rule 31(c).

Second, the history of Rule 31(c) supports the adoption of the elements approach. The Rule, which has not been amended since its adoption in 1944, is the most recent derivative of the common-law practice that permitted a jury to find a defendant "guilty of any lesser offense necessarily included in the offense charged." *Beck v. Alabama*, 447 U.S. 625, 633 (1980). Over a century ago, Congress codified the common law for federal criminal trials, providing in the Act of June 1, 1872, ch. 255, § 9, 17 Stat. 198, that "in all criminal causes the defendant may be found guilty of any offence the commission of which is necessarily included in that with which he is charged in the indictment." Rule 31(c) was intended to be a restatement of this "pre-existing law." See *Keeble v. United States*, 412 U.S. 205, 208, n. 6 (1973). Accordingly, prevailing practice at the time of the Rule's promulgation informs our understanding of its terms, and, specifically, its limitation of lesser included offenses to those "necessarily included in the offense charged."

The nature of that prevailing practice is clear. In *Giles v. United States*, 144 F. 2d 860 (1944), decided just three months before the adoption of Rule 31(c), the Court of Appeals for the Ninth Circuit unequivocally applied the elements test to determine the propriety of a lesser included offense instruction: " 'To be necessarily included in the greater offense the lesser must be such that it is impossible to commit the greater without first having committed the lesser.' " *Id.*, at 861, quoting *House v. State*, 186 Ind. 593, 595–596, 117 N. E. 647, 648 (1917). This approach, moreover, was applied consistently by state courts. Indeed, in *State v. Henry*, 98 Me. 561, 564, 57 A. 891, 892 (1904), the Supreme Judicial Court of Maine concluded that "a practically universal rule prevails, that the verdict may be for a lesser crime which is included in a greater charged in the indictment, the test being that the evidence required to establish the greater would prove the lesser offense as a necessary element." The California Supreme Court in *People v. Kerrick*, 144 Cal. 46, 47, 77 P. 711, 712 (1904), stated: "To be 'necessarily included' in the offense charged, the lesser offense must not only be part of the greater in fact, but it must be embraced within the legal definition of the greater as a part thereof." See also *State v. Marshall*, 206 Iowa 373, 375, 220 N. W. 106 (1928); *People ex rel. Wachowicz v. Martin*, 293 N. Y. 361, 364, 57 N. E. 2d 53, 54–55 (1944). This Court's decision in *Stevenson v. United States*, 162 U.S. 313 (1896), reflects the "practically universal" practice. There, in holding that the defendant in a murder charge was entitled to a lesser included offense instruction on manslaughter under the statutory predecessor to Rule 31(c), the Court engaged in a careful comparison of the statutory elements of murder and manslaughter to determine if the latter was a lesser included offense of the former. *Id.*, at 320. In short, the elements approach was settled doctrine at the time of the Rule's promulgation and for more than two decades thereafter. In its restatement of "pre-existing law," *Keeble v. United States*, 412 U.S., at 208, n. 6, Rule 31(c) incorporated this established practice.

Third, the elements test is far more certain and predictable in its application than the inherent relationship approach. Because the elements approach involves a textual comparison of criminal statutes and does not depend on inferences that may be drawn from evidence introduced at trial, the elements approach permits both sides to know in advance what jury instructions will be available and to plan their trial strategies accordingly. The objective elements approach, moreover, promotes judicial economy by providing a clearer rule of decision and by permitting appellate courts to decide whether jury instructions were wrongly refused without reviewing the entire evidentiary record for nuances of inference.

The inherent relationship approach, in contrast, is rife with the potential for confusion. Finding an inherent relationship between offenses requires a determination that the offenses protect the same interests and that "in general" proof of the lesser "necessarily" involves proof of the greater. In the present case, the Court of Appeals appropriately noted: "These new layers of analysis add to the uncertainty of the propriety of an instruction in a particular case: not only are there more issues to be resolved, but correct resolution involves questions of degree and judgment, with the attendant probability that the trial and appellate courts may differ." 840 F. 2d, at 389–390. This uncertainty was illustrated here. The three judges of the original appellate panel split in their application of the inherent relationship test to the offenses of mail fraud and odometer tampering. 776 F. 2d, at 1373–1375 (opinion concurring in part and dissenting in part). In the context of rules of criminal procedure, where certainty and predictability are desired, we prefer the clearer standard for applying Rule 31(c).

* * *

Rule 31. Jury Verdict

(d) **Jury Poll.** After a verdict is returned but before the jury is discharged, the court must on a party's request, or may on its own, poll the jurors individually. If the poll reveals a lack of unanimity, the court may direct the jury to deliberate further or may declare a mistrial and discharge the jury.

* * *

Other Issues Related to Jury Verdicts

Just as defendants may present inconsistent defenses, *see Matthews v. United States*, 485 U.S. 58 (1988), the government may present alternative theories of guilt to the jury, as long as they do not implicate separate offenses. *See Schad v. Arizona*, 501 U.S. 624 (1991). Also, inconsistent verdicts returned by a jury do not constitute error. *See United States v. Powell*, 469 U.S. 57 (1984); *Dunn v. United States*, 284 U.S. 390 (1932).

When there are multiple theories of guilt, the jury may return a general verdict of guilty even if there is inadequate evidence to support one of the theories. *See Griffin v. United States*, 502 U.S. 46 (1991). In contrast, a general verdict of guilty cannot stand in this context if one of the alternate theories is constitutionally or legally inadequate. *See id.*; *see also Bravo-Fernandez v. United States*, 137 S.Ct. 352 (2016) (no preclusion under Double Jeopardy Clause when jury returns inconsistent verdicts of convictions and acquittals and convictions are later vacated).

Special jury verdict interrogatories pose specific questions to the jurors bearing on the criminal liability of the defendant, and may be useful in complex cases such as those involving numerous predicate acts and multiple defendants, or narcotics quantities as predicates for mandatory sentences. Although courts generally frown upon special interrogatories in criminal cases, they may be used as long as they do not work a prejudice against the defendant. *See* Note, *Beyond "Guilty" or "Not Guilty": Giving Special Verdicts in Criminal Jury Trials*, 21 YALE L. & POL'Y REV. 263 (2003).

Jury Nullification—Power and Right?

Finally, juries may return a verdict not supported by the evidence. If the jury convicts, there are certain tools to address the problematic verdict, including a motion for judgment of acquittal under Rule 29, discussed in Chapter 16 *infra*. However, if the verdict acquits the defendant, there is nothing that can be done, as the Double Jeopardy Clause forever shields the defendant from prosecution for the same offense. *See* U.S. CONST., amend. V ("[N]or shall any person be subject for the same offence to be twice put in jeopardy of life or limb.").

Many call this latter phenomenon jury nullification. *See* BLACK'S LAW DICTIONARY 936 (9th ed. 2009) (defining jury nullification as "[the] knowing and deliberate rejection of the evidence or refusal to apply the law either because the jury wants to send a message about some social issue that is larger than the case itself or because the result dictated by law is contrary to the [juror's] sense of justice, morality, or fairness").

Is jury nullification a power of the jury, a right of the jury, or both? Most courts to have considered the issue reject the notion that a defendant is entitled to have a jury instructed on its ability to nullify. *See, e.g.*, *United States v. Kerley*, 838 F.2d 932 (7th Cir. 1988); *United States v. Trujillo*, 714 F.2d 102, 105 (11th Cir. 1983). Is jury nullification consistent with the jury's role and the rule of law? *Compare* Paul Butler, *Racially Based Jury Nullification: Black Power in the Criminal Justice System*, 105 YALE L.J. 677 (1995); Andrew D. Leipold, *Rethinking Jury Nullification*, 82 VA. L. REV. 253 (1996); Darryl K. Brown, *Jury Nullification Within the Rule of Law*, 81 MINN. L. REV. 1149 (1997); Nancy S. Marder, *The Myth of the Nullifying Jury*, 93 NW. U. L. REV. 877 (1999). If you think it is problematic, how would you protect against it?

III. MISTRIAL

Federal Rule of Criminal Procedure 26.3 governs mistrials.

Rule 26.3. Mistrial

Before ordering a mistrial, the court must give each defendant and the government an opportunity to comment on the propriety of the order, to state whether that party consents or objects, and to suggest alternatives.

The court's decision to declare a mistrial can be prompted by any number of events, including attorney, party, or juror misconduct, loss of the requisite number of jurors, external influence on the jury, or, as discussed earlier, the inability of the jurors to reach a verdict. As Rule 26.3 provides, the parties must be given the opportunity to weigh in before the court declares a mistrial.

Mistrials and the Double Jeopardy Clause

The Double Jeopardy Clause may apply to bar a prosecution after a mistrial has been declared, but it depends upon the context. As the U.S. Supreme Court explained in *United States v. Scott*, 437 U.S. 82 (1978):

> When a trial court declares a mistrial, it all but invariably contemplates hat the prosecutor will be permitted to proceed anew notwithstanding the defendant's plea of double jeopardy. * * * Such a motion ma be granted upon the initiative of either party or upon the court's own initiative. The fact that the trial judge contemplates that there will be a new trial is not conclusive on the issue of double jeopardy; in passing on the propriety of a declaration of mistrial granted at the behest of the prosecutor or on the court's own motion, this Court has balanced 'the valued right of a defendant to have his trial completed by the particular tribunal summoned to sit in judgment on him' * * * against the public interest in insuring that justice is meted out to offenders. * * * Where, in the other hand, a *defendant* successfully seeks to avoid his trial prior to its conclusion by a motion for mistrial, the Double Jeopardy Clause is not offended by a second prosecution.

Id. at 92–93.

Thus, the key inquiry is whether the mistrial came about pursuant to the government's motion, or *sua sponte* by the court. In either case, the defendant's interest in having the case resolved in the first trial is balanced against the public's interest in justice, and the Double Jeopardy Clause bar on retrial generally applies only if there was not "manifest necessity" for the mistrial, in light of that balancing. *See Scott*, 437 U.S. at 93. On the other hand, if the defendant moves for a mistrial, that "is deemed to be a deliberate election on his part to forego his valued right to have his guilt or innocence determined before the first trier of fact." *Id.* However, an important qualification on that rule is explained in *Oregon v. Kennedy*, 456 U.S. 667 (1982), in which the U.S. Supreme Court held that the Double Jeopardy Clause may apply to bar re-prosecution following a defendant's motion for mistrial if the government or court engaged in conduct intended to provoke the defendant into moving for mistrial.

CHAPTER 16

POST-TRIAL MOTIONS

I. MOTION FOR JUDGMENT OF ACQUITTAL

Despite the strong presumption in favor of having the fact-finder arrive at a verdict, there may be the situation when the evidence introduced by the government simply is insufficient—as a matter of law—to support a verdict of guilty. When defense counsel believes that the government's evidence has not reached the minimum threshold to support a guilty judgment, a motion for judgment of acquittal is appropriate.

In the federal system, Rule 29 governs such a motion.

Rule 29. Motion for a Judgment of Acquittal

(a) **Before Submission to the Jury.** After the government closes its evidence or after the close of all the evidence, the court on the defendant's motion must enter a judgment of acquittal of any offense for which the evidence is insufficient to sustain a conviction. The court may on its own consider whether the evidence is insufficient to sustain a conviction. If the court denies a motion for a judgment of acquittal at the close of the government's evidence, the defendant may offer evidence without having reserved the right to do so.

* * *

Note that the motion for judgment of acquittal is not exclusively a post-trial motion. In addition to the availability of the motion after the guilty verdict, the motion also may be made during trial at the close of the government's case-in-chief, or at the close of all evidence. If the evidence is insufficient to sustain a conviction on a count, the court *must* enter a judgment of acquittal on that count; the court has no discretion in the matter. In addition, under Rule 29, the court may consider the sufficiency of the evidence *sua sponte*.

(b) **Reserving Decision.** The court may reserve decision on the motion, proceed with the trial (where the motion is made before the close of all the evidence), submit the case to the jury, and decide the motion either before the jury returns a verdict or after it returns a verdict of guilty or is discharged without having returned a verdict. If the court reserves decision, it must decide the motion on the basis of the evidence at the time the ruling was reserved.

* * *

Rule 29(b) provides that the court may reserve its decision on the motion for judgment for acquittal and decide at a later point in the proceedings, either before or after the jury reaches a verdict. Obviously, the motion is rendered moot if the jury returns a verdict of not guilty on a count. If the jury returns a verdict of guilty, however, query whether this influences the court's decision on the motion for judgment of acquittal. Perhaps it is easier to grant such a motion when making the determination about what a hypothetical reasonable jury might do than when there is an actual verdict from a sitting jury.

ADVOCACY POINT

Note that if a court reserves its decision on the motion for judgment of acquittal, "it must decide the motion on the basis of the evidence at the time the ruling was reserved." This underscores the importance of making the motion at every opportunity, whether or not it is required as a procedural matter. Although defense counsel might expect that the defense case would weaken the government's evidence, sometimes the unexpected happens with a key defense witness or with physical evidence and the defense case unintentionally strengthens the government's case. However, if the court must confine the assessment of the evidence to the time when the ruling was reserved, defense counsel might escape the consequences of a damaging defense presentation.

(c) After Jury Verdict or Discharge.

(1) *Time for a Motion.* A defendant may move for a judgment of acquittal, or renew such a motion, within 14 days after a guilty verdict or after the court discharges the jury, whichever is later.

(2) *Ruling on the Motion.* If the jury has returned a guilty verdict, the court may set aside the verdict and enter an acquittal. If the jury has failed to return a verdict, the court may enter a judgment of acquittal.

(3) *No Prior Motion Required.* A defendant is not required to move for a judgment of acquittal before the court submits the case to the jury as a prerequisite for making such a motion after jury discharge.

* * *

Timing of the post-trial Rule 29 motion for judgment of acquittal is key. As the Rule provides, the motion must be made within 14 days of the later of the jury verdict or the discharge of the jury. This deadline generally may not be waived by the court. As the Supreme Court explained in *Carlisle v. United States*, 517 U.S. 416 (1996), "[t]here is simply no room in the text of Rule[ ] 29 . . . for the granting of an untimely postverdict motion for judgment of acquittal, regardless of whether the motion is accompanied by a claim of legal innocence, is filed before sentencing, or was filed late because of attorney error." The Court in *Carlisle* held that a court is without authority to consider a Rule 29 motion filed even one day late. *But see Kontrick v. Ryan*, 540 U.S. 443 (2004) (noting *Carlisle* did not characterize Rule 29 as jurisdictional).

However, Rules 29 and 45 (dealing with the computation and extension of time) were subsequently amended and the Advisory Committee notes now clarify that the court may entertain a request from the defendant for an extension of time to file the Rule 29 motion, but only if that request is filed within the 14-day filing period. Additionally, under Rule 45(b)(1)(B), a court has some discretion to extend the time for a Rule 29 motion filed late due to excusable neglect.

Regardless, it is incumbent upon defense counsel to remain aware of and meet the deadlines for post-trial motions. These deadlines are particularly susceptible to neglect because of the natural inclination of counsel to "decompress" after an intense and stressful trial. However, given the importance of post-trial motions for the client and the quality of justice delivered by the system, defense counsel must be vigilant regarding these obligations and deadlines before, during, and after trial.

Also note that, in the federal system, counsel need not make the motion for judgment of acquittal during trial in order for it to be made after the verdict. As discussed below, however, some jurisdictions require that the motion be made at earlier stages of the trial in order for it to be made after trial.

(d) Conditional Ruling on a Motion for a New Trial.

(1) *Motion for a New Trial.* If the court enters a judgment of acquittal after a guilty verdict, the court must also conditionally determine whether any motion for a new trial should be granted if the judgment of acquittal is later vacated or reversed. The court must specify the reasons for that determination.

(2) *Finality.* The court's order conditionally granting a motion for a new trial does not affect the finality of the judgment of acquittal.

(3) *Appeal.*

(A) Grant of a Motion for a New Trial. If the court conditionally grants a motion for a new trial and an appellate court later reverses the judgment of acquittal, the trial court must proceed with the new trial unless the appellate court orders otherwise.

(B) Denial of a Motion for a New Trial. If the court conditionally denies a motion for a new trial, an appellee may assert that the denial was erroneous. If the appellate court later reverses the judgment of acquittal, the trial court must proceed as the appellate court directs.

However, what is the standard the court should apply when considering whether to enter a judgment of acquittal? Under what circumstances should a court take the question of whether there is enough evidence to establish guilt away from the jury? The next case provides guidance to trial judges conducting this inquiry in the wake of *In re Winship, supra.*

Jackson v. Virginia

Supreme Court of the United States, 1979
443 U.S. 307

■ MR. JUSTICE STEWART delivered the opinion of the Court.

The Constitution prohibits the criminal conviction of any person except upon proof of guilt beyond a reasonable doubt. *In re Winship*, 397 U.S. 358, 90 S.Ct. 1068, 25 L.Ed.2d 368. The question in this case is what standard is to be applied in a federal habeas corpus proceeding when the claim is made that a person has been convicted in a state court upon insufficient evidence.

The petitioner was convicted after a bench trial in the Circuit Court of chesterfield County, Va., of the first-degree murder of a woman named Mary Houston Cole. Under Virginia law, murder is defined as "the unlawful killing of another with malice aforethought." *Stapleton v. Commonwealth*, 123 Va. 825, 96 S.E. 801. Premeditation, or specific intent to kill, distinguishes murder in the first from murder in the second degree; proof of this element is essential to conviction of the former offense, and the burden of proving it clearly rests with the prosecution. *Shiflett v. Commonwealth*, 143 Va. 609, 130 S.E. 777; *Jefferson v. Commonwealth*, 214 Va. 432, 201 S.E.2d 749.

That the petitioner had shot and killed Mrs. Cole was not in dispute at the trial. The State's evidence established that she had been a member of the staff at the local county jail, that she had befriended him while he was imprisoned there on a disorderly conduct charge, and that when he was released she had arranged for him to live in the home of her son and daughter-in-law. Testimony by her relatives indicated that on the day of the killing the petitioner had been drinking and had spent a great deal of time shooting at targets with his revolver. Late in the afternoon, according to their testimony, he had unsuccessfully attempted to talk the victim into driving him to North Carolina. She did drive the petitioner to a local diner. There the two were observed by several police officers, who testified that both the petitioner and the victim had been drinking. The two were observed by a deputy sheriff as they were preparing to leave the diner in her car. The petitioner was then in possession of his revolver, and the sheriff also observed a kitchen knife in the automobile. The sheriff testified that he had offered to keep the revolver until the petitioner sobered up, but that the latter had indicated that this would be unnecessary since he and the victim were about to engage in sexual activity.

Her body was found in a secluded church parking lot a day and a half later, naked from the waist down, her slacks beneath her body. Uncontradicted medical and expert evidence established that she had been shot twice at close range with the petitioner's gun. She appeared not to have been sexually molested. Six cartridge cases identified as having been fired from the petitioner's gun were found near the body.

After shooting Mrs. Cole, the petitioner drove her car to North Carolina, where, after a short trip to Florida, he was arrested several days later. In a postarrest statement, introduced in evidence by the prosecution, the petitioner admitted that he had shot the victim. He contended, however, that the shooting had been accidental. When asked to describe his condition at the time of the shooting, he indicated that he had not been drunk, but had been "pretty high." His story was that the victim had attacked him with a knife when he resisted her sexual advances. He said that he had defended himself by firing a number of warning shots into the ground, and had then reloaded his revolver. The victim, he said, then attempted to take the gun from him, and the gun "went off" in the ensuing struggle. He said that he fled without seeking help for the victim because he was afraid. At the trial, his position was that he had acted in self-defense. Alternatively, he claimed that in any event the State's own evidence showed that he had been too intoxicated to form the specific intent necessary under Virginia law to sustain a conviction of murder in the first degree.

The trial judge, declaring himself convinced beyond a reasonable doubt that the petitioner had committed first-degree murder, found him guilty of that offense. The petitioner's motion to set aside the judgment as contrary to the evidence was denied, and he was sentenced to serve a term of 30 years in the Virginia state penitentiary. A petition for writ of error to the Virginia Supreme Court on the ground that the evidence was insufficient to support the conviction was denied.

The petitioner then commenced this habeas corpus proceeding in the United States District Court for the Eastern District of Virginia, raising the same basic claim. Applying the "no evidence" criterion of *Thompson v. Louisville*, 362 U.S. 199, 80 S.Ct. 624, 4 L.Ed.2d 654, the District Court found the record devoid of evidence of premeditation and granted the writ. The Court of Appeals for the Fourth Circuit reversed the judgment. The court noted that a dissent from the denial of certiorari in a case in this Court had exposed the question whether the constitutional rule of *In re Winship*, 397 U.S. 358, 90 S.Ct. 1068, 25 L.Ed.2d 368, might compel a new criterion by which the validity of a state criminal conviction must be tested in a federal habeas corpus proceeding. See *Freeman v. Zahradnick*, 429 U.S. 1111, 97 S.Ct. 1150, 51 L.Ed.2d 566 (dissent from denial of certiorari). But the appellate court held that in the absence of further guidance from this Court it would apply the same "no evidence" criterion of *Thompson v. Louisville* that the District Court had adopted. The court was of the view that some evidence that the petitioner had intended to kill the victim could be found in the facts that the petitioner had reloaded his gun after firing warning shots, that he had had time to do so, and that the victim was then shot not once but twice. The court also concluded that the state trial judge could have found that the petitioner was not so intoxicated as to be incapable of premeditation.

We granted certiorari to consider the petitioner's claim that under *In re Winship, supra,* a federal habeas corpus court must consider not whether there was *any* evidence to support a state-court conviction, but whether there was sufficient evidence to justify a rational trier of the facts to find guilt beyond a reasonable doubt. 439 U.S. 1001, 99 S.Ct. 609, 58 L.Ed.2d 676.

II

Our inquiry in this case is narrow. The petitioner has not seriously questioned any aspect of Virginia law governing the allocation of the burden of production or persuasion in a murder trial. See *Mullaney v. Wilbur*, 421 U.S. 684, 95 S.Ct. 1881, 44 L.Ed.2d 508; *Patterson v. New York*, 432 U.S. 197, 97 S.Ct. 2319, 53 L.Ed.2d 281. As the record demonstrates, the judge sitting as factfinder in the petitioner's trial was aware that the State bore the burden of establishing the element of premeditation, and stated that he was applying the reasonable-doubt standard in his appraisal of the State's evidence. The petitioner, moreover, does not contest the conclusion of the Court of Appeals that under the "no evidence" rule of *Thompson v. Louisville, supra,* his conviction of first-degree murder is sustainable. And he has not attacked the sufficiency of the evidence to support a conviction of second-degree murder. His sole constitutional claim, based squarely upon *Winship*, is that the District Court and the Court of Appeals were in error in not recognizing that the question to be decided in this case is whether any rational factfinder could have concluded beyond a reasonable doubt that the killing for which the petitioner was convicted was premeditated. The question thus raised goes to the basic nature of the constitutional right recognized in the *Winship* opinion.

III

A

This is the first of our cases to expressly consider the question whether the due process standard recognized in *Winship* constitutionally protects an accused against conviction except upon evidence that is sufficient fairly to support a conclusion that every element of the crime has been established beyond a reasonable doubt. Upon examination of the fundamental differences between the constitutional underpinnings of *Thompson v. Louisville, supra*, and of *In re Winship, supra*, the answer to that question, we think, is clear.

It is axiomatic that a conviction upon a charge not made or upon a charge not tried constitutes a denial of due process. *Cole v. Arkansas*, 333 U.S. 196, 201, 68 S.Ct. 514, 517, 92 L.Ed. 644; *Presnell v. Georgia*, 439 U.S. 14, 99 S.Ct. 235, 58 L.Ed.2d 207. These standards no more than reflect a broader premise that has never been doubted in our constitutional system: that a person cannot incur the loss of liberty for an offense without notice and a meaningful opportunity to defend. *E. g., Hovey v. Elliott*, 167 U.S. 409, 416–420, 17 S.Ct. 841, 844–846, 42 L.Ed. 215. Cf. *Boddie v. Connecticut*, 401 U.S. 371, 377–379, 91 S.Ct. 780, 785–787, 28 L.Ed.2d 113. A meaningful opportunity to defend, if not the right to a trial itself, presumes as well that a total want of evidence to support a charge will conclude the case in favor of the accused. Accordingly, we held in the *Thompson* case that a conviction based upon a record wholly devoid of any relevant evidence of a crucial element of the offense charged is constitutionally infirm. See also *Vachon v. New Hampshire*, 414 U.S. 478, 94 S.Ct. 664, 38 L.Ed.2d 666; *Adderley v. Florida*, 385 U.S. 39, 87 S.Ct. 242, 17 L.Ed.2d 149; *Gregory v. Chicago*, 394 U.S. 111, 89 S.Ct. 946, 22 L.Ed.2d 134; *Douglas v. Buder*, 412 U.S. 430, 93 S.Ct. 2199, 37 L.Ed.2d 52. The "no evidence" doctrine of *Thompson v. Louisville* thus secures to an accused the most elemental of due process rights: freedom from a wholly arbitrary deprivation of liberty.

The Court in *Thompson* explicitly stated that the due process right at issue did not concern a question of evidentiary "sufficiency." 362 U.S., at 199, 80 S.Ct., at 625. The right established in *In re Winship*, however, clearly stands on a different footing. *Winship* involved an adjudication of juvenile delinquency made by a judge under a state statute providing that the prosecution must prove the conduct charged as delinquent—which in *Winship* would have been a criminal offense if engaged in by an adult—by a preponderance of the evidence. Applying that standard, the judge was satisfied that the juvenile was "guilty," but he noted that the result might well have been different under a standard of proof beyond a reasonable doubt. In short, the record in *Winship* was not totally devoid of evidence of guilt.

The constitutional problem addressed in *Winship* was thus distinct from the stark problem of arbitrariness presented in *Thompson v. Louisville*. In *Winship*, the Court held for the first time that the Due Process Clause of the Fourteenth Amendment protects a defendant in a criminal case against conviction "except upon proof beyond a reasonable doubt of every fact necessary to constitute the crime with which he is charged." 397 U.S., at 364, 90 S.Ct., at 1073. In so holding, the Court emphasized that proof beyond a reasonable doubt has traditionally been regarded as the decisive difference between criminal culpability and civil liability. *Id.*, at 358–362, 90 S.Ct., at 1068–1072. See *Davis v. United States*, 160 U.S. 469, 16 S.Ct. 353, 40 L.Ed. 499; *Brinegar v. United States*, 338 U.S. 160, 174, 69 S.Ct. 1302, 1310, 93 L.Ed. 1879; *Leland v. Oregon*, 343 U.S. 790, 72 S.Ct. 1002, 96 L.Ed. 1302; 9 J. Wigmore, Evidence § 2495, pp. 307–308 (3d ed. 1940). Cf. *Woodby v. INS*, 385 U.S. 276, 285, 87 S.Ct. 483, 487, 17 L.Ed.2d 362. The standard of proof beyond a reasonable doubt, said the Court, "plays a vital role in the American scheme of criminal procedure," because it operates to give "concrete substance" to the presumption of innocence to ensure against unjust convictions, and to reduce the risk of factual error in a criminal proceeding. 397 U.S., at 363, 90 S.Ct., at 1072. At the same time by impressing upon the factfinder the need to reach a subjective state of near certitude of the guilt of the accused, the standard symbolizes the significance that our society attaches to the criminal sanction and thus to liberty itself. *Id.*, at 372, 90 S.Ct., at 1076 (Harlan, J., concurring).

The constitutional standard recognized in the *Winship* case was expressly phrased as one that protects an accused against a conviction except on "*proof* beyond a reasonable doubt . . . ." In subsequent cases discussing the reasonable-doubt standard, we have never departed from this definition of the rule or from the *Winship* understanding of the central purposes it serves. See, *e. g., Ivan V. v. City of New York*, 407 U.S. 203, 204, 92 S.Ct. 1951, 1952, 32 L.Ed.2d 659; *Lego v. Twomey*, 404 U.S. 477, 486–487, 92 S.Ct. 619, 625–626, 30 L.Ed.2d 618; *Mullaney v. Wilbur*, 421 U.S. 684, 95 S.Ct. 1881, 44 L.Ed.2d 508; *Patterson v. New York*, 432 U.S. 197, 97 S.Ct. 2319, 53 L.Ed.2d 281; *Cool v. United States*, 409 U.S. 100, 104, 93 S.Ct. 354, 357, 34 L.Ed.2d 335. In short, *Winship* presupposes as an essential of the due process guaranteed by the Fourteenth Amendment that no person shall be made to suffer the onus of a criminal conviction except upon sufficient proof—defined as evidence necessary to convince a trier of fact beyond a reasonable doubt of the existence of every element of the offense.

B

Although several of our cases have intimated that the factfinder's application of the reasonable-doubt standard to the evidence may present a federal question when a state conviction is challenged, *Lego v. Twomey, supra*, 404 U.S., at 487, 92 S.Ct., at 625; *Johnson v. Louisiana*, 406 U.S. 356, 360, 92 S.Ct. 1620, 1623, 32 L.Ed.2d 152, the Federal Courts of Appeals have generally assumed that so long as the reasonable-doubt instruction has been given at trial, the no-evidence doctrine of *Thompson v. Louisville* remains the appropriate guide for a federal habeas corpus court to apply in assessing a state prisoner's challenge to his conviction as founded upon insufficient evidence. See, *e. g., Cunha v. Brewer*, 511 F.2d 894 (CA8). We cannot agree.

The *Winship* doctrine requires more than simply a trial ritual. A doctrine establishing so fundamental a substantive constitutional standard must also require that the factfinder will rationally apply that standard to the facts in evidence. A "reasonable doubt," at a minimum, is one based upon "reason." Yet a properly instructed jury may occasionally convict even when it can be said that no rational trier of fact could find guilt beyond a reasonable doubt, and the same may be said of a trial judge sitting as a jury. In a federal trial, such an occurrence has traditionally been deemed to require reversal of the conviction. *Glasser v. United States*, 315 U.S. 60, 80, 62 S.Ct. 457, 469, 86 L.Ed. 680; *Bronston v. United States*, 409 U.S. 352, 93 S.Ct. 595, 34 L.Ed.2d 568. See also, *e. g., Curley v. United States*, 81 U.S.App.D.C. 389, 392–393, 160 F.2d 229, 232–233. Under *Winship*, which established proof beyond a reasonable doubt as an essential of Fourteenth Amendment due process, it follows that when such a conviction occurs in a state trial, it cannot constitutionally stand.

A federal court has a duty to assess the historic facts when it is called upon to apply a constitutional standard to a conviction obtained in a state court. For example, on direct review of a state-court conviction, where the claim is made that an involuntary confession was used against the defendant, this Court reviews the facts to determine whether the confession was wrongly admitted in evidence. *Blackburn v. Alabama*, 361 U.S. 199, 205–210, 80 S.Ct. 274, 279–282, 4 L.Ed.2d 242. Cf. *Drope v. Missouri*, 420 U.S. 162, 174–175, and n. 10, 95 S.Ct. 896, 905–906, and n. 10, 43 L.Ed.2d 103. The same duty obtains in federal habeas corpus proceedings. See *Townsend v. Sain*, 372 U.S. 293, 318, 83 S.Ct. 745, 759, 9 L.Ed.2d 770; *Brown v. Allen*, 344 U.S. 443, 506–507, 73 S.Ct. 397, 445–446, 97 L.Ed. 469 (opinion of Frankfurter, J.).

After *Winship* the critical inquiry on review of the sufficiency of the evidence to support a criminal conviction must be not simply to determine whether the jury was properly instructed, but to determine whether the record evidence could reasonably support a finding of guilt beyond a reasonable doubt. But this inquiry does not require a court to "ask itself whether *it* believes that the evidence at the trial established guilt beyond a reasonable doubt." *Woodby v. INS*, 385 U.S., at 282, 87 S.Ct., at 486(emphasis added). Instead, the relevant question is whether, after viewing the evidence in the light most favorable to the prosecution, *any* rational trier of fact could have found the essential elements of the crime beyond a reasonable doubt. See *Johnson v. Louisiana*, 406 U.S., at 362, 92 S.Ct., at 1624–1625. This familiar standard gives full play to the responsibility of the trier of fact fairly to resolve conflicts in the testimony, to weigh the evidence, and to draw reasonable inferences from basic facts to ultimate facts. Once a defendant has been found guilty of the crime charged, the factfinder's role as weigher of the evidence is preserved through a legal conclusion that upon judicial review *all of the evidence* is to be considered in the light most favorable to the prosecution. The criterion thus impinges upon "jury" discretion only to the extent necessary to guarantee the fundamental protection of due process of law.

That the *Thompson* "no evidence" rule is simply inadequate to protect against misapplications of the constitutional standard of reasonable doubt is readily apparent. "[A] mere modicum of evidence may satisfy a 'no evidence' standard . . . ." *Jacobellis v. Ohio*,378 U.S. 184, 202, 84 S.Ct. 1676, 1686, 12 L.Ed.2d 793 (Warren, C.J., dissenting). Any evidence that is relevant—that has any tendency to make the existence of an element of a crime slightly more probable than it would be without the evidence, cf. Fed.Rule Evid. 401—could be deemed a "mere modicum." But it could not seriously be argued that such a "modicum" of evidence could by itself rationally support a conviction beyond a reasonable doubt. The *Thompson* doctrine simply fails to supply a workable or even a predictable standard for determining whether the due process command of *Winship* has been honored.

C

Under 28 U.S.C. § 2254, a federal court must entertain a claim by a state prisoner that he or she is being held in "custody in violation of the Constitution or laws or treaties of the United States." Under the *Winship* decision, it is clear that a state prisoner who alleges that the evidence in support of his state conviction cannot be fairly characterized as sufficient to have led a rational trier of fact to find guilt beyond a reasonable doubt has stated a federal constitutional claim. Thus, assuming that state remedies have been exhausted, see 28 U.S.C. § 2254(b), and that no independent and adequate state ground stands as a bar, see *Estelle v. Williams*, 425 U.S. 501, 96 S.Ct. 1691, 48 L.Ed.2d 126; *Francis v. Henderson*, 425 U.S. 536, 96 S.Ct. 1708, 48 L.Ed.2d 149; *Wainwright v. Sykes*,433 U.S. 72, 97 S.Ct. 2497, 53 L.Ed.2d 594; *Fay v. Noia*, 372 U.S. 391, 438, 83 S.Ct. 822, 848, 9 L.Ed.2d 837, it follows that such a claim is cognizable in a federal habeas corpus proceeding. The respondents have argued, nonetheless, that a challenge to the constitutional sufficiency of the evidence should not be entertained by a federal district court under 28 U.S.C. § 2254.

In addition to the argument that a *Winship* standard invites replication of state criminal trials in the guise of § 2254 proceedings—an argument that simply fails to recognize that courts can and regularly do gauge the sufficiency of the evidence without intruding into any legitimate domain of the trier of fact—the respondents have urged that any departure from the *Thompson* test in federal habeas corpus proceedings will expand the number of meritless claims brought to the federal courts, will duplicate the work of the state appellate courts, will disserve the societal interest in the finality of state criminal proceedings, and will increase friction between the federal and state judiciaries. In sum, counsel for the State urges that this type of constitutional claim should be deemed to fall within the limit on federal habeas corpus jurisdiction identified in *Stone v. Powell*, 428 U.S. 465, 96 S.Ct. 3037, 49 L.Ed.2d 1067, with respect to Fourth Amendment claims. We disagree.

First, the burden that is likely to follow from acceptance of the *Winship* standard has, we think, been exaggerated. Federal-court challenges to the evidentiary support for state convictions have since *Thompson* been dealt with under § 2254. *E. g., Freeman v. Stone*, 444 F.2d 113 (CA9); *Grieco v. Meachum*, 533 F.2d 713 (CA1); *Williams v. Peyton*, 414 F.2d 776 (CA4). A more stringent standard will expand the contours of this type of claim, but will not create an entirely new class of cases cognizable on federal habeas corpus. Furthermore, most meritorious challenges to constitutional sufficiency of the evidence undoubtedly will be recognized in the state courts, and, if the state courts have fully considered the issue of sufficiency, the task of a federal habeas court should not be difficult. Cf. *Brown v. Allen*, 344 U.S., at 463, 73 S.Ct., at 410. And this type of claim can almost always be judged on the written record without need for an evidentiary hearing in the federal court.

Second, the problems of finality and federal-state comity arise whenever a state prisoner invokes the jurisdiction of a federal court to redress an alleged constitutional violation. A challenge to a state conviction brought on the ground that the evidence cannot fairly be deemed sufficient to have established guilt beyond a reasonable doubt states a federal constitutional claim. Although state appellate review undoubtedly will serve in the vast majority of cases to vindicate the due process protection that follows from *Winship*, the same could also be said of the vast majority of other federal constitutional rights that may be implicated in a state criminal trial. It is the occasional abuse that the federal writ of habeas corpus stands ready to correct. *Brown v. Allen, supra,* at 498–501, 73 S.Ct., at 441–443 (opinion of Frankfurter, J.).

The respondents have argued nonetheless that whenever a person convicted in a state court has been given a "full and fair hearing" in the state system—meaning in this instance state appellate review of the sufficiency of the evidence—further federal inquiry—apart from the possibility of discretionary review by this Court—should be foreclosed. This argument would prove far too much. A judgment by a state appellate court rejecting a challenge to evidentiary sufficiency is of course entitled to deference by the federal courts, as is any judgment affirming a criminal conviction. But Congress in § 2254 has selected the federal district courts as precisely the forums that are responsible for determining whether state convictions have been secured in accord with federal constitutional law. The federal habeas corpus statute presumes the norm of a fair trial in the state court and adequate state postconviction remedies to redress possible error. See 28 U.S.C. § 2254(b), (d). What it does not presume is that these state proceedings will always be without error in the constitutional sense. The duty of a federal habeas corpus court to appraise a claim that constitutional error did occur—reflecting as it does the belief that the "finality" of a deprivation of liberty through the invocation of the criminal sanction is simply not to be achieved at the expense of a constitutional right—is not one that can be so lightly abjured.

The constitutional issue presented in this case is far different from the kind of issue that was the subject of the Court's decision in *Stone v. Powell, supra.* The question whether a defendant has been convicted upon inadequate evidence is central to the basic question of guilt or innocence. The constitutional necessity of proof beyond a reasonable doubt is not confined to those defendants who are morally blameless. *E. g., Mullaney v. Wilbur,* 421 U.S., at 697–698, 95 S.Ct., at 1888–1889 (requirement of proof beyond a reasonable doubt is not "limit[ed] to those facts which, that if not proved, would wholly exonerate" the accused). Under our system of criminal justice even a thief is entitled to complain that he has been unconstitutionally convicted and imprisoned as a burglar.

We hold that in a challenge to a state criminal conviction brought under 28 U.S.C. § 2254—if the settled procedural prerequisites for such a claim have otherwise been satisfied—the applicant is entitled to habeas corpus relief if it is found that upon the record evidence adduced at the trial no rational trier of fact could have found proof of guilt beyond a reasonable doubt.

IV

Turning finally to the specific facts of this case, we reject the petitioner's claim that under the constitutional standard dictated by *Winship* his conviction of first-degree murder cannot stand. A review of the record in the light most favorable to the prosecution convinces us that a rational factfinder could readily have found the petitioner guilty beyond a reasonable doubt of first-degree murder under Virginia law.

There was no question at the trial that the petitioner had fatally shot Mary Cole. The crucial factual dispute went to the sufficiency of the evidence to support a finding that he had specifically intended to kill her. This question, as the Court of Appeals recognized, must be gauged in the light of applicable Virginia law defining the element of premeditation. Under that law it is well settled that premeditation need not exist for any particular length of time, and that an intent to kill may be formed at the moment of the commission of the unlawful act. *Commonwealth v. Brown*, 90 Va. 671, 19 S.E. 447. From the circumstantial evidence in the record, it is clear that the trial judge could reasonably have found beyond a reasonable doubt that the petitioner did possess the necessary intent at or before the time of the killing.

The prosecution's uncontradicted evidence established that the petitioner shot the victim not once but twice. The petitioner himself admitted that the fatal shooting had occurred only after he had first fired several shots into the ground and then reloaded his gun. The evidence was clear that the two shots that killed the victim were fired at close, and thus predictably fatal, range by a person who was experienced in the use of the murder weapon. Immediately after the shooting, the petitioner drove without mishap from Virginia to North Carolina, a fact quite at odds with his story of extreme intoxication. Shortly before the fatal episode, he had publicly expressed an intention to have sexual relations with the victim. Her body was found partially unclothed. From these uncontradicted circumstances, a rational factfinder readily could have inferred beyond a reasonable doubt that the petitioner, notwithstanding evidence that he had been drinking on the day of the killing, did have the capacity to form and had in fact formed an intent to kill the victim.

The petitioner's calculated behavior both before and after the killing demonstrated that he was fully capable of committing premeditated murder. His claim of self-defense would have required the trial judge to draw a series of improbable inferences from the basic facts, prime among them the inference that he was wholly uninterested in sexual activity with the victim but that she was so interested as to have willingly removed part of her clothing and then attacked him with a knife when he resisted her advances, even though he was armed with a loaded revolver that he had just demonstrated he knew how to use. It is evident from the record that the trial judge found this story, including the petitioner's belated contention that he had been so intoxicated as to be incapable of premeditation, incredible.

Only under a theory that the prosecution was under an affirmative duty to rule out every hypothesis except that of guilt beyond a reasonable doubt could this petitioner's challenge be sustained. That theory the Court has rejected in the past. *Holland v. United States*, 348 U.S. 121, 140, 75 S.Ct. 127, 137, 99 L.Ed. 150. We decline to adopt it today. Under the standard established in this opinion as necessary to preserve the due process protection recognized in *Winship*, a federal habeas corpus court faced with a record of historical facts that supports conflicting inferences must presume—even if it does not affirmatively appear in the record—that the trier of fact resolved any such conflicts in favor of the prosecution, and must defer to that resolution. Applying these criteria, we hold that a rational trier of fact could reasonably have found that the petitioner committed murder in the first degree under Virginia law.

For these reasons, the judgment of the Court of Appeals is affirmed.

It is so ordered.

The Jackson *Standard for Sufficiency of the Evidence*

The Court, in *Jackson*, rejected the *Thompson v. Louisville* "no evidence" standard in favor of a more robust standard:

> [T]he relevant question is whether, after viewing the evidence in the light most favorable to the prosecution, *any* rational trier of fact could have found the essential elements of the crime beyond a reasonable doubt. * * * This familiar standard gives full play to the responsibility of the trier of fact fairly to resolve conflicts in the testimony, to weigh the evidence, and to draw reasonable inferences from basic facts to ultimate facts.

Note that, under the *Jackson* standard, the evidence is viewed in the light most favorable to the prosecution, which, of course, carries the burden of proof. *See Wright v. West*, 505 U.S. 277 (1992). In the context of an affirmative defense for which the defendant has the burden of persuasion, the reviewing court will determine whether any rational factfinder could have *rejected* the evidence supporting the defense.

Also, it is important to understand that a court considering a motion for judgment of acquittal does not determine whether it would find the evidence sufficient to support a conviction, but rather, whether *any* rational factfinder would do so. Indeed, courts examining the sufficiency of the evidence must defer to the factfinder's prerogative to assess the credibility of witnesses, and to weigh and make reasonable inferences from the evidence presented in the case.

The *Jackson* standard is used both for consideration of motions for judgment of acquittal during and after trial, and for sufficiency of the evidence claims on appeal. As a general matter, there must have been a motion for judgment of acquittal made in the trial court in order to preserve the sufficiency of the evidence claim on appeal. An attorney's failure to make the motion waives the issue on appeal. The exception is in the context of a bench trial. *See, e.g., United States v. Atkinson*, 990 F.2d 501, 503 (9th Cir. 1993) ("[N]o motion for acquittal is necessary in a bench trial in order to preserve for appeal a challenge to the sufficiency of the evidence.").

ADVOCACY POINT

Given that failure to make a motion for judgment of acquittal can waive the defendant's right to raise a sufficiency of the evidence claim on appeal, remembering to make such a motion is of paramount importance. Treating the making of such a motion as the first step of the defense case presentation after the government's case-in-chief may help avoid a costly oversight.

NOTE ON STATE PRACTICE

Unlike under Rule 29(c)(3), some jurisdictions require that defense counsel make a motion for judgment of acquittal after the government's case-in-chief, at the close of all evidence, and after a guilty verdict. Failure to make the motion at all of these various stages in these jurisdictions will be treated as a waiver of the argument that the verdict must be overturned because of insufficiency of the evidence. The basic rationale is one of efficiency. If there is cause to end the prosecution for lack of evidence, it should be discovered during or just after the trial, rather than on appeal after many additional court and other resources have been expended. What is the rule in the jurisdiction in which you plan to practice?

Judgments of Acquittal and the Double Jeopardy Clause

As the U.S. Supreme Court explained succinctly in *North Carolina v. Pearce*, 395 U.S. 711 (1969), the Double Jeopardy Clause "protects against a second prosecution for the same offense after acquittal. It protects against a second prosecution for the same offense after conviction. And it protects against multiple punishments for the same offense." *Id.* at 717. You will note that this list excludes protection against re-prosecution after a successful appeal resulting in the overturning of a conviction. However, a defendant may invoke the

Double Jeopardy Clause in these circumstances if the appeal was won on the ground that there was insufficient evidence to support the conviction. *See Burks v. United States*, 437 U.S. 1, 18 (1978); *United States v. Ball*, 163 U.S. 662, 672 (1896). Likewise, a defendant may not be retried after a court enters a judgment of acquittal before verdict, as long as that decision was final. *See, e.g., Smith v. Massachusetts*, 543 U.S. 462 (2005). However, the Double Jeopardy Clause does *not* bar the reinstatement of a jury verdict of guilty after a trial or appellate court erroneously sets aside that guilty verdict. *See id.* at 467.

COUNSEL EXERCISE 16A: Motion for Judgment of Acquittal (Prosecution and Defense)

Assume for purposes of this exercise that the government has presented its case-in-chief at trial and has rested. Attorneys for the defendant immediately made an oral motion for judgment of acquittal under Rule 29 on all counts of the indictment. Before ruling on the motion (or deciding to reverse judgment), the court orders the defense to put its motion in writing and orders both sides to brief their position on the motion.

II. MOTION FOR A NEW TRIAL

Despite best efforts and the fact that a case was tried to completion and verdict, there sometimes may be a compelling need to have a new trial. A new trial might be necessitated by any number of reasons. For example, the court may have erred making a legal ruling on the admissibility of a key piece of evidence, or the jury may have been given incorrect instructions on the elements of the charged offense, or the prosecutor may have made improper remarks to the jury.

Obviously, after the time and expense of a trial, courts often are reluctant to simply start over, particularly given that no trial is likely to be perfect and completely fair. However, where there are issues with a trial that substantially undermine the legality and fairness of a conviction, it not only serves the interests of due process to provide the defendant with a new trial but it promotes efficiency by granting an inevitable new trial without going through the added procedural step of an appeal and remand.

Federal Rule of Criminal Procedure 33 governs the motion for a new trial.

Rule 33. New Trial

(a) **Defendant's Motion.** Upon the defendant's motion, the court may vacate any judgment and grant a new trial if the interest of justice so requires. If the case was tried without a jury, the court may take additional testimony and enter a new judgment.

* * *

Standards Governing Motions for a New Trial

The standard governing the motion for a new trial is different from that governing the motion for judgment of acquittal. Whereas the latter context requires the court to examine the evidence in the light most favorable to the government and with deference to the factfinder's credibility determinations, the motion for a new trial has the court make its *own* determination of the weight and credibility of the evidence and testimony. However, the bar is higher for a motion for a new trial in that the court must determine that a miscarriage of justice would result if a new trial is not granted.

Rule 33. New Trial

* * *

(b) **Time to File.**

(1) *Newly Discovered Evidence.* Any motion for a new trial grounded on newly discovered evidence must be filed within 3 years after the verdict or finding of guilty. If an appeal is pending, the court may not grant a motion for a new trial until the appellate court remands the case.

* * *

Motions for New Trial Based upon Newly Discovered Evidence

Although under Rule 33(b)(2), a motion for a new trial generally must be filed within 14 days of the guilty verdict, there is a much lengthier time frame—three years—for the deadline for such a motion based upon newly discovered evidence. However, there is a high threshold that must be met for evidence to be considered newly discovered for these purposes. Generally, a court will only grant a motion for a new trial under Rule 33(b)(1)'s newly discovered evidence provision if:

(1) the evidence [has] been discovered since trial; (2) the party seeking the new trial [has] show[n] diligence in the attempt to procure the newly discovered evidence; (3) the evidence relied on [is] not merely cumulative or impeaching; (4) [the evidence

is] material to the issues involved; and (5) [the evidence is] of such nature that in a new trial it would probably produce an acquittal.

United States v. Lafayette, 983 F.2d 1102, 1105 (D.C. Cir.1993).

It is important to note that evidence the defendant knew about during trial does not qualify as newly discovered, even if it only becomes available after trial, such as when a witness previously protected from testifying by privilege is later willing to take the stand.

What do you think about the notion that a defendant claiming to have newly discovered evidence of actual innocence might not have recourse in the courts? Is executive clemency sufficient to safeguard against the possibility that an innocent defendant could lose his liberty or even his life? *See Herrera v. Collins*, 506 U.S. 390 (1993) (holding that defendant's claim of actual innocence did not entitle him to habeas corpus relief in federal court, but noting that executive clemency is a "fail-safe" for innocence claims based on newly-discovered evidence not cognizable by the courts).

NOTE ON STATE PRACTICE

It should be noted that although Rule 33(b)(1) provides a three-year limit for newly discovered evidence, some jurisdictions have drastically shorter timeframes for new trial motions even when based upon newly discovered evidence. What is the deadline for a motion for a new trial in the state in which you plan to practice? Is the deadline different for motions based upon newly discovered evidence?

Rule 33. New Trial

* * *

(b) Time to File.

* * *

(2) *Other Grounds.* Any motion for a new trial grounded on any reason other than newly discovered evidence must be filed within 14 days after the verdict or finding of guilty.

* * *

The Court in *Eberhart v. United States*, 546 U.S. 12 (2005), held that the time requirement in Rule 33 is a "claims processing rule" that is mandatory (meaning the relief is unavailable if the motion is not filed within the deadline) but, unlike, a jurisdictional rule, can be forfeited if the government fails to object to the missed deadline.

> **COUNSEL EXERCISE 16B: Motion for a New Trial
> (Prosecution and Defense)**
>
> Assume that the defendant was convicted of the charged offenses after a jury trial. Defense counsel should draft and file a timely motion for a new trial making arguments relevant to the standard the court must apply when considering relief. The prosecutor should draft a pleading opposing the motion. Included with the motion should be a supporting brief or memorandum of law, a proposed order, and a certificate of service.

III. MOTION TO ARREST JUDGMENT

Under Federal Rule of Criminal Procedure 34, a defendant may move to arrest judgment on the ground that the court is without jurisdiction over the offense for which the defendant was convicted.

Rule 34. Arresting Judgment

(a) In General. Upon the defendant's motion or on its own, the court must arrest judgment if the court does not have jurisdiction of the charged offense.

(b) Time to File. The defendant must move to arrest judgment within 14 days after the court accepts a verdict or finding of guilty, or after a plea of guilty or nolo contendere.

IV. MOTION FOR BAIL AFTER CONVICTION

Although there is no constitutional requirement that the court grant bail to a convicted defendant who appeals the conviction, *see McKane v. Durston*, 153 U.S. 684 (1894), Fed. R. Crim. P. 46 and the Bail Reform Act, discussed in Chapter 3 *supra*, give the court discretionary authority to do so in certain circumstances.

Rule 46. Release from Custody; Supervising Detention

* * *

(c) Pending Sentencing or Appeal. The provisions of 18 U.S.C. § 3143 govern release pending sentencing or appeal. The burden of establishing that the defendant will not flee or pose a danger to any other person or to the community rests with the defendant.

As Federal Rule of Criminal Procedure 46(c) provides, Section 3143 guides the court's authority in this context. Where a defendant has been convicted, sentenced to a term of imprisonment, and is appealing, there is a requirement that the court detain the defendant unless: (1) the court finds "clear and convincing evidence that the person is not likely to flee or pose a danger to the safety of any other person or the community"; (2) "that the appeal is not for the purpose of delay"; and (3) the appeal "raises a substantial question of law or fact likely to result in—(i) reversal, (ii) an order for a new trial, (iii) a sentence that does not include a term of imprisonment, or (iv) a reduced sentence to a term of imprisonment less than the total of the time already served plus the expected duration of the appeal process." 18 U.S.C. § 3143(b).

Notwithstanding these factors, when a defendant is appealing a conviction for one of the more serious offenses enumerated in Section 3142(f)(1)(A)-(C), and has been sentenced to a term of incarceration, the court must detain the defendant pending appeal.

A separate provision of the Bail Reform Act governs consideration of a defendant who has been convicted but not yet sentenced. *See* 18 U.S.C. § 3143(a)). As with Section 3143(b), there is a presumption in favor of detention absent the court's finding of specific factors.

V. STAY OF SENTENCE PENDING APPEAL

Related to the issue whether a defendant will be released pending appeal, Federal Rule of Criminal Procedure 38 governs the stay of sentences pending appeal. Note that under Rule 38, the court must, for obvious reasons, stay a death sentence if the defendant appeals.

Rule 38. Staying a Sentence or a Disability

(a) Death Sentence. The court must stay a death sentence if the defendant appeals the conviction or sentence.

(b) Imprisonment.

(1) *Stay Granted.* If the defendant is released pending appeal, the court must stay a sentence of imprisonment.

(2) *Stay Denied; Place of Confinement.* If the defendant is not released pending appeal, the court may recommend to the Attorney General that the defendant be confined near the place of the trial or appeal for a period reasonably necessary to permit the defendant to assist in preparing the appeal.

(c) Fine. If the defendant appeals, the district court, or the court of appeals under Federal Rule of Appellate Procedure 8, may stay a sentence to pay a fine or a fine and costs. The court may stay the sentence on any terms considered appropriate and may require the defendant to:

(1) deposit all or part of the fine and costs into the district court's registry pending appeal;

(2) post a bond to pay the fine and costs; or

(3) submit to an examination concerning the defendant's assets and, if appropriate, order the defendant to refrain from dissipating assets.

(d) Probation. If the defendant appeals, the court may stay a sentence of probation. The court must set the terms of any stay.

(e) Restitution and Notice to Victims.

(1) *In General.* If the defendant appeals, the district court, or the court of appeals under Federal Rule of Appellate Procedure 8, may stay—on any terms considered appropriate—any sentence providing for restitution under 18 U.S.C. § 3556 or notice under 18 U.S.C. § 3555.

(2) *Ensuring Compliance.* The court may issue any order reasonably necessary to ensure compliance with a restitution order or a notice order after disposition of an appeal, including:

(A) a restraining order;

(B) an injunction;

(C) an order requiring the defendant to deposit all or part of any monetary restitution into the district court's registry; or

(D) an order requiring the defendant to post a bond.

(f) Forfeiture. A stay of a forfeiture order is governed by Rule 32.2(d).

(g) Disability. If the defendant's conviction or sentence creates a civil or employment disability under federal law, the district court, or the court of appeals under Federal Rule of Appellate Procedure 8, may stay the disability pending appeal on any terms considered appropriate. The court may issue any order reasonably necessary to protect the interest represented

by the disability pending appeal, including a restraining order
or an injunction.

CHAPTER 17

APPEAL

Why is the availability of appeal in a criminal case important? How does the appeal serve due process rights? What would our system of criminal justice look like in the absence of appeal? These are key questions to consider both as a matter of procedural design and of constitutional fairness. However, many would be surprised to learn that the Constitution does not provide a right to an appeal. As the Supreme Court explained in *Abney v. United States*, 431 U.S. 651 (1977):

> [I]t is well settled that there is no constitutional right to an appeal. *McKane v. Durston*, 153 U.S. 684, 14 S.Ct. 913, 38 L.Ed. 87 (1894). Indeed, for a century after this Court was established, no appeal as of right existed in criminal cases, and, as a result, appellate review of criminal convictions was rarely allowed. As the Court described this period in *Reetz v. Michigan*, 188 U.S. 505, 23 S.Ct. 390, 47 L.Ed. 563 (1903):
>
> > "(T)rials under the Federal practice for even the gravest offences ended in the trial court, except in cases where two judges were present and certified a question of law to this court." Id., at 508, 23 S.Ct., at 392.
>
> The right of appeal, as we presently know it in criminal cases, is purely a creature of statute; in order to exercise that statutory right of appeal one must come within the terms of the applicable statute in this case, 28 U.S.C. § 1291.

* * *

The statute creating the right to appeal in federal criminal cases, 28 U.S.C. § 1291 provides, in relevant part:

> The courts of appeals (other than the United States Court of Appeals for the Federal Circuit) shall have jurisdiction of appeals from all final decisions of the district courts of the United States, the United States District Court for the District of the Canal Zone, the District Court of Guam, and the District Court of the Virgin Islands, except where a direct review may be had in the Supreme Court.

Final Decisions

The fact that the statute provides the right to appeal from "final" decisions of the district court is significant. If a decision is not yet final, it may not be appealed. As the Supreme Court explained in *Abney*, *supra*:

[S]ince appeals of right have been authorized by Congress in criminal cases, as in civil cases, there has been a firm congressional policy against interlocutory or "piecemeal" appeals and courts have consistently given effect to that policy. Finality of judgment has been required as a predicate for federal appellate jurisdiction.

"The general principle of federal appellate jurisdiction, derived from the common law and enacted by the First Congress, requires that review of nisi prius proceedings await their termination by final judgment." * * * This principle is currently embodied in 28 U.S.C. § 1291 which grants the federal courts of appeals jurisdiction to review "all final decisions of the district courts," both civil and criminal.

Adherence to this rule of finality has been particularly stringent in criminal prosecutions because "the delays and disruptions attendant upon intermediate appeal," which the rule is designed to avoid, "are especially inimical to the effective and fair administration of the criminal law." * * *

Interlocutory Appeals and the Double Jeopardy Clause

There are certain circumstances in which a court's decision, though not technically "final," is subject to interlocutory appellate review. For example, the government may immediately appeal a court's decision to suppress evidence in a criminal case. This should make sense, given that, if the defendant is acquitted at trial, the Double Jeopardy Clause would bar a retrial. On the other hand, a defendant does not have the same right of interlocutory appeal of an order denying her motion to suppress evidence; a defendant must wait until after she is convicted to appeal the court's failure to suppress evidence.

However, a defendant may appeal a pretrial order to dismiss an indictment on double jeopardy grounds. *See Abney v. United States*, 431 U.S. 651 (1977) (noting that "the rights conferred on a criminal accused by the Double Jeopardy Clause would be significantly undermined if appellate review of double jeopardy claims were postponed until after conviction and sentence").

The Double Jeopardy Clause yields many complex doctrinal questions that go well beyond the basic notion that "subjecting the defendant to postacquittal factfinding proceedings going to guilt or innocence violates the Double Jeopardy Clause." *Smith v. Massachusetts*, 543 U.S. 462 (2005) (quoting *Smails v. Pennsylvania*, 476 U.S, 140, 145 (1986)). For more on double jeopardy, *see* Akhil Reed Amar, *Double Jeopardy Law Made Simple*, 106 YALE L.J. 1807 (1997).

I. PROCEDURAL ISSUES

A. FEDERAL RULE OF APPELLATE PROCEDURE 4

Appeals in criminal cases are governed not by the Federal Rules of Criminal Procedure, but by the Federal Rules of Appellate Procedure.

Rule 4. Appeal as of Right

* * *

(b) Appeal in a Criminal Case.

(1) *Time for Filing a Notice of Appeal.*

(A) In a criminal case, a defendant's notice of appeal must be filed in the district court within 14 days after the later of:

(i)   the entry of either the judgment or the order being appealed; or

(ii) the filing of the government's notice of appeal.

(B) When the government is entitled to appeal, its notice of appeal must be filed in the district court within 30 days after the later of:

(i)   the entry of the judgment or order being appealed; or

(ii) the filing of a notice of appeal by any defendant.

(2) *Filing Before Entry of Judgment.* A notice of appeal filed after the court announces a decision, sentence, or order—but before the entry of the judgment or order—is treated as filed on the date of and after the entry.

(3) *Effect of a Motion on a Notice of Appeal.*

(A) If a defendant timely makes any of the following motions under the Federal Rules of Criminal Procedure, the notice of appeal from a judgment of conviction must be filed within 14 days after the entry of the order disposing of the last such remaining motion, or within 14 days after the entry of the judgment of conviction, whichever period ends later. This provision applies to a timely motion:

(i)   for judgment of acquittal under Rule 29;

(ii) for a new trial under Rule 33, but if based on newly discovered evidence, only if the motion is made no later than 14 days after the entry of the judgment; or

(iii) for arrest of judgment under Rule 34.

(B) A notice of appeal filed after the court announces a decision, sentence, or order—but before it disposes of any of the motions referred to in Rule 4(b)(3)(A)—becomes effective upon the later of the following:

(i) the entry of the order disposing of the last such remaining motion; or

(ii) the entry of the judgment of conviction.

(C) A valid notice of appeal is effective—without amendment—to appeal from an order disposing of any of the motions referred to in Rule 4(b)(3)(A).

(4) *Motion for Extension of Time.* Upon a finding of excusable neglect or good cause, the district court may—before or after the time has expired, with or without motion and notice—extend the time to file a notice of appeal for a period not to exceed 30 days from the expiration of the time otherwise prescribed by this Rule 4(b).

(5) *Jurisdiction.* The filing of a notice of appeal under this Rule 4(b) does not divest a district court of jurisdiction to correct a sentence under Federal Rule of Criminal Procedure 35(a), nor does the filing of a motion under 35(a) affect the validity of a notice of appeal filed before entry of the order disposing of the motion. The filing of a motion under Federal Rule of Criminal Procedure 35(a) does not suspend the time for filing a notice of appeal from a judgment of conviction.

(6) *Entry Defined.* A judgment or order is entered for purposes of this Rule 4(b) when it is entered on the criminal docket.

(c) Appeal by an Inmate Confined in an Institution.

(1) If an inmate confined in an institution files a notice of appeal in either a civil or a criminal case, the notice is timely if it is deposited in the institution's internal mail system on or before the last day for filing. If an institution has a system designed for legal mail, the inmate must use that system to receive the benefit of this rule. Timely filing may be shown by a declaration in

compliance with 28 U.S.C. § 1746 or by a notarized statement, either of which must set forth the date of deposit and state that first-class postage has been prepaid.

(2) If an inmate files the first notice of appeal in a civil case under this Rule 4(c), the 14-day period provided in Rule 4(a)(3) for another party to file a notice of appeal runs from the date when the district court dockets the first notice.

(3) When a defendant in a criminal case files a notice of appeal under this Rule 4(c), the 30-day period for the government to file its notice of appeal runs from the entry of the judgment or order appealed from or from the district court's docketing of the defendant's notice of appeal, whichever is later.

(d) Mistaken Filing in the Court of Appeals. If a notice of appeal in either a civil or a criminal case is mistakenly filed in the court of appeals, the clerk of that court must note on the notice the date when it was received and send it to the district clerk. The notice is then considered filed in the district court on the date so noted.

* * *

While familiarity with the entire rule is important, it bears noting two provisions in particular. First, the deadline for filing the appeal is determined by the context in which the appeal is being made. Thus, the deadline may be a certain number of days after the court disposes of a motion or enters a judgment of conviction, or it may be a certain number of days after the opposing party files a notice of appeal. In addition, although it may be counterintuitive, the notice of appeal is filed not with the court of appeals, but with the district court.

B. PRESERVING ISSUES FOR APPEAL

Whether a court will entertain an issue on appeal is sometimes determined by whether the party seeking review first raised the issue before the trial court. Efficiency concerns militate in favor of presenting issues to the trial court where they often can be remedied by the tribunal with the greatest access to the factual and procedural background and without the added delay and expense of remand after appellate review. Although, historically, appellate rules required that an objection be made during trial in order to preserve an issue for appeal, the requirement of making formal exceptions to rulings of the trial judge has been relaxed.

Rule 51. Preserving Claimed Error

(a) Exceptions Unnecessary. Exceptions to rulings or orders of the court are unnecessary.

(b) Preserving a Claim of Error. A party may preserve a claim of error by informing the court—when the court ruling or order is made or sought—of the action the party wishes the court to take, or the party's objection to the court's action and the grounds for that objection. If a party does not have an opportunity to object to a ruling or order, the absence of an objection does not later prejudice that party. A ruling or order that admits or excludes evidence is governed by Federal Rule of Evidence 103.

II. STANDARDS OF REVIEW

When there has been an error at trial, how does the appellate court determine whether the defendant is entitled to a new trial? Professor Fairfax explains the concept of harmless error in *Harmless Constitutional Error and the Institutional Significance of the Jury*, 76 FORDHAM L. REV. 2027 (2008):

> The U.S. Constitution does not guarantee a criminal defendant a trial free from error. The doctrine of harmless error, which saves a flawed criminal conviction from reversal, generally permits a conviction to stand where the reviewing court believes the defect in the proceeding was harmless beyond a reasonable doubt. A twentieth-century innovation prompted primarily by concerns of efficiency and finality, the harmless error rule applies to all trial errors, save for a narrow class of constitutional errors deemed to be structural. A criminal conviction infected by structural error is immune to harmless error review and, therefore, is subject to automatic reversal. Conversely, if the constitutional error of which the criminal defendant complains is not deemed structural, the appellate court may both acknowledge the conviction was tainted with constitutional error and, at the same time, affirm the conviction.

> The Supreme Court has been sparing in its designation of errors as structural, thus far admitting only a handful of constitutional defects into the category of errors requiring automatic reversal. What remains in the vast number of errors that can be deemed harmless would surprise most casual observers; everything from Fourth Amendment violations to the erroneous admission of a coerced confession may be

deemed harmless for purposes of appellate review of criminal convictions.

A. HARMLESS ERROR

From where did the rule of harmless error originate? Why would an error at trial *not* lead to reversal of a conviction and a new trial? The historic development of the harmless error review is helpful to an understanding of the role it plays in appellate review of criminal cases. Professor Fairfax offers a brief historical exegesis of how the harmless error rule became central to the efforts to reform American criminal justice in the early 20th century in the following excerpt from *A Fair Trial Not a Perfect One: The Early Twentieth-Century Campaign for the Harmless Error Rule*, 93 MARQUETTE L. REV. 433 (2009):

> Why was there such a strong emphasis on a harmless error rule within the early twentieth-century criminal reform agenda? We may lack appreciation today for how criminal appeals looked to the early twentieth-century reformers. After all, for the past forty years, we have operated under a regime in which the Supreme Court has explicitly approved the state and federal appellate courts' application of harmless error review to most federal constitutional errors. This sits in stark contrast to the dominant criminal appellate practice in the early twentieth century, in which virtually any error—pleading errors, evidentiary errors, and constitutional errors—would be deemed presumptively prejudicial and often would prompt automatic reversal of the conviction and the granting of a new trial to the defendant.

> This approach derived from English practice. An 1835 English case in the Court of Exchequer is thought by most to be the beginning of an era in which error at trial was thought to be presumptively prejudicial or subject to automatic reversal. Almost forty years later, in 1873, Parliament authorized English courts to implement a harmless error rule in civil cases. Nearly thirty-five years after that, Parliament passed the Criminal Appeal Act of 1907, imposing a harmless error rule in criminal cases, although English judges took slowly to the idea of applying the harmless error rule.

> American courts were broadly influenced by the old Exchequer rule of automatic reversal followed by English courts in the nineteenth century. By the beginning of the nineteenth century, it is fair to say, the prevalent approach in American courts was to apply a presumption of prejudice or a strict rule of automatic reversal in criminal (and civil) cases upon a finding of error below. As one might imagine, such an

approach, whatever its merits, led to absurd results, such as granting convicted murderers new trials because of the misspelling of non-essential words or other typographical errors in the indictment, or minor and inconsequential evidentiary errors at trial. Such instances were widely reported and often sensationalized in the media, which led to growing public outcry over perceived "technicalities" and "formalism" in criminal appellate practice.

Nevertheless, American legislatures were slow to follow Parliament's lead in the late nineteenth century and early twentieth century to rid the old Exchequer rule of automatic reversal from criminal appellate practice. As American reformers often complained (with regard to the harmless error rule and a number of other items on the criminal procedural reform agenda), American courts and legislatures seemed to adhere steadfastly to practices inherited from the English, long after the English had discarded the approach as unsatisfactory. American appellate courts of this era were described as "impregnable citadels of technicality," which created an environment where "the fear of reversal hangs as a sword of Damocles over the heads of prosecutors and trial judges."

Against this backdrop, the criminal procedural reform project's campaign for the harmless error rule was set in motion. For these reformers, the adoption of a harmless error rule in American criminal appellate practice would lead to improved efficiency of, and enhanced public confidence in, the criminal process. In addition, the formalistic rules and requirements, the violation of which frequently triggered reversals and grants of new trials, were themselves often the target of the reform agenda.

Federal Rules of Criminal Procedure 52(a) implements a harmless error rule in federal criminal cases.

Rule 52. Harmless and Plain Error

(a) Harmless Error. Any error, defect, irregularity, or variance that does not affect substantial rights must be disregarded.

* * *

This harmless error rule went into effect with the advent of the Federal Rules of Criminal Procedure in 1946. *See* Fairfax, *A Fair Trial, Not a Perfect One, supra.* The promulgation of the rule had been significant because federal judges had been reluctant to apply the harmless error doctrine despite a "harmless error statute" that had been on the books since 1919. *See* Act of Feb. 26, 1919, Pub. L. No. 65–281, 40 Stat, 1181 (amending Judicial Code section 269, 36 Stat. 1163). This statute, which can today be found at 28 U.S.C. § 2111, provides, "On the hearing of any appeal or writ of certiorari in any case, the court shall give judgment after an examination of the record without regard to errors or defects which do not affect the substantial rights of the parties."

The same year that the Federal Rules of Criminal Procedure embraced the harmless error rule, the Supreme Court, in *Kotteakos v. United States*, 328 U.S. 750 (1946), affirmed the notion that federal courts could ignore certain errors if the reviewing court "is sure that the error did not influence the jury or had but very slight effect."

Harmless Error Doctrine and Constitutional Errors

However, the *Kotteakos* Court was careful to point out that the harmless error rule might not apply when the error is not simply an evidentiary or other technical error, but instead represented a violation of "a constitutional norm or a specific command of Congress." *Id.* For over twenty years after *Kotteakos*, courts did not apply harmless error to trial errors of *constitutional* dimension. This all changed when the Court decided *Chapman v. California*, 386 U.S. 18 (1967). Professor Fairfax describes the *Chapman* Court's expansion of the harmless error doctrine to constitutional errors in the following excerpt from *Harmless Constitutional Error and the Institutional Significance of the Jury*, 76 FORDHAM L. REV. 2027 (2008):

> One thing was certain both before and after *Kotteakos*—the harmless error rule did not apply to constitutional errors at trial. Prior to the Supreme Court's 1967 decision in *Chapman v. California*, constitutional errors prompted the automatic reversal of a conviction. Indeed, the notion that an error implicating a federal constitutional right could be harmless was not even taken seriously until the 1960s, when a significant expansion in the rights of criminal defendants was underway. A five-justice majority in the 1963 case of *Fahy v. Connecticut* avoided the question of whether a constitutional error could ever be harmless, a question the four dissenters answered in the affirmative. Four years later, in *Chapman*, the Court made clear that automatic reversal is not required to remedy federal constitutional error.
>
> Petitioner Ruth Elizabeth Chapman had been convicted at a state trial infected with a clear federal constitutional violation and the state supreme court upheld the conviction pursuant to the harmless error rule contained in California's constitution.

After determining that review of federal constitutional errors is governed by federal law, the Court turned to the question of whether a federal constitutional error can ever be harmless. The Court noted that a harmless error rule operates in each of the fifty states and the federal system, and that none of those rules distinguished between errors of statute or rules on the one hand and constitutional error on the other. Emphasizing the core purpose of harmless error review—avoiding the "setting aside [of] convictions for small errors or defects that have little, if any, likelihood of having changed the result of the trial"—the Court expanded the harmless error doctrine to federal constitutional error:

> We conclude that there may be some constitutional errors which in the setting of a particular case are so unimportant and insignificant that they may, consistent with the Federal Constitution, be deemed harmless, not requiring the automatic reversal of the conviction.

Chapman then advanced a standard for judging the harmlessness of a constitutional error, declaring that, "before a federal constitutional error can be held harmless, the court must be able to declare a belief that it was harmless beyond a reasonable doubt."

After *Chapman*, even where the defendant raises a timely objection to a constitutional error below, the appellate court may affirm the conviction in cases where it is clear beyond a reasonable doubt that such error did not affect the outcome of the proceedings or "did not contribute to the verdict obtained." Two years later, the Supreme Court muddied the waters by allowing a conviction to stand despite constitutional error because of the "overwhelming" evidence of the defendant's guilt. Since then, the Court has shifted between the two standards—harmlessness based upon whether the error contributed to the verdict and harmlessness based upon whether the residual evidence was overwhelming—in applying the harmless error rule to federal constitutional error.

* * *

"Structural" Constitutional Errors

Thus, after *Chapman*, harmless error review may be applied to both non-constitutional and constitutional errors. However, the *Chapman* Court noted that "there are some constitutional rights so basic to a fair trial that their infraction can never be treated as harmless error." *See Chapman*, 386 U.S. at 23 n.8. This final excerpt from Professor Fairfax's article explains how the Court has determined which constitutional errors are structural and, thus, cannot be deemed harmless:

> Although the Supreme Court has made plain that "most constitutional errors can be harmless," the *Chapman* Court noted its "prior cases have indicated that there are some constitutional rights so basic to a fair trial that their infraction can never be treated as harmless error," citing cases involving a biased trial judge, the evidentiary admission of a coerced confession, and the denial of the right to counsel at trial. Beyond setting out these three precedents, the *Chapman* Court provided no guidance for the future ascertainment of those rights "so basic to a fair trial that their infraction can never be treated as harmless error." The Court subsequently "adopted an ad hoc approach which resulted in the vast majority of constitutional errors being held subject to harmless error analysis." Thus, in the wake of *Chapman*, we knew that harmless error review could be applied to many, but not all types of constitutional error; however, there was no principled way of determining into which category a specific constitutional error would fall.

> Finally, nearly twenty-five years after *Chapman*, the Court offered a framework for determining which constitutional errors were subject to automatic reversal and which were subject to harmless error review. The Court, in *Arizona v. Fulminante*, attempted to draw a principled distinction between the numerous constitutional errors it had made subject to harmless error review and those constitutional errors the Court had deemed to be reversible per se. This attempt yielded the trial error/structural error dichotomy to which the Court adheres today.

> The Court, in *Fulminante*, distinguished those errors susceptible to harmless error review by making a distinction between "trial" errors, "which may . . . be quantitatively assessed in the context of the other evidence," and "structural" errors, which "affect[ ] the framework within which the trial proceeds, rather than simply an error in the trial process itself." To be sure, the term "structural error" does not refer to constitutional structure; instead, it corresponds to the "infrastructure" within which a criminal case is tried. Only those constitutional errors that "transcend[ ] the criminal process," and implicate that trial infrastructure or framework, according to *Fulminante*, were reversible per se.

> Grafting this explanation onto the Court's precedents that had designated certain constitutional errors as not subject to

harmless error review, the *Fulminante* majority carved out a category of rights giving rise to such structural errors, a category including the right to a public trial, the right to pro se representation, the right not to have members of one's race excluded from a grand jury, the right to an unbiased judge, and the right to counsel. This list of structural errors pales in comparison to the remainder of constitutional errors, most of which presumably are deemed to be trial error and, therefore, subject to harmless error review. Indeed, the Court has been miserly in its own designation of constitutional errors subject to automatic reversal. A full decade-and-a-half after *Fulminante*'s inventory of those structural constitutional errors subject to automatic reversal, only two additions—a defective reasonable doubt instruction and deprivation of counsel of one's choice—have been made.

Not surprisingly, the dichotomy between trial error and structural error has been the subject of much criticism. Some commentators take issue with the manner in which the Court distinguishes between trial and structural errors, arguing that the Court is far too simplistic, and ultimately unpersuasive, in its approach to the complex task of determining which errors are or are not reversible per se. Others attack the dichotomy itself, arguing that "[t]he Constitution does not create a hierarchy of rights or values," while others try to discern the Court's rationale for choosing certain rights over others in the designation of structural error. Some go as far as to condemn the application of harmless error review to any constitutional error, arguing that all constitutional error should be subject to automatic reversal because harmless error doctrine allows appellate courts to undermine constitutional decisions they are otherwise bound to apply.

* * *

Categories of Structural Constitutional Error

It should be noted that there are a number of other categories of. The U.S. Supreme Court, in *Weaver v. Massachusetts*, 137 S.Ct. 1899 (2017), recently took inventory of the three categories of constitutional errors it has recognized as qualifying as "structural" and, thus, not subject to harmless error review:

> The purpose of the structural error doctrine is to ensure insistence on certain basic, constitutional guarantees that should define the framework of any criminal trial. Thus, the defining feature of a structural error is that it "affect[s] the framework within which the trial proceeds," rather than being

"simply an error in the trial process itself." *Fulminante,* 499 U.S. at 310. For the same reason, a structural error "def[ies] analysis by harmless error standards." *Id.,* at 309 (internal quotation marks omitted). The precise reason why a particular error is not amenable to that kind of analysis—and thus the precise reason why the Court has deemed it structural—varies in a significant way from error to error. There appear to be at least three broad rationales.

First, an error has been deemed structural in some instances if the right at issue is not designed to protect the defendant from erroneous conviction but instead protects some other interest. This is true of the defendant's right to conduct his own defense, which, when exercised, "usually increases the likelihood of a trial outcome unfavorable to the defendant." *McKaskle v. Wiggins,* 465 U.S. 168, 177, n. 8, 104 S.Ct. 944, 79 L.Ed.2d 122 (1984). That right is based on the fundamental legal principle that a defendant must be allowed to make his own choices about the proper way to protect his own liberty. See *Faretta v. California,* 422 U.S. 806, 834, 95 S.Ct. 2525, 45 L.Ed.2d 562 (1975). Because harm is irrelevant to the basis underlying the right, the Court has deemed a violation of that right structural error. See *United States v. Gonzalez-Lopez,* 548 U.S. 140, 149, n. 4, 126 S.Ct. 2557, 165 L.Ed.2d 409 (2006).

Second, an error has been deemed structural if the effects of the error are simply too hard to measure. For example, when a defendant is denied the right to select his or her own attorney, the precise "effect of the violation cannot be ascertained." *Ibid.* (quoting *Vasquez v. Hillery,* 474 U.S. 254, 263, 106 S.Ct. 617, 88 L.Ed.2d 598 (1986)). Because the government will, as a result, find it almost impossible to show that the error was "harmless beyond a reasonable doubt," *Chapman, supra,* at 24, 87 S.Ct. 824, the efficiency costs of letting the government try to make the showing are unjustified.

Third, an error has been deemed structural if the error always results in fundamental unfairness. For example, if an indigent defendant is denied an attorney or if the judge fails to give a reasonable-doubt instruction, the resulting trial is always a fundamentally unfair one. See *Gideon v. Wainwright,* 372 U.S. 335, 343–345, 83 S.Ct. 792, 9 L.Ed.2d 799 (1963) (right to an attorney); *Sullivan v. Louisiana,* 508 U.S. 275, 279, 113 S.Ct. 2078, 124 L.Ed.2d 182 (1993) (right to a reasonable-doubt instruction). It therefore would be futile for the government to try to show harmlessness.

These categories are not rigid. In a particular case, more than one of these rationales may be part of the explanation for why an error is deemed to be structural. See *e.g., id.,* at 280–282, 113 S.Ct. 2078. For these purposes, however, one point is critical: An error can count as structural even if the error does not lead to fundamental unfairness in every case. See *Gonzalez-Lopez, supra,* at 149, n. 4, 126 S.Ct. 2557 (rejecting as "inconsistent with the reasoning of our precedents" the idea that structural errors "always or necessarily render a trial fundamentally unfair and unreliable" (emphasis deleted)).

Id. at 1907–08.

B. PLAIN ERROR

As discussed above, appellate rules often require that an issue had been raised at trial in order to obtain review on appeal. When a party fails to object to a decision or raise an issue at trial, appellate courts may either deny or curtail review of the issue on appeal. Despite the rule that causes an appellate court to refuse review of an issue for failure to raise it below, there may be a limited exception for certain glaring or "plain" errors that the trial court should have caught even without the objection of counsel. Federal Rule of Criminal Procedure 52(b) provides for appellate review of "plain error" in such a situation:

Rule 52. Harmless and Plain Error

* * *

(b) Plain Error. A plain error that affects substantial rights may be considered even though it was not brought to the court's attention.

However, it can be difficult to determine when a Court has authority under Rule 52(b) to notice a "plain error." The Supreme Court provides a guide in the following case.

United States v. Olano
Supreme Court of the United States, 1993
507 U.S. 725

■ JUSTICE O'CONNOR Delivered the opinion of the Court.

The question in this case is whether the presence of alternate jurors during jury deliberations was a "plain error" that the Court of Appeals was authorized to correct under Federal Rule of Criminal Procedure 52(b).

I

Each of the respondents, Guy W. Olano, Jr., and Raymond M. Gray, served on the board of directors of a savings and loan association. In 1986, the two were indicted in the Western District of Washington on multiple federal charges for their participation in an elaborate loan "kickback" scheme. Their joint jury trial with five other codefendants commenced in March 1987. All of the parties agreed that 14 jurors would be selected to hear the case, and that the 2 alternates would be identified before deliberations began.

On May 26, shortly before the end of the 3-month trial, the District Court suggested to the defendants that the two alternate jurors, soon to be identified, might be allowed to attend deliberations along with the regular jurors:

> ". . . I'd just like you to think about it, you have a day, let me know, it's just a suggestion and you can-if there is even one person who doesn't like it we won't do it, but it is a suggestion that other courts have followed in long cases where jurors have sat through a lot of testimony, and that is to let the alternates go in but not participate, but just to sit in on deliberations.

> "It's strictly a matter of courtesy and I know many judges have done it with no objections from counsel. One of the other things it does is if they don't participate but they're there, if an emergency comes up and people decide they'd rather go with a new alternate rather than 11, which the rules provide, it keeps that option open. It also keeps people from feeling they've sat here for three months and then get just kind of kicked out. But it's certainly not worth—unless it's something you all agree to, it's not worth your spending time hassling about, you know what I mean? You've got too much else on your mind. I don't want it to be a big issue; it's just a suggestion. Think about it and let me know." App. 79.

The matter arose again the next day, in an ambiguous exchange between Gray's counsel and the District Court:

> "THE COURT: [H]ave you given any more thought as to whether you want the alternates to go in and not participate, or do you want them out?

> "MR. ROBISON [counsel for Gray]: We would ask they not.

> "THE COURT: Not." App. 82.

> One day later, on May 28, the last day of trial, the District Court for a third time asked the defendants whether they wanted the alternate jurors to retire into the jury room.

Counsel for defendant Davy Hilling gave an unequivocal, affirmative answer.

"THE COURT: Well, Counsel, I received your alternates. Do I understand that the defendants now-it's hard to keep up with you, Counsel. It's sort of a day by day-but that's all right. You do all agree that all fourteen deliberate?

"Okay. Do you want me to instruct the two alternates not to participate in deliberation?

"MR. KELLOGG [counsel for Hilling]: That's what I was on my feet to say. It's my understanding that the conversation was the two alternates go back there instructed that they are not to take part in any fashion in the deliberations." App. 86.

This discussion, like the preceding two, took place outside the hearing of the jurors. As before, both Gray's counsel and Olano's counsel were present. Gray, too, attended all three discussions. Olano may not have attended the third-he claims that the Marshal failed to return him to the courtroom in time-but he was present at the first two.

The District Court concluded that Hilling's counsel was speaking for the other defendants as well as his own client. None of the other counsel intervened during the colloquy between the District Court and Hilling's counsel on May 28, nor did anyone object later the same day when the court instructed the jurors that the two alternates would be permitted to attend deliberations. The court instructed:

"We have indicated to you that the parties would be selecting alternates at this time. I am going to inform you who those alternates are, but before I do, let me tell you, I think it was a difficult selection for all concerned, and since the law requires that there be a jury of twelve, it is only going to be a jury of twelve. But what we would like to do in this case is have all of you go back so that even the alternates can be there for the deliberations, but according to the law, the alternates must not participate in the deliberations. It's going to be hard, but if you are an alternate, we think you should be there because things do happen in the course of lengthy jury deliberations, and if you need to step in, we want you to be able to step in having heard the deliberations. But we are going to ask that you not participate.

"The alternates are Norman Sargent and Shirley Kinsella. I am going to ask at this time now, ladies and gentlemen, that you retire to the jury room and begin your deliberations." App. 89–90.

During deliberations, one of the alternate jurors was excused at his request. The other alternate remained until the jury returned with its verdict.

Both respondents were convicted on a number of charges. They appealed to the United States Court of Appeals for the Ninth Circuit. 934 F.2d 1425 (1991). The Court of Appeals reversed certain counts for insufficient evidence and then considered whether the presence of alternate jurors during jury deliberations violated Federal Rule of Criminal Procedure 24(c):

> "The court may direct that not more than 6 jurors in addition to the regular jury be called and impanelled to sit as alternate jurors. Alternate jurors in the order in which they are called shall replace jurors who, prior to the time the jury retires to consider its verdict, become or are found to be unable or disqualified to perform their duties. . . . An alternate juror who does not replace a regular juror shall be discharged after the jury retires to consider its verdict."

Because respondents had not objected to the alternates' presence, the court applied a "plain error" standard under Rule 52(b). Noting that "[w]e have not previously directly resolved the question of the validity of a verdict when alternate jurors are permitted to be present during the jury's deliberations," the court relied on the "language of Rule 24(c), Rule 23(b), the Advisory Committee Notes to Rule 23, and related Ninth Circuit precedent" to hold that Rule 24(c) barred alternate jurors from attending jury deliberations unless the defendant, on the record, explicitly consented to their attendance. 934 F.2d, at 1436–1437. The court found that Rule 24(c)was violated in the instant case, because "the district court did not obtain individual waivers from each defendant personally, either orally or in writing." *Id.*, at 1438. It then held that the presence of alternates in violation of Rule 24(c) was "inherently prejudicial" and reversible *per se. Ibid.*

> "We cannot fairly ascertain whether in a given case the alternate jurors followed the district court's prohibition on participation. However, even if they heeded the letter of the court's instructions and remained *orally* mute throughout, it is entirely possible that their attitudes, conveyed by facial expressions, gestures or the like, may have had some effect upon the decision of one or more jurors." *Ibid.* (internal quotation marks and brackets omitted).

Finally, in a footnote, the court decided that "[b]ecause the violation is inherently prejudicial and because it infringes upon a substantial right of the defendants, it falls within the plain error doctrine." *Id.*, at 1439, n. 23.

The Court of Appeals vacated respondents' remaining convictions and did not reach the other "substantial issues" that they had raised. *Id.*, at 1428, n. 3. We granted certiorari to clarify the standard for "plain error" review by the courts of appeals under Rule 52(b). 504 U.S. 908, 112 S.Ct. 1935, 118 L.Ed.2d 542 (1992).

II

"No procedural principle is more familiar to this Court than that a constitutional right," or a right of any other sort, "may be forfeited in criminal as well as civil cases by the failure to make timely assertion of the right before a tribunal having jurisdiction to determine it." *Yakus v. United States*, 321 U.S. 414, 444, 64 S.Ct. 660, 677, 88 L.Ed. 834 (1944). Federal Rule of Criminal Procedure 52(b), which governs on appeal from criminal proceedings, provides a court of appeals a limited power to correct errors that were forfeited because not timely raised in district court. The Rule has remained unchanged since the original version of the Criminal Rules, and was intended as "a restatement of existing law." Advisory Committee's Notes on Fed.Rule Crim.Proc. 52, 18 U.S.C.App., p. 833. It is paired, appropriately, with Rule 52(a), which governs nonforfeited errors. Rule 52 provides:

> "(a) HARMLESS ERROR. Any error, defect, irregularity or variance which does not affect substantial rights shall be disregarded.

> "(b) PLAIN ERROR. Plain errors or defects affecting substantial rights may be noticed although they were not brought to the attention of the court."

Although "[a] rigid and undeviating judicially declared practice under which courts of review would invariably and under all circumstances decline to consider all questions which had not previously been specifically urged would be out of harmony with ... the rules of fundamental justice," *Hormel v. Helvering*, 312 U.S. 552, 557, 61 S.Ct. 719, 721, 85 L.Ed. 1037 (1941), the authority created by Rule 52(b) is circumscribed. There must be an "error" that is "plain" and that "affect[s] substantial rights." Moreover, Rule 52(b) leaves the decision to correct the forfeited error within the sound discretion of the court of appeals, and the court should not exercise that discretion unless the error " 'seriously affect[s] the fairness, integrity or public reputation of judicial proceedings.' " *United States v. Young*, 470 U.S. 1, 15, 105 S.Ct. 1038, 1046, 84 L.Ed.2d 1 (1985) (quoting *United States v. Atkinson*, 297 U.S. 157, 160, 56 S.Ct. 391, 392, 80 L.Ed. 555 (1936)).

A

Rule 52(b) defines a single category of forfeited-but-reversible error. Although it is possible to read the Rule in the disjunctive, as creating two separate categories—"plain errors" and "defects affecting substantial rights"—that reading is surely wrong. See *Young*, 470 U.S., at 15, n. 12, 105 S.Ct., at 1046, n. 12 (declining to adopt disjunctive reading). As we explained in *Young*, the phrase "error or defect" is more simply read as "error." *Ibid.* The forfeited error "may be noticed" only if it is "plain" and "affect[s] substantial rights." More precisely, a court of appeals may *correct* the error (either vacating for a new trial, or reversing outright) only if it meets these criteria. The appellate court must consider the error, putative or real, in deciding whether the judgment below should be overturned, but cannot provide that remedy unless Rule 52(b) applies (or unless some other provision authorizes the error's correction, an issue that respondents do not raise).

The first limitation on appellate authority under Rule 52(b) is that there indeed be an "error." Deviation from a legal rule is "error" unless the rule has been waived. For example, a defendant who knowingly and voluntarily pleads guilty in conformity with the requirements of Rule 11 cannot have his conviction vacated by court of appeals on the grounds that he ought to have had a trial. Because the right to trial is waivable, and because the defendant who enters a valid guilty plea waives that right, his conviction without a trial is not "error."

Waiver is different from forfeiture. Whereas forfeiture is the failure to make the timely assertion of a right, waiver is the "intentional relinquishment or abandonment of a known right." *Johnson v. Zerbst*, 304 U.S. 458, 464, 58 S.Ct. 1019, 1023, 82 L.Ed. 1461 (1938); see, *e.g.*, *Freytag v. Commissioner*, 501 U.S. 868, 894, n. 2, 111 S.Ct. 2631, 2647, n. 2, 115 L.Ed.2d 764 (1991) (SCALIA, J., concurring in part and concurring in judgment) (distinguishing between "waiver" and "forfeiture"); Spritzer, Criminal Waiver, Procedural Default and the Burger Court, 126 U.Pa.L.Rev. 473, 474–477 (1978) (same); Westen, Away from Waiver: A Rationale for the Forfeiture of Constitutional Rights in Criminal Procedure, 75 Mich.L.Rev. 1214, 1214–1215 (1977) (same). Whether a particular right is waivable; whether the defendant must participate personally in the waiver; whether certain procedures are required for waiver; and whether the defendant's choice must be particularly informed or voluntary, all depend on the right at stake. See, *e.g.*, 2 W. LaFave & J. Israel, Criminal Procedure § 11.6 (1984) (allocation of authority between defendant and counsel); Dix, Waiver in Criminal Procedure: A Brief for More Careful Analysis, 55 Texas L.Rev. 193 (1977) (waivability and standards for waiver). Mere forfeiture, as opposed to waiver, does not extinguish an "error" under Rule 52(b). Although in theory it could be argued that "[i]f the question was not presented to the trial court no error was committed by the trial court, hence there is nothing to review," Orfield, The Scope of Appeal in Criminal Cases, 84 U.Pa.L.Rev. 825, 840 (1936), this is not the theory that Rule 52(b) adopts. If a legal rule was violated during the district court proceedings, and if the defendant did not waive the rule, then there has been an "error" within the meaning of Rule 52(b) despite the absence of a timely objection.

The second limitation on appellate authority under Rule 52(b) is that the error be "plain." "Plain" is synonymous with "clear" or, equivalently, "obvious." See *Young, supra,* 470 U.S., at 17, n. 14, 105 S.Ct. at 1047, n. 14; *United States v. Frady,* 456 U.S. 152, 163, 102 S.Ct. 1584, 1592, 71 L.Ed.2d 816 (1982). We need not consider the special case where the error was unclear at the time of trial but becomes clear on appeal because the applicable law has been clarified. At a minimum, court of appeals cannot correct an error pursuant to Rule 52(b) unless the error is clear under current law.

The third and final limitation on appellate authority under Rule 52(b) is that the plain error "affec[t] substantial rights." This is the same language employed in Rule 52(a), and in most cases it means that the error must have been prejudicial: It must have affected the outcome of the district court proceedings. See, *e.g., Bank of Nova Scotia v. United States,* 487 U.S. 250, 255–257, 108 S.Ct. 2369, 2373–2374, 101 L.Ed.2d 228 (1988); *United States v. Lane,* 474 U.S. 438, 454–464, 106 S.Ct. 725, 734–739, 88 L.Ed.2d 814 (1986) (Brennan, J., concurring in part and dissenting in part); *Kotteakos v. United States,* 328 U.S. 750, 758–765, 66 S.Ct. 1239, 1244–1248, 90 L.Ed. 1557 (1946). When the defendant has made a timely objection to an error and Rule 52(a) applies, a court of appeals normally engages in a specific analysis of the district court record-a so-called "harmless error" inquiry-to determine whether the error was prejudicial. Rule 52(b) normally requires the same kind of inquiry, with one important difference: It is the defendant rather than the Government who bears the burden of persuasion with respect to prejudice. In most cases, a court of appeals cannot correct the forfeited error unless the defendant shows that the error was prejudicial. See *Young, supra,* 470 U.S., at 17, n. 14, 105 S.Ct., at 1047 n. 14 ("[F]ederal courts have consistently interpreted the plain-error doctrine as requiring an appellate court to find that the claimed error . . . had [a] prejudicial impact on the jury's deliberations"). This burden shifting is dictated by a subtle but important difference in language between the two parts of Rule 52: While Rule 52(a) precludes error correction only if the error "does *not* affect substantial rights" (emphasis added), Rule 52(b) authorizes no remedy unless the error *does* "affec[t] substantial rights." See also Note, Appellate Review in a Criminal Case of Errors Made Below Not Properly Raised and Reserved, 23 Miss.L.J. 42, 57 (1951) (summarizing existing law) ("The error must be real and such that it probably influenced the verdict . . .").

We need not decide whether the phrase "affecting substantial rights" is always synonymous with "prejudicial." See generally *Arizona v.*

Fulminante, 499 U.S. 279, 310, 111 S.Ct. 1246, 1265, 113 L.Ed.2d 302 (1991) (constitutional error may not be found harmless if error deprives defendant of the " 'basic protections [without which] a criminal trial cannot reliably serve its function as a vehicle for determination of guilt or innocence, and no criminal punishment may be regarded as fundamentally fair' ") (quoting *Rose v. Clark*, 478 U.S. 570, 577–578, 106 S.Ct. 3101, 3106, 92 L.Ed.2d 460 (1986)). There may be a special category of forfeited errors that can be corrected regardless of their effect on the outcome, but this issue need not be addressed. Nor need we address those errors that should be presumed prejudicial if the defendant cannot make a specific showing of prejudice. Normally, although perhaps not in every case, the defendant must make a specific showing of prejudice to satisfy the "affecting substantial rights" prong of Rule 52(b).

B

Rule 52(b) is permissive, not mandatory. If the forfeited error is "plain" and "affect[s] substantial rights," the court of appeals has authority to order correction, but is not required to do so. The language of the Rule ("may be noticed"), the nature of forfeiture, and the established appellate practice that Congress intended to continue all point to this conclusion. "[I]n criminal cases, where the life, or as in this case the liberty, of the defendant is at stake, the courts of the United States, in the exercise of a sound discretion, may notice [forfeited error]." *Sykes v. United States*, 204 F. 909, 913–914 (CA8 1913). Accord, *Crawford v. United States*, 212 U.S. 183, 194, 29 S.Ct. 260, 264, 53 L.Ed. 465 (1909); former Supreme Court Rule 27.6 (1939) (cited in Advisory Committee's Notes on Fed.Rule Crim.Proc.Rule 52(b), 18 U.S.C.App., p. 833) (" '[T]he court, at its option, may notice a plain error not assigned or specified' ").

We previously have explained that the discretion conferred by Rule 52(b) should be employed " 'in those circumstances in which a miscarriage of justice would otherwise result.' " *Young*, 470 U.S., at 15, 105 S.Ct., at 1046 (quoting *Frady, supra*, 456 U.S., at 163, n. 14, 102 S.Ct., at 1592, n. 14). In our collateral-review jurisprudence, the term "miscarriage of justice" means that the defendant is actually innocent. See, *e.g., Sawyer v. Whitley*, 505 U.S. 333, 339–340, 112 S.Ct. 2514, 2519, 120 L.Ed.2d 269 (1992). The court of appeals should no doubt correct a plain forfeited error that causes the conviction or sentencing of an actually innocent defendant, see, *e.g., Wiborg v. United States*, 163 U.S. 632, 16 S.Ct. 1127, 41 L.Ed. 289 (1896), but we have never held that a Rule 52(b) remedy is *only* warranted in cases of actual innocence.

Rather, the standard that should guide the exercise of remedial discretion under Rule 52(b) was articulated in *United States v. Atkinson*, 297 U.S. 157, 56 S.Ct. 391, 80 L.Ed. 555 (1936). The Court of Appeals should correct a plain forfeited error affecting substantial rights if the error "seriously affect[s] the fairness, integrity or public reputation of judicial proceedings." *Id.*, at 160, 56 S.Ct., at 392. As we explained in *Young*, the "standard laid down in *United States v. Atkinson* [was] codified in Federal Rule of Criminal Procedure 52(b)," 470 U.S., at 7, 105 S.Ct., at 1042, and we repeatedly have quoted the *Atkinson* language in describing plain-error review, see *id.*, at 15, 105 S.Ct., at 1046; *Frady, supra*, 456 U.S., at 163, n. 13, 102 S.Ct., at 1592, n. 13; *Silber v. United States*, 370 U.S. 717, 718, 82 S.Ct. 1287, 1288, 81 L.Ed.2d 798 (1962) *(per curiam); Johnson v. United States*, 318 U.S. 189, 200, 63 S.Ct. 549, 554, 87 L.Ed. 704 (1943); *United States v. Socony-Vacuum Oil Co.*, 310 U.S. 150, 239, 60 S.Ct. 811, 851, 84 L.Ed. 1129 (1940); see also *Connor v. Finch*, 431 U.S. 407, 421, n. 19, 97 S.Ct. 1828, 1837, n. 19, 52 L.Ed.2d 465 (1977) (civil appeal). An error may "seriously affect the fairness, integrity or public reputation of judicial proceedings" independent of the defendant's innocence. Conversely, a plain error affecting substantial rights does not, without more, satisfy the *Atkinson* standard, for otherwise the discretion afforded by Rule 52(b) would be illusory.

With these basic principles in mind, we turn to the instant case.

III

The presence of alternate jurors during jury deliberations is no doubt a deviation from Rule 24(c). The Rule explicitly states: "An alternate juror who does not replace a regular juror shall be discharged after the jury retires to consider its verdict." It is a separate question whether such deviation amounts to "error" when the defendant consents to the alternates' presence. The Government supposes that there was indeed an "error" in this case, on the premise that Rule 24(c) is nonwaivable, see Reply Brief for United States 9, n. 4, and we assume without deciding that this premise is correct. The Government also essentially concedes that the "error" was "plain." See *id.*, at 8–9, and n. 4.

We therefore focus our attention on whether the error "affect [ed] substantial rights" within the meaning of Rule 52(b), and conclude that it did not. The presence of alternate jurors during jury deliberations is not the kind of error that "affect[s] substantial rights" independent of its prejudicial impact. Nor have respondents made a specific showing of prejudice. Finally, we see no reason to presume prejudice here.

Assuming *arguendo* that certain errors "affec[t] substantial rights" independent of prejudice, the instant violation of Rule 24(c) is not such an error. Although the presence of alternate jurors does contravene " 'the cardinal principle that the deliberations of the jury shall remain private and secret,' " Advisory Committee's Notes on Fed.Rule Crim.Proc. 23(b), 18 U.S.C.App., p. 785 (quoting *United States v. Virginia Erection Corp.*, 335 F.2d 868, 872 (CA4 1964)), the primary if not exclusive purpose of jury privacy and secrecy is to protect the jury's deliberations from improper influence. "[I]f no harm resulted from this intrusion [of an alternate juror into the jury room,] reversal would be pointless." *United States v. Watson*, 669 F.2d 1374, 1391 (CA11 1982). We generally have analyzed outside intrusions upon the jury for prejudicial impact. See, *e.g., Parker v. Gladden*, 385 U.S. 363, 87 S.Ct. 468, 17 L.Ed.2d 420 (1967) (*per curiam*) (bailiff's comments to jurors, such as "Oh that wicked fellow he is guilty," were prejudicial); *Patton v. Yount*, 467 U.S. 1025, 104 S.Ct. 2885, 81 L.Ed.2d 847 (1984) (pretrial publicity was not prejudicial); *Holbrook v. Flynn*, 475 U.S. 560, 106 S.Ct. 1340, 89 L.Ed.2d 525 (1986) (presence of uniformed state troopers in courtroom was not prejudicial). A prime example is *Remmer v. United States*, 347 U.S. 227, 74 S.Ct. 450, 98 L.Ed. 654 (1954), where an outsider had communicated with a juror during a criminal trial, appearing to offer a bribe, and the Federal Bureau of Investigation then had investigated the incident. We noted that "[t]he sending of an F.B.I. agent in the midst of a trial to investigate a juror as to his conduct is bound to impress the juror," and remanded for the District Court to "determine the circumstances, the impact thereof upon the juror, and whether or not it was prejudicial, in a hearing with all interested parties permitted to participate." *Id.*, at 229–230, 74 S.Ct., at 451.

This "intrusion" jurisprudence was summarized in *Smith v. Phillips*, 455 U.S. 209, 102 S.Ct. 940, 71 L.Ed.2d 78 (1982):

> "[D]ue process does not require a new trial every time a juror has been placed in a potentially compromising situation. Were that the rule, few trials would be constitutionally acceptable. . . . [I]t is virtually impossible to shield jurors from every contact or influence that might theoretically affect their vote. Due process means a jury capable and willing to decide the case solely on the evidence before it, and a trial judge ever watchful to prevent prejudicial occurrences and to determine the effect of such occurrences when they happen." *Id.*, at 217, 102 S.Ct., at 946.

There may be cases where an intrusion should be presumed prejudicial, see, *e.g., Patton, supra*, 467 U.S., at 1031–1035, 104 S.Ct., at 2888–2890; *Turner v. Louisiana*, 379 U.S. 466, 85 S.Ct. 546, 13 L.Ed.2d 424 (1965), but a presumption of prejudice as opposed to a specific analysis does not change the ultimate inquiry: Did the intrusion affect the jury's deliberations and thereby its verdict? We cannot imagine why egregious comments by a bailiff to a juror *(Parker)* or an apparent bribe followed by an official investigation *(Remmer)* should be evaluated in terms of "prejudice," while the mere *presence* of alternate jurors during jury deliberations should not. Of course, the issue here is whether the alternates' presence sufficed to establish remedial authority under Rule

52(b), not whether it violated the Sixth Amendment or Due Process Clause, but we see no reason to depart from the normal interpretation of the phrase "affecting substantial rights."

The question, then, is whether the instant violation of Rule 24(c) prejudiced respondents, either specifically or presumptively. In theory, the presence of alternate jurors during jury deliberations might prejudice a defendant in two different ways: either because the alternates actually participated in the deliberations, verbally or through "body language"; or because the alternates' presence exerted a "chilling" effect on the regular jurors. See *Watson, supra*, at 1391; *United States v. Allison*, 481 F.2d 468, 472 (CA5 1973). Conversely, "if the alternate in fact abided by the court's instructions to remain orally silent and not to otherwise indicate his views or attitude . . . and if the presence of the alternate did not operate as a restraint upon the regular jurors' freedom of expression and action, we see little substantive difference between the presence of [the alternate] and the presence in the jury room of an unexamined book which had not been admitted into evidence." *Id.*, at 472.

Respondents have made no specific showing that the alternate jurors in this case either participated in the jury's deliberations or "chilled" deliberation by the regular jurors. We need not decide whether testimony on this score by the alternate jurors or the regular jurors, through affidavits or at a *Remmer*-like hearing, would violate Federal Rule of Evidence 606(b), compare *Watson, supra*, at 1391–1392, and n. 17, with *United States v. Beasley*, 464 F.2d 468 (CA10 1972), or whether the courts of appeals have authority to remand for *Remmer*-like hearings on plain-error review. Respondents have never requested a hearing, and thus the record before us contains no direct evidence that the alternate jurors influenced the verdict. On this record, we are not persuaded that the instant violation of Rule 24(c) was actually prejudicial.

Nor will we presume prejudice for purposes of the Rule 52(b) analysis here. The Court of Appeals was incorrect in finding the error "inherently prejudicial." 934 F.2d, at 1439. Until the close of trial, the 2 alternate jurors were indistinguishable from the 12 regular jurors. Along with the regular jurors, they commenced their office with an oath, see Tr. 212 (Mar. 2, 1987), received the normal initial admonishment, see *id.*, at 212–218, heard the same evidence and arguments, and were not identified as alternates until *after* the District Court gave a final set of instructions, see App. 89–90. In those instructions, the District Court specifically enjoined the jurors that "according to the law, the alternates must not participate in the deliberations," and reiterated, "we are going to ask that you not participate." *Ibid.* The Court of Appeals should not have supposed that this injunction was contravened. "[It is] the almost invariable assumption of the law that jurors follow their instructions." *Richardson v. Marsh*, 481 U.S. 200, 206, 107 S.Ct. 1702, 1707, 95 L.Ed.2d 176 (1987). "[We] presum[e] that jurors, conscious of the gravity of their task, attend closely the particular language of the trial court's instructions in a criminal case and strive to understand, make sense of, and follow the instructions given them." *Francis v. Franklin*, 471 U.S. 307, 324, n. 9, 105 S.Ct. 1965, 1976, n. 9, 85 L.Ed.2d 344 (1985). See also *Strickland v. Washington*, 466 U.S. 668, 694, 104 S.Ct. 2052, 2068, 80 L.Ed.2d 674 (1984) (in assessing prejudice for purposes of ineffective-assistance claim, "a court should presume . . . that the judge or jury acted according to law"). Nor do we think that the mere presence of alternate jurors entailed a sufficient risk of "chill" to justify a presumption of prejudice on that score.

In sum, respondents have not met their burden of showing prejudice under Rule 52(b). Whether the Government could have met its burden of showing the absence of prejudice, under Rule 52(a), if respondents had not forfeited their claim of error, is not at issue here. This is a plain-error case, and it is respondents who must persuade the appellate court that the deviation from Rule 24(c) was prejudicial.

Because the conceded error in this case did not "affec[t] substantial rights," the Court of Appeals had no authority to correct it. We need not consider whether the error, if prejudicial, would have warranted correction under the *Atkinson* standard as "seriously affect[ing] the fairness, integrity or public reputation of judicial proceedings." The judgment of the Court of Appeals is reversed, and the case is remanded for further proceedings consistent with this opinion.

So ordered.

Difficulty of Satisfying Plain Error Standard

The Court has been consistent in its strict application of the *Olano* standard. The threshold for having an appellate court review issues not raised before the trial court is very difficult to meet. *See, e.g., Puckett v. United States*, 556 U.S. 129, 135 (2009) ("Meeting all four prongs [of the *Olano* standard] is difficult, as it should be.") (quotations omitted); *but see Henderson v. United States*, 568 U.S. 266 (2013). The U.S. Supreme Court has the opportunity to clarify further the threshold for satisfying the *Olano* standard in a pending case, *Rosales-Mireles v. United States*, No. 16–9493 (whether *Olano* requires that the plain error "would shock the conscience of the common man, serve as a powerful indictment against our system of justice, or seriously call into question the competence or integrity of the district judge" as the Fifth Circuit has held).

ADVOCACY POINT

Given Rule 52 and the strict Olano standard set forth by the U.S. Supreme Court, it is crucially important that errors are raised in the trial court. Although it does not receive the same attention as examination of witnesses and moving of exhibits, a defense attorney should maintain focus on "making a record" by objecting to rulings of the trial court to which counsel takes exception. Even if counsel believes the objection to be futile, Rule 52 and Olano demonstrate that raising the issue is sometimes indispensable to having the appellate court notice the error.

COUNSEL EXERCISE 17: Appeal
(Prosecution and Defense)

Assume that the defendant was convicted of the charged offenses after a jury trial. Defense counsel should draft and file an appellate brief making a sufficiency of the evidence claim. The prosecutor should draft a brief in opposition.

CHAPTER 18

SENTENCE AND JUDGMENT

After the sometimes-lengthy process of moving a criminal matter through pretrial proceedings, discovery, motions, and—in the relatively rare case in which the case is not resolved by guilty plea—trial, the sentencing phase begins.

Before delving into the particulars of sentencing, it is important to place the sentencing process in its larger context. Although the judge ultimately decides upon and imposes a criminal sentence, many other actors play significant roles. The legislature, which creates the criminal prohibition in the first instance, attaches a prescribed punishment for violation of the law, including any minimum or maximum terms of incarceration. Law enforcement officials and prosecutors determine which laws will be enforced and which crimes will be prosecuted, thus determining the extent of punishment exposure for the offender. Prosecutors and defense attorneys will help to shape the record—both at trial or plea colloquy, and at the sentencing hearing—upon which the court's sentencing decision will rest. Probation or pretrial services officers will investigate the offender's background, circumstances of the offense, characteristics of the victim, and other factors relevant to the court's sentencing decision. Finally, even after the judge makes a sentencing decision—whether pursuant to guidelines in "determinate" sentencing jurisdictions, or with broad discretion within the statutory maxima and minima in "indeterminate" sentencing jurisdictions—parole boards or commissions may alter the sentence.

I. FORMS OF PUNISHMENT

A. INCARCERATION

A sentence may impose various forms of punishment. Obviously, incarceration is the form of punishment that receives the most attention. The United States has the highest rate of incarceration in the world, a rate that has tripled over the past several decades. Although the United States makes up about 5% of the world's population, we house about 25% of the world's prisoners in our prisons and jails. Despite modest declines in prison populations over the past several years, approximately 1 out of every 131 people—over two million total—are imprisoned in state and federal prisons and jails. Racial disparities are rampant and the rate of annual increase in numbers of incarcerated women continues to outpace that of incarcerated men by a substantial amount. As extraordinary as those numbers are, over 700,000 are released from prisons and jails back into the community each year, with nearly five million people under non-custodial criminal justice supervision. *See, e.g.,* THE SENTENCING PROJECT, TRENDS IN U.S. CORRECTIONS (June 2017). For distinct views on the causes of mass incarceration in the United States, *see* MICHELLE ALEXANDER, THE NEW JIM CROW: MASS INCARCERATION IN THE AGE OF COLORBLINDNESS (2010); JOHN PFAFF, LOCKED IN: THE TRUE CAUSES OF MASS INCARCERATION—AND HOW TO ACHIEVE REAL REFORM (2017).

The imposition of a sentence of incarceration in federal court is governed by 18 U.S.C. § 3582 and the U.S. Sentencing Guidelines Manual, as described *infra*.

B. PROBATION

Although this state of "mass incarceration" in the United States is the result of enforcement and sentencing strategies heavily reliant on incarceration, there are other forms of punishment utilized in the criminal justice system. One such alternative to incarceration is probation. Under probation, a court may impose certain conditions on a convicted defendant, such as not violating any federal, state, or local laws, not using banned substances or alcohol, and the requirement that the defendant meet regularly with a probation officer. Probation officers will monitor the progress of individuals sentenced to probation and will report alleged violations of the terms of probation to the court. The court may decide to revoke probation and impose a term of incarceration if the defendant is found to have violated one of these conditions.

In the federal system, probation is governed by 18 U.S.C. § 3561. Probation is authorized—unless precluded by the statute—for less serious felonies, misdemeanors, and infractions. For Class C or D felonies, a term of probation of 1 to 5 years may be imposed. For misdemeanors, any term of probation up to 5 years may be imposed. In the case of a mere infraction, a term of probation of not more than 1 year may be imposed. Probation is not authorized for Class A or Class B felony offenses. Section 3563 of Title 18 provides for the mandatory and discretionary imposition of certain conditions in connection with a sentence of probation.

C. SUPERVISED RELEASE

It is important to distinguish probation from supervised release, a mechanism utilized in the federal system and some state systems in lieu of parole. Unlike with probation, a term of supervised release follows a term of incarceration, and its serves the purpose of supervising the ex-offender's transition back to the community. Under 18 U.S.C. § 3583, the court will set certain conditions of supervised release—some mandatory—and the defendant who violates such conditions is subject to additional incarceration for the term of supervised release.

Terms of supervised release (and the resulting period of exposure to addition prison time) can be lengthy. For Class A and Class B felonies, the term of supervised release can be up to five years; for Class C and D felonies, up to three years; and for Class E felonies and non-petty misdemeanors, up to one year. Given the exposure to additional incarceration, there must be a hearing before supervised release is revoked.

Federal Rule of Criminal Procedure 32.1 governs supervised release (and probation) revocation hearings in federal court.

Rule 32.1. Revoking or Modifying Probation or Supervised Release

(a) Initial Appearance.

(1) *Person In Custody.* A person held in custody for violating probation or supervised release must be taken without unnecessary delay before a magistrate judge.

(A) If the person is held in custody in the district where an alleged violation occurred, the initial appearance must be in that district.

(B) If the person is held in custody in a district other than where an alleged violation occurred, the initial appearance must be in that district, or in an adjacent district if the appearance can occur more promptly there.

(2) *Upon a Summons.* When a person appears in response to a summons for violating probation or supervised release, a magistrate judge must proceed under this rule.

(3) *Advice.* The judge must inform the person of the following:

(A) the alleged violation of probation or supervised release;

(B) the person's right to retain counsel or to request that counsel be appointed if the person cannot obtain counsel; and

(C) the person's right, if held in custody, to a preliminary hearing under Rule 32.1(b)(1).

(4) *Appearance in the District With Jurisdiction.* If the person is arrested or appears in the district that has jurisdiction to conduct a revocation hearing—either originally or by transfer of jurisdiction—the court must proceed under Rule 32.1(b)–(e).

(5) *Appearance in a District Lacking Jurisdiction.* If the person is arrested or appears in a district that does not have jurisdiction to conduct a revocation hearing, the magistrate judge must:

(A) if the alleged violation occurred in the district of arrest, conduct a preliminary hearing under Rule 32.1(b) and either:

(i) transfer the person to the district that has jurisdiction, if the judge finds probable cause to believe that a violation occurred; or

(ii) dismiss the proceedings and so notify the court that has jurisdiction, if the judge finds no probable cause to believe that a violation occurred; or

(B) if the alleged violation did not occur in the district of arrest, transfer the person to the district that has jurisdiction if:

(i) the government produces certified copies of the judgment, warrant, and warrant application, or produces copies of those certified documents by reliable electronic means; and

(ii) the judge finds that the person is the same person named in the warrant.

(6) *Release or Detention.* The magistrate judge may release or detain the person under 18 U.S.C. § 3143(a)(1) pending further proceedings. The burden of establishing by clear and convincing evidence that the person will not flee or pose a danger to any other person or to the community rests with the person.

(b) Revocation.

(1) *Preliminary Hearing.*

(A) In General. If a person is in custody for violating a condition of probation or supervised release, a magistrate judge must promptly conduct a hearing to determine whether there is probable cause to believe that a violation occurred. The person may waive the hearing.

(B) Requirements. The hearing must be recorded by a court reporter or by a suitable recording device. The judge must give the person:

(i)   notice of the hearing and its purpose, the alleged violation, and the person's right to retain counsel or to request that counsel be appointed if the person cannot obtain counsel;

(ii) an opportunity to appear at the hearing and present evidence; and

(iii) upon request, an opportunity to question any adverse witness, unless the judge determines that the interest of justice does not require the witness to appear.

(C) Referral. If the judge finds probable cause, the judge must conduct a revocation hearing. If the judge does not find probable cause, the judge must dismiss the proceeding.

(2) *Revocation Hearing.* Unless waived by the person, the court must hold the revocation hearing within a reasonable time in the district having jurisdiction. The person is entitled to:

(A) written notice of the alleged violation;

(B) disclosure of the evidence against the person;

(C) an opportunity to appear, present evidence, and question any adverse witness unless the court determines that the interest of justice does not require the witness to appear;

(D) notice of the person's right to retain counsel or to request that counsel be appointed if the person cannot obtain counsel; and

(E) an opportunity to make a statement and present any information in mitigation.

(c) Modification.

(1) *In General.* Before modifying the conditions of probation or supervised release, the court must hold a hearing, at which the person has the right to counsel and an opportunity to make a statement and present any information in mitigation.

(2) *Exceptions.* A hearing is not required if:

(A) the person waives the hearing; or

(B) the relief sought is favorable to the person and does not extend the term of probation or of supervised release; and

(C) an attorney for the government has received notice of the relief sought, has had a reasonable opportunity to object, and has not done so.

(d) Disposition of the Case. The court's disposition of the case is governed by 18 U.S.C. § 3563 and § 3565 (probation) and § 3583 (supervised release).

(e) Producing a Statement. Rule 26.2(a)–(d) and (f) applies at a hearing under this rule. If a party fails to comply with a Rule 26.2 order to produce a witness's statement, the court must not consider that witness's testimony.

* * *

It should be noted that revocation may be triggered by, of course, criminal conduct (e.g., violating a federal, state, or local law), but it also may be triggered by non-criminal conduct, such as failure to contact a probation officer at a prescribed time, or leaving the jurisdiction without obtaining prior permission.

Do you recognize how the revocation procedures set out in Rule 32.1 are a microcosm of the procedural framework of the larger federal criminal process? The defendant is entitled to an initial appearance and advice of rights, a transfer of district, a detention decision under 18 U.S.C. § 3143, and a preliminary hearing. Additionally, the revocation hearing itself, described in Rule 32.1(b)(2) is very similar to a trial, with the right to counsel and notice of allegations, disclosure of evidence and Jencks Act procedures, opportunity to appear, present evidence, cross-examine government witnesses, and present evidence in mitigation.

D. FINES

Courts may also impose fines on defendants where authorized by statute. For corporate entity defendants, obviously, fines are the primary form of punishment. Criminal fines are regulated by the Eighth Amendment's Excessive Fines Clause and it is a violation of the Equal Protection Clause to impose a sentence of imprisonment in lieu of a fine for those unable to pay. *See, e.g., Tate v. Short,* 401 U.S. 395 (1971); *see also Williams v. Illinois,* 399 U.S. 235 (1970) . Criminal fines in federal court are governed by 18 U.S.C. § 3571, which authorizes the imposition of a fine up to the maximum amount permitted under the statute of conviction or the maximum amounts set out in section 3571.

Section 3572 sets out certain factors the court must consider when determining whether a fine will be imposed and the particulars of any such fine:

(a) FACTORS TO BE CONSIDERED.—In determining whether to impose a fine, and the amount, time for payment, and method of payment of a fine, the court shall consider, in addition to the factors set forth in section 3553(a)—

(1)

the defendant's income, earning capacity, and financial resources;

(2)

the burden that the fine will impose upon the defendant, any person who is financially dependent on the defendant, or any other person (including a government) that would be responsible for the welfare of any person financially dependent on the defendant, relative to the burden that alternative punishments would impose;

(3)

any pecuniary loss inflicted upon others as a result of the offense;

(4)

whether restitution is ordered or made and the amount of such restitution;

(5)

the need to deprive the defendant of illegally obtained gains from the offense;

(6)

the expected costs to the government of any imprisonment, supervised release, or probation component of the sentence;

(7)

whether the defendant can pass on to consumers or other persons the expense of the fine; and

(8)

if the defendant is an organization, the size of the organization and any measure taken by the organization to discipline any officer, director, employee, or agent of the organization responsible for the offense and to prevent a recurrence of such an offense.

18 U.S.C. § 3572.

For insight on the difficulties criminal justice fines impose on those unable to pay, *see, e.g.,* HARVARD LAW SCHOOL CRIMINAL JUSTICE POLICY PROGRAM, CONFRONTING CRIMINAL JUSTICE DEBT: A GUIDE FOR POLICY REFORM (2016).

E. FORFEITURES

When property is utilized in connection with criminal conduct, it may be seized or "forfeited" upon the requisite showing. A forfeiture action can be brought civilly against a piece of property (*in rem*) or its owner (*in personam*), or it can be brought criminally upon conviction of the defendant. Regardless of whether the forfeiture action is civil or criminal, the Excessive Fines Clause proportionality principle applies and forfeitures cannot be excessive. *See United States v. Bajakajian*, 524 U.S. 321 (1998); *Austin v. United States*, 509 U.S. 602 (1993). In addition, due process requirements such as notice and the opportunity to be heard apply in the forfeiture arena. *See, e.g., United States v. James Daniel Good Real Property*, 510 U.S. 43 (1993).

Criminal forfeiture in the federal system is governed by Federal Rule of Criminal Procedure 32.2. The defendant must have been placed on notice in the indictment or information if property is to be forfeited, *see, e.g., Kadonsky v. United States*, 216 F.3d 499, 506 (5th Cir. 2000), as the following excerpt from the rule provides.

Rule 32.2. Criminal Forfeiture

(a) Notice to the Defendant. A court must not enter a judgment of forfeiture in a criminal proceeding unless the indictment or information contains notice to the defendant that the government will seek the forfeiture of property as part of any sentence in accordance with the applicable statute. The notice should not be designated as a count of the indictment or information. The indictment or information need not identify the property subject to forfeiture or specify the amount of any forfeiture money judgment that the government seeks.

Civil Forfeiture

In addition to criminal forfeiture, there is also civil forfeiture, where the government seeks, in a civil action, to seize assets or property allegedly used in a prohibited way. See, e.g., 18 U.S.C. § 981. As you might imagine, there are some key differences in the two contexts. Although one defending a civil forfeiture action might have access to more robust civil discovery tools and dispositive pretrial motions to resolve the matter more expeditiously, a defendant in a criminal forfeiture proceeding typically already has counsel (either retained or appointed) who can defend the criminal forfeiture action in the course of representation on the substantive criminal charges against the individual. One who is subject to a civil forfeiture action presumably would have to retain counsel solely for the purpose of defending the civil proceeding.

Civil forfeiture statutes have come under increasing scrutiny on Due Process Clause grounds and are likely to be the subject of U.S. Supreme Court case law in the near future. *See, e.g., Leonard v. Texas,* 580 U.S. ___, 137 S.Ct. 847 (2017 (statement of Thomas, J. on the denial of certiorari); *see also* Caleb Nelson, *The Constitutionality of Civil Forfeiture,* 125 YALE L.J. 2182 (2016).

> ### Application for a Warrant to Seize Property Subject to Forfeiture
>
> http://www.uscourts.gov/sites/default/files/ao108.pdf
>
> ### Warrant to Seize Property Subject to Forfeiture
>
> http://www.uscourts.gov/sites/default/files/ao109.pdf

F. RESTITUTION

A court may also impose a requirement that the defendant pay restitution to the victim as part of a sentence. Certain federal statutes authorize or mandate the imposition of restitution as part of a criminal sentence. *See* Mandatory Victim's Restitution Act, 18 U.S.C. § 3663 et seq.; Victim and Witness Protection Act, 18 U.S.C. § 3579; U.S. Department of Justice, *The Restitution Process for Victims of Federal Crime,* http://www.justice.gov/sites/default/files/usao-ndia/legacy/2014/10/08/Restitution.pdf.

G. PRETRIAL DIVERSION AND PROBATION BEFORE JUDGMENT

Pretrial diversion and probation before judgment are designed to have the offender focus on and correct the behavior or conditions which gave rise to the criminal violation. Typically, substance abuse or other counseling will be a feature of the diversionary arrangement. Successful completion of the program allows the defendant to avoid incarceration and possibly even a criminal conviction. One example in the federal system can be found in 18 U.S.C. § 3607, dealing with special probation and expungement procedures for drug possessors. *See also* UNITED STATES SENTENCING COMMISSION, FEDERAL ALTERNATIVE-TO-INCARCERATION PROGRAMS (Sept. 2017).

Probation Order Under 18 U.S.C. § 3607

http://www.uscourts.gov/sites/default/files/ao246.pdf

Order of Discharge and Dismissal Under 18 U.S.C. § 3607

http://www.uscourts.gov/sites/default/files/ao246A.pdf

II. CONSTITUTIONAL LIMITS ON SENTENCING

Although sentencing is driven by the statutes that prescribe punishments for crimes, and the statutes and rules creating sentencing procedures, there are various constitutional limitations on the substance and procedure of sentencing. As discussed in Chapter 14 *supra*, the Sixth Amendment right to jury trial is violated when a court imposes a sentence above the statutory maximum based on facts not found by the jury. The constitutional issues at the heart of the distinction between elements and sentencing factors will be revisited later in the chapter.

A. CRUEL AND UNUSUAL PUNISHMENTS CLAUSE

However, there are other constitutional issues implicated by sentencing. As you may remember from your Criminal Law course, the Eighth Amendment's Cruel and Unusual Punishments Clause regulates the type of sentences that can be imposed for a particular crime. Although the Clause is clearly understood to prohibit "barbaric" punishments, the Supreme Court has engaged in a long-running debate over the extent to which the Clause requires that sentences are proportional to the crime.

In *Solem v. Helm*, 463 U.S. 277 (1983), the Court endorsed the view that "a criminal sentence must be proportionate to the crime for which the defendant has been convicted," in holding that life without parole for a seventh conviction for a non-violent offense violated the Cruel and Unusual Punishments Clause. However, eight years later in *Harmelin v. Michigan*, 501 U.S. 957 (1991), a fractured Court seemed to back away from the proportionality principle, giving a nod to legislative judgment in determining sentences. Over a decade after *Harmelin*, in *Ewing v. California*, 538 U.S. 11 (2003), the Court reemphasized the need for deference to legislative prerogative in fashioning sentences for crimes in holding that a sentence of 25 years to life for a "third strike" offense of theft of golf clubs was not violative of the Cruel and Unusual Punishments Clause.

Although the Court has not declared that capital punishment violates the Eighth Amendment's Cruel and Unusual Punishments Clause *per se*, it has determined that the death penalty cannot be imposed for certain offenses. *See, e.g., Enmund v. Florida*, 458 U.S. 782 (1982) (death penalty for an accomplice without intent to commit homicide violates Eighth Amendment); *Coker v. Georgia*, 433 U.S. 584 (1977) (death penalty for non-fatal sexual assault violates the Eighth Amendment). There are also requirements that the decision to impose the death penalty must be reached in an individualized manner, *see, e.g., Gregg v. Georgia*, 428 U.S. 153 (1976); *Furman v. Georgia*, 408 U.S. 238 (1972), with due consideration of properly-articulated aggravating and mitigating circumstances, *see, e.g. Maynard v. Cartwright*, 486 U.S. 356 (1988); *Lockett v. Ohio*, 438 U.S. 586 (1978).

A series of relatively recent cases from the Supreme deal with the imposition of sentences on defendants who were juveniles at the time of the criminal conduct. In *Roper v. Simmons*, 543 U.S. 551 (2005), the Court held that the Eighth Amendment prohibited the imposition of the death penalty on an offender who was under 18 years of age at the time of the offense. Five years later, the Court extended the Eighth Amendment's prohibition to sentences of life without parole for juveniles who committed a non-homicide offense. See *Graham v. Florida*, 560 U.S. 48 (2010). Most recently, in the companion cases of *Miller v. Alabama*, 567 U.S. 460 (2012) and *Jackson v. Hobbs*, 565 U.S. 1013 (2012), the Court held that the Cruel and Unusual Punishments Clause prohibits mandatory life without parole for a juvenile, regardless of the nature of the offense. The Court made this prohibition retroactive in *Montgomery v. Louisiana*, 136 S.Ct. 718 (2016).

B. EQUAL PROTECTION CLAUSE

The Equal Protection Clause can come into play when there are claims of sentencing disparities based on protected class status. However, it has been difficult to obtain relief on such claims. The Supreme Court in *McClesky v Kemp*, 481 U.S. 279 (1987), held that a study showing a disparity in the rate of imposition of the death penalty depending on the race of the victim and the race of the defendant was insufficient to demonstrate a violation of the Equal Protection Clause. The Court reasoned that the study provided no evidence that the decisionmakers in the petitioner's case acted with discriminatory purpose in imposing the death penalty.

There have also been equal protection challenges to the disparity in crack and powder cocaine sentencing. Prior to the passage and signing of the Fair Sentencing Act of 2010, Pub. L. 111–220, there was a 100 to 1 ratio for the sentencing severity for powder cocaine vs. crack cocaine under the federal sentencing guidelines. Because well over 90% of crack cocaine prosecutions were being initiated against African American defendants, there existed a substantial racial disparity in sentencing for cocaine offenses in the United States. However, challenges to the sentencing scheme on equal protection grounds were unsuccessful in every court of appeals in which they were brought. *See, e.g., United States v. Edwards*, 98 F.3d 1364 (D.C. Cir. 1996). The Fair Sentencing Act of 2010 reduced the ratio from 100 to 1, to 18 to 1, although the law does not apply retroactively to defendants sentenced before the law became effective. For background on the passage of the Fair Sentencing Act of 2010, see Jelani Jefferson Exum, *Forget Sentencing Equality: Moving From the "Cracked Cocaine" Debate Toward Particular Purpose Sentencing*, 18 LEWIS & CLARK L. REV. 95 (2014).

C. FIRST AMENDMENT

There have been First Amendment challenges to laws authorizing enhanced sentences for crimes motivated by racial animus. However, the Supreme Court held, in *Wisconsin v. Mitchell*, 508 U.S. 476 (1993), that hate crime sentencing enhancements do not run afoul of the First Amendment as long as they punish not abstract beliefs, but the actual motive behind the commission of the offense. *Compare Dawson v. Delaware*, 503 U.S. 159 (1992) (holding admission regarding defendant's affiliation with white supremacist gang violated defendant's First Amendment rights because "the evidence proved nothing more than [the defendant's] abstract beliefs,"), *with Mitchell*, 508 U.S. at 486 (upholding Wisconsin penalty-enhancement statute that increased sentences for bias-inspired hate crimes because the statute focused on the defendant's motive for committing that crime). However, as discussed in *Apprendi v. New Jersey*, Chapter 14 *supra* (which happened to involve a hate crime sentencing enhancement), facts that raise the sentence above a statutory maximum must be proven to a jury beyond a reasonable doubt.

III. SENTENCING GUIDELINES

A. THE SENTENCING REFORM ACT OF 1984

The Sentencing Reform Act of 1984 created the United States Sentencing Commission, which was charged with promulgating sentencing guidelines for federal offenses. The rationale for the Act's creation of the Commission and the Guidelines is described in the following case upholding the constitutionality of the Sentencing Guidelines.

Mistretta v. United States

Supreme Court of the United Sates, 1989
488 U.S. 361

■ JUSTICE BLACKMUN delivered the opinion of the Court.

In this litigation, we granted certiorari before judgment in the United States Court of Appeals for the Eighth Circuit in order to consider the constitutionality of the Sentencing Guidelines promulgated by the United States Sentencing Commission. The Commission is a body created under the Sentencing Reform Act of 1984 (Act), as amended, 18 U.S.C. § 3551 *et seq.* (1982 ed., Supp. IV), and 28 U.S.C. §§ 991–998 (1982 ed., Supp. IV). * * *

I

A

Background

For almost a century, the Federal Government employed in criminal cases a system of indeterminate sentencing. Statutes specified the penalties for crimes but nearly always gave the sentencing judge wide discretion to decide whether the offender should be incarcerated and for how long, whether he should be fined and how much, and whether some lesser restraint, such as probation, should be imposed instead of imprisonment or fine. This indeterminate-sentencing system was supplemented by the utilization of parole, by which an offender was returned to society under the "guidance and control" of a parole officer. See *Zerbst v. Kidwell*, 304 U.S. 359, 363, 58 S.Ct. 872, 874, 82 L.Ed. 1399 (1938).

Both indeterminate sentencing and parole were based on concepts of the offender's possible, indeed probable, rehabilitation, a view that it was realistic to attempt to rehabilitate the inmate and thereby to minimize the risk that he would resume criminal activity upon his return to society. It obviously required the judge and the parole officer to make their respective sentencing and release decisions upon their own assessments of the offender's amenability to rehabilitation. As a result, the court and the officer were in positions to exercise, and usually did exercise, very broad discretion. See Kadish, The Advocate and the Expert-Counsel in the Peno-Correctional Process, 45 Minn.L.Rev. 803, 812–813 (1961). This led almost inevitably to the conclusion on the part of a reviewing court that the sentencing judge "sees more and senses more" than the appellate court; thus, the judge enjoyed the "superiority of his nether position," for that court's determination as to what sentence was appropriate met with virtually unconditional deference on appeal. See Rosenberg, Judicial Discretion of the Trial Court, Viewed From Above, 22 Syracuse L.Rev. 635, 663

(1971). See *Dorszynski v. United States*, 418 U.S. 424, 431, 94 S.Ct. 3042, 3047, 41 L.Ed.2d 855 (1974). The decision whether to parole was also "predictive and discretionary." *Morrissey v. Brewer*, 408 U.S. 471, 480, 92 S.Ct. 2593, 2600, 33 L.Ed.2d 484 (1972). The correction official possessed almost absolute discretion over the parole decision. See, *e.g.*, *Brest v. Ciccone*, 371 F.2d 981, 982–983 (CA8 1967); *Rifai v. United States Parole Comm'n*, 586 F.2d 695 (CA9 1978).

Historically, federal sentencing-the function of determining the scope and extent of punishment-never has been thought to be assigned by the Constitution to the exclusive jurisdiction of any one of the three Branches of Government. Congress, of course, has the power to fix the sentence for a federal crime, *United States v. Wiltberger*, 18 U.S. (5 Wheat.) 76, 5 L.Ed. 37 (1820), and the scope of judicial discretion with respect to a sentence is subject to congressional control. *Ex parte United States*, 242 U.S. 27, 37 S.Ct. 72, 61 L.Ed. 129 (1916). Congress early abandoned fixed-sentence rigidity, however, and put in place a system of ranges within which the sentencer could choose the precise punishment. See *United States v. Grayson*, 438 U.S. 41, 45–46, 98 S.Ct. 2610, 2613–14, 57 L.Ed.2d 582 (1978). Congress delegated almost unfettered discretion to the sentencing judge to determine what the sentence should be within the customarily wide range so selected. This broad discretion was further enhanced by the power later granted the judge to suspend the sentence and by the resulting growth of an elaborate probation system. Also, with the advent of parole, Congress moved toward a "three-way sharing" of sentencing responsibility by granting corrections personnel in the Executive Branch the discretion *365 to release a prisoner before the expiration of the sentence imposed by the judge. Thus, under the indeterminate-sentence system, Congress defined the maximum, the judge imposed a sentence within the statutory range (which he usually could replace with probation), and the Executive Branch's parole official eventually determined the actual duration of imprisonment. See *Williams v. New York*, 337 U.S. 241, 248, 69 S.Ct. 1079, 1083, 93 L.Ed. 1337 (1949). See also *Geraghty v. United States Parole Comm'n*, 719 F.2d 1199, 1211 (CA3 1983), cert. denied, 465 U.S. 1103, 104 S.Ct. 1602, 80 L.Ed.2d 133 (1984); *United States v. Addonizio*, 442 U.S. 178, 190, 99 S.Ct. 2235, 2243, 60 L.Ed.2d 805 (1979); *United States v. Brown*, 381 U.S. 437, 443, 85 S.Ct. 1707, 1712, 14 L.Ed.2d 484 (1965) ("[I]f a given policy can be implemented only by a combination of legislative enactment, judicial application, and executive implementation, no man or group of men will be able to impose its unchecked will").

Serious disparities in sentences, however, were common. Rehabilitation as a sound penological theory came to be questioned and, in any event, was regarded by some as an unattainable goal for most cases. See N.

Morris, The Future of Imprisonment 24–43 (1974); F. Allen, The Decline of the Rehabilitative Ideal (1981). In 1958, Congress authorized the creation of judicial sentencing institutes and joint councils, see 28 U.S.C. § 334, to formulate standards and criteria for sentencing. In 1973, the United States Parole Board adopted guidelines that established a "customary range" of confinement. See *United States Parole Comm'n v. Geraghty*, 445 U.S. 388, 391, 100 S.Ct. 1202, 1206, 63 L.Ed.2d 479 (1980). Congress in 1976 endorsed this initiative through the Parole Commission and Reorganization Act, 18 U.S.C. §§ 4201– 4218, an attempt to envision for the Parole Commission a role, at least in part, "to moderate the disparities in the sentencing practices of individual judges." *United States v. Addonizio*, 442 U.S., at 189, 99 S.Ct., at 2242. That Act, however, did not disturb the division of sentencing responsibility among the three Branches. The judge continued to exercise discretion and to set the sentence within the statutory range fixed by Congress, while the prisoner's actual release date generally was set by the Parole Commission.

This proved to be no more than a way station. Fundamental and widespread dissatisfaction with the uncertainties and the disparities continued to be expressed. Congress had wrestled with the problem for more than a decade when, in 1984, it enacted the sweeping reforms that are at issue here.

Helpful in our consideration and analysis of the statute is the Senate Report on the 1984 legislation, S.Rep. No. 98–225 (1983), U.S.Code Cong. & Admin.News 1984, p. 3182 (Report).[3] The Report referred to the "outmoded rehabilitation model" for federal criminal sentencing, and recognized that the efforts of the criminal justice system to achieve rehabilitation of offenders had failed. *Id.*, at 38. It observed that the indeterminate-sentencing system had two "unjustifi[ed]" and "shameful" consequences. *Id.*, at 38, 65. The first was the great variation among sentences imposed by different judges upon similarly situated offenders. The second was the uncertainty as to the time the offender would spend in prison. Each was a serious impediment to an evenhanded and effective operation of the criminal justice system. The Report went on to note that parole was an inadequate device for overcoming these undesirable consequences. This was due to the division of authority between the sentencing judge and the parole officer who often worked at cross purposes; to the fact that the Parole Commission's own guidelines did not take into account factors Congress regarded as important in sentencing, such as the sophistication of the offender and the role the offender played in an offense committed with others, *id.*, at 48; and to the fact that the Parole Commission had only limited power to adjust a sentence imposed by the court. *Id.*, at 47.

Before settling on a mandatory-guideline system, Congress considered other competing proposals for sentencing reform. It rejected strict determinate sentencing because it concluded that a guideline system would be successful in reducing sentence disparities while retaining the flexibility needed to adjust for unanticipated factors arising in a particular case. *Id.*, at 78–79, 62. The Judiciary Committee rejected a proposal that would have made the sentencing guidelines only advisory. *Id.*, at 79.

B

The Act

The Act, as adopted, revises the old sentencing process in several ways:

1.   It rejects imprisonment as a means of promoting rehabilitation, 28 U.S.C. § 994(k), and it states that punishment should serve retributive, educational, deterrent, and incapacitative goals, 18 U.S.C. § 3553(a)(2).

2.   It consolidates the power that had been exercised by the sentencing judge and the Parole Commission to decide what punishment an offender should suffer. This is done by creating the United States Sentencing Commission, directing that Commission to devise guidelines to be used for sentencing, and prospectively abolishing the Parole Commission. 28 U.S.C. §§ 991, 994, and 995(a)(1).

3.   It makes all sentences basically determinate. A prisoner is to be released at the completion of his sentence reduced only by any credit earned by good behavior while in custody. 18 U.S.C. §§ 3624(a) and (b).

4.   It makes the Sentencing Commission's guidelines binding on the courts, although it preserves for the judge the discretion to depart from the guideline applicable to a particular case if the judge finds an aggravating or mitigating factor present that the Commission did not adequately consider when formulating guidelines. §§ 3553(a) and (b). The Act also requires the court to state its reasons for the sentence imposed and to give "the specific reason" for imposing a sentence different from that described in the guideline. § 3553(c).

5.   It authorizes limited appellate review of the sentence. It permits a defendant to appeal a sentence that is above the defined range, and it permits the Government to appeal a sentence that is below that range. It also permits either side to appeal an incorrect application of the guideline. §§ 3742(a) and (b).

Thus, guidelines were meant to establish a range of determinate sentences for categories of offenses and defendants according to various specified factors, "among others." 28 U.S.C. §§ 994(b), (c), and (d). The maximum of the range ordinarily may not exceed the minimum by more than the greater of 25% or six months, and each sentence is to be within the limit provided by existing law. §§ 994(a) and (b)(2).

C

The Sentencing Commission

The Commission is established "as an independent commission in the judicial branch of the United States." § 991(a). It has seven voting members (one of whom is the Chairman) appointed by the President "by and with the advice and consent of the Senate." "At least three of the members shall be Federal judges selected after considering a list of six judges recommended to the President by the Judicial Conference of the United States." *Ibid.* No more than four members of the Commission shall be members of the same political party. The Attorney General, or his designee, is an ex officio non-voting member. The Chairman and other members of the Commission are subject to removal by the President "only for neglect of duty or malfeasance in office or for other good cause shown." *Ibid.* Except for initial staggering of terms, a voting member serves for six years and may not serve more than two full terms. §§ 992(a) and (b).

D

The Responsibilities of the Commission

In addition to the duty the Commission has to promulgate determinative-sentence guidelines, it is under an obligation periodically to "review and revise" the guidelines. § 994(o). It is to "consult with authorities on, and individual and institutional representatives of, various aspects of the Federal criminal justice system." *Ibid.* It must report to Congress "any amendments of the guidelines." § 994(p). It is to make recommendations to Congress whether the grades or maximum penalties should be modified. § 994(r). It must submit to Congress at least annually an analysis of the operation of the guidelines. § 994(w). It is to issue "general policy statements" regarding their application. § 994(a)(2). And it has the power to "establish general policies . . . as are necessary to carry out the purposes" of the legislation, § 995(a)(1); to "monitor the performance of probation officers" with respect to the guidelines, § 995(a)(9); to "devise and conduct periodic training programs of instruction in sentencing techniques for judicial and probation personnel" and others, § 995(a)(18); and to "perform such other functions as are required to permit Federal courts to meet their responsibilities" as to sentencing, § 995(a)(22).

We note, in passing, that the monitoring function is not without its burden. Every year, with respect to each of more than 40,000 sentences, the federal courts must forward, and the Commission must review, the presentence report, the guideline worksheets, the tribunal's sentencing statement, and any written plea agreement.

* * *

We conclude that in creating the Sentencing Commission-an unusual hybrid in structure and authority-Congress neither delegated excessive legislative power nor upset the constitutionally mandated balance of powers among the coordinate Branches. The Constitution's structural protections do not prohibit Congress from delegating to an expert body located within the Judicial Branch the intricate task of formulating sentencing guidelines consistent with such significant statutory direction as is present here. Nor does our system of checked and balanced authority prohibit Congress from calling upon the accumulated wisdom and experience of the Judicial Branch in creating policy on a matter uniquely within the ken of judges. Accordingly, we hold that the Act is constitutional.

* * *

It is so ordered.

For more on the legislative background of the federal sentencing guidelines, *see* Kate Stith & Steve Y. Koh, *The Politics of Sentencing Reform: The Legislative History of the Federal Sentencing Guidelines,* 28 WAKE FOREST L. REV. 223 (1993).

B. UNITED STATES SENTENCING GUIDELINES

Although the Guidelines Manual is lengthy and contains literally thousands of provisions and commentary notes, the basic operation of the federal sentencing guidelines is fairly straightforward.

1. HOW SERIOUS IS THE OFFENSE?

The first step is to determine how serious the offense is. The Guidelines assign what is called a "base offense level" to the various categories of federal crimes. Higher base offense levels correspond with more serious offenses, and lower base offense levels correspond with less serious offenses.

2. DO ANY CHARACTERISTICS OF THE OFFENSE AFFECT ITS SERIOUSNESS?

There may be "specific offense characteristics" that may increase or decrease the base offense level. For example, some financial crimes have associated offense characteristics related to the amount of loss suffered by the victims. When determining the presence or absence of such characteristics, the court may consider all "relevant" conduct including conduct for which the defendant has not been charged or has been acquitted. *See* USSG, Section 1B1.3.

3. DO ANY GENERAL ADJUSTMENTS APPLY TO THE OFFENSE LEVEL?

Certain general "adjustments" apply to all crimes. These adjustments may apply depending upon the defendant's role in the offense, certain characteristics of the victims of the crime, or the defendant's conduct as it relates to the integrity of the proceedings, such as obstruction of justice or perjury.

In addition, there may be adjustments made to the offense level when a defendant has been convicted of more than one offense, or whether the defendant accepted responsibility. Factors the court will consider in determining whether the acceptance of responsibility adjustment applies include whether the defendant made an admission of culpability, made pre-conviction restitution, and whether the defendant pled guilty as opposed to going to trial. Does the premium placed upon the guilty plea in order to obtain an acceptance of responsibility downward adjustment unduly burden any of the defendant's constitutional rights? What about the fact that the sentencing court may consider conduct for which the defendant has been acquitted but for which the court finds the defendant responsible by a preponderance of the evidence? For a spirited argument against the use of acquitted conduct in sentencing, *see* Dillon Malar, *Not Guilty But Might as Well Be: Ending Acquitted Conduct Sentencing*, AM. BAR ASS'N, CRIMINAL LITIGATION, Sept. 17, 2015, available at http://apps. americanbar.org/litigation/committees/criminal/articles/fall2015-0915-not-guilty-but-might-well-be-ending-acquitted-conduct-sentencing.html.

4. WHAT IS THE DEFENDANT'S CRIMINAL HISTORY?

After the offense level has been calculated, factoring in any specific offense characteristics and adjustments, the defendant's criminal record is evaluated to determine his or her criminal history. Defendants with the least extensive criminal records will be in Criminal History Category I, and more serious records will be assigned higher criminal history categories up through Criminal History Category VI, the most serious.

5. WHAT IS THE GUIDELINE RANGE?

Once the offense level and criminal history category have been calculated, the Sentencing Table can be consulted to determine the guidelines range. The Criminal History Categories run along the X-axis, and the Offense Levels run along the Y-axis. The appropriate guideline range, expressed in a range of months, can be found at the intersection of the two. The sentencing range will fall into one of four designated zones (A, B, C, or D) that constrain the sentencing options the court can exercise. For example, straight probation is an option if the range is within Zone A, probation with conditions is available for Zone B, a split sentence between incarceration and home confinement if the range is within Zone C, and exclusively incarceration if the range is within Zone D.

U.S. Sentencing Guideline Manual— Sentencing Table

https://www.ussc.gov/sites/default/files/pdf/guidelines-manual/2016/Sentencing_Table.pdf

---

The "Advisory" Federal Sentencing Guidelines

As discussed in Chapter 14 *supra*, the Court's holding in *Apprendi* that the Sixth Amendment requires that any fact that would increase a sentence above the statutory maximum must be proved to a jury beyond a reasonable doubt seemed to have profound implications for sentencing guidelines systems that, like the federal system, relied on judicial factfinding. When the Court struck down the Washington state sentencing guidelines in *Blakely v. Washington*, 542 U.S. 296 (2004), many legal commentators waited for the other shoe to drop. The concern was that the federal sentencing guidelines were similarly designed and, therefore, unconstitutional. The Supreme Court faced the question head-on in the *United States v. Booker*, 543 U.S. 220 (2005). As you read the case, note that there are *two* separate majority opinions, which is unusual. The first, authored by Justice Stevens, addressed whether the federal sentencing guidelines scheme is sufficiently similar to that ruled unconstitutional in *Blakeley*. The second majority opinion, authored by Justice Breyer, addressed whether the guidelines could be salvaged in light of the holding in the first majority opinion.

United States v. Booker

Supreme Court of the United States, 2005
543 U.S. 220

■ JUSTICE STEVENS delivered the opinion of the Court in part.

The question presented in each of these cases is whether an application of the Federal Sentencing Guidelines violated the Sixth Amendment. In each case, the courts below held that binding rules set forth in the Guidelines limited the severity of the sentence that the judge could lawfully impose on the defendant based on the facts found by the jury at his trial. In both cases the courts rejected, on the basis of our decision in *Blakely v. Washington*, 542 U.S. 296, 124 S.Ct. 2531, 159 L.Ed.2d 403 (2004), the Government's recommended application of the Sentencing Guidelines because the proposed sentences were based on additional facts that the sentencing judge found by a preponderance of the evidence. We hold that both courts correctly concluded that the Sixth Amendment as construed in Blakely does apply to the Sentencing Guidelines. In a separate opinion authored by Justice BREYER, the Court concludes that in light of this holding, two provisions of the Sentencing Reform Act of 1984 (SRA) that have the effect of making the Guidelines mandatory must be invalidated in order to allow the statute to operate in a manner consistent with congressional intent.

I

Respondent Booker was charged with possession with intent to distribute at least 50 grams of cocaine base (crack). Having heard evidence that he had 92.5 grams in his duffel bag, the jury found him guilty of violating 21 U.S.C. § 841(a)(1). That statute prescribes a minimum sentence of 10 years in prison and a maximum sentence of life for that offense. § 841(b)(1)(A)(iii).

Based upon Booker's criminal history and the quantity of drugs found by the jury, the Sentencing Guidelines required the District Court Judge to select a "base" sentence of not less than 210 nor more than 262 months in prison. See United States Sentencing Commission, Guidelines Manual §§ 2D1.1(c)(4), 4A1.1 (Nov. 2003) (USSG). The judge, however, held a post-trial sentencing proceeding and concluded by a preponderance of the evidence that Booker had possessed an additional 566 grams of crack and that he was guilty of obstructing justice. Those findings mandated that the judge select a sentence between 360 months and life imprisonment; the judge imposed a sentence at the low end of the range. Thus, instead of the sentence of 21 years and 10 months that the judge could have imposed on the basis of the facts proved to the jury beyond a reasonable doubt, Booker received a 30-year sentence.

Over the dissent of Judge Easterbrook, the Court of Appeals for the Seventh Circuit held that this application of the Sentencing Guidelines conflicted with our holding in *Apprendi v. New Jersey*, 530 U.S. 466, 490, 120 S.Ct. 2348, 147 L.Ed.2d 435 (2000), that "[o]ther than the fact of a prior conviction, any fact that increases the penalty for a crime beyond the prescribed statutory maximum must be submitted to a jury, and proved beyond a reasonable doubt." 375 F.3d 508, 510 (2004). The majority relied on our holding in *Blakely*, 542 U.S. 296, 124 S.Ct. 2531, that "the 'statutory maximum' for *Apprendi* purposes is the maximum sentence a judge may impose *solely on the basis of the facts reflected in the jury verdict or admitted by the defendant.*" *Id.*, at 303, 124 S.Ct., at

2537. The court held that the sentence violated the Sixth Amendment, and remanded with instructions to the District Court either to sentence respondent within the sentencing range supported by the jury's findings or to hold a separate sentencing hearing before a jury.

Respondent Fanfan was charged with conspiracy to distribute and to possess with intent to distribute at least 500 grams of cocaine in violation of 21 U.S.C. §§ 846, 841(a)(1), and 841(b)(1)(B)(ii). He was convicted by the jury after it answered "Yes" to the question "Was the amount of cocaine 500 or more grams?" App. C to Pet. for Cert. in No. 04–105, p. 15a. Under the Guidelines, without additional findings of fact, the maximum sentence authorized by the jury verdict was imprisonment for 78 months.

A few days after our decision in *Blakely*, the trial judge conducted a sentencing hearing at which he found additional facts that, under the Guidelines, would have authorized a sentence in the 188-to-235-month range. Specifically, he found that respondent Fanfan was responsible for 2.5 kilograms of cocaine powder, and 261.6 grams of crack. He also concluded that respondent had been an organizer, leader, manager, or supervisor in the criminal activity. Both findings were made by a preponderance of the evidence. Under the Guidelines, these additional findings would have required an enhanced sentence of 15 or 16 years instead of the 5 or 6 years authorized by the jury verdict alone. Relying not only on the majority opinion in *Blakely*, but also on the categorical statements in the dissenting opinions and in the Solicitor General's brief in *Blakely*, see App. A to Pet. for Cert. in No. 04–105, pp. 6a–7a, the judge concluded that he could not follow the particular provisions of the Sentencing Guidelines "which involve drug quantity and role enhancement," *id.*, at 11a. Expressly refusing to make "any blanket decision about the federal guidelines," he followed the provisions of the Guidelines that did not implicate the Sixth Amendment by imposing a sentence on respondent "based solely upon the jury verdict in this case." *Ibid.*

Following the denial of its motion to correct the sentence in Fanfan's case, the Government filed a notice of appeal in the Court of Appeals for the First Circuit, and a petition in this Court for a writ of certiorari before judgment. Because of the importance of the questions presented, we granted that petition, 542 U.S. 956, 124 S.Ct. 2531, 159 L.Ed.2d 403 (2004), as well as a similar petition filed by the Government in Booker's case, *ibid.* In both petitions, the Government asks us to determine whether our *Apprendi* line of cases applies to the Sentencing Guidelines, and if so, what portions of the Guidelines remain in effect.

In this opinion, we explain why we agree with the lower courts' answer to the first question. In a separate opinion for the Court, Justice BREYER explains the Court's answer to the second question.

II

It has been settled throughout our history that the Constitution protects every criminal defendant "against conviction except upon proof beyond a reasonable doubt of every fact necessary to constitute the crime with which he is charged." *In re Winship*, 397 U.S. 358, 364, 90 S.Ct. 1068, 25 L.Ed.2d 368 (1970). It is equally clear that the "Constitution gives a criminal defendant the right to demand that a jury find him guilty of all the elements of the crime with which he is charged." *United States v. Gaudin*, 515 U.S. 506, 511, 115 S.Ct. 2310, 132 L.Ed.2d 444 (1995). These basic precepts, firmly rooted in the common law, have provided the basis for recent decisions interpreting modern criminal statutes and sentencing procedures.

In *Jones v. United States*, 526 U.S. 227, 230, 119 S.Ct. 1215, 143 L.Ed.2d 311 (1999), we considered the federal carjacking statute, which provides three different maximum sentences depending on the extent of harm to the victim: 15 years in jail if there was no serious injury to a victim, 25 years if there was "serious bodily injury," and life in prison if death resulted. 18 U.S.C. § 2119 (1988 ed., Supp. V). In spite of the fact that the statute "at first glance has a look to it suggesting [that the provisions relating to the extent of harm to the victim] are only sentencing provisions," 526 U.S., at 232, 119 S.Ct. 1215, we concluded that the harm to the victim was an element of the crime. That conclusion was supported by the statutory text and structure, and was influenced by our desire to avoid the constitutional issues implicated by a contrary holding, which would have reduced the jury's role "to the relative importance of low-level gatekeeping." *Id.*, at 244, 119 S.Ct. 1215. Foreshadowing the result we reach today, we noted that our holding was consistent with a "rule requiring jury determination of facts that raise a sentencing ceiling" in state and federal sentencing guidelines systems. *Id.*, at 251–252, n. 11, 119 S.Ct. 1215.

In *Apprendi v. New Jersey*, 530 U.S. 466, 120 S.Ct. 2348, 147 L.Ed.2d 435 (2000), the defendant pleaded guilty to second-degree possession of a firearm for an unlawful purpose, which carried a prison term of 5-to-10 years. Thereafter, the trial court found that his conduct had violated New Jersey's "hate crime" law because it was racially motivated, and imposed a 12-year sentence. This Court set aside the enhanced sentence. We held: "Other than the fact of a prior conviction, any fact that increases the penalty for a crime beyond the prescribed statutory maximum must be submitted to a jury, and proved beyond a reasonable doubt." *Id.*, at 490, 120 S.Ct. 2348.

The fact that New Jersey labeled the hate crime a "sentence enhancement" rather than a separate criminal act was irrelevant for constitutional purposes. *Id.*, at 478, 120 S.Ct. 2348. As a matter of simple justice, it seemed obvious that the procedural safeguards designed to protect Apprendi from punishment for the possession of a firearm should apply equally to his violation of the hate crime statute. Merely using the label "sentence enhancement" to describe the latter did not provide a principled basis for treating the two crimes differently. *Id.*, at 476, 120 S.Ct. 2348.

In *Ring v. Arizona*, 536 U.S. 584, 122 S.Ct. 2428, 153 L.Ed.2d 556 (2002), we reaffirmed our conclusion that the characterization of critical facts is constitutionally irrelevant. There, we held that it was impermissible for "the trial judge, sitting alone" to determine the presence or absence of the aggravating factors required by Arizona law for imposition of the death penalty. *Id.*, at 588–589, 122 S.Ct. 2428. "If a State makes an increase in a defendant's authorized punishment contingent on the finding of a fact, that fact—no matter how the State labels it—must be found by a jury beyond a reasonable doubt." *Id.*, at 602, 122 S.Ct. 2428.Our opinion made it clear that ultimately, while the procedural error in Ring's case might have been harmless because the necessary finding was implicit in the jury's guilty verdict, *id.*, at 609, n. 7, 122 S.Ct. 2428, "the characterization of a fact or circumstance as an 'element' or a 'sentencing factor' is not determinative of the question 'who decides,' judge or jury," *id.*, at 605, 122 S.Ct. 2428.

In *Blakely v. Washington*, 542 U.S. 296, 124 S.Ct. 2531, 159 L.Ed.2d 403 (2004), we dealt with a determinate sentencing scheme similar to the Federal Sentencing Guidelines. There the defendant pleaded guilty to kidnaping, a class B felony punishable by a term of not more than 10 years. Other provisions of Washington law, comparable to the Federal Sentencing Guidelines, mandated a "standard" sentence of 49-to-53 months, unless the judge found aggravating facts justifying an exceptional sentence. Although the prosecutor recommended a sentence in the standard range, the judge found that the defendant had acted with " 'deliberate cruelty' " and sentenced him to 90 months. *Id.*, at 300, 124 S.Ct., at 2534.

For reasons explained in *Jones, Apprendi*, and *Ring*, the requirements of the Sixth Amendment were clear. The application of Washington's sentencing scheme violated the defendant's right to have the jury find the existence of " 'any particular fact' " that the law makes essential to his punishment. 542 U.S., at 301, 124 S.Ct., at 2536. That right is implicated whenever a judge seeks to impose a sentence that is not solely based on "facts reflected in the jury verdict or admitted by the defendant." *Id.*, at 303, 124 S.Ct., at 2537 (emphasis deleted). We rejected the State's argument that the jury verdict was sufficient to authorize a sentence within the general 10-year sentence for class B felonies, noting that under Washington law, the judge was *required* to find additional facts in order to impose the greater 90-month sentence. Our precedents, we explained, make clear "that the 'statutory maximum' for *Apprendi* purposes is the maximum sentence a judge may impose *solely on the basis of the facts reflected in the jury verdict or admitted by the defendant.*" *Ibid.* (emphasis in original). The determination that the defendant acted with deliberate cruelty, like the determination in *Apprendi* that the defendant acted with racial malice, increased the sentence that the defendant could have otherwise received. Since this fact was found by a judge using a preponderance of the evidence standard, the sentence violated Blakely's Sixth Amendment rights.

As the dissenting opinions in *Blakely* recognized, there is no distinction of constitutional significance between the Federal Sentencing Guidelines and the Washington procedures at issue in that case. See, *e.g.*, 542 U.S., at 325, 124 S.Ct., at 2540 (opinion of O'CONNOR, J.) ("The structure of the Federal Guidelines likewise does not, as the Government halfheartedly suggests, provide any grounds for distinction. ... If anything, the structural differences that do exist make the Federal Guidelines more vulnerable to attack"). This conclusion rests on the premise, common to both systems, that the relevant sentencing rules are mandatory and impose binding requirements on all sentencing judges.

If the Guidelines as currently written could be read as merely advisory provisions that recommended, rather than required, the selection of particular sentences in response to differing sets of facts, their use would not implicate the Sixth Amendment. We have never doubted the authority of a judge to exercise broad discretion in imposing a sentence within a statutory range. See *Apprendi*, 530 U.S., at 481, 120 S.Ct. 2348; *Williams v. New York*, 337 U.S. 241, 246, 69 S.Ct. 1079, 93 L.Ed. 1337 (1949). Indeed, everyone agrees that the constitutional issues presented by these cases would have been avoided entirely if Congress had omitted from the SRA the provisions that make the Guidelines binding on district judges; it is that circumstance that makes the Court's answer to the second question presented possible. For when a trial judge exercises his discretion to select a specific sentence within a defined range, the defendant has no right to a jury determination of the facts that the judge deems relevant.

The Guidelines as written, however, are not advisory; they are mandatory and binding on all judges. While subsection a) of § 3553 of the sentencing statute lists the Sentencing Guidelines as one factor to be considered in imposing a sentence, subsection (b) directs that the court "*shall* impose a sentence of the kind, and within the range" established by the Guidelines, subject to departures in specific, limited cases. (Emphasis added.) Because they are binding on judges, we have consistently held that the Guidelines have the force and effect of laws. See, *e.g., Mistretta v. United States*, 488 U.S. 361, 391, 109 S.Ct. 647,

102 L.Ed.2d 714 (1989); *Stinson v. United States*, 508 U.S. 36, 42, 113 S.Ct. 1913, 123 L.Ed.2d 598 (1993).

The availability of a departure in specified circumstances does not avoid the constitutional issue, just as it did not in *Blakely* itself. The Guidelines permit departures from the prescribed sentencing range in cases in which the judge "finds that there exists an aggravating or mitigating circumstance of a kind, or to a degree, not adequately taken into consideration by the Sentencing Commission in formulating the guidelines that should result in a sentence different from that described." 18 U.S.C. § 3553(b)(1) (2000 ed., Supp. IV). At first glance, one might believe that the ability of a district judge to depart from the Guidelines means that she is bound only by the statutory maximum. Were this the case, there would be no *Apprendi* problem. Importantly, however, departures are not available in every case, and in fact are unavailable in most. In most cases, as a matter of law, the Commission will have adequately taken all relevant factors into account, and no departure will be legally permissible. In those instances, the judge is bound to impose a sentence within the Guidelines range. It was for this reason that we rejected a similar argument in *Blakely*, holding that although the Washington statute allowed the judge to impose a sentence outside the sentencing range for " 'substantial and compelling reasons,' " that exception was not available for Blakely himself. 542 U.S., at 299, 124 S.Ct., at 2535. The sentencing judge would have been reversed had he invoked the departure section to justify the sentence.

Booker's case illustrates the mandatory nature of the Guidelines. The jury convicted him of possessing at least 50 grams of crack in violation of 21 U.S.C. § 841(b)(1)(A)(iii) based on evidence that he had 92.5 grams of crack in his duffel bag. Under these facts, the Guidelines specified an offense level of 32, which, given the defendant's criminal history category, authorized a sentence of 210-to-262 months. See USSG § 2D1.1(c)(4). Booker's is a run-of-the-mill drug case, and does not present any factors that were inadequately considered by the Commission. The sentencing judge would therefore have been reversed had he not imposed a sentence within the level 32 Guidelines range.

Booker's actual sentence, however, was 360 months, almost 10 years longer than the Guidelines range supported by the jury verdict alone. To reach this sentence, the judge found facts beyond those found by the jury: namely, that Booker possessed 566 grams of crack in addition to the 92.5 grams in his duffel bag. The jury never heard any evidence of the additional drug quantity, and the judge found it true by a preponderance of the evidence. Thus, just as in *Blakely*, "the jury's verdict alone does not authorize the sentence. The judge acquires that authority only upon finding some additional fact." 542 U.S., at 305, 124 S.Ct., at 2538. There is no relevant distinction between the sentence imposed pursuant to the Washington statutes in *Blakely* and the sentences imposed pursuant to the Federal Sentencing Guidelines in these cases.

In his dissent, *post*, at 803–804, Justice BREYER argues on historical grounds that the Guidelines scheme is constitutional across the board. He points to traditional judicial authority to increase sentences to take account of any unusual blameworthiness in the manner employed in committing a crime, an authority that the Guidelines require to be exercised consistently throughout the system. This tradition, however, does not provide a sound guide to enforcement of the Sixth Amendment's guarantee of a jury trial in today's world.

It is quite true that once determinate sentencing had fallen from favor, American judges commonly determined facts justifying a choice of a heavier sentence on account of the manner in which particular defendants acted. *Apprendi*, 530 U.S., at 481, 120 S.Ct. 2348. In 1986, however, our own cases first recognized a new trend in the legislative regulation of sentencing when we considered the significance of facts selected by legislatures that not only authorized, or even mandated, heavier sentences than would otherwise have been imposed, but increased the range of sentences possible for the underlying crime. See *McMillan v. Pennsylvania*, 477 U.S. 79, 87–88, 106 S.Ct. 2411, 91 L.Ed.2d 67 (1986). Provisions for such enhancements of the permissible sentencing range reflected growing and wholly justified legislative concern about the proliferation and variety of drug crimes and their frequent identification with firearms offenses.

The effect of the increasing emphasis on facts that enhanced sentencing ranges, however, was to increase the judge's power and diminish that of the jury. It became the judge, not the jury, who determined the upper limits of sentencing, and the facts determined were not required to be raised before trial or proved by more than a preponderance.

As the enhancements became greater, the jury's finding of the underlying crime became less significant. And the enhancements became very serious indeed. See, *e.g., Jones*, 526 U.S., at 230–231, 119 S.Ct. 1215 (judge's finding increased the maximum sentence from 15 to 25 years); respondent Booker's (from 262 months to a life sentence); respondent Fanfan's (from 78 to 235 months); *United States v. Rodriguez*, 73 F.3d 161, 162–163 (C.A.7 1996) (Posner, C.J., dissenting from denial of rehearing en banc) (from approximately 54 months to a life sentence); *United States v. Hammoud*, 381 F.3d 316, 361–362 (C.A.4 2004) (en banc) (Motz, J., dissenting) (actual sentence increased from 57 months to 155 years).

As it thus became clear that sentencing was no longer taking place in the tradition that Justice BREYER invokes, the Court was faced with the issue of preserving an ancient guarantee under a new set of circumstances. The new sentencing practice forced the Court to address the question how the right of jury trial could be preserved, in a meaningful way guaranteeing that the jury would still stand between the individual and the power of the government under the new sentencing regime. And it is the new circumstances, not a tradition or practice that the new circumstances have superseded, that have led us to the answer first considered in *Jones* and developed in *Apprendi* and subsequent cases culminating with this one. It is an answer not motivated by Sixth Amendment formalism, but by the need to preserve Sixth Amendment substance.

III

The Government advances three arguments in support of its submission that we should not apply our reasoning in *Blakely* to the Federal Sentencing Guidelines. It contends that *Blakely* is distinguishable because the Guidelines were promulgated by a Commission rather than the Legislature; that principles of *stare decisis* require us to follow four earlier decisions that are arguably inconsistent with *Blakely;* and that the application of *Blakely* to the Guidelines would conflict with separation-of-powers principles reflected in *Mistretta v. United States*, 488 U.S. 361, 109 S.Ct. 647, 102 L.Ed.2d 714 (1989). These arguments are unpersuasive.

* * *

IV

All of the foregoing supports our conclusion that our holding in *Blakely* applies to the Sentencing Guidelines. We recognize, as we did in *Jones, Apprendi*, and *Blakely*, that in some cases jury factfinding may impair the most expedient and efficient sentencing of defendants. But the interest in fairness and reliability protected by the right to a jury trial—a common-law right that defendants enjoyed for centuries and that is now enshrined in the Sixth Amendment—has always outweighed the interest in concluding trials swiftly. *Blakely*, 542 U.S., at 313, 124 S.Ct., at 2542–2543. As Blackstone put it:

> "[H]owever *convenient* these [new methods of trial] may appear at first, (as doubtless all arbitrary powers, well executed, are the most *convenient*) yet let it be again remembered, that delays, and little inconveniences in the forms of justice, are the price that all free nations must pay for their liberty in more substantial matters; that these inroads upon this sacred bulwark of the nation are fundamentally opposite to the spirit of our constitution; and that, though begun in trifles, the precedent may gradually increase and spread, to the utter

disuse of juries in questions of the most momentous concerns."
4 Commentaries on the Laws of England 343–344 (1769).

Accordingly, we reaffirm our holding in *Apprendi:* Any fact (other than a prior conviction) which is necessary to support a sentence exceeding the maximum authorized by the facts established by a plea of guilty or a jury verdict must be admitted by the defendant or proved to a jury beyond a reasonable doubt.

■ JUSTICE BREYER delivered the opinion of the Court in part.

The first question that the Government has presented in these cases is the following:

> "Whether the Sixth Amendment is violated by the imposition of an enhanced sentence under the United States Sentencing Guidelines based on the sentencing judge's determination of a fact (other than a prior conviction) that was not found by the jury or admitted by the defendant." Pet. for Cert. in No. 04–104, p. (I).

The Court, in an opinion by Justice STEVENS, answers this question in the affirmative. Applying its decisions in *Apprendi v. New Jersey*, 530 U.S. 466, 120 S.Ct. 2348, 147 L.Ed.2d 435 (2000), and *Blakely v. Washington*, 542 U.S. 296, 124 S.Ct. 2531, 159 L.Ed.2d 403 (2004), to the Federal Sentencing Guidelines, the Court holds that, in the circumstances mentioned, the Sixth Amendment requires juries, not judges, to find facts relevant to sentencing. See *ante*, at 746, 756 (STEVENS, J., opinion of the Court).

We here turn to the second question presented, a question that concerns the remedy. We must decide whether or to what extent, "as a matter of severability analysis," the Guidelines "as a whole" are "inapplicable . . . such that the sentencing court must exercise its discretion to sentence the defendant within the maximum and minimum set by statute for the offense of conviction." Pet. for Cert. in No. 04–104, p. (I).

We answer the question of remedy by finding the provision of the federal sentencing statute that makes the Guidelines mandatory, 18 U.S.C. § 3553(b)(1) (Supp. IV), incompatible with today's constitutional holding. We conclude that this provision must be severed and excised, as must one other statutory section, § 3742(e) (2000 ed. and Supp. IV), which depends upon the Guidelines' mandatory nature. So modified, the federal sentencing statute, see Sentencing Reform Act of 1984 (Sentencing Act), as amended, 18 U.S.C. § 3551 *et seq.*, 28 U.S.C. § 991 *et seq.*, makes the Guidelines effectively advisory. It requires a sentencing court to consider Guidelines ranges, see 18 U.S.C.A. § 3553(a)(4) (Supp.2004), but it permits the court to tailor the sentence in light of other statutory concerns as well, see § 3553(a).

* * *

V

In respondent Booker's case, the District Court applied the Guidelines as written and imposed a sentence higher than the maximum authorized solely by the jury's verdict. The Court of Appeals held *Blakely* applicable to the Guidelines, concluded that Booker's sentence violated the Sixth Amendment, vacated the judgment of the District Court, and remanded for resentencing. We affirm the judgment of the Court of Appeals and remand the case. On remand, the District Court should impose a sentence in accordance with today's opinions, and, if the sentence comes before the Court of Appeals for review, the Court of Appeals should apply the review standards set forth in this opinion.

In respondent Fanfan's case, the District Court held *Blakely* applicable to the Guidelines. It then imposed a sentence that was authorized by the jury's verdict—a sentence lower than the sentence authorized by the Guidelines as written. Thus, Fanfan's sentence does not violate the Sixth Amendment. Nonetheless, the Government (and the defendant should he so choose) may seek resentencing under the system set forth in today's opinions. Hence we vacate the judgment of the District Court and remand the case for further proceedings consistent with this opinion.

As these dispositions indicate, we must apply today's holdings—both the Sixth Amendment holding and our remedial interpretation of the Sentencing Act—to all cases on direct review. See *Griffith v. Kentucky*, 479 U.S. 314, 328, 107 S.Ct. 708, 93 L.Ed.2d 649 (1987) ("[A] new rule for the conduct of criminal prosecutions is to be applied retroactively to all cases . . . pending on direct review or not yet final, with no exception for cases in which the new rule constitutes a 'clear break' with the past"). See also *Reynoldsville Casket Co. v. Hyde*, 514 U.S. 749, 752, 115 S.Ct. 1745, 131 L.Ed.2d 820 (1995) (civil case); *Harper v. Virginia Dept. of Taxation*, 509 U.S. 86, 97, 113 S.Ct. 2510, 125 L.Ed.2d 74 (1993) (same). That fact does not mean that we believe that every sentence gives rise to a Sixth Amendment violation. Nor do we believe that every appeal will lead to a new sentencing hearing. That is because we expect reviewing courts to apply ordinary prudential doctrines, determining, for example, whether the issue was raised below and whether it fails the "plain-error" test. It is also because, in cases not involving a Sixth Amendment violation, whether resentencing is warranted or whether it will instead be sufficient to review a sentence for reasonableness may depend upon application of the harmless-error doctrine.

It is so ordered.

The Role of the Federal Sentencing Guidelines After Booker

After *Booker*, the federal sentencing guidelines are advisory, but "district courts, while not bound to apply the Guidelines, must . . . take them into account when sentencing." *Booker*, 543 U.S. at 264. Section 3553(a) reads as follows:

18 U.S.C. § 3553. Imposition of a Sentence

(a) Factors To Be Considered in Imposing a Sentence. The court shall impose a sentence sufficient, but not greater than necessary, to comply with the purposes set forth in paragraph (2) of this subsection. The court, in determining the particular sentence to be imposed, shall consider—

(1) the nature and circumstances of the offense and the history and characteristics of the defendant;

(2) the need for the sentence imposed—

(A) to reflect the seriousness of the offense, to promote respect for the law, and to provide just punishment for the offense;

(B) to afford adequate deterrence to criminal conduct;

(C) to protect the public from further crimes of the defendant; and

(D) to provide the defendant with needed educational or vocational training, medical care, or other correctional treatment in the most effective manner;

(3) the kinds of sentences available;

(4) the kinds of sentence and the sentencing range established for—

(A) the applicable category of offense committed by the applicable category of defendant as set forth in the guidelines—

(i) issued by the Sentencing Commission pursuant to section 994 (a)(1) of title 28, United States Code, subject to any amendments made to such guidelines by act of Congress (regardless of whether such amendments have yet to be incorporated by the Sentencing Commission into amendments issued under section 994 (p) of title 28); and

(ii) that, except as provided in section 3742 (g), are in effect on the date the defendant is sentenced; or

(B) in the case of a violation of probation or supervised release, the applicable guidelines or policy statements issued by the Sentencing Commission pursuant to section 994 (a)(3) of title 28, United States Code, taking into account any amendments made to such guidelines or policy statements by act of Congress (regardless of whether such amendments have yet to be incorporated by the Sentencing Commission into amendments issued under section 994 (p) of title 28);

(5) any pertinent policy statement—

(A) issued by the Sentencing Commission pursuant to section 994 (a)(2) of title 28, United States Code, subject to any amendments made to such policy statement by act of Congress (regardless of whether such amendments have yet to be incorporated by the Sentencing Commission into amendments issued under section 994 (p) of title 28); and

(B) that, except as provided in section 3742 (g), is in effect on the date the defendant is sentenced.

(6) the need to avoid unwarranted sentence disparities among defendants with similar records who have been found guilty of similar conduct; and

(7) the need to provide restitution to any victims of the offense.

* * *

Thus, although section 3553(b)(2), which requires that "the court shall impose a sentence of the kind, and within the range, referred to in subsection (a)(4)" was declared unconstitutional, the Court left intact Section 3553(a)(4), which simply requires the sentencing court to *consider* the Guidelines. In the years since *Booker*, the Court has reiterated the need for sentencing courts to "include the Guidelines range in the array of factors warranting consideration," *Kimbrough v. United States*, 582 U.S. 85 (2007), and declared that "[a]s a matter of administration and to secure nationwide consistency, the Guidelines should be the starting point and initial benchmark" for the sentencing court. *Gall v. United Sates*, 552 U.S. 38, 49 (2007).

Appellate Review of Sentencing

The appellate review of sentencing is governed by 18 U.S.C. § 3742, excerpted below.

18 U.S.C. § 3742. Review of a Sentence

(a) Appeal by a defendant. A defendant may file a notice of appeal in the district court for review of an otherwise final sentence if the sentence—

(1) was imposed in violation of law;

(2) was imposed as a result of an incorrect application of the sentencing guidelines; or

(3) is greater than the sentence specified in the applicable guideline range to the extent that the sentence includes a greater fine or term of imprisonment, probation, or supervised release than the maximum established in the guideline range, or includes a more limiting condition of probation or supervised release under section 3563(b)(6) or (b)(11) than the maximum established in the guideline range; or

(4) was imposed for an offense for which there is no sentencing guideline and is plainly unreasonable.

(b) Appeal by the Government. The Government may file a notice of appeal in the district court for review of an otherwise final sentence if the sentence—

(1) was imposed in violation of law;

(2) was imposed as a result of an incorrect application of the sentencing guidelines;

(3) is less than the sentence specified in the applicable guideline range to the extent that the sentence includes a lesser fine or term of imprisonment, probation, or supervised release than the minimum established in the guideline range, or includes a less limiting condition of probation or supervised release under section 3563(b)(6) or (b)(11) than the minimum established in the guideline range; or

(4) was imposed for an offense for which there is no sentencing guideline and is plainly unreasonable.

The Government may not further prosecute such appeal without the personal approval of the Attorney General, the

Solicitor General, or a deputy solicitor general designated by the Solicitor General.

* * *

The *Booker* Court excised a provision of Section 3742 making the failure to sentence within the Guidelines a focus of appellate review. The *Booker* Court held that sentences handed down in the new advisory Guidelines regime would be reviewed on appeal for "unreasonableness." Two years later, the Court made clear that, if a sentence imposed by the district court is within the Guidelines range, the court of appeals *may* apply a presumption that the sentence is reasonable. *See Rita v. United States*, 551 U.S. 338 (2007).

IV. THE SENTENCING PROCESS

A. FEDERAL RULE OF CRIMINAL PROCEDURE 32

Federal Rule of Criminal Procedure 32 governs the sentencing process in federal court.

Rule 32. Sentencing and Judgment

(a) [Reserved.]

(b) Time of Sentencing.

(1) *In General.* The court must impose sentence without unnecessary delay.

(2) *Changing Time Limits.* The court may, for good cause, change any time limits prescribed in this rule.

(c) Presentence Investigation.

(1) *Required Investigation.*

(A) In General. The probation officer must conduct a presentence investigation and submit a report to the court before it imposes sentence unless:

(i) 18 U.S.C. § 3593 (c) or another statute requires otherwise; or

(ii) the court finds that the information in the record enables it to meaningfully exercise its sentencing authority under 18 U.S.C. § 3553, and the court explains its finding on the record.

(B) Restitution. If the law permits restitution, the probation officer must conduct an investigation and submit a report that contains sufficient information for the court to order restitution.

(2) *Interviewing the Defendant.* The probation officer who interviews a defendant as part of a presentence investigation must, on request, give the defendant's attorney notice and a reasonable opportunity to attend the interview.

(d) Presentence Report.

(1) *Applying the Advisory Sentencing Guidelines.* The presentence report must:

(A) identify all applicable guidelines and policy statements of the Sentencing Commission;

(B) calculate the defendant's offense level and criminal history category;

(C) state the resulting sentencing range and kinds of sentences available;

(D) identify any factor relevant to:

(i) the appropriate kind of sentence, or

(ii) the appropriate sentence within the applicable sentencing range; and

(E) identify any basis for departing from the applicable sentencing range.

(2) *Additional Information.* The presentence report must also contain the following:

(A) the defendant's history and characteristics, including:

(i) any prior criminal record;

(ii) the defendant's financial condition; and

(iii) any circumstances affecting the defendant's behavior that may be helpful in imposing sentence or in correctional treatment;

(B) information that assesses any financial, social, psychological, and medical impact on any victim;

(C) when appropriate, the nature and extent of nonprison programs and resources available to the defendant;

(D) when the law provides for restitution, information sufficient for a restitution order;

(E) if the court orders a study under 18 U.S.C. § 3552 (b), any resulting report and recommendation;

(F) a statement of whether the government seeks forfeiture under Rule 32.2 and any other law; and

(G) any other information that the court requires, including information relevant to the factors under 18 U.S.C. § 3553 (a).

(3) *Exclusions.* The presentence report must exclude the following:

(A) any diagnoses that, if disclosed, might seriously disrupt a rehabilitation program;

(B) any sources of information obtained upon a promise of confidentiality; and

(C) any other information that, if disclosed, might result in physical or other harm to the defendant or others.

(e) Disclosing the Report and Recommendation.

(1) *Time to Disclose.* Unless the defendant has consented in writing, the probation officer must not submit a presentence report to the court or disclose its contents to anyone until the defendant has pleaded guilty or nolo contendere, or has been found guilty.

(2) *Minimum Required Notice.* The probation officer must give the presentence report to the defendant, the defendant's attorney, and an attorney for the government at least 35 days before sentencing unless the defendant waives this minimum period.

(3) *Sentence Recommendation.* By local rule or by order in a case, the court may direct the probation officer not to disclose to anyone other than the court the officer's recommendation on the sentence.

(f) Objecting to the Report.

(1) *Time to Object.* Within 14 days after receiving the presentence report, the parties must state in writing any objections, including objections to material information, sentencing guideline ranges, and policy statements contained in or omitted from the report.

(2) *Serving Objections.* An objecting party must provide a copy of its objections to the opposing party and to the probation officer.

(3) *Action on Objections.* After receiving objections, the probation officer may meet with the parties to discuss the objections. The probation officer may then investigate further and revise the presentence report as appropriate.

(g) Submitting the Report. At least 7 days before sentencing, the probation officer must submit to the court and to the parties the presentence report and an addendum containing any unresolved objections, the grounds for those objections, and the probation officer's comments on them.

* * *

The Presentence Investigation Report

The Presentence Investigation Report ("PSR" or "PSIR") is completed by United States Probation Office staff. Under 18 U.S.C. § 3661, "[n]o limitation shall be placed on the information concerning the background, character, and conduct of a person convicted of an offense which a court of the United States may receive and consider for the purpose of imposing an appropriate sentence." Probation Officers typically will conduct a thorough investigation, obtaining documents and interviewing individuals regarding, *inter alia*, the defendant's background and criminal history, circumstances of the crime, the victim's injures and losses.

> **Order for a Presentence Investigation and Report**
>
> http://www.uscourts.gov/sites/default/files/ao246B.pdf

* * *

Rule 32. Sentencing and Judgment

* * *

(h) Notice of Possible Departure from Sentencing Guidelines. Before the court may depart from the applicable sentencing range on a ground not identified for departure either in the presentence report or in a party's prehearing submission, the court must give the parties reasonable notice that it is contemplating such a departure. The notice must specify any ground on which the court is contemplating a departure.

* * *

Departures and Variances from the Guidelines Range

If a court chooses a sentence outside of the guidelines range, it will be characterized as either a "departure" or a "variance." Departures typically are made pursuant to approved processes and criteria set forth in the Guidelines Manual and, therefore, most departures are well-established.

One frequent basis for downward departure is the defendant's provision of "substantial assistance" to the government. Under Section 5K1.1 of the Sentencing Guidelines, the court may entertain a motion for a downward departure due to the defendant's cooperation with the government's investigation and prosecution of other individuals. The court may also reward a cooperating defendant within a limited time after sentencing under 18 U.S.C. § 3553(e), and Fed. R. Crim. P. 35(b).

A variance, on the other hand, describes an out-of-guidelines sentence imposed for reasons other than those recognized in the Guidelines Manual, typically the statutory sentencing factors found at 18 U.S.C. § 3553(a). For more on departures and variances, *see* U.S. SENTENCING COMMISSION, PRIMER ON DEPARTURES AND VARIANCES (June 2016).

* * *

(i) Sentencing.

    (1) *In General.* At sentencing, the court:

        (A) must verify that the defendant and the defendant's attorney have read and discussed the presentence report and any addendum to the report;

        (B) must give to the defendant and an attorney for the government a written summary of—or summarize in camera—any information excluded from the presentence report under Rule 32(d)(3) on which the court will rely in sentencing, and give them a reasonable opportunity to comment on that information;

        (C) must allow the parties' attorneys to comment on the probation officer's determinations and other matters relating to an appropriate sentence; and

        (D) may, for good cause, allow a party to make a new objection at any time before sentence is imposed.

    (2) *Introducing   Evidence;   Producing   a Statement.* The court may permit the parties to introduce evidence on the objections. If a witness testifies at sentencing, Rule 26.2(a)–(d) and (f) applies. If a party fails to comply with a Rule 26.2 order to produce a witness's statement, the court must not consider that witness's testimony.

(3) *Court Determinations.* At sentencing, the court:

(A) may accept any undisputed portion of the presentence report as a finding of fact;

(B) must—for any disputed portion of the presentence report or other controverted matter—rule on the dispute or determine that a ruling is unnecessary either because the matter will not affect sentencing, or because the court will not consider the matter in sentencing; and

(C) must append a copy of the court's determinations under this rule to any copy of the presentence report made available to the Bureau of Prisons.

(4) *Opportunity to Speak.*

(A) By a Party. Before imposing sentence, the court must:

(i) provide the defendant's attorney an opportunity to speak on the defendant's behalf;

(ii) address the defendant personally in order to permit the defendant to speak or present any information to mitigate the sentence; and

(iii) provide an attorney for the government an opportunity to speak equivalent to that of the defendant's attorney.

(B) By a Victim. Before imposing sentence, the court must address any victim of the crime who is present at sentencing and must permit the victim to be reasonably heard.

(C) In Camera Proceedings. Upon a party's motion and for good cause, the court may hear in camera any statement made under Rule 32(i)(4).

(j) Defendant's Right to Appeal.

(1) *Advice of a Right to Appeal.*

(A) Appealing a Conviction. If the defendant pleaded not guilty and was convicted, after sentencing the court must advise the defendant of the right to appeal the conviction.

(B) *Appealing a Sentence.* After sentencing—regardless of the defendant's plea—the court must advise the defendant of any right to appeal the sentence.

(C) *Appeal Costs.* The court must advise a defendant who is unable to pay appeal costs of the right to ask for permission to appeal in forma pauperis.

(2) *Clerk's Filing of Notice.* If the defendant so requests, the clerk must immediately prepare and file a notice of appeal on the defendant's behalf.

(k) Judgment.

(1) *In General.* In the judgment of conviction, the court must set forth the plea, the jury verdict or the court's findings, the adjudication, and the sentence. If the defendant is found not guilty or is otherwise entitled to be discharged, the court must so order. The judge must sign the judgment, and the clerk must enter it.

(2) *Criminal Forfeiture.* Forfeiture procedures are governed by Rule 32.2.

* * *

Note that the sentencing court is required to make findings under Rule 32(i)(3). These findings are found by a preponderance of the evidence standard, not a beyond a reasonable doubt standard. Recall that the Guidelines are no longer binding and the sentence must be below the statutory maximum, so there is no violation of the defendant's Sixth Amendment or due process rights.

Judgment in a Criminal Case

http://www.uscourts.gov/sites/default/files/ao245B.pdf

Amended Judgment in a Criminal Case

http://www.uscourts.gov/sites/default/files/ao246C.pdf

Judgment in a Criminal Case (For Revocation of Probation or Supervised Release)

http://www.uscourts.gov/sites/default/files/ao245D.pdf

Judgment in a Criminal Case (Statement of Reasons)

http://www.uscourts.gov/sites/default/files/ao245SOR.pdf

B. FEDERAL RULE OF CRIMINAL PROCEDURE 35

After the sentencing process has been completed there may arise circumstances that necessitate the correction or reduction of a sentence. Federal Rule of Criminal Procedure 35 provides authority to the court to correct errors in sentences or to reduce a sentence as a reward to a defendant who has cooperated with the government in the investigation or prosecution of another.

Rule 35. Correcting or Reducing a Sentence

(a) Correcting Clear Error. Within 14 days after sentencing, the court may correct a sentence that resulted from arithmetical, technical, or other clear error.

(b) Reducing a Sentence for Substantial Assistance.

(1) *In General.* Upon the government's motion made within one year of sentencing, the court may reduce a sentence if the defendant, after sentencing, provided substantial assistance in investigating or prosecuting another person.

(2) *Later Motion.* Upon the government's motion made more than one year after sentencing, the court may reduce a sentence if the defendant's substantial assistance involved:

(A) information not known to the defendant until one year or more after sentencing;

(B) information provided by the defendant to the government within one year of sentencing, but which did not become useful to the government until more than one year after sentencing; or

(C) information the usefulness of which could not reasonably have been anticipated by the defendant until more than one year after sentencing and which was promptly provided to the government after its usefulness was reasonably apparent to the defendant.

(3) *Evaluating Substantial Assistance.* In evaluating whether the defendant has provided substantial assistance, the court may consider the defendant's presentence assistance.

(4) *Below Statutory Minimum.* When acting under Rule 35(b), the court may reduce the sentence to a level below the minimum sentence established by statute.

(c) "Sentencing" Defined. As used in this rule, "sentencing" means the oral announcement of the sentence.

* * *

ADVOCACY POINT

Prosecutors wishing to make a motion under Rule 35(b) must be mindful of the one-year time deadline for having the court evaluate the defendant's post-sentencing assistance. It is advisable for defense counsel to insist on a provision of the plea agreement in which the government agrees to make a timely Rule 35(b) motion, and to ensure that such a motion is filed within the deadline.

Nᴏᴛᴇ ᴏɴ Sᴛᴀᴛᴇ Pʀᴀᴄᴛɪᴄᴇ

Some jurisdictions permit the sentencing court to re-evaluate the sentence after a certain amount of time has elapsed following sentencing. Does the jurisdiction in which you plan to practice have such a procedure? If so, what is the time threshold for requesting review. Also, if a defendant pursues a sentence review, is there the possibility that the sentence can be *increased* in your state? *See, e.g.,* Md. Rule 4–344; Mass. Crim. P. R. 29.

COUNSEL EXERCISE 18: Sentencing
(Prosecution and Defense)

Assume that the defendant has been convicted at trial on all
counts in the indictment, and that the presentence report (PSR)
has been filed. Each side is to draft a sentencing memorandum to
the court, arguing for a specific sentence. The sentencing
memorandum should reference, *inter alia*: any statutory
maximum sentences and federal sentencing guidelines provisions
and calculations related to the charged offenses; victim impact
concerns; the defendant's family circumstances, job prospects, and
future dangerousness to the community; evidence of community
support for, or opposition to, a lenient sentence.

INDEX

References are to Pages
